ISAIAH

PREACHING THE WORD
Edited by R. Kent Hughes

(((PREACHING *the* WORD)))

ISAIAH

GOD SAVES SINNERS

RAYMOND C. ORTLUND, JR.

R. Kent Hughes,
Series Editor

WHEATON, ILLINOIS

Isaiah

Copyright © 2005 by Raymond C. Ortlund Jr.

Published by Crossway
      1300 Crescent Street
      Wheaton, Illinois 60187

Cover design: Jon McGrath, Simplicated Studio

Cover image: Adam Greene, illustrator

First printing 2005

Reprinted with new cover 2012

Printed in the United States of America

Scripture quotations marked RSV are from *The Revised Standard Version*. Copyright © 1946, 1952, 1971, 1973 by the Division of Christian Education of the National Council of the Churches of Christ in the U.S.A.

Scripture quotations marked NRSV are from the *Holy Bible, New Revised Standard Version*, copyright © 1989 by the Division of Christian Education of the National Council of the Churches of Christ in the U.S.A.

Scripture quotations marked KJV are from the King James Version of the Bible.

Scripture quotations marked NKJV are from *The New King James Version*. Copyright © 1982, Thomas Nelson, Inc. Used by permission.

Scripture references marked NLT are from *The Holy Bible, New Living Translation*, copyright © 1996, 2004. Used by permission of Tyndale House Publishers, Inc., Wheaton, IL, 60189. All rights reserved.

Scripture references marked NIV are taken from *The Holy Bible, New International Version*®, NIV®. Copyright © 1973, 1978, 1984, 2011 by Biblica, Inc.™ Used by permission. All rights reserved worldwide.

Scripture quotations marked NASB are from *The New American Standard Bible*®. Copyright © The Lockman Foundation 1960, 1962, 1963, 1968, 1971, 1972, 1973, 1975, 1977. Used by permission.

All emphases in Scripture quotations have been added by the author.

ISBN–13: 978-1-4335-3547-5
ISBN–10: 1-433-5-3547-5
PDF ISBN: 978-1-4335-1269-8
Mobipocket ISBN: 978-1-4335-0826-4
ePub ISBN: 978-1-4335-1730-3

Library of Congress Cataloging-in-Publication Data

Ortlund, Raymond C., Jr.
   Isaiah : God saves sinners / Raymond C. Ortlund, Jr. ; R. Kent
     Hughes, general editor.
     p. cm. (Preaching the word)
   Includes indexes.
   ISBN 13: 978-1-58134-727-2 (hc : alk. paper)
   ISBN 10: 1-58134-727-8
   1. Bible. O.T. Isaiah—Commentaries. I. Hughes, R. Kent. II.
Title. III. Series.
BS1515.53.O78   2005
224'.1077—dc22   2005004960

Crossway is a publishing ministry of Good News Publishers.

VP   28 27 26 25 24 23 22 21 20
15   14   13   12   11   10   9 8 7 6 5 4

For my lovely wife
Jani

"Turn to me and be saved,
all the ends of the earth!
For I am God,
and there is no other."
ISAIAH 45:22

Contents

Abbreviations

ANET Pritchard, James B., editor. *Ancient Near Eastern Texts Relating to the Old Testament.* Third edition with supplement. Princeton, NJ: Princeton University Press, 1969.

ARAB Luckenbill, Daniel David. *Ancient Records of Assyria and Babylonia.* 2 volumes. Chicago: University of Chicago Press, 1926–1927.

BDB Brown, Francis; Driver, S. R.; Briggs, Charles A. *A Hebrew and English Lexicon of the Old Testament.* Oxford, UK: The Clarendon Press, 1907.

BHS *Biblia Hebraica Stuttgartensia* Stuttgart, Germany: Deutsche Bibelgesellschaft, 1977.

ESV The English Standard Version (2001).

GKC Kautzsch, E., editor; Cowley, A. E., reviser. *Gesenius' Hebrew Grammar.* Oxford, UK: The Clarendon Press, 1910.

IBHS Waltke, Bruce K., and O'Connor, M. *An Introduction to Biblical Hebrew Syntax.* Winona Lake, IN: Eisenbrauns, 1990.

KB3 Koehler, Ludwig, and Baumgartner, Walter. *The Hebrew and Aramaic Lexicon of the Old Testament.* 5 volumes. Translated from the third edition by M. E. J. Richardson. Leiden, Netherlands: E. J. Brill, 1994–1999.

Motyer Motyer, J. Alec. *The Prophecy of Isaiah: An Introduction & Commentary.* Downers Grove, IL: InterVarsity, 1993.

NASB The New American Standard Bible (1971).

NEB The New English Bible (1970).

NIV The New International Version (1978).

NJPS The New Jewish Publication Society Translation (1988).

NKJV The New King James Version (1982).

NLT The New Living Translation (1996).

NRSV The New Revised Standard Version (1989).

Oswalt Oswalt, John N. *The Book of Isaiah.* The New International Commentary on the Old Testament. 2 volumes. Grand Rapids, MI: William B. Eerdmans, 1986, 1998.

REB The Revised English Bible (1989).

RSV The Revised Standard Version (1952).

Wehr Wehr, Hans. *A Dictionary of Modern Written Arabic.* Fourth edition. Edited by J. Milton Cowan. Wiesbaden: Otto Harrassowitz, 1979.

A Word to Those Who Preach the Word

There are times when I am preaching that I have especially sensed the pleasure of God. I usually become aware of it through the unnatural silence. The ever-present coughing ceases, and the pews stop creaking, bringing an almost physical quiet to the sanctuary—through which my words sail like arrows. I experience a heightened eloquence, so that the cadence and volume of my voice intensify the truth I am preaching.

There is nothing quite like it—the Holy Spirit filling one's sails, the sense of his pleasure, and the awareness that something is happening among one's hearers. This experience is, of course, not unique, for thousands of preachers have similar experiences, even greater ones.

What has happened when this takes place? How do we account for this sense of his smile? The answer for me has come from the ancient rhetorical categories of *logos*, *ethos*, and *pathos*.

The first reason for his smile is the *logos*—in terms of preaching, God's Word. This means that as we stand before God's people to proclaim his Word, we have done our homework. We have exegeted the passage, mined the significance of its words in their context, and applied sound hermeneutical principles in interpreting the text so that we understand what its words meant to its hearers. And it means that we have labored long until we can express in a sentence what the theme of the text is—so that our outline springs from the text. Then our preparation will be such that as we preach, we will not be preaching our own thoughts about God's Word, but God's actual Word, his *logos*. This is fundamental to pleasing him in preaching.

The second element in knowing God's smile in preaching is *ethos*— what you are as a person. There is a danger endemic to preaching, which is having your hands and heart cauterized by holy things. Phillips Brooks illustrated it by the analogy of a train conductor who comes to believe that he has been to the places he announces because of his long and loud heralding of them. And that is why Brooks insisted that preaching must be "the bringing of truth through personality." Though we can never *perfectly* embody the truth we preach, we must be subject to it, long for it, and make it as much a part of our ethos as possible. As the Puritan William Ames said, "Next to the Scriptures, nothing makes a sermon more to pierce, than when it comes out of the inward affection of the heart without any affectation." When a preacher's *ethos* backs up his *logos*, there will be the pleasure of God.

Last, there is *pathos*—personal passion and conviction. David Hume, the Scottish philosopher and skeptic, was once challenged as he was seen going to hear George Whitefield preach: "I thought you do not believe in the gospel." Hume replied, "I don't, but *he does*." Just so! When a preacher believes what he preaches, there will be passion. And this belief and requisite passion will know the smile of God.

The pleasure of God is a matter of *logos* (the Word), *ethos* (what you are), and *pathos* (your passion). As you *preach the Word* may you experience his smile—the Holy Spirit in your sails!

R. Kent Hughes
Wheaton, Illinois

Preface

God saves sinners. We don't believe that. We bank our happiness on other things. But God says to us, "I'm better than you think. You're worse than you think. Let's get together."

The prophet Isaiah wants to show us more of God and more of ourselves than we've ever seen before. He wants us to know what it means for us to be saved. Do we have the courage to listen? We might as well. Our friends disappoint us. Our own good intentions let us down. Sooner or later our very bodies will give out. But God has opened a way for us to swim eternally in the ocean of his love. Our part is to look beyond ourselves and stake everything on God, who alone saves sinners.

If you aren't a Christian believer, I dare you to give Isaiah a hearing. God speaks through this prophet even today. How else can you explain the fact that after 2,700 years there is still a market for books on Isaiah? Why are you holding this book right now? God wants to speak to *you* through Isaiah. If you're a new Christian, Isaiah offers you a God-centered confidence that can face anything. If you're an experienced Christian, Isaiah will challenge you to trust God in new ways. And if you're suffering, Isaiah will help you reach out and grasp God's mighty hand on your behalf.

You will find this more meaningful if you open up a Bible and follow Isaiah's text as you read along. I have used the English Standard Version. Any variations from the ESV are my own translations of the Hebrew text.

As a pastor, it's not my job to protect people from the living God. My job is to bring people to God, and leave them there. Martyn Lloyd-Jones, the British minister, asked, "What is the chief end of preaching?" His answer was, "It is to give men and women a sense of God and his presence."[1] How did he attempt that?

> His approach is habitually Isaianic: having surveyed man's pretensions, his fancied greatness and adequacy, moral, religious, cultural, intellectual, he punctures them, humbling man and exposing his weakness, futility and sin, in order then to exalt God as the only Savior.[2]

All prophetic preaching takes that approach. If all you want is

Christianity Lite, this book is not for you. But if your interest in God is sincere enough not to set preconditions, you may well find a sense of God here.

I owe a special debt of gratitude to the commentaries on Isaiah by J. Alec Motyer and John N. Oswalt. Their influence is pervasive here. Some quotations, from older works especially, I have edited slightly, in line with current idiom.

I thank Dr. Kent Hughes for the privilege of contributing the *Isaiah* volume to his Preaching the Word series. I thank the Session of Christ Presbyterian Church for their partnership in this project. I thank all my friends at Christ Pres for their loving prayers.

Jani, this book is for you. And it's about time.

Raymond C. Ortlund, Jr.
Christ Presbyterian Church
Nashville, Tennessee

1

Introduction to Isaiah

ISAIAH 1:1

*Who can tell us whether this awful and mysterious silence, in which
the Infinite One has wrapped himself, portends mercy or wrath?
Who can say to the troubled conscience whether He, whose laws
in nature are inflexible and remorseless, will pardon sin? Who can
answer the anxious inquiry whether the dying live on or whether
they cease to be? Is there a future state? And if so, what is the nature
of that untried condition of being? If there be immortal happiness,
how can I attain it? If there be an everlasting woe, how can it be
escaped? Let the reader close his Bible and ask himself seriously
what he knows upon these momentous questions apart from its
teachings. What solid foundation has he to rest upon in regard to
matters which so absolutely transcend all earthly experience and
are so entirely out of the reach of our unassisted faculties? A man
of facile faith may perhaps delude himself into the belief of what
he wishes to believe. He may thus take upon trust God's unlimited
mercy, his ready forgiveness of transgressors, and eternal happiness after death. But this is all a dream. He knows nothing, he can
know nothing about it, except by direct revelation from heaven.*[1]

WE CAN KNOW, BECAUSE GOD HAS SPOKEN. Into our troubled world,
God has spoken to us "from the borders of another world."[2] Our needs go
deeper than the remedies on sale in the marketplace of ideas today. Whether
you are a believer or an unbeliever, wouldn't you agree that "the solution of
the riddle of life in space and time lies *outside* space and time"?[3] No matter
how many experts we consult or how much research we do, the ultimate
questions of life remain unanswerable unless God speaks. And God *has*
spoken to us, in plain language. Surprisingly, his message is good news for
bad people like us. Will you listen to him thoughtfully, patiently?

God spoke eloquently through Isaiah. If you have any interest in the
Bible at all, Isaiah will reward a close reading. It is "the most theologi-

17

cally significant book in the Old Testament."⁴ "Of all the books in the Old Testament, Isaiah is perhaps the richest."⁵ "From ancient times Isaiah has been considered the greatest of the Old Testament prophets."⁶ The scholars who know what they are talking about prize Isaiah. What Bach's first biographer said about his music applies to Isaiah's prophecy:

> [Bach's music] is not merely agreeable, like other composers', but transports us to the regions of the ideal. It does not arrest our attention momentarily but grips us the stronger the oftener we listen to it so that, after a thousand hearings, its treasures are still unexhausted and yield fresh beauties to excite our wonder.⁷

Isaiah deserves better than to be a "classic"—a famous book nobody reads anymore. His prophecy isn't always easy to understand. But every day all around the world people take on challenges, from climbing the Matterhorn to learning Japanese to launching a new business. If God has spoken to us through Isaiah, let's explore this literary Matterhorn. Let's enjoy the view from the very top, and even the effort of getting there. Let's reach out for new understandings.

Let us begin: "The vision of Isaiah the son of Amoz, which he saw concerning Judah and Jerusalem in the days of Uzziah, Jotham, Ahaz, and Hezekiah, kings of Judah" (1:1). This heading invites three questions: What? Who? When?

What?

"The *vision* of Isaiah . . . which he *saw* . . ." This book is a prophetic vision. Not that Isaiah went into a trance, for 2:1 says that Isaiah saw a "*word*" from God. But this book puts before us *a way of seeing*. And it isn't our own brainstorm. God is the one offering us a new perspective on everything.

Left to ourselves, we live on the level of impressions and hunches and gut reactions. We are blind to the things we most need to know. But a prophet was enabled to see beyond the immediate. A prophet was not fooled or stampeded. He was a *seer*.

For example, Elisha was surrounded one night in Dothan by the army of the Syrians (2 Kings 6:15–17). A young man was with him there—a prophet-in-training. He got up one morning to find the area swarming with enemy troops. He was terrified. But when he alerted Elisha, the old man didn't panic. Elisha said, "Do not be afraid, for those who are with us are more than those who are with them." His young friend must have thought, *This old guy is past his prime! He doesn't appreciate the gravity of the situation.* But what did the prophet do? He prayed, "O Lord, please open his eyes that he may see." God did. And the young man *saw* that the surrounding mountains were filled with horses and chariots of fire. The prophet could see through appearances into reality, which is why the prophets were misunderstood.

Isaiah himself was enabled to see the divine King enthroned in the heavenly court (Isaiah 6). What he never could have stumbled onto, God revealed to him. This makes the prophetic vision of the Bible our clearest view into reality. Our natural outlook focuses on everything secondary. But in the Bible God is the central, unavoidable figure everywhere. All the basic questions of life are, in fact, God-questions. As John Calvin put it, "The Christian must surely be so disposed and minded that he feels within himself it is with God he has to deal throughout his life."[8] That is a prophetic way of seeing. But this awareness clashes with our intuitive sense of things. We dislike God's word and defend ourselves against it. But Isaiah begs us, "Come, let us walk in the light of the LORD" (2:5). Let's respect God enough to be open and think it through.

The heading in Isaiah 1:1 alerts us that his book will interrupt our familiar ways of thinking. Isaiah walks up to us, taps us on the shoulder as we struggle with our problems, and says, "There's another way to look at all this. Interested?" God is disruptive. Without his word, we are confined to our own pretenses and bluffs. With his word, new realities open up. But if we want to get anything out of Isaiah, we have to be ready to adjust.

The other thing we should see about the *What* is this: The verse says "the vision" (singular), not "the visions" (plural). That is surprising. Why? Because this book is an anthology of Isaiah's lifetime of prophetic work. He preached many sermons and made declarations for God on many occasions. What we have in this book is an edited collection of his whole career. Toward the end of his life, Isaiah gathered his papers and notes and memories together and wove them into one coherent presentation. So the unfolding sections of this book come from who knows how many different occasions, and not always in chronological order. But they all unite as one compelling new way of seeing everything. "The vision . . . which he saw . . ."

Who?

There are two answers to the *Who* question. The first is obvious: "Isaiah the son of Amoz." The Bible does not tell us who his father Amoz was, but rabbinic tradition claims that Amoz was brother to Amaziah, King of Judah, putting Isaiah into the royal family.[9] We know that Isaiah was a married man with children. We think he was a resident of Jerusalem. We can see he was a literary genius. But the most important thing about Isaiah is his name.

His Hebrew name means "The Lord saves." This man's very identity announces grace from beyond ourselves. We don't like that. We want to retain control, save face, set our own terms, pay our own way. Every day we treat God as incidental to what really matters to us, and we live by our own strategies of self-salvation. We don't think of our choices that way, but Isaiah can see that our lives are infested with fraudulent idols. Any hope that isn't from God is an idol of our own making.

Idolatry is Isaiah's primary concern about us. This is offensive, because we thought we left idolatry behind centuries ago. But Isaiah, who understands the power of God, also understands the power of non-gods. It works on our minds. Every day we shift our deepest fears around behind amusements, professional achievements, and even lesser fears. As we drive slowly around a serious car accident, we think, *It wasn't* me, to distance ourselves mentally. We think, *They must have been driving recklessly*, because blaming feels reassuring. We sense how vulnerable we are.[10] But any evasion of plain dealing with God is idol-manufacture. And we do not let go of our idols easily.

In heaping our idolatries together, we assemble a culture—a brilliant, collaborative quest to prove ourselves. Our modern culture rarely represents itself with religious language. But Ernest Becker, in his Pulitzer Prize-winning book *The Denial of Death*, explained how we serve it every day with faithful devotion:

> We disguise our struggle by piling up figures in a bank book to reflect privately our sense of heroic worth. Or by having only a little better home in the neighborhood, a bigger car, brighter children. But underneath throbs the ache of cosmic specialness, no matter how we mask it in concerns of smaller scope.[11]

We crave reassurance that our lives are not zeroes. But unless we are resting in God, our uncertainty generates "a blind drivenness that burns people up; in passionate people, a screaming for glory as uncritical and reflexive as the howling of a dog."[12] No idol can truthfully say, "My yoke is easy" (Matthew 11:30).

In today's increasingly dangerous world, our cheery but demanding idols, with their empty promises, are failing us. The fact is, death watches us, stalks us, takes aim, and shoots straight. There is no safe place, not even in America, the land of optimism. We have terrorist hijackers, drive-by shootings, tainted blood transfusions, gun-toting kids at school, and weapons of mass destruction in the hands of maniacs. William James, in *The Varieties of Religious Experience*, put it vividly:

> Let sanguine healthy-mindedness do its best with its strange power of living in the moment and ignoring and forgetting, still the evil background is really there to be thought of, and the skull will grin in at the banquet.[13]

Ignoring and forgetting is *why* we hold this banquet called the American Dream. Isn't it time, with all other hopes proving false, to reach out for the strong hand of God?

A salvation we don't even know how to define, Isaiah is an expert at explaining to us. He wants to lead us into a life that outlasts our earthly expiration date. J. I. Packer puts into words the greatness of the Isaianic message:

> *God saves sinners. God*—the Triune Jehovah, Father, Son and Holy Spirit; three Persons working together in sovereign wisdom, power and love to achieve the salvation of a chosen people, the Father electing, the Son fulfilling the Father's will by redeeming, the Spirit executing the purpose of the Father and Son by renewing. *Saves*—does everything, first to last, that is involved in bringing man from death in sin to life in glory: plans, achieves and communicates redemption, calls and keeps, justifies, sanctifies, glorifies. *Sinners*—men as God finds them, guilty, vile, helpless, powerless, blind, unable to lift a finger to do God's will or better their spiritual lot. *God saves sinners. . . .* Sinners do not save themselves in any sense at all, but salvation, first and last, whole and entire, past, present and future, is of the Lord, to whom be glory forever, amen![14]

God is announcing to us through Isaiah: *The Lord*, for all that he is, *saves*, for all that's worth, *sinners*, for all that we need. That truth is better than we give it credit for.

The people of Isaiah's day had an unrealistic appraisal of themselves, with little awareness of their own fatal salvations. They went through the motions of Biblical faith. But when it came to the hardball of everyday life, they saw no relevance in God's help. But their brilliant stupidity only played into the hands of their enemies, as we will see. The Lutheran Church, in their service of Affirmation of Baptism, asks new members, "Do you renounce all the forces of evil, the devil, and all his empty promises?"[15] That may sound quaint. But *the* question on which our lives turn, moment by moment, is whether we are banking on God's promises of salvation or on the empty promises of the false salvations pressing in upon us all around. If we are not letting God save us, we are exposing ourselves to forces of evil, more than we know. But as the truth of "The Lord saves" breaks upon us with prophetic clarity, it becomes a powerful resource for living.

In Isaiah's day, his message was unpopular. A prophet with his name ("the Lord saves")—well, the people could see a mile away what he stood for, and not many listened. Their hearts were too dead to resonate with the greatest thing in the universe. And so it is today. If the gospel that you cannot be your own savior, but God can save you totally, does not thrill you, it's probably an irritant to your self-importance, lust for control, and moral superiority. Even in the church, the more clearly the good news is preached and the more directly it is applied, the more inevitably it sparks controversy. So be it. "The Lord saves" is the improbable truth we've been looking for but resisting all our lives.

This book is also about, secondly, "Judah and Jerusalem." Isaiah will address other nations too. His message is for everyone. But God is most present among the people of his choosing, and the revival of his people is the hope of the nations. That is Isaiah's primary concern. So we should apply Isaiah's vision today not to America or any other political entity but, first and foremost, to the Christian church. Jesus said to his followers, "*You* are the salt of the earth. . . . *You* are the light of the world" (Matthew 5:13, 14). Nothing is more important to the state of the world than the state of the church. God speaks first to believers, so that his overflowing salvation can spread to all. The world cannot impede the expansion of salvation; the mediocrity of the church can and does. If the world is not experiencing the grace of God, the church is being untrue to its destiny. What the world most needs is the church so obviously saved that the church is an alternative to convert *to*. If Isaiah were alive today, he would say to Christian believers, "The Lord saves, beginning with us."

When?

". . . in the days of Uzziah, Jotham, Ahaz, and Hezekiah, kings of Judah." Isaiah preached in the southern kingdom of Judah during the closing decades of the eighth-century B.C. It was the best of times; it was the worst of times. When Isaiah began his work about 740 B.C., Judah was still basking in long-sustained prosperity. But the good times were nearly over, and the people sensed it. They lived in a pivotal moment and in a threatening world. *The* crisis of their generation was the rising Assyrian empire to the east, and these four kings of Judah proved how mixed the nation's response was—trust in God complicated by deeper trust in themselves. You can read more about it in 2 Kings 15—20. But the Assyrian threat was the point at which these leaders and their people would decide whether God would save them or whether they had to develop their own strategies of self-salvation. Every generation is tested at some point of felt urgency, and to us today God freely offers himself as our most powerful ally. Whether or not we choose him is *the* story of our generation, and nothing else ultimately matters.

Why did Isaiah keep speaking out? Few people took him seriously. As thanks for his ministry, according to an ancient tradition, he was sawn in two.[16] How did he carry on? There is only one answer. What he saw is real.

We need to see it too. We need to embrace it rather than push it away. We can discover in our crises today what it means to be saved by grace from God. Others in the past have trusted him, and he more than kept his word. Now it's our turn. But we don't have forever to make up our minds.

Let's rethink everything from this prophetic viewpoint: *God saves sinners*. It's the most underrated truth in all the world.

2

Our Urgent Need:
A New Self-Awareness I

ISAIAH 1:2–9

PAUL TOURNIER, THE SWISS PSYCHIATRIST, OBSERVED, "A diffuse and vague guilt feeling kills the personality, whereas the conviction of sin gives life to it."[1] Isaiah begins with life-giving conviction of sin. It's our first step back to God.

We need a sense of sin. We shouldn't fear it or resent it. It is not destructive. It is life-giving, if we have the courage to let Christ save us. We are often told—or just whispered to—that what we need is more self-esteem. That is false. What we need is more humility and more Christ-esteem.

William Kilpatrick distinguishes self-esteem, with its non-judgmentalism, from self-awareness, with its clear consciousness of sin:

> A colleague at Boston College . . . once asked members of his philosophy class to write an anonymous essay about a personal struggle over right and wrong, good and evil. Most of the students, however, were unable to complete the assignment. "Why?" he asked. "Well," they said—and apparently this was said without irony—"we haven't done anything wrong." We can see a lot of self-esteem here, but little self-awareness.[2]

We may feel good about ourselves. But what if *God* thinks we've done wrong, a lot of wrong, and not much right? What if he wants to talk to us about it because he also has a remedy for us? What if he can see that our self-protection is really self-imprisonment? God lovingly confronts us with truths embarrassing enough to save us.

What is conviction of sin? It is not an oppressive spirit of uncertainty or paralyzing guilt feelings. Conviction of sin is the lance of the divine Surgeon piercing the infected soul, releasing the pressure, letting the infection pour out. Conviction of sin is a health-giving injury. Conviction of sin is the Holy Spirit being kind to us by confronting us with the light we don't want to see and the truth we're afraid to admit and the guilt we prefer to ignore. Conviction of sin is the severe love of God overruling our compulsive dishonesty, our willful blindness, our favorite excuses. Conviction of sin is the violent sweetness of God opposing the sins lying comfortably undisturbed in our lives. Conviction of sin is the merciful God declaring war on the false peace we settle for. Conviction of sin is our escape from malaise to joy, from attending church to worship, from faking it to authenticity. Conviction of sin, with the forgiveness of Jesus pouring over our wounds, is *life*.

In Isaiah chapter 1, God is telling us the truth about ourselves. Let's not be fooled by our polished appearances and our stylish theories of the darling self. They'll be the death of us. The unflattering portrait of Isaiah 1 is God's way of disturbing us until we start asking the courageous Godward questions that can breathe life back into us.

The first chapter of Isaiah shows us the "before" picture—what we are, left to ourselves. Later prophecies in the book piece together the "after" picture—what God promises to make of everyone he saves. By the end of the book, what God achieves is not simply a patched-up version of you and me. His grace will create new heavens and a new earth (65:17; 66:22). Isaiah 1 opens the way to our God-glorification by deconstructing our self-glorification.

Isaiah crafted his message with literary care, as we'll see throughout his work. At first glance he may seem to be meandering—confused and confusing. Martin Luther said that the prophets "have a queer way of talking, like people who, instead of proceeding in an orderly manner, ramble off from one thing to the next, so that you cannot make head or tail of them or see what they are getting at."[3] But a closer look at Isaiah's text reveals a purposeful genius underneath that first impression.[4] His first chapter is structured like this:

1. Three views of God's uncomprehending people (1:2–26)
   A The tragedy of their humiliation: "Ah, sinful nation" (1:2–9)
      B The hypocrisy of their worship: "Bring no more vain offerings" (1:10–20)
         C The corruption of their character: "Everyone loves a bribe" (1:21–26)
2. The alternatives confronting God's people (1:27–31)

Robert Burns, the poet of Scotland, wrote, "O, wad some Pow'r the giftie gie us, to see oursels as others see us."[5] That wouldn't do us any harm, would it? But even better is to see ourselves as *God* sees us. According to John Calvin, we need to know two things to make meaningful contact with reality. We need to know God and ourselves. A new self-awareness "leads us by the hand," Calvin says, to find God.[6] Isaiah begins there, with our most urgent need—a new self-awareness through the conviction of sin.

Isaiah chapter 1 is so important that we'll devote three studies to it—chapters 2, 3, and 4 in this book. We begin now with Isaiah 1:2–9. The prophet shows us God's broken heart (1:2, 3), our broken strength (1:4–8), and God's unbroken grace (1:9).

God's Broken Heart

> Hear, O heavens, and give ear, O earth;
>   for the Lord has spoken. (Isaiah 1:2a)

I watched a television interview with the Shah of Iran after he was deposed in the 1970s. With deep sorrow in his voice he said, "It would take no one less than a Homer to tell the story of how I was betrayed." But it takes the heavens and the earth, it takes the entire cosmos, to witness the enormity of our offenses against God. How dimly we grasp the significance of our lives. We shrink our self-awareness down to the sequential passing of one moment after another, thinking piecemeal, rarely looking beyond, unaware of the magnitude of what we are before God. We trivialize our choices. We don't think they matter that much. But God does not trivialize us. To him, there is no greater tragedy in the universe than his own children in rebellion against him.

> "Children have I reared and brought up,
>   but they have rebelled against me." (v. 2b)

What hinders God's blessing in the world today is not Hollywood or Washington. What hinders God's blessing is his own children in rebellion against him. The reason we see so little repentance in the world is that the world sees so little repentance in the church. And the measure of our wrong against God is the measure of his love invested in us: "*Children* have I reared and brought up, but *they* have rebelled against me." Do we *feel* rebellious? Rarely. We may feel "more sinned against than sinning" (*King Lear*). We may feel that God is picking on us here. "After all, we're doing the best we can, and life is hard. What is he expecting of us?"

Wait a minute. Examine that thought. When that impulse pops into our minds, we're proving God's point. That very attitude is rebellion. Whenever we resist his claims upon us and make peace with our mediocrity, we are rebelling against our Father—which is to say, we live *often* in open defiance against God. We don't intend to. But we don't need to intend to. Defiance is the way we are. We settle for a watered-down experience of God. We don't even *want* that much of God. But we think of ourselves as good people, because it feels better that way. We need to be awakened to the prophetic truth. And the truth is, this verse is a cry of pain from Heaven. What wounds the heart of God is that we are as rebellious against him as we are blessed by him.

> "The ox knows its owner,
>   and the donkey its master's crib,
> but Israel does not know,
>   my people do not understand." (v. 3)

God's children make animals look intelligent. Oxen and donkeys are stupid. Even as animals, they're dense. But they know enough to go find their master. After all, he feeds them. But we are often unmoved by God's love. We wander from one false master to another—hungry, empty, frustrated, wondering why God seems unreal. But the name "Israel" declares that God still longs to bless us (cf. Genesis 32:22–29; 35:9–12). The words "my people" show how closely God identifies with us. What madness is this, that we treat God our generous Father as a problem to work around, while we get on with the real business of life! The prophet is saying, "That's *stupid*." And it breaks God's heart.

Our Broken Strength

> Ah, sinful nation,
>   a people laden with iniquity,
> offspring of evildoers,
>   children who deal corruptly! (Isaiah 1:4a)

The prophet sees God's people missing the point of life ("sinful nation"), oppressed with failure ("laden with iniquity"),[7] going from bad to worse ("offspring of evildoers, children who deal corruptly"). But he isn't railing. The word "Ah!" signals that this is a lament. Hear that in the prophet's tone. He is not nagging; he is weeping. It is a solemn thing to see God's children, called to greatness, dissolving into the opposite. How does this happen? Isaiah sees through the infestation of surface-level sins, down to the root.

> They have forsaken the Lord,
>   they have despised the Holy One of Israel,
>   they are utterly estranged. (v. 4b)

Do we really forsake the Lord and despise the Holy One? From his point of view, yes. How so? To forsake the Lord is to treat him as the last resort rather than as the fountainhead. To despise God is to disrelish him, to put a discount on God while valuing other things. And that condition of the heart estranges us from God because of who God is—"the Holy One of Israel." He is both *the* Holy One and *our* Holy One. Jonathan Edwards explains the moral significance of that:

> Our obligation to love, honor and obey any being is in proportion to his loveliness, honor and authority. Therefore, sin against God, being a violation of infinite obligations, must be a crime infinitely heinous and so deserving infinite punishment. If there is any evil in sin against God, it is infinite evil.[8]

This is why theft, murder, terrorism, and other outward sins are mere fleabites compared with the mega-sin of forsaking and despising God. But the latter is common, even in the church.

> For many, Christianity has become the grinding out of general doctrinal laws from collections of biblical facts. But childlike wonder and awe have died. The scenery and poetry and music of the majesty of God have dried up like a forgotten peach at the back of the refrigerator.[9]

Grinding it out, grinding it out—that kind of Christianity offends God and injures us more than we realize.

Isaiah uses two images to help us see how clueless we can be. The first image is a beaten man who doesn't feel his own wounds enough to get help.

> Why will you still be struck down?
>   Why will you continue to rebel?
> The whole head is sick,
>   and the whole heart faint.
> From the sole of the foot even to the head,
>   there is no soundness in it,
> but bruises and sores
>   and raw wounds;
> they are not pressed out or bound up
>   or softened with oil. (vv. 5, 6)

This man has been so clobbered, there isn't a square inch on his body *not* sore and bleeding. But he doesn't feel it. So he keeps going back for more punishment and gets beaten to a pulp again and again and never learns his lesson. Isaiah is saying, "This is you—never comprehending why or even imagining that things could be better."

The biggest obstacle to our spiritual progress is that we feel healthy, even successful. We do not sense that we're like the boxer in the film *Rocky*—one massive wound from head to toe. We have so little expectation of how invigorating God is that we keep on forsaking and despising the very one who binds up the brokenhearted (Isaiah 61:1). The prophet looks at us in amazement and asks, "Why? If your aim is to make yourselves miserable, haven't you accomplished that by now? Wouldn't you rather start to heal?"

Isaiah's other image of our need for God is an invaded country that does not see its own humiliation. Some interpreters read verses 7, 8 as literal. In Isaiah's day they came close to being literal. But the similes in verse 8, signaled by the word "like," argue that Isaiah is still speaking figuratively:

> Your country lies desolate;
>   your cities are burned with fire;
> in your very presence foreigners devour your land;
>   it is desolate, as overthrown by foreigners.
> And the daughter of Zion is left
>   like a booth in a vineyard,
> like a lodge in a cucumber field,
>   like a besieged city.

Compare that with how the Bible describes believers at their best: a chosen race, a royal priesthood, a holy nation, a people for God's own possession, so that we may proclaim the excellencies of him who called us out of darkness into his marvelous light (1 Peter 2:9). But Isaiah saw God's people in his day reduced to something like a shack in the midst of a field picked over by invading robbers. The church on the defensive, the church pitiable, exposed, cornered, her influence diminished—helplessness is not God's will for the people he intends to be redemptive in this world (Deuteronomy 26:18, 19; 28:1). The church needs a Savior too.

God's Unbroken Grace

> If the LORD of hosts
>   had not left us a few survivors,
> we should have been like Sodom,
>   and become like Gomorrah. (Isaiah 1:9)

It's a miracle that the church survives at all. But not because God is weak. He is the omnipotent "LORD of hosts." The church survives because God saves sinners. He sees what we would become, left to ourselves, and in mercy he stretches out his hand and says, "I will not let you go." That is why the evil inside every one of us doesn't explode with its actual power, to our destruction (Romans 9:29). Apart from God's preserving grace, we would relive the story of Sodom and Gomorrah. We *are* what they *were*. We *deserve* what they *got*. That's what God says. And the only reason we're still here is his overruling mercy saving us from ourselves.

Isaiah 1:2–9 awakens us to God's broken heart, our broken strength, and his unbroken grace. God is saying:

> See now that I, even I, am he,
>> and there is no god beside me;
> I kill and I make alive;
>> I wound and I heal;
>> and there is none that can deliver out of my hand. (Deuteronomy 32:39)

This is the God we have to deal with. He can wound us, and he can heal us; but he would rather heal us. Will we come to our senses and turn to him? Here is good news for wounded people: Jesus was wounded too. "He was pierced for our transgressions; he was crushed for our iniquities; upon him was the chastisement that brought us peace, and with his wounds we are healed" (Isaiah 53:5). Our wounds are healed by his wounds.

Isaiah intends to convict us of our sins. But we can feel convicted of a million sins without experiencing any healing from God. *The only conviction of sin that ends up healing us is when we see how we have despised and forsaken the very One who died to save us.* Conviction of that super-sin opens up healing for all our other sins.

So, what is your conscience telling you? If you will trust God enough to admit it and open up to his grace, he will start healing your broken heart more than you can imagine.

3

Our Urgent Need:
A New Self-Awareness II

Isaiah 1:10–20

THE BIBLE SAYS, "Draw near to God, and he will draw near to you" (James 4:8). But how do we draw near to God so that he draws near to us? That question is being debated today. The debate gets so hot, it's sometimes called "the worship wars." Some churches are fighting for traditional forms of worship, and others are fighting for contemporary forms of worship. The traditional people accuse the contemporary people of being superficial, and the contemporary people accuse the traditional people of being irrelevant.

Isaiah points the way out of our wars into God's peace by helping us think in God's categories. His categories are not traditional versus contemporary worship but, more profoundly, acceptable versus unacceptable worship. And he has told us what kind of worship he considers acceptable: "The sacrifice acceptable to God is a broken spirit" (Psalm 51:17, NRSV). Acceptable worship is sweetened with a spirit of repentance.

Isaiah 1:10–20 is about two things at once: worship and repentance. In essence, God puts them together this way: "I want you to repent of your worship. Your worship is unacceptable unless it is the overflow of repentance."

What is repentance? Repentance is not morbid introspection. It is not self-punishment. True repentance is a privilege, given by the Holy Spirit, opening our eyes not only to how costly our sins are but, more searchingly, how evil our sins are.[1] Repentance is not afraid of wholesome self-suspicion, because it feels an urgency to be right with God at any cost. Repentance is a power giving us traction for newness of life. It isn't piecemeal or selective, doctoring up this problem or that. As Martin Luther taught in the first of his

95 Theses, "The whole life of believers should be penitence."[2] Repentance is an honest new self renouncing the shifty old self. And, as Isaiah teaches here, repentance turns from mere forms of worship, whatever they are, to authenticity with God.

Isaiah chapter 1 is holding before us a mirror, so that we can see ourselves more realistically. The rest of the book shows how God saves people like us, so that we become the New Jerusalem. But Isaiah begins the good news of the gospel with the bad news of the gospel, because it's when we place ourselves under God's judgment that we experience his salvation.

Just as chapter 1 introduces the book, verse 2 sets the tone for that chapter: "Children have I reared and brought up, but they have rebelled against me." The verb "rebelled" also appears in the last verse of the book (66:24). The whole prophecy is framed within these two appearances of "rebelled." Rebellion against God is our problem. But God saves rebels. And true worship is rebels like us waving the white flag of surrender before our rightful Lord in repentance.

Isaiah is portraying God's uncomprehending people. Now he exposes the hypocrisy of their worship. His analysis takes four steps: confrontation (1:10), accusation (1:11–15), invitation (1:16–18), decision (1:19, 20).

Confrontation

> Hear the word of the Lord,
>   you rulers of Sodom!
> Give ear to the teaching of our God,
>   you people of Gomorrah! (Isaiah 1:10)

In verse 9 Isaiah said that, apart from God's preserving grace, we would all end up like Sodom and Gomorrah, in both guilt and destruction. We can imagine how Isaiah's contemporaries responded to that, along with everything else in verses 2–9. "What do you mean, Isaiah, that we're rebellious and uncomprehending and sick and desolate? We're the people of God! Any problems we have are more than compensated for by our splendid worship here in Jerusalem. You're overlooking something very much to our credit. How can you say we're like Sodom and Gomorrah?" They must have felt misunderstood. Their feelings must have been hurt. I think Isaiah stopped, thought it over a minute, and then said, "You're right. You're not *like* Sodom and Gomorrah. You *are* Sodom and Gomorrah!" He now intensifies the confrontation. Why? Because we rarely listen the first time.

But it's a sign of God's grace when all of us, both "rulers" and "people," start asking ourselves new questions like, "What have we become?

Are we living proof of what it means to be saved? In our homes, in our professional influence, in our deepest thoughts, *what have we become?*" Only when our confidence is shaken can we hear the word of the Lord afresh. What is he saying?

Accusation

With unsparing honesty, God tells us how he judges our worship. One commentator says, "Of all prophetic outbursts at religious unreality, this is the most powerful and sustained. Its vehemence is unsurpassed."[3] The way God evaluates our worship goes far deeper than the outward forms churches prize so fiercely.

> "What to me is the multitude of your sacrifices?
>   says the Lord;
> I have had enough of burnt offerings of rams
>   and the fat of well-fed beasts;
> I do not delight in the blood of bulls,
>   or of lambs, or of goats." (v. 11)

The key is "I have had enough . . ." The *New Living Translation* puts it bluntly: "I am sick of your sacrifices." Today we'd say, "I've had it up to here!" Then there's that word "your" in the first line: ". . . *your* sacrifices." "Wait a minute, God," the people would have said. "We didn't come up with this form of worship. It was your idea. We're just doing what the book of Leviticus tells us to do. They're *your* sacrifices, Lord." But God is saying, "No, I don't identify with what you're doing, however 'Biblical' it may be." And do you see the lavish inventory of worship materials here? "Sacrifices . . . burnt offerings of rams . . . the fat of well-fed beasts . . . the blood of bulls, or of lambs, or of goats." This careful catalog of sacrifices shows how bountiful, how outwardly impressive, how unselfish (in a way) their worship was. But God says, "I have had enough." Why? We don't know yet. He'll explain later.

> "When you come to appear before me,
>   who has required of you
>   this trampling of my courts?" (v. 12)

Here is the heart of worship: "When you come to appear before me." After all, what *is* worship? It is drawing near to God, entering into his felt presence. He himself calls it "com[ing] to appear before me." But that beautiful thing can be trampled underfoot. Jesus too was offended by the vulgarization of worship (Mark 11:15, 16). When the immediacy of God fades away, no matter how proper our observances may be, God is saying that, to him, such worship has been spoiled as a "trampling of my courts"—it's just the noise of feet shuffling on the pavement or of car doors slamming in the parking lot. Real encounter with God is easily lost.

> "Bring no more vain offerings;
>> incense is an abomination to me.
> New moon and Sabbath and the calling of convocations—
>> I cannot endure iniquity and solemn assembly." (Isaiah 1:13)

Isaiah is probing down to the root of the problem. There are two clues, one in the first line and another in the last line. God does not want "vain offerings"—literally, "offerings of nothing." That's the first clue. What offends God is hollowed-out worship. If we force together "iniquity and solemn assembly"—the second clue—God calls our worship "offerings of nothing." God is not saying, "I cannot endure iniquity." He is saying, "I cannot endure *iniquity and solemn assembly*." We might think, "Sure, I have these unconfessed sins in my life. But it has nothing to do with my worship." But God is saying, "Your unconfessed sins make your worship unendurable to me, because your sins reveal what you really think of me." So, which claims the greater sense of urgency in our hearts—the form of our worship or the quality of our lives? Are we at least as eager to repent of our sins as we are to preserve our form of worship, whatever it may be? *Where does our sense of urgency lie?*

> "Your new moons and your appointed feasts
>> my soul hates;
> they have become a burden to me;
>> I am weary of bearing them." (v. 14)

Let's ask ourselves, what do we think is unbearably repulsive to God, to his very soul, right down to the depths of the Divine Being? We might answer, hard-core crime, the exploitation of children, terrorist mayhem—that sort of thing. It might not occur to us that what the soul of God hates and is burdened and wearied by is the worship we offer him, if we are not in repentance.

What does God see that we don't? The worship he is rejecting is the worship of himself. It's not the worship of a pagan idol. The worship he is rejecting is his own authorized, Levitical worship. It isn't some ludicrous human invention. What kind of God-directed worship does his soul *hate*? What kind of Biblical worship makes God complain, "Do I have to go church today?" We finally see the answer:

"When you spread out your hands,
   I will hide my eyes from you;
even though you make many prayers,
   I will not listen;
   your hands are full of blood." (v. 15)

God makes his most damning charge in rejecting the most pure worship of all—prayer, which doesn't even require an outward form. Even in prayer, however frequent, however fervent, bloody hands turn God's face away.

Our hands bloody? Jesus said that murder can take many forms, including anger, cutting words, and unresolved relational tension (Matthew 5:21–24).[4] Character assassination, backstabbing, and "dividing wall[s] of hostility" (Ephesians 2:14) at church create a life-depleting social atmosphere rather than the life-enriching environment God wants. Are our hands bloody? Maybe more than we thought. That could be why, even in prayer, God seems aloof. A church hostile to people is a church hostile to God, whether that church knows it or not. The hard truth is this: "The curse of a godless man can sound more pleasant in God's ears than the Hallelujah of the pious."[5]

Why is God so blunt? Because he wants to save us. For our worship to be saved, it isn't a matter of fine-tuning our outward performances. It's a matter of repentance.

Invitation

"Wash yourselves; make yourselves clean;
   remove the evil of your deeds from before my eyes;
cease to do evil,
   learn to do good;
seek justice,
   correct oppression;
bring justice to the fatherless,
   plead the widow's cause." (Isaiah 1:16, 17)

Isn't it striking how simple and direct these imperatives are, compared with the elaborate descriptions of the worship in verses 11–15? God is calling us to repent in obvious ways. He's saying, "Clean up your lives." He emphasizes our own active repentance, because our whole problem is our active worship concealing our passive repentance. He is telling us that treating people well beautifies our worship of him. He is saying that true worship doesn't substitute for obedience; it inspires obedience.

God does not say, "Remove your evil deeds from before my eyes."

Some translations give that impression. But the wording of the English Standard Version is accurate and significant: "Remove *the evil of* your deeds from before my eyes." Repentance is not just removing evil deeds; it goes the second mile and, after the deeds have passed, goes back to clean up the residual evil, the damage done. True repentance makes things *right* again. God is saying, "If you want your worship to please me, do this. Become actively creative in compassion and justice for the people you have hurt, especially the people nobody else cares about, people who can't pay you back, people who might not thank you. Set right again the wrongs you've been tolerating. Then your worship will be beautiful to me, and then I will be real to you again."

As always, God is more ready to meet us with grace than we thought. His invitation is irresistible:

> "Come now, let us reason together, says the Lord:
> though your sins are like scarlet,
>   they shall be as white as snow;
> though they are red like crimson,
>   they shall become like wool." (v. 18)

God is saying, "Come on, let's talk this over. Give me a chance. Here's my invitation. You present your blood-red hands to me in open confession, I'll wash you clean in the blood of Jesus, and your worship will come alive."

Richard Lovelace reminds us that the grace of God is the only power that can free us from our hypocrisies:

> Many areas of the church which contain a great deal of legal thunder and lightning, exposing at least the surfaces of sin, are full of desperately anxious and bitterly contentious people. Law without grace provokes sin . . . and aggravates it into some of its ugliest expressions. . . . Psychoanalysts speak of the "resistance" patients have toward the discovery of traumatic material hidden in the unconscious. The same automatic fear of having repressed problems uncovered will grip and bind Christians unless they are deeply assured that they are "accepted in the Beloved," received by God as if they were perfectly righteous because their guilt is canceled by the righteousness of Christ laid to their account. . . . God simply wants honesty, openness and a trusting reliance on Christ our Savior.[6]

The problem with worship—it must take some form or other—is this: The more Biblical and beautiful its form becomes, the more useful it is as a mechanism for evading honest dealings with God and the more plausible as a substitute for repentance. God sees that. So he assures us, "Let's talk it over. Let's open our hearts to one another. I only want to save you. Will you let me?"

Decision

"If you are willing and obedient,
    you shall eat the good of the land;
but if you refuse and rebel,
    you shall be eaten by the sword;
    for the mouth of the Lord has spoken." (vv. 19, 20)

The simple clarity here implies one thing: All that keeps us from renewal with God is our own stubbornness. It isn't as though the path forward is mysteriously hard to find. Is God's appeal unreasonable or irrelevant? He isn't demanding that we be perfect. All he wants is that we be open and responsive. Is that asking too much?

What makes worship acceptable, through Christ, is repentance—in other words, cleaning up our lives with compassion toward people and tenderness toward God. Thomas Watson, the Puritan pastor, offers us incentives to say yes to God:

Have you repented? God looks upon you as if you had not offended. He becomes a friend, a father. He will now bring forth the best robe and put it on you. God is pacified towards you and will, with the father of the prodigal, fall upon your neck and kiss you. . . . Have you been penitentially humbled? The Lord will never upbraid you with your former sins. After Peter wept, we never read that Christ upbraided him with his denial of him. God has cast your sins into the depth of the sea. How? Not as cork, but as lead. . . . O the music of conscience! Conscience is turned into a paradise, and there a Christian sweetly solaces himself and plucks the flowers of joy. The repenting sinner can go to God with boldness in prayer and look upon him not as a Judge but as a Father. He is born of God and is heir to a kingdom. He is encircled with promises. He no sooner shakes the tree of the promise but some fruit falls.[7]

Don't we know what's there for us when we turn back to our Father in repentance? The best robe, a ring, and a kiss. *What are we waiting for?*

4

Our Urgent Need:
A New Self-Awareness III

ISAIAH 1:21–31

DO YOU REMEMBER THE SCENE IN CASABLANCA, with Humphrey Bogart and Ingrid Bergman, when the customers at Rick's Café burst out singing the *Marseillaise* in defiance of the Nazis? They poke the Nazi bullies right in the eye. At one point the camera catches a French woman standing to sing passionately and movingly. Earlier in the story, she had been hanging on the arm of a Nazi soldier as his date. But when the opportunity came, she took her stand and redeemed herself.

Redemption is beautiful. To see a new human being rise from wreckage is moving. The gospel is about redemptive newness for you and me. But the difference between redemption in *Casablanca* and redemption in the Bible is that the stories in the Bible do not inspire us to redeem ourselves. The gospel offers redemption *by God*.

What is redemption? Redemption explains *how* God saves us. How does he? By paying a personal price. In real life, we sin our way right into bondage, and there's no easy way out. If we try to cover it up or make excuses, we dig ourselves in deeper. Every day we create the conditions in which we literally deserve Hell. But what does God do? He offers to get us out of trouble *at his own expense*. He offers to absorb within himself the consequences we have set in motion. He pays the price, so that we don't have to, because we can't anyway. That's redemption. If you have sinned your way into helplessness, where you deserve to reap what you have sown, you can be redeemed. God is not only willing to pay the price, he already has—at the cross of Christ. You can enter into redemption freely, by his grace.

Isaiah puts all his hope in redemption: "Zion shall be *redeemed* by justice, and those in her who repent, by righteousness" (1:27). That's where he wants to take us—through the conviction of sin into repentance, where we experience redemption.

Isaiah 1:21–31 falls into two major sections. In verses 21–26, the prophet laments our corruption. He asks *What?* What have we become, and what does God do with people like us? He shows us both our corruption and God's redeeming purpose. Verse 21 says, "How the faithful city has become a whore." Verse 26 resolves that tension: "Afterward you shall be called the city of righteousness, the faithful city." Verses 21–26 come full circle, from a faithful city to a whore to a faithful city again. That's redemption.

Then in verses 27–31, the prophet asks *How?* How does God lead us into redemption? We must understand that verses 21–26 stand back and envision the whole sweep of history. Looking from the disasters of Old Testament Israel through the failures of the Christian church, Isaiah foresees "the faithful city" of Revelation 21, 22. But verses 27–31 speak directly to every successive generation along the way. We face a decision: Will *we* choose to enter into the redemptive ways of God? Isaiah aims to sober us with who we are, give us hope in who God is, and urge upon us an unblinking realism about how we experience redemption. His vision is both beautiful and terrible.

Our Corruption

How the faithful city
    has become a whore,
        she who was full of justice! (Isaiah 1:21a)

Christian believers are engaged to be married to Jesus Christ (2 Corinthians 11:1–3). His love for us is no platonic attachment; it is a passionate, marital love, claiming us for himself alone. We are the Bride of Christ (Ephesians 5:22–33). He isn't just flirting with us; he wants to go all the way. We should long for that day when he will present us to himself in splendor (Revelation 19:6–9; 21:2, 9–11). But right now, whenever we form other allegiances we are committing spiritual adultery (Hosea 1—3).[1] That's why the word "How" stands at the beginning of verse 21. That same word begins the book of Lamentations. It signals that verses 21–26 of Isaiah 1 are a prophetic *lament*. Something heart-breaking has happened.

Martyn Lloyd-Jones wrote, "Every institution tends to produce its opposite."[2] Look at the church's record. Again and again it has produced the opposite of what God wants. When the church is not "full of justice"—modeling the way human life is meant to be—we hear a heart-cry of sorrow from Heaven.

Righteousness lodged in her,
  but now murderers. (Isaiah 1:21b)

Isaiah's Hebrew wording implies that in this world righteousness is like a lonely traveler in hostile surroundings. In the Israel of Isaiah's forefathers, righteousness once found a welcome: "Righteousness lodged in her." But by his time things have changed. The spiritual neighborhood has gone bad, because unfaithfulness to *God* destroys the bonds that hold *people* together: "but now murderers."

Whittaker Chambers was a Communist spy in the U.S. who eventually turned against Communism. In his book *Witness*, he recalls this conversation:

> The daughter of a former German diplomat in Moscow was trying to explain to me why her father, who as an enlightened modern man had been extremely pro-Communist, had become an implacable anti-Communist. . . . "He was immensely pro-Soviet," she said, "and then—you will laugh at me—but you must not laugh at my father—and then—one night—in Moscow—he heard screams. That's all. Simply one night he heard screams."[3]

In the church, the city of God, do we ever hear screams? Those screams are one reason why there are ex-Christians. They heard screams where they should have heard songs. The Bible says, "Everyone who hates his brother is a murderer" (1 John 3:15).

Your silver has become dross,
  your best wine mixed with water. (Isaiah 1:22)

Sin promises to spice up our lives, but it dilutes everything. Simone Weil was a French Jewish intellectual who died in England during World War II after putting herself on the rations of her fellow-Frenchmen who were suffering under Nazi occupation. She understood the difference between good and evil:

> Nothing is so beautiful, nothing is so continually fresh and surprising, so full of sweet and perpetual ecstasy as the good. No deserts are so dreary, monotonous and boring as evil. But with fantasy it is the other way round. Fictional good is boring and flat, while fictional evil is varied, intriguing, attractive and full of charm.[4]

We need God to tell us the truth, or dreariness will feel exciting and freshness will seem lackluster. Isaiah now contrasts the influence of man (1:23) with the intervention of God (1:24).

Rebellious Leaders, the Mighty Lord

> Your princes are rebels
>   and companions of thieves.
> Everyone loves a bribe
>   and runs after gifts.
> They do not bring justice to the fatherless,
>   and the widow's cause does not come to them. (v. 23)

Salvation is a community experience. That means leadership is involved, which creates levels of responsibility to one another. The ancient Jewish paraphrase of the Old Testament called Targum shows how verse 23 can work out in real life: "All of them love to accept a bribe, saying—a man to his neighbor—'Assist me in my case, so that I will repay you in your case.'"[5] Today we say, "You scratch my back, and I'll scratch yours." That's how the gears of everyday life are lubricated. It gets things done. But when it overrides justice, it's wrong, no matter how well it works. When responsible people choose expediency, they are not judges; they are auctioneers, with the "truth" going to the highest bidder. That is why helpless people get stepped on—powerful people lose their sense of God. When the only ones who matter are successful, formidable people, life becomes savage. If people do not believe that the very hairs of their head are numbered by a loving Father in Heaven (Matthew 10:30), they have no logical reason to care about anyone else. This is why the most important thing about us is our sense of God.

> Therefore the Lord declares,
>   the LORD of hosts,
>   the Mighty One of Israel:
> "Ah, I will get relief from my enemies
>   and avenge myself on my foes." (Isaiah 1:24)

To his glory, no matter what we do, God just won't go away. He will never un-God himself. There is a Lord in Heaven, the Lord of hosts, the Mighty One of Israel, who cares deeply about his own offended justice. And his commitment to his own cause is our hope. He will get relief from his enemies. He will avenge himself on his foes. Nobody is getting away with anything, and redemption will never be defeated.

Now, after the charges in verse 23 and God's angry resolve in verse 24, wouldn't we expect him to follow up with total annihilation? But redemption is surprising.

Our Redemption

"I will turn my hand against you
and will smelt away your dross as with lye
and remove all your alloy.
And I will restore your judges as at the first,
and your counselors as at the beginning.
Afterward you shall be called the city of righteousness,
the faithful city." (Isaiah 1:25, 26)

God has industrial-strength cleansing agents ("as with lye") to remove the deep stains of our long-standing, well-established sins. He is able to re-create our lost purity. He takes his people into a refining fire, all the way through to restoration as a "faithful city." The people of God at their best will be seen again, and we can be a part of it.

But the Hebrew text does something more here. The words "I will turn" (1:25) and "I will restore" (1:26) translate the same verb (*'ašîḇâh*). We translate this with different English verbs, "turn" and "restore," because our idiom requires it. But Isaiah is implying that one God, acting in one way, is able to accomplish two things at once. When God turns his hand against us, it isn't a disaster; it's an act of restoration. The discipline of God achieves just what he intends, in purification and in restoration, both at the same time. We can expect the goodness of God to show up in unlikely experiences. When he turns his hand against us to purify us, let's trust him to restore us.

Verses 27–31 conclude the passage, but not with the cutesy ending of a TV sitcom. These verses are hard-hitting. Why are they here? Because Isaiah doesn't want us to misunderstand. He has been saying that God will restore his people. The church's glory is not passing; it's her corruption that is passing. But for us in our generation, how are we redeemed out of our failures? Isaiah wants us to know. He wants us to feel the weight of the decision we face. In verses 21–26 he fortified us with confidence that God will purify his Bride, so that now, in verses 27–31, we will dare to follow God into the refining fire and stay there long enough for his purpose to be fulfilled in us.

The Decision Before Us

Zion shall be redeemed by justice,
and those in her who repent, by righteousness.
But rebels and sinners shall be broken together,
and those who forsake the LORD shall be consumed. (Isaiah 1:27, 28)

God does not redeem us by casually sweeping his standards aside. God pays the price demanded by his own justice and righteousness. This is the magnitude of his achievement at the cross of Christ. Redemption comes not by God's leniency but by his justice and righteousness fully satisfied in Christ. The Bible says that "our great God and Savior Jesus Christ . . . gave himself for us to redeem us from all lawlessness and to purify for himself a people for his own possession" (Titus 2:13, 14). We are redeemed at a cost to God that we will never understand. At the cross he put the real moral guilt of sinners onto Christ, the perfect substitute. God honored his own moral government of the universe. Our part, Isaiah tells us, is to repent: ". . . and those in her who repent."

How could it be otherwise? We add nothing to the value of Jesus' sacrifice, but his love does claim all that we are. The flip side of God paying the price is that we are no longer our own (1 Corinthians 6:19b, 20a). What else can we do but repent? We need to repent of our sins every day. We need to repent of our fifth-rate righteousness every day. We need to receive afresh, with the empty hands of faith, real righteousness from Jesus Christ every day. The cross becomes a redeeming power for us as we learn what it means to repent.

There is no way around repentance. The only alternative is in verse 28: "But rebels and sinners shall be broken together, and those who forsake the Lord shall be consumed." That is the decision before us. Will we repent and be redeemed, or rebel and be consumed? God will redeem his people, and he wants to redeem you and me. He has already paid the price at the cross. The question is, will we turn to God in repentance, even if he leads us into a refining fire (v. 25)? If we decide against repentance, we will be consumed. If we decide for repentance, we will be redeemed.

Finally, in verses 29–31, Isaiah begs us to embrace repentance by showing us what will happen if we refuse God.

The Reality Confronting Us

> For you[6] shall be ashamed of the oaks
>   that you desired;
> and you shall blush for the gardens
>   that you have chosen.
> For you shall be like an oak
>   whose leaf withers,
>   and like a garden without water.
> And the strong shall become tinder,
>   and his work a spark,
> and both of them shall burn together,
>   with none to quench them. (vv. 29–31)

Why are these verses so confrontational? God isn't slapping us around. He is pressing his point. We think, "It doesn't matter. My decisions, my attitudes and thoughts and feelings—do they really make that much difference?" But God is saying, "Every moment of your life matters to me. Your choices have lasting repercussions. *That's* why I am confronting you with the truth."

If we set the course of our lives by the earthly things we foolishly desire and choose, we will end up with nothing. The key to the metaphors in verses 29, 30 is verse 31: "the strong . . . and his work." The "oaks" and "gardens" are metaphors for human strength and potential and preference. The point is that our own brilliance and desire will be the death of us. But repentance opens up life. In the ways of God, the weakness of repentance is how we experience the power of redemption.

Conviction of sin, repentance, and redemption—this is the way into salvation. It's a good way, because there is a Redeemer. Whatever gets us closer to him can only be good. The New Testament scholar Everett F. Harrison wrote,

> No word in the Christian vocabulary deserves to be held more precious than Redeemer, for even more than Savior it reminds the child of God that his salvation has been purchased at a great and personal cost, for the Lord has given himself for our sins in order to deliver us from them.[7]

You may be wondering which way to go. You may be far from God. You may have lost your purity. What you must know is that there is a Redeemer. Go to him with honest dealings about your real problems. He will save you from them all.

5

The Transforming Power
of Hope and Humility

ISAIAH 2:1–22

WHERE DO WE MODERN PEOPLE typically find our incentives for living? In the present. The future threatens to rob us of all we have and hope to have. We trust in God, in a way. But more than we realize, our sense of stability is not grounded in God alone but in our pleasant surroundings. If we successful people have nothing beyond the status quo, we will respond to earthly loss with rage and despair. Have we worked so hard, only to create our own vulnerability? World events are forcing us to think about that. Every day terrorist fanatics are plotting to murder us. Even if we get to them first, how do we save ourselves from the powers of nature that slammed Asia with killer tsunami waves in late 2004? Left to ourselves, we are defenseless before the buffetings of life.

That is when Christ comes to us. Through him our losses can become pathways to hope. For us privileged people in the Western world, the supreme privilege of life is when we find that God himself is all we really need.

Isaiah helps us set our hearts on God. The key is not just what we *believe* but what we *value*. Prophetic eyes look beyond the world as it is now to a new world in the future (2:2–4). We can live now in the power of that future (2:5). Our well-being does not depend on our present social construct, which Isaiah views with contempt (2:6–21). He invites us to join him in his unblinking realism about all false hopes (2:22). He is saying to us, "Relocate your happiness in the future, in a world that doesn't exist yet except in the promise of God. If you do that, you won't be devastated when the idols of human pride are trashed, as they will be. In God you can possess both the present and the future." Here are the terms: "Aim at heaven and you will get earth 'thrown in'; aim at earth and you will get neither."[1]

Verse 1 of Isaiah's second chapter marks the literary seam between the introduction (chapter 1) and the body (chapters 2—66) of his book. What follows in the rest of chapter 2 is a poem on the transforming power of hope and humility. Why does Isaiah link hope with humility? Because we use the idol of self-advancement to stabilize ourselves. But God can replace our fear and pride with hope and humility.

1. The transforming power of hope (2:2–5)
   A The hope (2:2–4)
      B The transforming power: "Let us walk in the light of the LORD"
        (2:5)
2. The transforming power of humility (2:6–22)
   A The humility (2:6–21)
      1 The church: full but empty (2:6–9)
      2 The world: high but low (2:10–19)
         a^1 Man is defenseless before God (2:10)
           b^1 The Lord alone will be exalted (2:11)
             c God will defeat all pride (2:12–16)
           b^2 The Lord alone will be exalted (2:17)
         a^2 Man's idols are defenseless before God (2:18, 19)
      3 The idols: precious but contemptible (2:20, 21)
   B The transforming power: "Stop regarding man" (2:22)

As we come alive to God's promised future, we dethrone our idols, and the Lord alone is exalted within us.

The Power of Hope

> It shall come to pass in the latter days
>   that the mountain of the house of the LORD
> shall be established as the highest of the mountains,
>   and shall be lifted up above the hills. (Isaiah 2:2a)

The words "in the latter days" could be translated "in the end of the days." Isaiah may be playing on the words "In the beginning" from Genesis 1:1—*bᵉrêšît* there answered with *bᵉ'aḥᵃrît* here.[2] Isaiah looks from the beauty of the beginning, through the wreckage of history, all the way forward to the glory of the consummation. What does he foresee?

Isaiah sees the worship of God enthused over, while all the religions of man are humbled into nothing. In Isaiah's day people located their shrines on hills and mountaintops, closer to Heaven. But God chose a measly little hilltop in the land of Israel to be the place where he should be worshiped. It wasn't impressive by the usual standards. And today the church is rarely impressive in the eyes of man (1 Corinthians 1:26). But in the latter days the nations will abandon their worldviews and ideologies and gladly give to the church their esteem as the world's leader in worship.

> And all the nations shall flow to it,
>   and many peoples shall come, and say:
> "Come, let us go up to the mountain of the LORD,
>   to the house of the God of Jacob,
> that he may teach us his ways
>   and that we may walk in his paths."
> For out of Zion shall go forth the law,
>   and the word of the Lord from Jerusalem. (Isaiah 2:2b, 3)

I love the anti-gravitational anomaly of this human river flowing uphill to worship God. He is promising a worldwide miracle as the nations, far from being forced, gladly hurry to worship him and learn his ways. They set no preconditions. They are eager and open. This miracle has already begun. It started at Pentecost 2,000 years ago (Acts 2), it is going on today through Christian missions, and it will be consummated in the latter days with an overflowing river of conversions to Christ.

When verse 3 says, "out of Zion," the implication is "out of Zion *only*." But today we are told that the exclusive claim of the gospel is intolerant. We are told that we should admit all religions as valid ways to God, so that people can be true to themselves. But those in this prophetic vision remain multicultural *as* "all the nations" and "many peoples." What changes is that, in all their beautiful diversity, they find their greatest delight in a new devotion. And if the whole world freely chooses to rally around Jesus Christ by the irresistible force of his dying love, who would deny them that choice? *That* would be oppression.

Look how desirable it is, from a universally human point of view, to be allured to Christ:

> He shall judge between the nations,
>   and shall decide disputes for many peoples;
> and they shall beat their swords into plowshares,
>   and their spears into pruning hooks;
> nation shall not lift up sword against nation,
>   neither shall they learn war anymore. (Isaiah 2:4)

When the gospel finally sweeps over the world, there will be neither the practice of nor even the inclination to engage in war. No widows and orphans will be left behind by a fallen soldier, no money consumed on military hardware, as Jesus settles our disputes with perfectly satisfying justice and mercy. All that money and talent and genius and effort will be deployed for life-enriching purposes.[3] That is God's promise. It is our only hope. And what is the power of that hope right now?

> O house of Jacob,
>   come, let us walk
>   in the light of the LORD. (v. 5)

Verse 5 echoes verse 3. What Isaiah says in verse 5 resembles what the nations say in verse 3: "Come, let us go up to the mountain of the LORD . . . that we may walk in his paths. . . . Come, let us walk in the light of the LORD." The difference is the prepositions—"to" and "in." The nations come *to* the worship of God. Believers walk *in* the light. We Christians become a prophetic presence in our generation as the nations can see their own most deeply desired future in our life together. "O house of Jacob, come, let us walk in the light of the LORD." In other words, "Let the promises of God have their full impact on us now."

The Power of Humility

We need hope. But we also need humility. Isaiah is no dreamy idealist. He sees human pride as the great impediment to the world as it should be.

He discerns pride among God's people, pride in the world, and pride in the worship of idols. First, pride among God's people (2:6–9). The key words here are "full" in verse 6 and "filled" repeated three times in verses 7, 8. The church can be *full* of worldly wisdom, *filled* with money, *filled* with power, and *filled* with idols—filled with everything but the Holy Spirit. When believers stuff their lives full of false ideals and comforts, it's because they feel empty within. They have lost their sense of God.[4] Isaiah arrives at a shocking conclusion for his own generation:

> So people are humbled,
>   and each one is brought low—
>   do not forgive them! (v. 9)

If we fill ourselves with anything other than God, we are not enriched; we are brought low. There can come a point of no return, where God's people are so filled with the wrong things and so empty of a sense of God that forgiveness becomes unthinkable, and God moves on.[5] "You have rejected your people," Isaiah says (v. 6). It's not that God doesn't love them anymore. But if any generation of his people along the way becomes full of pride, he would do them no favor by visiting them with blessing. It would only reinforce their self-salvation. Their first need is to be emptied of their fullness. Isaiah understands that ". . . proud, self-sufficient Israel can become the witness to the greatness of God only when she has been reduced to helplessness by his just judgment and then restored to life by his unmerited grace."[6]

Secondly, Isaiah sees the pride in the world (2:10–19). The words "against all" or "against every"—the same words in the Hebrew text—appear ten times in verses 12–16, the heart of this section. *Everything* in the world that exalts itself against God is brought low when his kingdom comes. But why does God insist that he alone be exalted in that day (2:11, 17)? Is God a megalomaniac who can't stand to see others succeed? No. The reason is that God's glory entails both his own happiness and our happiness. Our egocentric self-exaltation degrades us, but humility before God heaps honors upon us. This is the salvation we don't believe in.

No individual, not even the whole world together, can rob God of his glory. The Bible says, "The LORD is high above all nations, and his glory above the heavens!" (Psalm 113:4). You and I are no threat to him. He isn't insecure when he insists upon the triumph of his glory alone. The problem is that we *think* that his glory and our joy do not lie together in the depths of his heart. We *think* we have to compete with his will to fulfill our own potential. That is pride. We think too well of ourselves and too poorly of God to believe that his love for his glory and his love for us are *one* love, drawing him on to the final day when we will be forever happy with his glory alone. But how could it be otherwise? Human fulfillment *is* union with God. Jonathan Edwards wisely wrote:

> God is glorified not only by His glory's being seen, but by its being rejoiced in. When those that see it delight in it, God is more glorified than if they only see it. His glory is then received with the whole soul, both by the understanding and by the heart. God made the world that he might communicate, and the creature receive, His glory.[7]

Isaiah is telling us, "Strip away all the surface problems. Our deepest disorder is that the human race arrogantly perceives God as a threat, when in fact his glory is another word for *Heaven*. Therefore, God has set aside a day on the calendar of human history to destroy with a terrible finality every proud barrier to the only true joy that exists for the human heart. The Lord alone will be exalted in that day. And this is the best news imaginable."

When we read about "the terror of the LORD" in verses 10 and 19, we feel uneasy. We should. But the worst that can happen is not the terror of the Lord deconstructing the whole world. The worst that can happen is not the loss of retirement investments, the loss of health, the loss of face. The worst that can happen to us is the loss of delight in the glory of God alone. And the best that can happen to us is to be awakened to his glory as our joy, even if we must be humbled to experience that awakening. John Donne (1573–1631) understood this:

> Batter my heart, three-personed God, for you
> As yet but knock, breathe, shine, and seek to mend;
> That I may rise and stand, o'erthrow me, and bend
> Your force to break, blow, burn and make me new. . . .
> Take me to you, imprison me, for I
> Except you enthrall me, never shall be free,
> Nor ever chaste, except you ravish me.[8]

Thirdly, the prophet discerns pride among the idols (2:20, 21). The key here is the incongruity of "their idols of silver and their idols of gold" being thrown like trash "to the moles and to the bats." Pride deceives people into assembling an idol-filled culture, because idolatry gives people a feeling of control and power. They *make* the things they worship. But when the Lord stands forth in unmistakable glory, it will be terrible for those who do not delight in his control and his power. They will see how worthless their most dearly cherished idols really are, and they will have nothing left worth having.

Idols are precious. They are always our hard-won silver and gold. That's why we prize them. They are beautiful, but also contemptible. J. R. R. Tolkien portrayed this in The Lord of the Rings. Everyone who wears the golden ring of power morphs into something weirdly subhuman, like Gollum, who cherishes it as "My Precious." So for Middle-earth to be saved, the ring must be thrown into the fire of Mount Doom and destroyed forever. Tolkien understood that the key to life is not only what we lay hold of but also what we throw away. Paul wrote, "I have suffered the loss of all things and count them as rubbish, in order that I may gain Christ" (Philippians 3:8). What golden idols do we cherish as essential to our happiness? What must we throw away, to possess the one treasure we really cannot live without—Christ, who will not make us weird but beautiful, like himself?

That humbling experience of self-exposure is a breakthrough into valuing everything in a new way. Isaiah explains the power of humility:

> Stop regarding man
>   in whose nostrils is breath,

for of what account is he? (Isaiah 2:22)

We think of ourselves as sophisticated, but the fact is, we are too easily impressed. Our self-confidence keeps us from walking in the light of the Lord. So God is calling us to take a bold step. "The greatest need of man is to reject man"[9] and humbly to live for the glory of God alone.

Do you believe that there is enough glory in God to make you happy forever? If you don't, why? What failing have you found in God? The gospel promises that his glory will remake the whole world. Stop valuing the idols you not only might lose but inevitably must lose. Learn to enjoy God. The triumph of his glory is enough to make your complete happiness forever invincible.

6

The Enriching Power of Loss and Gain

ISAIAH 3:1—4:6

WILLIAM BUTLER YEATS understood our modern world. In "The Second Coming" he wrote:

> Things fall apart; the centre cannot hold;
> Mere anarchy is loosed upon the world,
> The blood-dimmed tide is loosed, and everywhere
> The ceremony of innocence is drowned.[1]

Yeats wrote that in 1919. The engines of militarism, uncoupled from the restraints of mercy, had unleashed the bloodiest century of history so far.

Isaiah looks even more deeply into the social disintegration we fear, and he sees God there. God's work is both terrible and beautiful. He leads us into loss in order to enrich us with lasting gain.

The whole section of Isaiah 2:1—4:6 has two bookends: the prophecy of the nations attracted to God's people (2:2–5) and the prophecy of God's people visited by him (4:2–6). In between, God speaks bluntly about the mess that his people are right now (2:6—4:1). His confrontation is real, but it stands within a larger context of grace. He will save his people. He will bless the whole world. He is moving us toward the Day of the Lord,[2] when he will reveal himself with finality. Isaiah explains how God calculates loss and gain in our experience as he prepares us for that day.

1. Loss: The Lord will remove all stability (3:1–15)
    A¹ Social upheaval as leadership collapses (3:1–7)
        B¹ The root cause: "defying his glorious presence" (3:8–11)
    A² "My people" stumble in confusion (3:12)
        B² The root cause: "It is *you* . . ." (3:13–15)
2. Loss: The Lord will remove all arrogant finery (3:16—4:1)
    A¹ The haughty women humiliated (3:16, 17)
        B¹ Cleaning out the glut (3:18–23)
            C A new wardrobe! (3:24)
        B² Replacing the glut with emptiness (3:25, 26)
    A² The humiliated women desperate (4:1)
3. Gain: The Lord will create true beauty and security (4:2–6)
    A Our only beauty and pride: the Messiah (4:2–4)
        B Our only security and refuge: the Presence (4:5, 6)

In 3:1 God says he is "taking away" something from his people. Then again in 3:18 he says he will "take away" something further. But in 4:2–6, the gain section, he doesn't say what we expect. He doesn't say that he will give something back. He promises to "create" something new. That is our gain—better than we expect or deserve.

God knows how to enrich us through loss. Sometimes he takes away more than we wish he would, but only to give us more of himself forever. Jim Elliot said, "He is no fool who gives up what he cannot keep to gain what he cannot lose."[3] And we will not gain what we cannot lose *without* giving up what we cannot keep. Loss for the sake of gain—this is the way of God for us.

If God seems severe at times, it's only because his love is so intense, his imagination so colorful, that he settles for nothing less than our complete salvation. C. S. Lewis pictures it with Isaianic vividness:

> Imagine yourself living in a house. God comes in to rebuild that house. At first, perhaps, you can understand what he is doing. He is getting the drains right and stopping the leaks in the roof and so on; you knew that those jobs needed doing and so you are not surprised. But presently he starts knocking the house about in a way that hurts abominably and does not seem to make sense. What on earth is he up to? The explanation is that he is building quite a different house from the one you thought of—throwing out a new wing here, putting on an extra floor there, running up towers, making courtyards. You thought you were going to be made into a decent little cottage; but he is building a palace. He intends to come and live in it himself.[4]

That is exactly the force of Isaiah 3:1—4:6.

Loss of Stability

> For behold, the Lord GOD of hosts
>   is taking away from Jerusalem and from Judah
> support and supply,
>   all support of bread,
>   and all support of water. (Isaiah 3:1)

This section is surrounded by "the Lord GOD of hosts" in 3:1 and 15. The prophet envisions this powerful Lord taking something away from his people. What do they stand to lose? "Support and supply." These two words translate one Hebrew word repeated in Isaiah's text, once in the masculine form, then again in the feminine form—*mash'ēn* and *maš'ēnâh*. The Lord is taking away *everything* that stabilizes the corporate life of Isaiah's generation: "*all* support of bread, and *all* support of water." He is talking about Assyrian invasion, with all its destabilizing impact.

Then God explains the meltdown. He is taking away their leaders (vv. 2, 3) and replacing them with irresponsible "boys" (v. 4), so that social cohesion dissolves into chaos (v. 5). In their desperation, the people will look around for someone, for anyone, to provide guidance and courage. But no one will be willing (vv. 6, 7). The warning for every generation is this: One way God judges his people is by depriving them of worthy leaders. The center no longer holds.

Mayor Rudolph Giuliani is respected today because on September 11, 2001, when part of New York City literally became "this heap of ruins," he stepped forward with courage. But what if Mayor Guliani had lost his nerve that day? What if there had been no one to accept responsibility, lift morale, coordinate the effort? Trustworthy leaders are gifts from God. The New Testament says that God gave us the most important leaders of all—apostles, prophets, evangelists, and pastor-teachers (Ephesians 4:11–16)—to lead us to himself. That is the heart of spiritual leadership. But sometimes that isn't what God's people want.

In verses 8–11, the prophet identifies the reason for the malaise of his time. The key is the last line of verse 8:

> For Jerusalem has stumbled,
>   and Judah has fallen,
> because their speech and their deeds are against the LORD,
>   defying his glorious presence.

Literally this reads, "defying the eyes of his glory." Isaiah's contemporaries resisted God's relevance to the whole of life—"the eyes of his glory." To be forgiven, yes. To be protected, yes. But beyond that, they didn't want

God to be *too* real. They wanted a compartmentalized God, not an omnipresent God, and this is what did them in. The pagan cultures were not the problem. Why blame external forces when the people of God bring evil on themselves (v. 9)? God is still present, still at work (vv. 10, 11). But we either delight in his glorious presence or we defy his glorious presence. Everything else hinges on this.

In verses 12–15 the Lord exposes the leaders. They too answer to God because he loves his people. We feel his love in the words "my people," seen twice in verse 12 and again in verse 15, along with "his people" in verse 14.[5] It breaks his heart when his people are oppressed by opportunists: "It is you [elders and princes] who have devoured the vineyard" (v. 14). Rather than living to enrich others, false leaders ride on the backs of others. Verse 15 asks, "What do you mean by crushing my people, by grinding the face of the poor?" Do you hear the loving indignation in God's voice?

Jesus was like this. He said, "The thief comes only to steal and kill and destroy. I came that they may have life and have it abundantly. I am the good shepherd. The good shepherd lays down his life for the sheep" (John 10:10, 11). That is leadership. That is the love we can trust.

One of the marks of revival is not just high-octane worship, which costs us no self-denial and might even reinforce our selfishness. True revival awakens a new sense of our responsibility to one another, which is contrary to our selfishness and therefore a more revealing indicator of the presence of the Holy Spirit.[6] When John the Baptist was announcing the coming of God's kingdom, the people asked him what they should do. He told them, "Whoever has two tunics is to share with him who has none, and whoever has food is to do likewise" (Luke 3:11). If we love God's presence, we will not say, "The poor aren't my responsibility." We will help them. And those of us who lead should exert this influence. In our personalities and lifestyles, we should be life-enrichers, not life-depleters.

In verses 1–15, then, the prophet foresees loss for his generation—the loss of stability as real leaders disappear and the people stumble into confusion. But this loss God remedies with a great gain. He gives a Messiah, as we will see in the climax of the passage. In his second major section Isaiah says that God is taking something else away. In 3:16—4:1, the women of Judah stand to lose the outward finery they have flaunted in self-display. Another way in which God can judge his people is to replace their absurd arrogance with everything they dread.

Loss of Finery

The key words appear in 3:24, the heart of this section. Five times we see "instead of":

Instead of perfume there will be rottenness;
    and instead of a belt, a rope;
and instead of well-set hair, baldness;
    and instead of a rich robe, a skirt of sackcloth;
    and branding instead of beauty.

God is describing capture and exile and abuse. This actually happened. Why? Isaiah 3:16 explains, "Because the daughters of Zion are haughty . . ." How dimly they felt the evil of pride! But pride is what made an angel into the devil (1 Timothy 3:6). It is "the complete anti-God state of mind."[7] When their pride forced him to it, God exchanged ("instead of") pretense with reality, and life tailed off into unspeakable sadness as "wealthy women, secure in their luxury and their allure, are reduced to scabrous hags begging to belong to someone."[8]

The inventory of jewels and fancy clothes in 3:18–23 stands parallel with the list of big-shot leaders in 3:2, 3. Both the men and the women, in their own ways, fell short of the glory of God. To swagger the way men do, to display false beauty the way women do—that is not the glory God created us for. The secret beauty of a Christian woman is a persona radiant with the Holy Spirit (1 Timothy 2:9, 10; 1 Peter 3:4). The world does not have a category for that beauty, but it's real. A God-filled woman is beautiful, whatever her age or features. She is dressed properly for The Occasion—that coming day when the Lord alone will be exalted (Isaiah 2:11, 17).

The desperation of these tragic women in 4:1 stands parallel with the desperate men of 3:6. A man takes hold of his brother in a pitiful attempt to escape social chaos, and women take hold of a man in a pitiful attempt to escape personal shame. Both images merge in 3:25, 26, where Isaiah describes a metaphorical lady, Jerusalem herself. God has taken away her "support and supply," with all her finery, and "empty, she shall sit on the ground" (3:26).[9]

God's people suffer loss upon loss, *and God is the one doing it*. He is taking away what they need to stabilize and beautify their lives. Does this say anything to us? The risen Jesus says to his church,

You say, I am rich, I have prospered, and I need nothing, not realizing that you are wretched, pitiable, poor, blind, and naked. I counsel you to buy from me gold refined by fire, so that you may be rich, and white garments so that you may clothe yourself and the shame of your nakedness may not be seen, and salve to anoint your eyes, so that you may see. Those whom I love, I reprove and discipline, so be zealous and repent. (Revelation 3:17–19)

I will come to you and take away your lampstand from its place, unless you repent. (Revelation 2:5b)

What losses must we suffer, so that we prize Christ as our only true gain?

Gain of Perfection

> In that day the branch of the LORD shall be beautiful and glorious, and the fruit of the land shall be the pride and honor of the survivors of Israel. (Isaiah 4:2)

This vision is as beautiful as the preceding has been terrible. We read the words "In that day" as it opens, and we wince. After the painful stripping of 3:1—4:1, what's next? But God threatens no further loss. Instead he creates something new, better than what he took away.

"The branch of the LORD," with the parallel "the fruit of the land," is a metaphor for the Messiah.[10] Isaiah is contrasting the beautiful humility of our Messiah—just a sprout, a twig, growing from the Davidic line—with the absurd magnificence of Jerusalem's women. Later the prophet will write, "He had no form or majesty that we should look at him, and no beauty that we should desire him" (Isaiah 53:2). But Jesus replaces false beauty with true desirability: "The branch of the LORD shall be beautiful and glorious" (Isaiah 4:2).

But not everyone will enjoy him. He will be "the pride and honor of *the survivors* of Israel." There will be no rival agendas and pet causes and swollen egos crowding the church of Jesus Christ then. On the Day of the Lord, the Spirit will wash the church clean with judgment and burning (4:4). That is significant. It means we do not find hope in avoiding judgment but in going through judgment. Without it, we remain as we are. But if we submit to God's "spirit of judgment and . . . spirit of burning," we change and become holy (4:3). Jesus himself will stand forth as our only beauty and pride. Then God will create something new—a cloud by day and a flaming fire by night (4:5). What is that? Exodus 40:34–38 says that the glory of God filled the tabernacle this way. First Kings 8:10, 11 says that the glory of God filled the temple this way. Isaiah is thinking of the manifest presence of God, but now with a difference. On this final Day of the Lord the glory will not just fill a tabernacle or a temple; it will cover "the whole site of Mount Zion" and "her assemblies." God is moving us toward a time when his glorious presence will cover his whole church and all local gatherings of believers. And over all the glory will be a wedding canopy, according to verse 5, hinting at our intimacy and joy with God. The display of his glory will not be intimidating, as it was on Mount Sinai (Exodus 19:16). We will feel, and we will be, sheltered in his presence forever (4:6). And everything will finally be *perfect*.

I need the help of a sensitive imagination like Jonathan Edwards's to convey the beauty of this:

There the glorious God is manifested and shines forth in full glory, in beams of love. And there this glorious fountain forever flows forth in streams, yea, in rivers of love and delight. And these rivers swell, as it were, to an ocean of love, in which the souls of the ransomed may bathe with the sweetest enjoyment and their hearts, as it were, be deluged with love![11]

He is no fool who gives up what he cannot keep to gain this, which he can never lose.

7

Receiving the Grace
of God in Vain

ISAIAH 5:1–30

IN 2 CORINTHIANS 6:1 the Apostle Paul says a strange thing: "We appeal to you not to receive the grace of God in vain." How can *grace* be received in vain? Isn't grace God's all-forgiving kindness to us? Doesn't God's grace compensate even for our halfhearted responses to God? Why then does Paul urge us not to receive the grace of God in vain? Because God's grace not only accepts us, it also transforms us. But if all we want out of God is acceptance without transformation, we are receiving his grace in vain and our Christianity is worthless.

The power of grace is not automatic. Each of us lives out of an inner world with its own moral and conceptual and emotional topography. The obstacles to God there are formidable. Our intuitive ways of thinking, the tilt of our very desires—these powerful internal structures can hinder the advance of God. Isaiah 5 helps us by identifying six ways we resist God's grace, so we can turn those obstacles into avenues. And Isaiah 5 solemnizes us by identifying four ways in which God disciplines grace-resistant people if we don't. Verses 1–7 are Isaiah's parable of the vineyard. That's about the grace of God. Then verses 8–30 are about the tragedy of receiving his grace in vain.

1. Grace: What more could God have done? (5:1–7)
2. Tragedy: Six laments over God's unresponsive people (5:8–30)
      A¹ Reckless ambition yields little (5:8–10)
         B¹ Self-indulgence misses the obvious (5:11, 12)
            (1) Therefore, God's uncomprehending people suffer deprivation (5:13)

(2) Therefore, God's humbled people prove his holiness
(5:14–17)
C¹ Deliberate sinning defies the Holy One (5:18, 19)
C² Willful perversion rationalizes evil (5:20)
B² Self-admiration redefines reality (5:21)
A² Reckless excess produces injustice (5:22, 23)
(1) Therefore, God's enfeebled people prove his holiness
(5:24)
(2) Therefore, God's helpless people suffer his anger (5:25–30)

You know the popular caricature of the ranting Hebrew prophet? It will not do. The structure of the literature shows how reasonable Isaiah was. The "woes" argue his case with evidences, and the "therefores" draw out inescapable conclusions. Isaiah is explaining how we disempower the gospel. He is logical and fair and helpful.

Isaiah is tenderhearted as well. The word "woe" itself, appearing six times in the passage, does not just *denounce* our sins, it *laments* our sins. The same word is translated "Ah!" in Isaiah 1:4 and "Alas!" in 1 Kings 13:30. Remember that "woe" is the opposite of the word "blessed" (cf. Luke 6:20–26). "Blessed" exclaims joy, but "woe" mingles solemnity with sorrow. Is there warning here? Yes, but not stridency. The prophet's reasonableness and sympathy are meant to win from us a fruitful response to the grace of God.

Grace

Let me sing for my beloved my love song concerning his vineyard:
My beloved had a vineyard
    on a very fertile hill.
He dug it and cleared it of stones,
    and planted it with choice vines;
he built a watchtower in the midst of it,
    and hewed out a wine vat in it;
and he looked for it to yield grapes,
    but it yielded wild grapes. (Isaiah 5:1, 2)

Isaiah starts with a harmless piece of entertainment, a popular love song. But like Nathan confronting David in 2 Samuel 12, the prophet is taking us somewhere. He is contrasting God's lavish bestowments of grace with the disappointing outcomes on our end. In the prophet's imaginative scenario, a man is cultivating a vineyard with every appropriate provision. He has a right to expect a good crop. But what comes of his efforts? "Wild grapes,"

Isaiah says. Actually, the Hebrew word suggests stinking grapes. They are not merely wild, they are rancid.

What went wrong? The owner of the vineyard did everything he could. Where was the breakdown? Verse 3 offers only two possibilities: "Judge between *me* and *my vineyard.*" The failure lies either with the owner or with the vineyard. And verses 1, 2 have shown how generous and intelligent and purposeful was his investment. In fact, in verse 4 the owner himself invites us to find fault with him: "What more was there to do for my vineyard, that I have not done in it?" The key word in verses 1–7 appears next: "When I looked for it to yield grapes, *why* did it yield wild grapes?" Why? Why are we not more fruitful? Is it God's fault?

We tell ourselves, "If only I had more time, if only I had a better wife/husband, if only I were married, if only my job weren't so demanding, if only I had more money, I'd really live for the Lord." We tell ourselves, "If only we had contemporary music in our church, if only we'd keep that contemporary music out of our church, we'd be the church we ought to be." "If only this, if only that . . ." These are all excuses. At bottom each one implies a criticism of God, as if he hasn't already given us all we need to live well for him (2 Peter 1:3).

What has God done for us? Think of Romans 8 alone. God has removed all condemnation from us through our union with Christ. He has made a new arrangement for us, the New Covenant, so that the righteousness of the Law will be fulfilled in our actual moral character by the Spirit's power. Christ now lives in us, as the Holy Spirit imparts life to our personalities now and to our bodies at the resurrection. We are being led forward in this new life by the Spirit, who awakens in us a sense of God's fatherly love for us. He has made us co-heirs with Christ of the new heavens and the new earth, where all our hopes will be fulfilled. And right now the Spirit helps us to press on even when we're too weak to pray. God is working all things for our good along the way, according to his eternal plan, and nothing will ever be able to separate us from the love of God in Christ Jesus our Lord. And that is just Romans 8.

God has been busy on our behalf! The question is, what have we *done* with his outpouring of grace?[1] Are we parlaying his blessing into fruitful outcomes? Are we a good investment? Dr. Robert E. Coleman travels the globe constantly and has his finger on the pulse of worldwide Christianity. Several years ago he told me that in the previous fifteen years real church growth in North America was zero percent. And we North Americans have astonishing resources to work with—not only the riches of Romans 8, which all believers have, but also a ministry infrastructure unprecedented in Christian history. We have churches and schools and colleges and seminaries and radio stations and conferences and new translations of the Bible and publishing companies and magazines and Bible study materials and on and on. And in fifteen years, the result? *Zero net growth.* There is only one word for that outcome: failure. But the church in Asia and Africa and Latin America is growing by leaps and bounds. We must ask ourselves the same question Isaiah asked his generation: *Why?* The problem is not a failure in God.

We can't hide behind our identity as God's people. He isn't offering that identity as a refuge from embarrassing questions. Verse 7 says, "The vineyard of the LORD of hosts is the house of Israel, and the men of Judah are his pleasant planting." They were the people of God too, but it didn't exempt them from God's expectation of fruitful results; it made them responsible for fruitful results. God takes a practical outlook because his grace works with a practical power. We shouldn't minimize the strengths in the church. But God himself is telling us to face our weaknesses. So let's stop thinking how successful we are and figure out what it's going to take to go to the next level of productivity. And when by grace we get there, then let's ask how to go to the next level above that, and so forth. We must take full advantage of the opportunity God has given us, or we will lose it (vv. 5, 6).

It gets worse. When we are unfruitful in response to God's grace, we become fruitful with "wild grapes." In verse 7 God translates the parable into literal reality:

> . . . and he looked for justice,
> but behold, bloodshed;
> for righteousness,
> but behold, an outcry!

The note in the margin of the English Standard Version tells us that Isaiah is using a word play here. One commentator tries to convey it in English this way: "Did he find right? Nothing but riot! Did he find decency? Only despair."[2] One of the anomalies of our age is how the lives of professing Christians are often little distinguished from the lives of others. The question we must ask is not, "Is our generation of the church bearing fruit?" The question is, "Are we bearing the *sweet* fruit consistent with the beauty of grace, and are we yielding an *abundant* harvest commensurate with the abundant grace God has invested in us?" If the answers to those questions are not encouraging, let's have the honesty to ask ourselves why.

Tragedy

Isaiah helps us think it all through. He holds up six clusters of wild grapes, as it were, to illustrate what's going wrong, six ways we resist the grace of God, six answers to the question "Why?" Each is presented with a "Woe."

Woe to those who join house to house,
   who add field to field,
until there is no more room,
   and you are made to dwell alone
   in the midst of the land. (v. 8)

The rich were getting richer, and the poor were getting squeezed out. But there was more to it. God had said that the land was his, and all the people were living there by his gracious permission (Leviticus 25). And he wanted the land to be handed down along family lines, to prevent a permanent underclass. So when the wealthy of Judah were amassing property to themselves, they were living as if God were worthless and as if they were not their brother's keeper. It was more than social injustice; it was practical atheism. It made a difference. The law of unintended consequences kicked in. As these people enlarged their estates, they ended up isolating themselves: "And you are made to dwell *alone* in the midst of the land." In the land, the place of blessing, what is their condition? They are alone. And the *much* they have grabbed comes to a *little* they cannot increase (Isaiah 5:10). Isaiah is saying that greed disempowers grace and dissolves into emptiness. One scholar asks, "How many of the world's great castles and mansions have been lived in for any appreciable time? They are simply too pretentious to be borne."[3] Remember that Hell, in C. S. Lewis's *The Great Divorce*, is an enormous city, with mansions set off at vast distances from one another, because nobody likes anybody else and they end up living alone.[4] Let's beware what we build.

The second bunch of wild grapes appears with the "Woe" in verse 11. Here the obstacle to the transforming power of grace is a refusal to think.

Woe to those who rise early in the morning,
   that they may run after strong drink,
who tarry late into the evening
   as wine inflames them!
They have lyre and harp,
   tambourine and flute and wine at their feasts,
but they do not regard the deeds of the LORD,
   or see the work of his hands. (Isaiah 5:11, 12)

God's people refused to face facts, and Isaiah knew why. The word "inflames" is significant. The passion inflaming them was not the Holy Spirit. Something else stirred their intensity.

The gospel explains that there are basically two kinds of people in the world: sensate and spiritual (Romans 8:5, 6).[5] The sensate mentality is drawn to entertainment, while the spiritual mentality is drawn to worship. Isaiah condemned Judah's unreasoning passion for one thrill after another, because a visceral approach to life quenches the Holy Spirit. The gospel says, "Do not get drunk with wine . . . but be filled with the Spirit" (Ephesians 5:18). The power of grace does not lie in spiritual moderation but in deep, repeated gulps of the Spirit. And that kind of excess does not dull our minds; it sharpens our awareness, so that God becomes real to us.

In verses 13–17 Isaiah transitions into a subsection. He matches his two "woes" with two "therefores." He is setting forth in a logical way how the grace-diminishing patterns of life in verses 8–12 impact actual experience. The "Therefore" of verse 13 draws out the irony that their drinking and excesses lead to hunger and thirst. The land will spit them out in exile. And the "Therefore" of verses 14–17 reveals the further irony that the land-grabbers will themselves be swallowed up. Sheol enlarges its appetite for them and opens its mouth (v. 14). So now we discover what the exile threatened in verse 13 really amounts to. It's more than military conquest and deportation. It's a kind of death, a descent into Sheol, a depressing underworld, far from God's presence. And where is God himself in this picture? According to verse 16, he is proving his holiness as he disciplines his people. The gospel says, "Do not be deceived: God is not mocked, for whatever one sows, that will he also reap" (Galatians 6:7). Rather than assume that our Christianity is what God had in mind when he started this movement, let's think about what he's saying here. He is calling us to courageous change, to welcome the progress of his grace.

In the third cluster of wild grapes, the metaphor is so absurd it must be true.

> Woe to those who draw iniquity with cords of falsehood,
>   who draw sin as with cart ropes,
> who say: "Let him be quick,
>   let him speed his work
>   that we may see it;
> let the counsel of the Holy One of Israel draw near,
>   and let it come near, that we may know it!" (Isaiah 5:18, 19)

Picture people, not horses, harnessed to a heavy wagon, pulling it along, straining with all their might. Isaiah understands the burden that sin is. But we do it to ourselves! Why? Because sin is deceitful. The prophet says, "Woe to those who draw iniquity *with cords of falsehood*." That's how it happens. Sin lies to us. It's not as though sin fulfills its promises to make life better. It's a drag. So why don't we throw off the harnesses and run free? Because we are deceived—doubly so, for even as we cling to our favorite sins, so heavy but so dear to us, we also wonder, "I'm so bored. I'm so disappointed. Why isn't God more real to me? And look at the condition of this whole wretched world. Where is God?" That is what Isaiah discerns in the human heart, according to verse 19—a mind that blames God, defies God, taunts God. Jesus said, "According to your faith be it unto you" (Matthew 9:29, KJV). He did not say, "According to your demand . . ." How could it be otherwise? Real faith gladly strains after *God*. And that is the faith that welcomes the impact of grace.

The fourth cluster of wild grapes appears in verse 20:

> Woe to those who call evil good
>   and good evil,
> who put darkness for light
>   and light for darkness,
> who put bitter for sweet
>   and sweet for bitter!

"We human beings don't make sense," a friend said to me the other day. However contrary to reason and experience, we find ways to rationalize sin. We redefine it. We change the labels. It is possible to lose one's sense of taste, the taste of the heart, not by age or injury but by choice, by rejecting the law of the Lord and despising the word of the Holy One (v. 24). If we do not discover sweet to be sweet but insist that reality be redesigned so that our taste for bitter can not only be satisfied but *called* sweet, how can the grace of God thrive under those conditions? Do we enjoy the right things? Do we call good and evil by their true names? Or is that passé?

The fifth cluster of wild grapes reveals a spirit of misplaced self-confidence:

> Woe to those who are wise in their own eyes,
>   and shrewd in their own sight! (v. 21)

Grace thrives when we feel how urgently we need to be saved from ourselves. Martyn Lloyd-Jones wrote:

> Sin is very clever; it always brings forward its reasons, its arguments. Sin knows us so well; it knows that we like to think of ourselves as highly intelligent people. So it does not just tell us, "Do this"; it gives us reasons for doing it, and they appear to be so wonderful. But the whole point is that in reality they are specious; they are empty and foolish. The reasoning is always false reasoning. The arguments are always wrong.[6]

But we start to see through the plausible arguments of compromise as we ask God to save us from our brilliant foolishness.

With the last cluster of wild grapes revealing a grace-resistant inner life, Isaiah draws a connection between two things we might not have put together:

Woe to those who are heroes at drinking wine,
and valiant men in mixing strong drink,
who acquit the guilty for a bribe,
and deprive the innocent of his right! (vv. 22, 23)

On the one hand, the prophet laments the corruption of society's elite. On the other hand, he laments the breakdown of social justice. The two go together. Personal excess cannot remain a merely private matter, with no impact on others. Reality doesn't work that way. There is a reason why people binge on escapism. They are medicating their despair. And how can self-induced delirium sustain social justice? Social justice thrives when people have such a sense of God that they embrace life as a meaningful whole, to the benefit of all around.

Isaiah closes his case with two "Therefores" in verses 24–30. The first goes down to the root of everything wrong with God's people in Isaiah's day: "Therefore . . . they have rejected the law of the LORD of hosts, and have despised the word of the Holy One of Israel" (v. 24). God delighted in them (Isaiah 5:7), but they did not delight in him. And when delight dies, despising takes over, and judgment descends.

The second "Therefore" reveals what form the judgment would take in Isaiah's situation: the army of Assyria. And God is the one bringing in the invading army (v. 26). That is Isaiah's way of exalting God as the architect of history and humbling Assyria as God's mere instrument. The God of Israel just whistles, and the Assyrian big shot comes running! What begins in verse 1 as a sweet little love song builds to a thundering climax, with the Assyrian hordes overrunning the people of God, "and none can rescue" (v. 29). They received the grace of God in vain.

John the Baptist told us how to receive grace: "Bear fruits in keeping with repentance. And do not begin to say to yourselves, 'We have Abraham as our father.' For I tell you, God is able from these stones to raise up children for Abraham. Even now the axe is laid to the root of the trees. Every tree therefore that does not bear good fruit is cut down and thrown into the fire" (Luke 3:8, 9). With God, it is not heritage that counts. He wants results—the fruit of the Holy Spirit (Galatians 5:22, 23).

But none of us receives the grace of God with a whole heart. That's why the final answer to all our failure is the one who said, "I am the *true* vine" (John 15:1). When Jesus said that, he meant, "I am replacing all human failure. I am the one who bears fruit for God. Without me, you can do nothing. If you abide in me, you will bear fruit that will last." Don't rely on your relationship with Jesus to explain away your fruitlessness. Look at your fruit, your results, and ask yourself about your relationship with Jesus. Are you abiding in him? Are you what you think you are? "By this my Father is glorified, that you bear much fruit and so prove to be my disciples" (John 15:8).

8

The Triumph of Grace over Our Failure: Isaiah

Isaiah 6:1–13

Give me a man in love; he knows what I mean. Give me one who yearns; give me one who is hungry; give me one far away in this desert, who is thirsty and sighs for the spring of the eternal country. Give me that sort of man; he knows what I mean. But if I speak to a cold man, he just does not know what I am talking about.[1]

AUGUSTINE SAID THAT IN A SERMON OVER 1,500 YEARS AGO. He understood that the response God longs to find in us is a heart in love. But what if your heart feels no love? If you don't know what Augustine—or Isaiah—is talking about, if your heart is cold, what remedy is there? What if your very capacity for response is dead? Isaiah answers that question now.

Chapters 1—5 describe the spiritual failure of God's people. In 2:5 the prophet appeals to them, "O house of Jacob, come, let us walk in the light of the LORD." But they refused. Chapter 5 concludes, "If one looks to the land, behold, darkness and distress; and the light is darkened by its clouds" (v. 30). If we prove unresponsive to his promises and warnings, so that darkness descends upon us, what's the remedy then? Only a radical act of God's grace. Chapters 6—11 display the awakening power of grace, starting with Isaiah himself.

Look how the symmetry of chapter 6 centers on God's gracious provision for our unresponsiveness in verses 6–10:

A¹ A great king dies, ending an era (6:1a)
   B¹ The King reigns in holiness (6:1b–4)
      C¹ The prophet despairs (6:5)
         D¹ The prophet is cleansed (6:6, 7)
         D² The prophet is sent (6:8–10)
      C² The prophet is dismayed (6:11a)
   B² The King reigns in judgment (6:11b–13a)
A² A humble remnant lives on, leading to Messiah (6:13b)

If God's grace is melting your natural God-resistance, you know it's the central experience in your life. If you don't know what Isaiah is talking about, this chapter will explain how radically you need God and what he can do for you.

A Great King Dies

> In the year that King Uzziah died . . . (Isaiah 6:1a)

We know from 2 Chronicles 26 that Uzziah's reign was long and prosperous. God lavished success on his people. But they didn't handle it well. They continued to affirm the traditional faith, but God himself became unreal to them. Uzziah sought God for a while; but when he was strong, "he grew proud, to his destruction" (2 Chronicles 26:5, 16). The whole nation followed their king into complacency, and God's patience with them finally ran out.

Uzziah's death marked the end of an era. It was like our own world in 1914. After decades of prosperity, Europe was free-falling into World War I, the seminal disaster of the disastrous twentieth century. Edward, Viscount Grey of Falloden, saw the significance of it: "The lamps are going out all over Europe; we shall not see them lit again in our lifetime." It was at just such a defining moment that Isaiah was called into the ministry—"in the year that King Uzziah died."

The King Reigns

> I saw the Lord sitting upon a throne, high and lifted up; and the train of his robe filled the temple. (Isaiah 6:1b)

Isaiah was worshiping in the temple one day when, for the first time, his vision was lifted beyond the familiar surroundings into the presence of God. The temple in Jerusalem represented the rule of God coming down to us. But on this day, for Isaiah, the earthly symbol merged into the heavenly reality. As the earthly king lay dying, the true Sovereign was reigning, holding court, and Isaiah *saw* it.

Above him stood the seraphim. Each had six wings: with two he covered his face, and with two he covered his feet, and with two he flew. (v. 2)

The throne room of God is a busy place. The King's angelic attendants are seraphim, which means something like "burning ones." They are living flames of pure, nuclear-powered praise. They are sinless, yet humbled before God because, as A. W. Tozer reminds us,

> We must not think of God as highest in an ascending order of beings, starting with the single cell and going on up from the fish to the bird to the animal to man to angel to cherub to God. God is as high above an archangel as above a caterpillar, for the gulf that separates the archangel from the caterpillar is but finite, while the gulf between God and the archangel is infinite.[2]

The seraphim hover in constant motion, ready to do God's will. Isaiah doesn't tell us how many there were; but when the Apostle John was lifted into Heaven, he saw "myriads of myriads and thousands of thousands" (Revelation 5:11)—that is, millions. Isaiah does tell us they were filling Heaven with their antiphonal worship.

> "Holy, holy, holy is the LORD of hosts;
> the whole earth is full of his glory." (Isaiah 6:3)

Back and forth to one another, the seraphim delight themselves in God for his infinite holiness and all-encompassing glory. What are they saying?

"Holy, holy, holy" is not just repetition; it is emphasis.[3] It isn't one + one + one; it's perfection x perfection x perfection. The holiness of God distinguishes him absolutely, even from the sinless angels. The Bible speaks of the splendor of God's holiness (Psalm 29:2), the majesty of God's holiness (Exodus 15:11), the incomparability of God's holiness (Isaiah 40:25). His holiness is simply his God-ness in all his attributes, works, and ways. And he is not just holy; he is "holy, holy, holy," each word boosting the force of the previous one exponentially. No other threefold adjective appears in all the Old Testament. It takes a unique linguistic contrivance to convey meaning beyond its meaning as the seraphim strain at the leash of language to say that God alone is *God*. He is not like us, only bigger and nicer. He is in a different category. He is holy.

And the holy God is filling the earth with his glory. He is not only out there; he is also down here. He is why there is a "down here." Think back to the beginning. Why did God create anything at all? Throughout eternity past, before time was launched, God was complete in himself. He was never lonely within the blazing fellowship of the Trinitarian Godhead. He has always been happy and full. Why does that kind of God *create* anything? Not to remedy a lack in himself, but to enjoy spreading his goodness. The delight that God feels in being God is so great that his exuberance spills over into a creation filled with his glory.

> Earth's crammed with heaven,
> And every common bush afire with God;
> And only he who sees, takes off his shoes;
> The rest sit round it and pluck blackberries,
> And daub their natural faces unaware.[4]

We are not just ordinary. Nothing is just ordinary. "The whole earth is full of his glory." We keep trying to fill it with monuments to our own glory—kingdoms, businesses, hit songs, athletic victories, and other mechanisms of self-salvation. But the truth is better than all that. Created reality is a continuous explosion of the glory of God. And history is the drama of his grace awakening in us dead sinners eyes to see and taste to enjoy and courage to obey.[5]

Do you realize that it is God's will to make this earth into an extension of his throne room in Heaven? Do you realize that it is God's will for his kingdom of glory to come into your life and for his will to be done in you as it is done in Heaven? Heaven is expanding, spreading in your direction. That is the meaning of your existence, if you will accept it and enter in. Heaven is taking over. Yield.

Plodding through our daily routines, we seldom feel God's glorious presence. We are absorbed in our own petty ambitions. But the truth is, God not only *deserves* to reign supreme, he *does* reign supreme. And his reign is glorious. Isaiah is enabled to sense the power of God's presence.

> And the foundations of the thresholds shook at the voice of him who called, and the house was filled with smoke. (Isaiah 6:4)

As a boy, I enjoyed Saturday morning television—Sky King, The Lone Ranger, Roy Rogers. What annoyed me was the weekend warriors of the Air National Guard flying their F-80 Shooting Stars over the house and interfering with the TV signal. Whenever they broke the sound barrier, the window panes of our family room would rattle. But even the temple shakes at the voice of just one seraph. So we should not think of God's seraphim as chubby babies with wings, like the angels in the art of Peter Paul Rubens. They were more like jet fighters breaking the sound barrier. And as the smoke from the incense altar fills the temple with the felt presence of God, Isaiah is overwhelmed. God is always more than we bargain for.

The Prophet Despairs

> And I said: "Woe is me! For I am lost; for I am a man of unclean lips, and
> I dwell in the midst of a people of unclean lips; for my eyes have seen the
> King, the LORD of hosts!" (Isaiah 6:5)

As sincere as his worship has always been, Isaiah has not been "a man
in love." His profession of faith has been orthodox but empty, with little
heart-awareness of the grandeur of God. Unlike the seraphim, Isaiah's lips
are unclean. In fact, he's no better than anyone else: "I am a man of unclean
lips, and I dwell in the midst of a people of unclean lips." The most telling indicator that God's grace is renewing us is not when we say all the
right things about his grace but when we stop putting ourselves above others, and even above God: "I'm not that bad. In fact, I'm better than most.
Heck, God's just lucky to have me for one whole hour every week." God's
awakening grace turns us completely around with new thoughts like, *My
opinion of myself doesn't matter. What matters is where I stand with God.
Here I am, breathing his glorious air, eating his glorious food, oblivious
to the continual display of his glory all around me—what right do I have
to be here?*

As this awareness forms in Isaiah's mind, he blurts out the obvious
conclusion: "Woe is me!" Those are the first words spoken by Isaiah himself in his book, and they pronounce a prophetic woe upon himself. He
doesn't saunter into God's presence. For the first time he really worships
God. For the first time his mouth speaks with "the highest sort of simplicity,
of *naiveté*, . . . the intuition of a soul which has seen itself in the light of the
divine holiness."[6] For the first time, he sees that he's typical of his generation, whose faith was unthinking and glib. Their mouths were not filled with
seraphic worship but with flippant repetitions and self-justifying excuses.
But now Isaiah sees himself, because he sees God. And something new is
entering his heart—humility.

The Prophet Is Cleansed

> Then one of the seraphim flew to me, having in his hand a burning coal
> that he had taken with tongs from the altar. And he touched my mouth and
> said: "Behold, this has touched your lips; your guilt is taken away, and
> your sin atoned for." (Isaiah 6:6, 7)

A seraph peels off from his flight path around the throne, diving
straight for Isaiah. He's holding a burning coal that he took from the altar
with tongs, but not because it is hot. After all, a seraph himself is a burning
one. He took this coal with tongs because it is a holy thing. It belongs to

the place of sacrifice and atonement and forgiveness. But this holy thing touches Isaiah's dirty mouth, and it does not hurt him, it heals him. What we must see, in the context of the whole Bible, is that this burning coal symbolizes the finished work of Christ on the cross. He went to the place of sacrifice. His dying love is the only power that can awaken people as dead to God as we are. And awaken us he does. He comes to us today through the Holy Spirit and says again, "Your guilt is taken away. Your sin is atoned for. Welcome into the overwhelming delight of my presence!" When the magnitude of that grace touches Isaiah, he is awakened to live for God.

The Prophet Is Sent

> And I heard the voice of the Lord saying, "Whom shall I send, and who will go for us?" Then I said, "Here I am! Send me." And he said, "Go, and say to this people:
>
> "Keep on hearing, but do not understand;
> keep on seeing, but do not perceive.'
> Make the heart of this people dull,
>   and their ears heavy,
>   and blind their eyes;
> lest they see with their eyes,
>   and hear with their ears,
> and understand with their hearts,
>   and turn and be healed." (vv. 8–10)

For the first time in the passage, God speaks. It's as if he says, "All right, everyone, I have some things to say to the human race. I need a spokesman, and not just anyone. I want someone who knows what it means to be forgiven. Who might that be?" Isaiah pipes up, "How about me?" And God says, "Go."

What silences Christians is a curious mingling of self-admiration with a guilty fear that God is against them. His remedy is the blood of Christ purifying our consciences, so that we serve the living God (Hebrews 9:14). A guilty conscience, liberated by grace, unleashes us. The gospel says to us, "That sin most damning to your conscience, that sin haunting your memory—Christ carried it far away to his cross, where it died under God's wrath. Justice has been satisfied. You are released!" The price we pay for this liberation is traumatic self-discovery before the all-holy God. We must be shocked into realizing that we're less Christian than we think we are, more American than we think we are, and unworthy of God. But that's when God comes, to experientialize to our hearts fresh cleansing in Christ. It is his grace alone that awakens us and qualifies us as his voices to our generation.

I began by asking what the remedy is when our very capacity to respond to God shuts down. Now the answer is clear. *The remedy for our deadness to God's grace is more grace.* The remedy is the touch of God himself, as the truth of the gospel breaks upon us with clarity. If God triumphs over us by his grace, we will live. If he doesn't, nothing in us will suffice, because our whole problem is our incapacity for self-renewal. This is how radically we need God.

God is fed up with Isaiah's generation (vv. 9, 10). So he sends the prophet to tell them that they won't listen. A strange mission. His message would save later generations, but not his own, because God would use Isaiah's preaching to *harden* his contemporaries. This is not an easy truth to accept. And today, if preachers speak from Isaiah 6, they usually stop at the end of verse 8. But the authors of the New Testament quoted verses 9, 10 at least five times.[7] They may be Isaiah's most frequently quoted verses in the New Testament. Why did the early Christians find them so meaningful? Because the young Christian movement was bitterly opposed for its gospel of grace, and the explanation for it stood out right here in these verses.

What's the insight? Simply this. Every time you hear the Word of God preached, you come away from that exposure to his truth either a little closer to God or a little further way from God, either more softened toward God or more hardened toward God. But you are never just the same. And if you think you can hold the gospel at arm's length in critical detachment, that very posture reveals that you are already deadened. The same truth enlivening someone else is hardening you. And don't tell yourself that if only God would perform a miracle in your life, you would believe and open up. Jesus performed miracles, and the people who saw them only became further hardened (John 12:37–41). And if God's Word isn't saving you, what will? "Receive with meekness the implanted word, which is able to save your souls" (James 1:21).

The Apostle Paul thought of his ministry as "the aroma of Christ." To some people, it came across as a fragrance of life; to others, it was the stench of death (2 Corinthians 2:15, 16). The same man, the same ministry, but two opposite responses. Obviously, it wasn't about Paul. It was about the people listening. And some people made themselves sermon-proof.

If we resist God, he may withdraw light from our understanding to the point that faith becomes impossible. Preachers are subject to God's judgment too, even a stricter judgment (James 3:1). But preaching that is true to the gospel is one way God *brings* judgment to those who have closed their hearts. Whether people accept the message or reject it, preaching God's Word is always a supernatural event. John Calvin helps us understand the implications:

If we have a zeal to serve and honor God and would desire peaceably that our Lord should have his royal throne in the midst of us, if we would be his people and dwell under his protection, if we desire to be built up in him and joined to him and persevere in him to the end, if (in brief) we desire salvation, we must learn to be humble disciples to receive the doctrine of the Gospel and to hear the pastors whom he has sent to us, as if Jesus Christ himself spoke to us in person.[8]

No preacher is always right. But when the Word of God comes to us through a human preacher, it remains the Word of God (1 Thessalonians 2:13). Let's not be impossible to please (Matthew 11:16–19). Let's not have "itching ears" (2 Timothy 4:3, 4). Simeon said to Mary that her Son was "appointed for the fall and rising of many in Israel" (Luke 2:34). Our response to the ministry of the gospel reveals our truest feelings about Jesus himself. And on him every one of us either falls or rises.

The Prophet Is Dismayed

Then I said, "How long, O Lord?" (Isaiah 6:11a)

Jesus wept over Jerusalem (Luke 19:41–44), and Isaiah anguished over his friends. He found no pleasure in the thought that his influence would be counter-redemptive. There was no feeling of self-righteous payback. He secretly hoped God might relent. So he wondered out loud to what extent this hardening would have its effect. How far would God go? "How long, O Lord? Three weeks? Five years? Then a big improvement, right? Where is this going, Lord?"

The King Reigns in Judgment

And he [the Lord] said,
"Until cities lie waste
   without inhabitant,
and houses without people,
   and the land is a desolate waste,
and the LORD removes people far away,
   and the forsaken places are many in the midst of the land.
And though a tenth remain in it,
   it will be burned again,
like a terebinth or an oak,
   whose stump remains
   when it is felled." (Isaiah 6:11b–13a)

The losses will be 90 percent. The people Isaiah preaches to will be devastated, like a forest cut down so that only stumps remain. And those stumps will then be burned over again. God is describing the eventual collapse of Judah, and all for one reason: They refused to listen to God. But even here his grace appears. What will the burning and the felling accomplish? They will clear the ground for new growth.

A Humble Remnant Lives On

The holy seed is its stump. (Isaiah 6:13b)

Isaiah concludes with an assurance of the finality of God's grace. God will judge his people, but not with finality. He will preserve a living remnant of people who are responsive to him. He will set them apart as holy and will use them for a great, though now hidden, purpose. Spiritual life will survive in one last stump, from which a little shoot of life will eventually sprout: "There shall come forth a shoot from the stump of Jesse, and a branch from his roots shall bear fruit . . . for the earth shall be full of the knowledge of the LORD as the waters cover the sea" (Isaiah 11:1, 9). God was finished with Isaiah's generation, but they did not defeat salvation. Jesus did come, and his grace will remake the whole world.

If your heart does not leap at God's grace in Christ, what you need is more grace. Nothing else can save you from your own deadness. Therefore, fear your own hardness of heart more than anything else.[9] Beware of rigidity, ingratitude, a demanding spirit. Beware of an unmelted heart that is never satisfied. Beware of a mind that looks for excuses not to believe. Beware of the impulse that always finds a reason to delay response. Beware of thinking how the sermon applies to someone *else*. God watches how you hear his Word. If you are ever again to receive it with at least the capacity for response that you have at this very moment, hear it *now*:

But this is the one to whom I will look:
    he who is humble and contrite in spirit
    and trembles at my word. (Isaiah 66:2)

9

The Triumph of Grace over Our Failure: Judah I

ISAIAH 7:1—8:8

IF ISAIAH HAD BEEN AN EIGHTEENTH-CENTURY MAN, he could have written a hymn like this one by John Newton:

> Let worldly minds the world pursue,
> It has no charms for me.
> Once I admired its trifles too,
> But grace has set me free.
>
> Its pleasures now no longer please,
> No more content afford;
> Far from my heart be joys like these,
> Now I have seen the Lord.
>
> As by the light of opening day
> The stars are all concealed,
> So earthly pleasures fade away,
> When Jesus is revealed.
>
> Creatures no more divide my choice,
> I bid them all depart.
> His name, and love, and gracious voice
> Have fixed my roving heart.

What was Newton saying? "Created things no longer so compel me that my heart is divided between them and God. I'm satisfied with God."

That happened to Isaiah when he saw the Lord. God took away his divided heart and gave him a united heart. But now in Isaiah 7 we encounter a man with a divided, roving heart—King Ahaz of Judah. What makes the difference between an Isaiah and an Ahaz? A big part of the answer is that Isaiah had a sense of the glory of Christ in his heart. His faith was not the heroic rejection of temptation, triumphant self-mastery over the flesh, stoic resistance toward the world, and so forth. Isaiah was given such a sense of Christ that he could say, "Here I am! Send me." That is Christianity.

Too often what passes for Christianity today is a life legislated by the good example of Jesus and frightened by the threat of divine punishment. But the person who is afraid of sinning because of hellfire isn't really afraid of sinning; he's only afraid of burning. He has no love for salvation. He has no stimulus for action except fear and pride. But true faith is swallowed up with such a sense of the glory of Christ that the heart transcends choice in the pleasures of surrender.

When you and I hover between the competing claims of good and evil, we're only proving how empty and divided we are. True faith is not the capacity for victorious choices when faced with two equally compelling alternatives. True faith is the capacity to act fully, joyfully, enthusiastically because our eyes have been opened to the glory of Christ.[1] "Creatures no more divide my choice." Isaiah experienced that, and it saved him. We can't be saved without it. Ahaz knew nothing of it. And his unbelief was his undoing.

When the promises and judgments of Isaiah 2—5 do not motivate us, what *can* liberate us to live for God? The answer lies in chapter 6: a new sense of the glory of Jesus imparted to us by God's grace. In 7:1—9:7 Isaiah makes the same point, but now at the corporate level—the nation of Judah. It's personal as well, as we see in Ahaz. But the implications address the whole church in our generation. God is preserving a remnant of people who really know what it means to be saved by grace.

God called Isaiah into the ministry "in the year that King Uzziah died" (6:1)—around 740 B.C. By the time we come to chapter 7, it's around 735 B.C. And *the* crisis of Isaiah's generation is exploding on the scene. After the death of Solomon, the ten Israelite tribal groups in the northern part of the country seceded and formed their own state. The Bible calls the breakaway kingdom Israel. Their capital city was Samaria. Only two tribes in the south remained loyal to the dynasty of David in Jerusalem, as five-sixths of the nation split off to go their own way.

Isaiah 7 locates us about 200 years into this massive dysfunction. By now the Assyrian empire at the eastern end of the Fertile Crescent is rising, growing, flexing its muscles, reaching, grabbing, dominating—"skilled and constant in systematic cruelty."[2] The little kingdoms of Palestine are no match for the new bully in town. So Israel joins forces with Syria, a northerly neighbor, in a pact of mutual defense against Assyria. They want the collaboration of Judah as well, for further reinforcement. In fact, they demand it. But King Ahaz is resisting this pressure. So the northern alliance is threatening to attack Judah, get rid of Ahaz, put their own puppet on the throne, and absorb Judah into their coalition. But from the start, the prophetic eye can see that their plan is doomed. God's covenant with the throne of David still stands, despite his people's failures. That's why Isaiah 7:1 states that the enemy could not mount an attack against Jerusalem.[3] The prophet wants us to know from the start that the threat will vanish. There is no need to panic. God is with his people.

Ahaz doesn't believe that. He doesn't want to believe it. He prefers dismay and hand-wringing. He feels more normal frantically devising his own salvation and lusting for the success of his own plans, rather than delighting in the victory of God. His heart is hard.

That's the setting—the defining crisis of Isaiah's generation, inflated in its emotional impact because their hearts are not filled with a sense of the glory of God.

Inevitably God brings us into crisis. Sooner or later this question presses itself upon us: If I put my trust in God, will he save me? Will he be true to his promises in the gospel when it really counts for *me*? Our answer to that question will either be an agonized struggle back and forth, as we are unable to make up our minds, or our answer will be a clear yes. And the larger point Isaiah is making is that God's people don't trust him as they should, and they pay a price for it. But his grace will have the last word on their behalf—the triumph of his grace over their failure.

The entire passage is lengthy enough (7:1—9:7) to require two studies here. The message of this first segment is that God is our true ally, he invites us to trust him, and not trusting him is a destructive choice.

1. Decision: Will we trust God or ourselves? (7:1–17)
    A^1 The people of God intimidated by attack (7:1, 2)
        B^1 A symbolic son and the attackers' plan (7:3–6)
            C^1 The Lord's overruling word of promise (7:7–9)
                D The response of distrust (7:10–12)
            C^2 The Lord's overruling sign of salvation (7:13–15)
        B^2 A symbolic son and the attackers' defeat (7:16)
    A^2 The people of God destined for attack (7:17)
2. Judgment: A rejected God rules over those who distrust him (7:18—8:8)
    A The thoroughness of God's judgment (7:18–25)

1. "In that day"—divine sovereignty effortless (7:18, 19)
2. "In that day"—the humiliation complete (7:20)
3. "In that day"—the people reduced to hardship (7:21, 22)
4. "In that day"—their accomplishments undone (7:23–25)

B The course of God's judgment (8:1–8)

1. Decreed: Judah's two enemies will soon be defeated (8:1–4)
2. Decreed: Judah herself will be nearly overwhelmed (8:5–8)

God is present in our crises. If we will trust him, he will save us. If we refuse him, he will discipline us. But he would rather save us.

Decision

> In the days of Ahaz the son of Jotham, son of Uzziah, king of Judah, Rezin the king of Syria and Pekah the son of Remaliah the king of Israel came up to Jerusalem to wage war against it, but could not mount an attack against it. When the house of David was told, "Syria is in league with Ephraim," the heart of Ahaz and the heart of his people shook as the trees of the forest shake before the wind. (Isaiah 7:1, 2)

The intimidating Syro-Ephraimite alliance, as historians call it, had its withering effect on Judah, who had already suffered from separate assaults by Syria and Ephraim (2 Chronicles 28:5–8). Now these two nations come together with renewed hostility toward little Judah. But God uses this crisis to call Ahaz to himself. He sends Isaiah with an appeal:

> And the LORD said to Isaiah, "Go out to meet Ahaz, you and Shear-jashub your son, at the end of the conduit of the upper pool on the highway to the Washer's Field." (Isaiah 7:3)

The king is out inspecting the city's water supply, preparing for the invasion. Ahaz is not thinking in terms of God; he's thinking in terms of stockpiling. But God wants to save him. So he tells Isaiah to go meet Ahaz, with his son Shear-jashub. The margin in your English Bible may tell you that name means "A remnant shall return." This is God's way of assuring Ahaz that even if the worst should happen, a remnant will return in victory.

God calls Ahaz to confidence: "Be careful, be quiet, do not fear, and do not let your heart be faint because of these two smoldering stumps of firebrands . . ." (v. 4). We might put it this way: "Stay calm before these two burned-out cigarette butts!" They are spent forces. God is saying, "These two nations coming at you are headed by mere men. I will not allow them to succeed. I've even set a drop-dead date for Israel" (7:7–9). And in fact God kept his word. Within three years Syria was crushed, and Israel fell ten years after that. By around 670 B.C., as the prophet had said, Israel's population was effaced from history.[4] God is offering Ahaz the opportunity of a lifetime to experience what it means to be saved by God. But that means Ahaz must treat God as God.

That matters. It matters to God. It matters to Ahaz, more than he realizes. So God explains to him what's at stake.

If you are not firm in faith,
    you will not be firm at all. (v. 9b)

The commentators try to capture the wordplay in English: "Hold God in doubt, and you'll not hold out." Or, "Unsure? Insecure!"[5] God literally says, "If you do not firm up, you will not be confirmed."[6] In other words, "You'll live by faith, or you won't live at all. But if you do want my support, all you have to do is lean on me." God is attracted to weakness and need and honesty. He is repelled by our self-assured pride.

Isaiah 7:9b makes faith in God the central, unavoidable question of our lives. What is faith? It has three components: *knowledge* of God, persuading us to *agree* with God, motivating us to *embrace* God. John Murray, the Scottish theologian, defines faith as "a whole-souled movement of intelligent, consenting and confiding self-commitment. . . . Intellect, feeling and will converge upon Christ. . . . There is a consensus of all the functions of man's heart and mind."[7] In other words, faith is the God-awakened capacity to respond fully to Christ. And if that is faith, then unfaith is the fragmentation and breakdown of our inner beings—intellect, feeling, and will. We know that God is more real than the earthly things immediately before us. We know he is more desirable than worldly attractions. We know he is faithful. We know we should live not out of what is but out of what is promised. We know our hearts must be grounded in finality if we hope to go the distance. And to refuse what we ourselves know to be true tears us apart inside. When we deny the truth we believe and refuse the consent we desire and withhold the trust we were created to enjoy, how can anything go right? The human being unravels. If we are not firm in faith, we are not firm at all. Everything in life, not just religion, flows out of our whole-souled movement toward Christ.

Something inside us—the Bible calls it sin—is spring-loaded to see God as a Hallmark-card sentimental glow for the warm moments of life. But God offers himself to us as our greatest ally at all times. With him, we can face anything. He is appealing to us here, "Lean on me, and you will stand. But treat me as irrelevant, and you will become irrelevant."

We need to think this through again and again, because living by faith in God rather than by faith in ourselves takes time to catch on to, and we lose focus quickly. Conversion to Christ is only the beginning. And how do we learn but in our crises? That's when God takes the training wheels off our bikes and teaches us to ride like the big kids. God is saying, "In your crisis, when it counts for you, trust me. I will keep my every promise. But if you treat me as unreal, you will not connect with reality at all."

The structure of the text focuses on verses 10–12, where Ahaz decides to go his own way and seals the fate of his generation. But look how fair God is. He doesn't just give Ahaz an ultimatum and that's that. He doesn't demand of Ahaz a nonrational "leap of faith." He invites Ahaz to ask for a sign, any sign he can think of, as evidence that God is serious about being his ally.

> Again the LORD spoke to Ahaz, "Ask a sign of the LORD your God; let it be as deep as Sheol or high as heaven." But Ahaz said, "I will not ask, and I will not put the LORD to the test." (vv. 10–12)

God hands him a blank check, but Ahaz refuses to cash it. Why? He doesn't *want* to trust God. Sure, he puts it in pious language (Deuteronomy 6:16). But it's all quick-thinking, diplomatic hypocrisy. He knows there are strings attached. If he lets God in, God will take control. And for Ahaz, that would mean using God's strategies to get through the crisis and giving God the glory for the outcome. Ahaz proves here that faith can be refused by the will, no matter how strong the evidences. If we don't want God, we can find a way to make our unbelief sound plausible, even pious.

But God can see when he's being rejected. In verse 11 Isaiah refers to God as "your God." "This is your God, Ahaz. He wants to save you. Will you let him?" But Ahaz declines. So in verse 13 Isaiah refers to God as "my God." "My God isn't on your side anymore, Ahaz. Your opportunity has passed."

God decides to send a sign of his own choosing. Not bolts of lightning falling from Heaven on the enemy armies. That would have come in handy! But God's token of his saving presence is improbable: "Behold, the young woman[8] shall conceive and bear a son, and shall call his name Immanuel" (7:14).

This is one of the outstanding verses of the Bible. But it isn't easy to understand. The problem is this. The New Testament says that this promise was fulfilled in the birth of Jesus centuries later (Matthew 1:18–25), but the context in Isaiah links it to Isaiah's own day (7:15, 16). When was God's promise fulfilled?

There is more to Isaiah 7:14 than at first meets the eye. The prophecy came true not in one but in two ways. First, it *predicted* the birth of Maher-shalal-hashbaz, Isaiah's own son. We read in Isaiah 8:1–4 that this boy's birth was tied to the fall of the Syro-Ephraimite alliance. The parallel of Isaiah 8:4 with 7:16 is unmistakable. The child's strange name means something like "The spoil speeds, the prey hastens," as the margin of your Bible may inform you. That message was as ominous as it sounds. Was God present with his people in their emergency? Yes, to fast-forward the undoing of the Syro-Ephraimite alliance. The message of Maher-shalal-hashbaz's young life was Immanuel, "God with us." The enemy forces are doomed because God is with his people.

But secondly, Isaiah 7:14 *prefigured* the birth of Jesus Christ. The Apostle Matthew read the Old Testament with an eye to how all its heroes, institutions, and events foreshadowed the coming Messiah.[9] He saw in Isaiah's prophecy of the Immanuel sign-child a picture of our ultimate salvation. We face a coalition of hostile powers far worse than Syria and Ephraim of old. We face the alliance of sin and death, they never go away, and we are no match for them. But at this ultimate level the baby Jesus fulfills the truest meaning of Immanuel, "God with us."

Political crises come and go, but God goes with us into battle against the enemies that can oppress us forever. This alliance of evil forces conquers all of us, destroying us utterly, for our sin is "the basic (if not always the immediate) cause of all other calamities."[10] It is *the* crisis of human existence. But here, most of all, God comes to us with a salvation that really counts: "You shall call his name Jesus, for he will save his people from their sins" (Matthew 1:21).

God stood by his promise to Ahaz that the two nations menacing him would fall. But Ahaz's unbelief was costly. His crisis was resolved by a more terrible enemy, the king of Assyria himself (7:15–17). Someone has said that this whole episode was like a mouse attacked by two rats, squeaking for the cat to come save him. The cat did (2 Kings 16:5–9). But the mouse ended up as dessert.

Trusting God to save us when we are assaulted by evil has no downside. He meets the weakness and foolishness of faith with his power and wisdom (1 Corinthians 1:18–25). Therefore, the question we should be asking each day is more profound than, Have I said a prayer? That's a good thing to do. But we should be asking ourselves, Am I trusting God right now, where it counts for me? If we welcome God as our ally and yield to his way, his timing, his control, his glory, he will fight for us. And we will have no regrets. He never lets faith go unmet. But if we set our own terms, we will fight alone. Jesus said, "According to your faith be it unto you" (Matthew 9:29, KJV). Moment by moment, that is the key to life.

Judgment

> The LORD spoke to me again: "Because this people [of Israel] have refused the waters of Shiloah that flow gently, and rejoice over Rezin and the son of Remaliah, therefore, behold, the Lord is bringing up against them the

waters of the River, mighty and many, the king of Assyria and all his glory. And it will rise over all its channels and go over all its banks, and it will sweep on into Judah, it will overflow and pass on, reaching even to the neck, and its outspread wings will fill the breadth of your land, O Immanuel. (Isaiah 8:5–8)

The judgment section of the passage unpacks the fullness of 7:17. Isaiah's thought unfolds in two movements: the thoroughness of God's judgment (7:18–25) and the course of God's judgment (8:1–8). Because Ahaz and his people have refused God, a day of reckoning is scheduled on their calendar ("In that day"—7:18, 20, 21, 23).

Isaiah brackets this section with "the land of Assyria" (7:18) and "your land, O Immanuel" (8:8). Assyria will rise like a flood, like the Euphrates overflowing its banks and rushing in to sweep Syria and Israel away. Poor little Judah will have to stand on tiptoe just to keep her head above water. The people will survive—barely. But Assyria will eventually fade from history, and Judah will remain the land of Immanuel. God will be with them through it all, more than they know. He will come to them in the fullness of time as a boy named Jesus, the Savior of the world.

The way to experience the saving presence of God is to look at the gently flowing trickle of water called Jesus Christ and say, "I will stake my life on that supply, and I will never thirst again, no matter how long I am under siege." The way to experience the saving presence of God is to look at the baby Jesus and say, "He will be my fiercest ally, and I will conquer, no matter what sin threatens me." The way to experience the saving presence of God in your crisis right now is to say yes to the improbable ways of God. The first business of our lives is to learn what it means to stop trying to save ourselves and venture all on God. He saves sinners. So be careful, be quiet, do not fear, and do not let your heart be faint. "God with us" is more than a name. He is a reality. And when you lean on him as *your* reality, what more do you need?

> Be still, my soul: The Lord is on thy side.
> Bear patiently the cross of grief or pain.
> Leave to thy God to order and provide;
> In every change, he faithful will remain.
> Be still, my soul: thy best, thy heavenly Friend
> Through thorny ways leads to a joyful end.

10

The Triumph of Grace over Our Failure: Judah II

ISAIAH 8:9—9:7

THE MOST WEIGHTY WORDS IN THIS TEXT COME AT THE END: "The zeal of the LORD of hosts will do this" (9:7). God is zealous. The idea of "gentle Jesus meek and mild" is not wrong, but it is incomplete. He is also "zealous Jesus brave and bold." And Isaiah is saying that the "this" God intends to accomplish will occur with a "zeal" from the heart of no one less than "the LORD of hosts." His passion is driving history toward the final triumph of grace in the messianic kingdom.

You and I will not achieve the victory of God in this world. We don't trust God that much. We rarely live fully for him. But God is solving our problem for us, because his heart is not divided. That is the guarantee of our salvation. When we are finally glorifying and enjoying him perfectly, we will look at one another and say, "*We* didn't do this. *God* did. This is the triumph of his zealous grace."

What does the word *zeal* tell us about God? My Hebrew lexicon defines this word as "ardor, zeal, jealousy."[1] This Hebrew word is cognate with an Arabic verb meaning "to become intensely red," suggesting the idea of color flooding a person's face with the flush of deep emotion within. This Hebrew word is used for a husband's jealousy for the love of his wife (Proverbs 6:34), for the envy that drives human effort (Ecclesiastes 4:4), for the love that burns in the hearts of a bride and groom (Song of Songs 8:6). But this very human word says something about God. It describes his *passion* for our salvation.

Isaiah 42:13 compares God with a warrior psyching himself up before going into battle: "He stirs up his zeal." Isaiah 63:15 sets in parallel "your zeal and your might" with "the stirring of your inner parts"—the emotions surging within the being of God. Zephaniah 1:18 and 3:8 speak of "the fire of his zeal." Psalm 79:5 looks with wonder at his zeal "burn[ing] like fire." The Bible says that our God is "a consuming fire, a zealous God" (Deuteronomy 4:24; Hebrews 12:29). And when Jesus threw the crooks out of the temple— the text says that he wove the whip himself—the Apostle John quotes Psalm 69:9 to explain Jesus' boldness: "Zeal for your house will consume me" (John 2:13–17). God is not a wishy-washy personality. He is on fire for the triumph of his grace: "The zeal of the LORD of hosts will do this."

This is the second half of Isaiah's sermon about God's grace overruling Judah's failure.

3. Grace: But God will preserve a trusting remnant (8:9–22)
    A A remnant is set apart by the presence of God (8:9, 10)
        B A remnant is set apart by the fear of God (8:11–15)
            C A remnant is set apart by the truth of God (8:16–18)
                D But hypocrites choose darkness (8:19–22)
4. Triumph: The light of Messiah will shine in our darkness (9:1–7)
    A The Messianic light portrayed (9:1–3)
        B The Messianic light explained (9:4–7)

Influenced by Ahaz, the people of Judah rejected God in the defining moment of their time, and God passed them by. But their unbelief did not defeat him. He has enough zeal in himself to bring salvation into fullness for all who will receive him.

Grace

Isaiah is showing us something new. God works with a remnant.[2] Why did Isaiah look for a remnant of real believers among the many with a Gallup-poll faith? There is something about us that requires this remnant concept. Sadly, God's people resist God's blessing. How many people who say they trust in Christ really open up to him with no preconditions? It takes the grace of God to preserve a trusting remnant among those who identify outwardly with him (Isaiah 1:9). The remnant is not a super-spiritual elite looking down on others, but they do dare to live by faith in God. The rest are careful not to risk too much on him. The difference shows. Jonathan Edwards describes a true Christian:

As he has more holy boldness, so he has less self-confidence. . . . As he is more sure than others of deliverance from hell, so he has a greater sense that he deserves it. He is less apt than others to be shaken in faith, but more apt than others to be moved by solemn warnings, God's frowns and the calamities of others. He has the firmest comfort, but the softest heart; richer than others, but poorest of all in spirit. He is the tallest and strongest saint, but the least and tenderest child among them.[3]

That beauty marks God's true people. Does it describe you, at least a little?

How then is the remnant set apart as God's true people? It isn't as simple as joining a certain church. The remnant is known, first, by the presence of God.

> Be broken, you peoples, and be shattered;
> give ear, all you far countries;
> strap on your armor and be shattered;
> strap on your armor and be shattered.
> Take counsel together, but it will come to nothing;
> speak a word, but it will not stand,
> for God is with us. (Isaiah 8:9, 10)

When Ahaz and his people were told of the Syro-Ephraimite forces coming against them, their hearts "shook as the trees of the forest shake before the wind" (Isaiah 7:2). But the remnant stands out with a defiant confidence. They actually experience "God . . . with us." So they look at the same crisis and say, "Do your worst. Strap on your armor. *But you will be shattered.*" In New Testament terms, "This is the victory that has overcome the world—our faith" (1 John 5:4).

Richard Williams, a young surgeon and Methodist lay preacher, and Anglican minister Allen Gardiner went as missionaries to Tierra del Fuego. In 1851 their ship was forced to winter in a cold and bitter bay, and the supply vessel never arrived. Everyone on board their ship died of cold and starvation. Even as they were suffering, on Good Friday, April 18, 1851, Williams wrote in his journal, "Poor and weak though we are, our abode is a very Bethel to our souls, and God we feel and know is here." Then on Wednesday, May 7, he wrote, "Should anything prevent my ever adding to this, let all my beloved ones at home rest assured that I was happy beyond description when I wrote these lines and would not have changed situations with any man living."[4] When your supply ship does not arrive, God can make your crisis a very Bethel to your soul (Genesis 28:10–19) as you find by faith that he is with you. He makes you happy beyond description.

Secondly, the remnant is set apart by the fear of God:

> For the LORD spoke thus to me with his strong hand upon me, and warned me not to walk in the way of this people, saying, "Do not call conspiracy

all that this people calls conspiracy, and do not fear what they fear, nor
be in dread. But the LORD of hosts, him you shall regard as holy. Let him
be your fear, and let him be your dread. And he will become a sanctuary
and a stone of offense and a rock of stumbling to both houses of Israel, a
trap and a snare to the inhabitants of Jerusalem. And many shall stumble
on it. They shall fall and be broken; they shall be snared and taken."
(Isaiah 8:11–15)

Isaiah was deeply impressed with this insight: ". . . with his strong
hand upon me." The message here is that a God-consciousness redefines
urgency: "Do not call conspiracy all that this people calls conspiracy, and
do not fear what they fear, nor be in dread" (v. 12). Ahaz and Judah were
wringing their hands over the Syro-Ephraimite threat, the way we fear
terrorists today. And God's remnant is not without fear. But their whole
approach is different. The way they see it, they dare not overlook *God*. They
see God at work in the events swirling around them. And in fearing him,
they stabilize themselves.

What does this fear of God look like? Verse 13 says: "The LORD of
hosts, him you shall regard as holy." In other words, "Dare to treat God as
God. Don't respond to life in a way that makes God look helpless and weak
and worthless." Living emotionally as if God were not really our Savior is
practical atheism.[5] If God is God, he is all that finally matters. The remnant
respects God enough to live that way.

How we treat God determines how we experience God, either as a sanctuary or a snare: "And he will become a sanctuary and . . . a snare to the
inhabitants of Jerusalem" (v. 14). Every one of us will experience God one
way or the other. If we take him into account as God, we will enter his
sanctuary and experience his presence. But if other things compel us—well,
God isn't going away. We end up colliding with him and tripping over him
as a snare. The New Testament explains that God is the most unavoidable
and the most dangerous in Jesus. He himself said, "The one who falls on
this stone will be broken to pieces; and when it falls on anyone, it will crush
him" (Matthew 21:44). Some people dismiss the gospel as irrelevant. They
stumble, fall, and are broken. But grace awakens the remnant to a trembling
faith.

Thirdly, the remnant is set apart by the truth of God (Isaiah 8:16–18).
In Ahaz's day, the gospel was not valued. So when Isaiah says, in verse
16, "Bind up the testimony; seal the teaching," he means, "Preserve this
neglected wisdom for a later generation who *will* listen." The prize the remnant discovers in God's Word is implied by the coherence of verses 16 and
17. Treasuring God's Word and finding hope in God himself are, to them,
inseparable: "Bind up the testimony . . . I will hope in [the Lord]." Erasmus
(1466–1536) wrote in the preface to his Greek New Testament, "On these

pages you will find the living Christ and you will see him more fully and more clearly than if he stood before you, before your very eyes."[6] That experience makes the remnant a prophetic presence in their generation (v. 18).

But hypocrites—the majority in Isaiah's day—choose a darkness that falls with increasing devastation (vv. 19–22). Our only safety is seen in verse 20: "To the teaching and to the testimony!" In other words, "*Run* to the truth!" And those who don't? "If they will not speak according to this word, it is because they have no dawn" (v. 20). Isaiah's people had the truth, but they didn't value it as their guide for life. Why? "They have no dawn"—no illumination within. Real faith and unreal faith are as different as light and darkness, even with the Bible open before us. But grace imparts to the remnant a Spirit of wisdom and of revelation in the knowledge of God, so that the eyes of their hearts are enlightened to all that he's worth, and they live in wealth and light (Ephesians 1:17, 18).

Isaiah 8:22, with its "gloom of anguish," transitions to the triumph section of the passage: "no gloom for her who was in anguish" (9:1). God promises his Old Testament remnant people a triumphant brightness they've never seen before.

Triumph

> But there will be no gloom for her who was in anguish. In the former time he brought into contempt the land of Zebulun and the land of Naphtali, but in the latter time he has made glorious the way of the sea, the land beyond the Jordan, Galilee of the nations.
>
> The people who walked in darkness
>   have seen a great light;
> those who dwelt in a land of deep darkness,
>   on them has light shone. (Isaiah 9:1, 2)

God came to his people first where they had suffered the most, and from that place he launched salvation for the world. Isaiah uses the metaphors of darkness and light for oppression and liberation. Whenever foreign armies marched over the Fertile Crescent to invade Israel, the first area to come under attack was "Galilee of the nations" in the north. The Galileans knew slavery and despair. But God turned invasion into mission by making the people of Galilee the first ones to see the light of Jesus (Matthew 4:12–17). That is how God ushered in the new era of triumphant grace. We made no contribution to it. The ones walking in darkness suddenly found themselves blinking under a new light they had never seen before. They deserved what had happened to them. But God was not satisfied with that. His zeal brought a Savior.

> You have multiplied the nation;
>   you have increased its joy;
> they rejoice before you
>   as with joy at the harvest,
>   as they are glad when they divide the spoil. (Isaiah 9:3)

The "you" here is God. He is spreading his light to more and more people, multiplying a remnant long ago into "a great multitude that no one could number, from every nation, from all tribes and peoples and languages . . . crying out with a loud voice, 'Salvation belongs to our God who sits on the throne, and to the Lamb!'" (Revelation 7:9, 10). Their joy is not meager. Isaiah compares it with the joy of workers at the harvest, a huge bonus on payday, and the gladness of soldiers dividing the spoil, like the locker room of the Super Bowl champions right after the game. The triumph of God's grace over our depressing failures is joy unspeakable and full of glory forever.

In verses 4–7 Isaiah explains—the word "for" appears three times—this miraculous joy's breaking upon the world. Our Liberator is fighting for us.

> For the yoke of his burden,
>   and the staff for his shoulder,
>   the rod of his oppressor,
>   you have broken as on the day of Midian. (v. 4)

Isaiah is thinking of a freedom fighter, like Gideon (Judges 6—8), breaking the power of all our oppressors. What is unique about his salvation is this: You and I are not the subject of any of the verbs in verses 4–7. True liberation comes from beyond ourselves. "The zeal of the LORD of hosts will do this."

But why "as on the day of Midian"? Because Gideon broke the power of the Midianite hordes. He was an unlikely hero. And God deliberately reduced the size of his army from 32,000 men to 300. Then God's strategy was an audacious bluff, with Gideon's men blowing trumpets and breaking jars and holding up torches in the night. But God threw the enemy into a panic, and they slaughtered their own men. Isaiah is looking ahead to a Liberator even better than Gideon.

> For every boot of the tramping warrior in battle tumult
>   and every garment rolled in blood
>   will be burned as fuel for the fire. (Isaiah 9:5)

Our Liberator will not only defeat all the forces of evil, he will put a final end to conflict itself. Every mechanism for tyranny will go into the bonfire of

God's grace. The passive voice "will be burned" whispers that this victory is not our accomplishment. We step onto the battlefield after the victory is won, and all we do is celebrate.

But who is this all-powerful, new figure striding across the world stage? Through what magnificent person does the zeal of the Lord renew the world forever?

> For to us a child is born,
>   to us a son is given;
> and the government shall be upon his shoulder,
>   and his name shall be called
> Wonderful Counselor, Mighty God,
>   Everlasting Father, Prince of Peace. (v. 6)

God's answer to everything that has ever terrorized us is a child. The power of God is so far superior to the Assyrias and all the big shots of this world that he can defeat them by coming as a mere child. His answer to the bullies swaggering through history is not to become an even bigger bully. His answer is Jesus.

When we get close enough to the secret of world peace to see it clearly, what do we discover? Against our expectations, we find weakness overwhelming power and foolishness outfoxing wisdom (1 Corinthians 1:18–25). Everything else has failed. However improbable, the gospel must be true. God does not need our strength or brains. Jesus Christ crucified is the only Savior and King of the world.

Look at Jesus. As the Wonderful Counselor, he has the best ideas and strategies. Let's follow him. As the Mighty God, he defeats his enemies easily. Let's hide behind him. As the Everlasting Father, he loves us endlessly. Let's enjoy him. As the Prince of Peace, he reconciles us while we are still his enemies. Let's welcome his dominion.

> He is a king of the most unparalleled clemency and grace. Never was any kingdom ruled by a government so mild and gentle and gracious. He is exceedingly gracious in the manner of his ruling his people by sweetly and powerfully influencing their hearts by his grace: not governing them against their wills, but powerfully inclining their wills.[7]

How can we defeat the One who is able to fly in under the radar of our prejudices and win our hearts? History is going his way.

> Of the increase of his government and of peace
>   there will be no end,

on the throne of David and over his kingdom,
   to establish it and to uphold it
with justice and with righteousness
   from this time forth and forevermore. (Isaiah 9:7)

This child is the King to end all kings, saving us from our failure, lifting us into his own justice and righteousness. He is Jesus Christ the Lord, our crucified, risen, reigning, and coming Savior. And he will not come back to tweak this problem and that. He will return with a massive correction of all systemic evil forever.

That is the best part. "Of the *increase* of his government and of peace *there will be no end*." The empire of grace will forever expand. If we will live by faith in him now, accepting his weakness as our strength and his folly as our wisdom, we will be there to enjoy his triumph, forever ascending, forever enlarging, forever accelerating, forever intensifying. There will never come one moment when we will say, "This is the limit. He can't think of anything new. We've seen it all." No. The finite will experience ever more wonderfully the infinite, and every new moment will be better than the last.

The zeal of the Lord of hosts will do this.

11

The Triumph of Grace over Our Failure: Israel I

ISAIAH 9:8—10:15

IN HIGH SCHOOL LIT, we read the famous sermon by Jonathan Edwards, "Sinners in the Hands of an Angry God." I didn't like it. "Sinners in the hands of an *angry* God"? Isn't that an old-fashioned concept of God? How is that helpful?

Isaiah must have thought it would be helpful. In this passage he has a lot to say about the anger of God: "For all this his anger has not turned away, and his hand is stretched out still" (9:12, 17, 21; 10:4). He also refers to God's "wrath" and "fury" (9:19; 10:5). This text is about sinners in the hands of an angry God. In fact, God, the most loving person in the Bible, is also the angriest person in the Bible.

What would we have preferred? Aristotle's Unmoved Mover, with no feelings about us at all?

> The God of Aristotle is little involved in the world; it would have been a sign of inferiority and imperfection for Him to be so. This reflected a typically Greek attitude. To be affected by something external to your self is an indication of weakness, and in Aristotle's ideal of the "Great-Minded Man" this is very marked—he will not be cruel to his inferiors just because they are beneath such notice.[1]

The wrath of God in the Bible reveals not cruelty but humility. He's willing to get involved. We matter to him. The Bible says, "God is love" (1 John 4:8, 16). It never says, "God is anger." But it couldn't say that God is love without his anger. Is our visceral offense at the wrath of God really wise? Has our thinking advanced beyond Isaiah? God is better than we think he is, in every respect—even his wrath.

Isaiah 1—5 describes the spiritual disaster that we are. Chapters 6—11 show us the triumph of God's grace over our failure. In chapter 6 we see the triumph of grace for Isaiah, in 7:1—9:7 the triumph of grace for Judah, and now in 9:8—11:16 the triumph of grace for Israel. Does Isaiah believe in the wrath of God? Yes. But he can see the wrath of God taking us further into his grace than we ourselves would ever go. The prophetic vision of the grace of God would be incomplete without the wrath of God.

What is the wrath of God? His wrath is his active, resolute opposition to all evil.[2] His delight is spontaneous and intrinsic to his being, but his wrath is provoked by the defiance of his creatures. His love will never make peace with our evil. What we must understand is that God's wrath is *perfect*, no less perfect than "the riches of his kindness and forbearance and patience" (Romans 2:4). His wrath is not moody vindictiveness; it is the solemn determination of a doctor cutting away the cancer that's killing his patient. And for God, the anger is personal, not detached and clinical. This Doctor hates the cancer, because he loves the carriers of the disease and he will rid the universe of all their afflictions. He has already scheduled "the day of wrath when God's righteous judgment will be revealed" (Romans 2:5). So let's forget our simplistic thoughts of God. The magnitude of the gospel prompts us to invent a word like "lovingangerkindness," to come to grips with who God is.[3] In his lovingangerkindness, God *destroyed* the guilt of sinners at the cross of Jesus. He will *destroy* all remaining sin in the hearts of those who take refuge in Jesus. He will *destroy* all injustice and suffering here in this world when the kingdom of Jesus creates a world better than our sentimentality could imagine.

The gospel sobers us even as it cheers us. It gets us asking serious questions about God that our breezy opinions would have overlooked.

> Who can stand before his indignation?
>   Who can endure the heat of his anger?
> His wrath is poured out like fire,
>   and the rocks are broken into pieces by him. (Nahum 1:6)

Then the kings of the earth and the great ones and the generals and the rich and the powerful, and everyone, slave and free, hid themselves in the caves and among the rocks of the mountains, calling to the mountains and rocks, "Fall on us and hide us from the face of him who is seated on the throne, and from the wrath of the Lamb, for the great day of their wrath has come, and who can stand?" (Revelation 6:15–17)

The tsunami waves that devastated Asia in December 2004 were triggered by an earthquake equal in power to about a million atomic bombs.[4] If the crust of this little fleck of the creation can generate such power, what is the Creator capable of?

Isaiah chooses strong words to show God to us. The word translated "anger" is used elsewhere to mean "nose," suggesting anger as a fuming rage. The word translated "wrath" means "outburst." The word translated "fury" means "indignation." These are very human words. But, removing all human distortion, the prophet finds these words useful for describing the perfect passion burning in the heart of God to defeat evil and bring us into the triumph of his grace. It is the vocabulary of God's fiery perfection.

His wrath works in two ways, with opposite results. On the one hand, his anger condemns those who finally reject him. They prefer Hell, and they get what they prefer. Still worse, as C. S. Lewis warns us, "It's not a question of God 'sending' us to Hell. In each of us there is something growing up which will of itself *be Hell* unless it is nipped in the bud. The matter is serious: let us put ourselves in His hands at once—this very day, this very hour."[5] On the other hand, God's anger purifies all who love him. His fatherly discipline enriches us in everything we long for in our own deepest intentions. This remedial anger does not afflict us as we deserve, but only as we need (Hebrews 12:5–13).

Our generation has almost completely lost sight of the wrath of God, but we cannot understand or respect our salvation without this awareness. So Isaiah explains the triumph of God's grace over our failure by dialing in God's wrath. The structure of his text mirrors his message to Judah in 7:1—9:7. Isaiah works with the same fourfold pattern of decision, judgment, grace, and triumph. Here are his first two points:

1. Decision: If God's people choose evil, his wrath works with unrelenting force (9:8—10:4)
    A Pride leads to humiliation (9:8–12)
        B Impenitence leads to irresponsible leaders (9:13–17)
            C Self-seeking leads to self-destruction (9:18–21)
                D Injustice leads to helplessness (10:1–4)
2. Judgment: God rules over his unwitting agents (10:5–15)
    A¹ God's wrath empowering Assyria (10:5)
        B¹ God's purpose deploying Assyria's ambition (10:6–11)
        B² God's finality punishing Assyria's pride (10:12–14)
    A² God's wrath humbling Assyria (10:15)

Isaiah is talking about the northern kingdom now: "... Jacob ... Israel
... Ephraim ... Samaria ..." (9:8, 9).

Decision

The outstanding feature of this section is the refrain repeated at the close of
each paragraph:

> For all this his anger has not turned away,
>   and his hand is stretched out still. (9:12, 17, 21; 10:4)

Isaiah is saying, "Yes, God has struck you. And he isn't finished yet."
This is why the outline reads, "God's wrath works with *unrelenting* force."
God has more resources for confronting us than we have tactics for evading
him.

First, in 9:8–12 Isaiah identifies Israel's basic problem: "... who say in
pride and in arrogance of heart" (v. 9). *What* were they saying in pride and
arrogance of heart?

> "The bricks have fallen,
>   but we will build with dressed stones;
> the sycamores have been cut down,
>   but we will put cedars in their place." (v. 10)

Apparently Israel has come under military attack. Bricks have fallen,
and sycamores have been cut down. But the people aren't thinking about
the meaning of their adversity. They're laughing it off. They see their setbacks as opportunities to rebuild the past, and even improve on it. But their
unthinking, self-exalting past is what got them into trouble in the first place.
Winston Churchill's final volume in his history of the Second World War
has this theme: "How the great democracies triumphed, and so were able to
resume the follies which had so nearly cost them their life."[6] No reflection,
no humility. But whether they come as sudden disaster or gradual decrepi-
tude, events have meaning, because God is at work in history.

> The Lord raises the adversaries of Rezin against him,
>   and stirs up his enemies. (v. 11)

The "adversaries of Rezin" are the Assyrians. The Lord himself raises
them up. Do you see the irony? The Lord matches Israel's uplifted pride and
newly erected buildings and freshly grown trees by raising up everyone's
nineteenth nervous breakdown, the Assyrians. Here is an axiom lying at the
very foundation of the moral order we live in: "God opposes the proud, but

gives grace to the humble" (James 4:6; 1 Peter 5:5). Israel ignored that truth. So God's hand was stretched out still.

Secondly, therefore, in Isaiah 9:13–17 their impenitence leads to irresponsible leaders. Why do I say impenitence? Because Isaiah laments,

> The people did not turn to him who struck them,
>   nor inquire of the LORD of hosts. (v. 13)

When God strikes you, the biggest mistake you can make is to turn away from him instead of turning to him and inquiring of him. When Jonathan Edwards's wife Sarah received word that her husband had died far away in Princeton, she was suffering from her own afflictions so deeply she could hardly hold her pen to write. But in a letter to her daughter she demonstrated how a Christian clings to God in God-sent adversity:

> What shall I say? A holy and good God has covered us with a dark cloud. Oh, that we may kiss the rod [of discipline], and lay our hands on our mouths! The Lord has done it. He has made me adore his goodness, that we had my husband so long. But my God lives, and he has my heart. Oh, what a legacy my husband, and your father, has left us! We are all given to God; and there I am, and love to be.[7]

In all our afflictions, the only way to run from God is to run to God. Israel chose foolishly. What came of it? "The LORD cut off from Israel head and tail" (v. 14)—that is, their leaders, under whose influence the nation was unraveling (v. 17). And God's hand was stretched out still.

Thirdly, therefore, in verses 18–21 self-seeking leads to self-destruction. Isaiah discerns the inherently destructive power of sin: "Wickedness burns like a fire" (v. 18). The pain sin brings is not an addition to sin, piled on top, but simply the outworking of sin itself. And there is a deeper meaning in that wildfire sweeping through a life, a family, a church, a company: "Through *the wrath of the LORD* of hosts the land is scorched" (v. 19). The wrath of God is *in* the damage that sin inflicts. For example, self-seeking people are devouring one another (vv. 19–21). Of the last six kings of Israel, five came to the throne by assassination.[8] Human sin was unleashing itself on humans. Does this address us? "If you bite and devour one another, watch out that you are not consumed by one another" (Galatians 5:15). And God's hand is stretched out still.

Finally, therefore, in Isaiah 10:1–4 injustice leads to helplessness. Isaiah envisions the corrupt elite of Israel huddling as prisoners of war or tossed onto a heap of dead bodies, as in fact happened when Assyria overran Israel in 722 B.C.:

Nothing remains but to crouch among the prisoners
  or fall among the slain. (v. 4)

And God's hand was stretched out still. You and I will never wear God down until he relents and we get our own way. In Almighty God we have met our match.

Whom should we fear? Whose favor should we cherish? We fear people and curry favor with them. This is all wrong. There is a God in Heaven who loves us more than they ever will. It is his wrath, not theirs, we should fear. It is his favor, not theirs, we should cherish. It is not the powers of this world with whom we have to deal, primarily. It is God, always.

Judgment

The ultimacy of God is Isaiah's point in 10:5–15. When we are beaten down by some Assyria or other, let's remember it is only a tool in the hand of God.

Woe to Assyria, the rod of my anger;
  the staff in their hands is my fury! (v. 5)

This is one of the most important passages in the Bible on the sovereignty of God. What is the sovereignty of God? It is his ultimacy as King of the universe. It is his glorious Throne, from which he rules all things in unfrustrated supremacy: "Our God is in the heavens; he does all that he pleases" (Psalm 115:3). Isaiah loved the sovereignty of God.[9] But the nation God used as the disciplinary rod in his hand was itself evil. The Assyrians have been called the Nazis of the ancient Near East. In fact, the problem is worse.

Against a godless nation I send him [Assyria],
  and against the people of my wrath I command him. (v. 6)

"Wait just one minute here!" Isaiah's readers in Israel would have said. "We aren't a godless nation. Assyria is! How can you say, Isaiah, that God is sending that cruel war-machine against us?" But God doesn't respect a double standard. The sins he judges out in the world he also judges among his own people (cf. Romans 2:11; 1 Peter 4:17). Belonging to God does not protect us from discipline; it makes us all the more accountable to obey. If we refuse, we are, in practical terms, "godless."

God is able to use godless worldly powers to discipline his godless covenant people. Human oppressors don't even have to be aware of God to be useful for his purifying purpose.

But he [Assyria] does not so intend,
    and his heart does not so think. (Isaiah 10:7)

Verses 8–11 reveal what Assyria *was* thinking. Not only were they salivating over the northern Israelite kingdom as a trophy of imperialistic expansion, they saw nothing to stop their advance all the way to Jerusalem in the south. The tool in God's hand was very impressed with itself. The annals of Adad-Nirari II (911–891 B.C.) openly express the Assyrian mentality:

> In these days, when at the command of the great gods my lordly sovereignty has manifested itself, going forth to plunder the goods of the lands, I am royal, I am lordly, I am mighty, I am honored, I am exalted, I am glorified, I am powerful, I am all powerful, I am brilliant, I am lion-brave, I am manly, I am supreme, I am noble.[10]

Right. But Isaiah can see two sovereignties at work in this world—the sovereignty of man and the greater sovereignty of God. And God's domain is able to use man's domain, whether man wants it that way or not. How can human power outflank a God like that?

Just because God deploys human ambition doesn't mean he condones human arrogance. Being used by God does not exempt anyone from humility before God. The truth here is twofold. On the one hand, God is on the side of the victor. The ebb and flow of this messy thing called human history follow the will of God. It was God's will in 722 B.C. that Assyria conquer Israel. It was God's will on September 11, 2001, that Muslim fanatics attack America. Therefore, when we are defeated, God is not defeated. But on the other hand, God is *not* on the side of the victor. God judges opportunistic people and nations, even if he uses them for his own higher purpose. God is able to use evil without being compromised by it. He holds every useful villain accountable, and no one is getting away with anything, not even arrogant speech and boastful looks.

> When the Lord has finished all his work on Mount Zion and on Jerusalem, he will punish the speech of the arrogant heart of the king of Assyria and the boastful look in his eyes. (v. 12)

God appoints days of reckoning here within history, and he has a day of final judgment waiting at the end of history (Acts 17:31). The ruins of Berlin in 1945 bore witness to the wrath of God in our time. But Berlin was given another chance. The divine wrath on that future day will not be remedial in its intention or its effects. It will be eternally devastating. What the Bible keeps saying to us is that God will never accept human pride. Its folly is unsustainable.

Shall the axe boast over him who hews with it,
or the saw magnify itself against him who wields it? (Isaiah 10:15)

God reasons with us, "What do you have that you did not receive? If then you received it, why do you boast as if you did not receive it?" (1 Corinthians 4:7).

God is no cardboard cutout. He is a real person with real anger and real love. He has wonderful things he wants to talk to us about. His grace can recover everything we have failed to be. But he will not negotiate with our self-exaltation. As we struggle against him, "Our relationship with God is a dramatic engagement, something like a bout of fencing, with its succession of offensives, retreats, feints and rallies."[11] God may walk up to you at some point and punch you right in the nose and knock you flat. And as you are sitting there on the ground wondering, "What was *that* all about?" he might kick you in the teeth. Think of Job. But why? Why does God blindside us at times? Because the only way we'll listen is the hard way. He would rather lead us gently beside still waters. But he will not settle for a polite religious unreality with us.

I asked the Lord that I might grow in faith and love and every grace,
Might more of his salvation know and seek more earnestly his face.

Twas he who taught me thus to pray and he, I trust, has answered prayer;
but it has been in such a way as almost drove me to despair.

I hoped that in some favored hour at once he'd answer my request,
And by his love's constraining power subdue my sins and give me rest.

Instead of this he made me feel the hidden evils of my heart,
And let the angry powers of hell assault my soul in every part.

Yea more, with his own hand he seemed intent to aggravate my woe,
Crossed all the fair designs I schemed, blasted my gourds, and laid me low.

Lord, why is this, I trembling cried, wilt thou pursue thy worm to death?
Tis in this way, the Lord replied, I answer prayer for grace and faith.

These inward trials I employ from self and pride to set thee free,
And break thy schemes of earthly joy, that thou mayest seek thy all in me.[12]

"Humble yourselves, therefore, under the mighty hand of God so that at the proper time he may exalt you" (1 Peter 5:6).

12

The Triumph of Grace over Our Failure: Israel II

ISAIAH 10:16—11:16

A. W. TOZER WROTE, "What comes into our minds when we think about God is the most important thing about us. . . . The gravest question before the Church is always God Himself, and the most portentous fact about any man is not what he at a given time may say or do, but what he in his deep heart conceives God to be like. We tend by a secret law of the soul to move toward our mental image of God."[1] The secret to who you really are, and the key to your future, is not your self-image but your God-image.

The gospel saves us by improving our God-image. It gets us thinking realistically about the wrath of God and longingly about the grace of God. There is a grace for us worthy of no one less than God, beyond all we can ask or imagine. Isaiah concludes his sermon about grace for Israel's failure with a vision of the messianic kingdom beautiful enough to heighten our God-esteem.

3. Grace: God moves history to preserve his remnant people (10:16–34)
   A¹ Therefore: vast Assyria made few (10:16–19)
      B¹ In that day: remnant Israel made pure (10:20–23)
   A² Therefore: fearful Zion made confident (10:24–26)
      B² In that day: haughty Assyria made low (10:27–34)
4. Triumph: The rule of Messiah will transform the world (11:1–16)
   A¹ The Davidic Messiah bringing peace to the world (11:1–9)

      1. The Messiah's powers (11:1–5)
      2. The Messiah's influence (11:6–9)
  A² The Divine Messiah attracting the nations (11:10)
    B¹ The Lord's hand regathering his exiled people (11:11)
    B² The Lord's hand destroying all opposition to his people's liberation
     (11:12–16)
        1. The exiles' fortunes reversed (11:12–14)
        2. His people's homecoming advanced (11:15, 16)

When we see God bending all his thought and will on our behalf, preparing a place for us, everything changes. How so? C. S. Lewis understands:

> If we consider the unblushing promises of reward and the staggering nature of the rewards promised in the Gospels [and the prophets], it would seem that Our Lord finds our desires, not too strong, but too weak. We are half-hearted creatures, fooling about with drink and sex and ambition when infinite joy is offered us, like an ignorant child who wants to go on making mud pies in a slum because he cannot imagine what is meant by the offer of a holiday at the sea. We are far too easily pleased.[2]

Isaiah's vision of God can stimulate in us such a longing that we stop settling for the mud pies of this slum and set our course for that holiday at the sea, far away in God's promised new world. To see God as our King of Grace, laboring to take us there despite what we deserve, makes the difference.

Grace

Isaiah floodlights God himself. He builds the subsections—A1, B1, A2, B2—on "the Lord GOD of hosts" (10:16, 23, 24, 33). He brings in other titles of God as well: "the Light of Israel" (10:17, NIV), "his Holy One" (10:17), "the LORD, the Holy One of Israel" (10:20), "the mighty God" (10:21), "the LORD of hosts" (10:26), and "the Majestic One" (10:34). There's a lot to God. Following him can be daunting, because the Lamb is also the Lion (Revelation 5:5, 6). But we become courageous enough to follow when our hearts are alive to the mighty grace of "the Lord GOD of hosts."

What does Isaiah see? First, the grace of the Lord God of hosts reduces vast Assyria to a few.

> The remnant of the trees of his forest [the Assyrian army] will be so few
>   that a child can write them down. (Isaiah 10:19)

In this paragraph Isaiah uses the metaphors of sickness and fire to describe how effectively God cuts the armies of Assyria down to a comically skimpy number—like a child counting on his fingers. What is Isaiah saying? If sickness is a malaise working slowly from within, and fire is a sudden disaster catching on from without, then God has *all* means at his disposal to do whatever he wants with the forces of this world opposing his grace. The human conqueror reaches into the nest of Israel and plunders the eggs nestled there (v. 14); but he doesn't see, until it's too late, that he's reaching into a plague with no antidote and a fire with no relief. This is why believers should never despair under the shocks of history. Whether the opposition to our joy is little "thorns and briers" (v. 17) or a vast "forest" (v. 18) makes no difference to the Fire.

Secondly, the grace of the Lord God of hosts purifies remnant Israel. When people are set apart by grace, they show it by a real faith.

> In that day the remnant of Israel and the survivors of the house of Jacob will no more lean on him who struck them, but will lean on the LORD, the Holy One of Israel, in truth. (v. 20)

Sometimes Christians cozy up to ideas, institutions, trends, and even emotions that strike at the heart of their faith. Paul wrote to the Corinthians, "If someone comes and proclaims another Jesus than the one we proclaimed, or if you receive a different spirit from the one you received, or if you accept a different gospel from the one you accepted, you put up with it readily enough" (2 Corinthians 11:4). We are more susceptible to alien saviors, spirits, and gospels than we know.

This is the question Isaiah wants each of us to think through: Where do I get my security, coping skills, confidence for the future? Many salvations are vying for our allegiance. And every false support we lean on turns around and bites us. We do lean on forces that strike us, abuse us, sneer at us. But Jesus never betrays our trust. Isaiah is helping us understand the difference that grace makes. We learn to examine ourselves: "When I am stricken with disillusionment, emptiness, self-hatred, when these emotional undercurrents are dragging me down, what false savior am I leaning on?"

To his glory, God will not put up with that humiliation. He wants you to know what it means to lean on him "in truth"—a practical faith in him alone—because that is your salvation. When he rips from your arms some false trust that has struck you a thousand times, and a thousand times you've gone back to it in servile compliance, and you're ready to go back again—when God tears it away, do you see what he is doing? His grace is setting you apart as one of his remnant, dear to his heart.

Another mark of God's remnant people is repentance: "A remnant will return, the remnant of Jacob, to the mighty God" (Isaiah 10:21). The key is "the mighty God," also used of the Messiah in Isaiah 9:6. This title means that he is the God of military prowess, the God who can fight and win. "Return" is repentance language. Coming back to this God, therefore, means that we repent of the way we fight our own battles, and we let him fight for us. He is well able to.

So the people of God are known by a courageous trust in him and a repentant willingness to let him be the Hero. All our happiness depends on it.

> For though your people Israel be as the sand of the sea, only a remnant of them will return. Destruction is decreed, overflowing with righteousness. (Isaiah 10:22)

God promised Abraham that his descendants would become numerous like the sand on the seashore (Genesis 22:17). But we have to read that promise according to the way God thinks. He was speaking from a heart that cares not about race but about grace (Romans 9:22–29). The true people of God are known not by ethnicity or institutional identity or historical roots but only by Abrahamic faith and repentance. What God cares about is that we have reality in our hearts, not that we're Presbyterian or Baptist or whatever in our lineage.

Thirdly, the grace of the Lord God of hosts makes fearful Zion confident.

> Therefore thus says the Lord GOD of hosts: "O my people, who dwell in Zion, be not afraid of the Assyrians when they strike with the rod and lift up their staff against you as the Egyptians did." (Isaiah 10:24)

God took up Assyria in his hand like a rod, to discipline his own people (Isaiah 10:5). But if the grace of God is at work even through the forces of evil, then nothing can separate us from his love but will only take us deeper (Romans 8:31–39). His secret strategy is this:

> And the LORD of hosts will wield against them a whip, as when he struck Midian at the rock of Oreb. And his staff will be over the sea, and he will lift it as he did in Egypt. (Isaiah 10:26)

Isaiah is alluding to two victories in Israel's history—over the Midianites, with Gideon and his little army (Judges 7:19–25), and over Egypt at the Red Sea (Exodus 14:15–31). What these two victories had in common was their improbable outcome. Gideon had only 300 men. At the Red Sea, Israel couldn't even mount an attack. But they won. Why? Because God's power is made perfect in our weakness (2 Corinthians 12:9). God has assembled reality in such a way that, for his remnant people, the ratchet turns only one way—toward the coming kingdom.

Finally, the grace of the Lord God of hosts brings haughty Assyria low.

The key is the last line of Isaiah 10:33: "and the lofty will be brought low." What could be more firmly established in this world than human pride? Isaiah sees the juggernaut of worldly arrogance bearing down on us in verses 28–32. The confident Assyrian army advances step by step, closing in on Zion with terrifying relentlessness, with God's people in full retreat.[3] But at the last moment God steps in and cuts that ego down. Back in verse 15 Assyria was the axe in God's hand. But now the Assyrians are themselves a forest being felled by an Axe (v. 34).

A day is coming when God will stop the whole Blitzkrieg of history dead in its tracks. And not just because God will police world politics. He will go down to the root of it all. Every injustice, every broken treaty, every national rape—it all stems from the boast, "I will force the world into a shape more to my liking, no matter what the cost to you." Hitler rationalized it as *Lebensraum*. Ego can always find some plausible excuse for imperialistic overreaching. But behind the highfalutin justifications, God sees human pride as *the* barrier to the world as it should be. That is why Christ came in humility, shaming our savagery. And at his second coming, the Majestic One will stand forth with his glory in full display, renewing the world as a kingdom of peace.

Triumph

The structure of Isaiah's thought in chapter 11 is intricate, but his central focus is clear. At the close of chapter 10, what do we see? The infestation of human pride like a vast forest cut down. God swings his axe, and the whole evil system falls. Bare stumps as far as the eye can see. No branches waving in the wind, no birds flitting around, no life, no movement, no sound. The world is dead. But wait. Something new appears:

> There shall come forth a shoot from the stump of Jesse,
>> and a branch from his roots shall bear fruit. (Isaiah 11:1)

From one stump a little shoot grows and becomes a branch and bears fruit. And the fruit it bears is a whole new world. Isaiah is thinking of a little boy, born in obscurity more than 2,000 years ago now, with no status but lineage in a failed ancient dynasty. And he is the only one who can save us from ourselves.

But Messiah has more than royal lineage. After all, Ahaz was a son of David, but he was spiritually bankrupt. Jesus also has the anointing of the Holy Spirit.

> And the Spirit of the LORD shall rest upon him,
>> the Spirit of wisdom and understanding,

the Spirit of counsel and might,
the Spirit of knowledge and the fear of the LORD. (v. 2)

Jesus does not need our mechanisms for power. He has another way to build the world of our dreams. He has the Spirit of wisdom and understanding for leadership, the Spirit of counsel and might for war, the Spirit of knowledge and the fear of the Lord for holiness. Unlike every other human leader in the sorry length of our history, Jesus is literally qualified to rule the world. We have nothing to fear from him. We are foolish to resist him. We can never be too loyal to him.

The anointing of Jesus with wisdom proves that the fullness of the Spirit is not just an emotional blowout. Richard Lovelace reminds us:

In our quest for the fullness of the Spirit, we have sometimes forgotten that a Spirit-filled intelligence is one of the powerful weapons for pulling down satanic strongholds.[4]

We think of Jesus as a very nice but, when it comes to real life, incompetent person. We think too much of ourselves, our worship patronizes him, and our lives set him aside. But the truth is, all the treasures of wisdom and knowledge are hidden in Christ (Colossians 2:3). His insight penetrates through appearances (Isaiah 11:3). The Apostle John saw him as having eyes "like a flame of fire" (Revelation 1:14). How many clever human leaders and judges have been deceived or misled, to the injury of many? But nobody is fooling the Anointed One. Along with his brilliance, he has a passion for justice. His rule will correct the massive wrongs we are forced to accept. But he will not step on the little people in pursuing his project. He will defend the meek and slay the wicked (Isaiah 11:4). When our own leaders trumpet their ideals, we have to be cautious. But the Messiah deserves our enthusiasm.

Righteousness shall be the belt of his waist,
and faithfulness the belt of his loins. (v. 5)

Isaiah means that Jesus is righteous and faithful just by being true to himself. He never needs to fear himself or correct himself. Unlike every other human leader, Jesus Christ is clothed not with the trappings of human ego but with righteousness and faithfulness. We can trust him without being guarded. If we do hold back, we're saying that we are more to be trusted than he is. We're saying that he is no better than a pompous Assyria or a wishy-washy Ahaz. That is our greatest sin—to think and act as our own saviors and to disrespect the Savior of the world. We have good intentions, but he has good judgment and all power. When we start to trust him more than we trust ourselves, we're beginning to understand what it means to trust him at all.

The wolf shall dwell with the lamb,
  and the leopard shall lie down with the young goat,
and the calf and the lion and the fattened calf together;
  and a little child shall lead them.
The cow and the bear shall graze;
  their young shall lie down together;
  and the lion shall eat straw like the ox.
The nursing child shall play over the hole of the cobra,
  and the weaned child shall put his hand on the adder's den.
They shall not hurt or destroy
  in all my holy mountain;
for the earth shall be full of the knowledge of the LORD
  as the waters cover the sea. (vv. 6–9)

The one anointed with the Spirit is the only one able to renew nature. He made this world. He loves it. He will transform it, so that "nature, red in tooth and claw" will be restful, secure, innocent. Every square inch of the world will be the "holy mountain" of the Lord.

"They shall not hurt or destroy" came to mind while I was reading a review of several books on the 1960s hippie movement, so significant to my generation. The reviewer described the 1967 "Summer of Love":

The Haight-Ashbury section of San Francisco was idyllic for about five minutes before the following famous flier was distributed: "Pretty little 16-year-old middle-class chick comes to the Haight to see what it's all about & gets picked up by a 17-year-old street dealer who spends all day shooting her full of speed again & again, then feeds her 3000 mikes & raffles off her temporarily unemployed body for the biggest Haight Street gang bang since the night before last. The politics & ethics of ecstasy." The "3000 mikes" there are micrograms of LSD and represent 12 times the "normal" dose. I still know people who undertook such voyages of the imagination, or had them inflicted upon themselves, and who never quite came back.[5]

When the earth is full of the knowledge of the Lord as the waters cover the sea, the scars of our ugly utopias will disappear forever under the overflowing healing of Christ. I long for my generation to join me there, where the human family will finally be one, the very environment will breathe with the peace of God, and we will never hurt one another again. Other revolutions have promised us liberation and instead oppressed us. But if we bow to the rule of Jesus Christ, he will lead us into everything safe and pleasant, with no dark side, no forced laughter, no guilty conscience, no unhealed wounds.

The triumph of Jesus will not be the rise of religion. His salvation is not confining that way, not even as private bliss. Nor will he set us in the clouds to play harps and sing in massed choirs forever. The victory of Jesus will be the awakening and purifying and restoring and gladdening of all things human. His kingdom is the only final answer to poverty, hunger, injustice, illiteracy, and all the other sorrows we have created. His grace will add sparkle to World Cup soccer, classical guitar, business ventures, Monopoly with the kids, *everything human*, to the greater glory of God.

The problem with this gospel is not that it is too small to deserve our faith. Its beauty and magnitude surpass our faith. But we have a reason to believe this audacious gospel. We saw the future glory in the resurrected Jesus on that Easter Sunday long ago. That is a knowable event in our past. And his immortal newness on that day was the future in advance, on public display.

Even now, the fullness of his kingdom is only an inch away. All that stands between the present moment and the promised future is the command of God. He is not waiting for favorable conditions in human social evolution. All he has to do is give the order, and Christ will come and judge and save and rule, because he is himself our peace.

Isaiah is not telling us *when*; he is telling us *who*, and that should be enough for us. This is the good news God is calling us to embrace today. Will we? Every human gospel is a slapdash mockery of our longings. But Christ has already been rejected by all our top people and condemned by our system, and raised by God to the immortal life that will renew the world. What can stop him now?

Isaiah adds an assurance, in verses 11–16, that when Christ comes again no earthly power can prevent his followers' joy. Whatever happens to us in the meantime, he will bring us safely home from all over the world in a second exodus, and no prison can hold us. His kingdom will fly no black flags for old comrades "missing in action." He will "assemble the banished of Israel, and gather the dispersed of Judah" (v. 12). We will forget our old denominational jealousies (v. 13), unite in victory over all evil (vv. 14, 15), and enjoy the happiest homecoming in history (v. 16).

> In that day the root of Jesse, who shall stand as a signal for the peoples—of him shall the nations inquire, and his resting place shall be glorious. (v. 10)

When Francis Scott Key wrote the American National Anthem, he was a prisoner on board a British ship during the War of 1812. The enemy ship fired on Fort McHenry all night long. "And the rocket's red glare, the bombs bursting in air, gave proof through the night that our flag was still there." That is the position believers are in now. The kingdom is established; the flag is flying. It will never fall, but it is opposed. Our part is to stay true.

The Messiah himself stands "as a signal for the peoples." The word "signal" means a banner or flag, drawing us in. What is this that compels our admiration? Jesus said, "And I, when I am lifted up from the earth, will draw all people to myself" (John 12:32). The signal is his cross. He wins us not with human swagger and intimidation, not even with human flash and cool, but with his own dying love. The power of his love accomplishes what human imperialism always destroys: the power of our own freely felt love in return.

Is the prophetic word changing your God-image?

13

Our Response to the
Triumph of Grace

ISAIAH 12:1–6

CHAPTER 12 BRINGS ISAIAH'S VISION of God's grace to a climax. Chapter 13 begins, "The oracle concerning Babylon which Isaiah the son of Amoz saw." That seam marks a division in the book. Chapter 13 will change the subject. But before he moves on, Isaiah shows us ourselves at our best, fully enjoying God in the kingdom of our Messiah.

As God catches us up into his purpose sweeping through history, what do we contribute? Nothing to be proud of. What does God contribute? Grace greater than all our sin—grace for Isaiah (6:6, 7), grace for Judah (8:9–22), grace for Israel (10:16–34), grace for us. Isaiah is saying, "We have all failed God. But he is not defeated. He has a remedy—his saving grace in our Messiah (9:1–7; 11:1–16). He will triumph."

When the Apostle Paul brings to a climax his argument about the overruling love of God, he asks us, "What then shall we say to these things?" (Romans 8:31). That is, how shall we respond to God? What can we say to him? We can't just sit here. "Love so amazing, so divine, demands my soul, my life, my all." That is where Isaiah takes us now. When we consider the grace of God restoring to us what we have bungled and giving us even better than what we had before, *what shall we say to these things?*

"You will say in that day" (Isaiah 12:1, 4). We are listening here to our own voices from the future. Isaiah is describing the revival of the church in the latter days.[1] He is not giving us details about the end times. He is creating an impression, giving us a foretaste of what it means to live in a spirit of praise. The structure of the text is simple:

A¹ Grace individually personalized: confident testimony (12:1, 2)
   B Grace deeply accessed: rich enjoyment (12:3)
A² Grace corporately proclaimed: universal mission (12:4–6)

What empowers the testimony of verses 1, 2 and the mission of verses 4–6 is the rich enjoyment in verse 3. Verse 3 is the key to a spirit of praise flooding our hearts. It is out of our delight in God that we find our prophetic voices. True Christianity isn't primarily a matter of control; primarily it's overflowing fullness. That is the triumph of grace.

The subtlety in Isaiah's text is this: English uses one word, *you*, the second person in both singular and plural. But Isaiah's Hebrew uses different linguistic forms for the second person singular and plural. The "you" in verse 1 is singular. Isaiah is saying, "In that day, each of you individually will say . . ." Hence, the pronouns "I," "me," and "my" in verses 1, 2. But the "you" in verses 3, 4 is plural. Here he is saying, "All of you together, as God's remnant people, will draw water from the wells of salvation. And in that day, out of that ever-fresh fullness, you will all say . . ." Then we see corporate worship and mission in verses 4–6.² So the difference between "you will say" in verses 1, 2 and verses 4–6 is the difference between personal testimony and corporate witness.³ Each of us will have a story to tell, and together we will fill the world with the praises of God.

Your Confident Testimony

First and foremost, God gives you your own experience of what it means to be saved. There is no secondhand salvation.

> I will give thanks to you, O LORD,
>   for though you were angry with me,
> your anger turned away,
>   that you might comfort me. (v. 1)

Our deepest problem is not whether we will love God, but whether God will love us. After all we have done to him, why shouldn't he hate us forever?

It would be interesting to poll Christians with the question, "What is the greatest wonder in all of your salvation?" Isaiah's answer would be, "God is your *former* enemy. Now he comes to comfort you." Have you transitioned from being frustrated with a reluctant God who isn't cooperating with your agenda to being comforted by a God who is lavishing you with grace upon grace? How does anyone turn that corner? By going back to the gospel that made us Christians in the first place.

Listen to it again. The wrath of God at our real guilt is warranted, even required for God to be true to himself. His condemnation does fall, and with full force, but not on us. It falls on our Substitute. In his great love for guilty people, Jesus changed places with us at the cross. His sacrifice is the reason why God's grace is morally entitled to treat us like royalty, which he does. If Jesus bears our condemnation far away, then all-forgiving grace toward us is not an extravagance; it is the morally beautiful meaning of our new relationship with God. For us to go boldly now into his presence for comfort, to receive mercy and find grace whenever we have a need, brings God's own purpose to fulfillment. He wants every one of us to be able to say to him, "You comfort me." If we will discover what that means for us now, we will be saying it forever.

> Behold, God is my salvation;
>   I will trust, and will not be afraid. (v. 2a)

Isaiah spent his life trying to persuade people to trust in God and not be afraid and not give themselves to false saviors. His book makes the question unavoidable for us today: Will we trust God through our crises? Or will we fearfully surround our trust in God with mechanisms of self-help, just in case God fails? Do we feel secure *with God alone*?

One of the striking things about this testimony, this voice out of the future, is its simplicity. We complicate our trust in God. We mix in other things. We trust in our trust in God. We trust in our theology of God. We trust in our worship of God. We cling to God *plus* whatever makes us feel comfortable and superior. And the more props we need, the more insecure we become. But when the grace of God overrules our folly, real faith comes alive, and our outlook is simplified so that we say, "Behold, God is my salvation. He is enough. Period." We then discover that we have been safe all along.

> For the LORD GOD is my strength and my song,
>   and he has become my salvation. (v. 2b)

When we experience how strong God really is on our behalf, better than we thought he'd be, he becomes our song. Remember the old musicals like *Singin' in the Rain*? Gene Kelly is walking down the street, happily sloshing in the rain and puddles, wonderfully in love, and he just starts singing. It's crazy. To enjoy that scene, we have to suspend belief just enough to play along with the movie. We have to let the spell come over us and identify with a grown man out in the rain, soaking wet and not caring at all and singing his head off. Why do people make films like that? Why do we watch them? The reason is that it isn't really crazy. God has put into our hearts that very capacity, the freedom to break out into song as the wonder of his saving love fills our hearts. That holy delight is what we were created for. We sense that is so. And in the kingdom we will glorify and enjoy God with unrestrained song.

The heart sings when we accept how little it matters that we are in control and how much it matters that God is in control for us, when we discover how little it matters that we are able and how much it suffices that God is able on our behalf. The day we step into the messianic kingdom and find that God has been true to his word, we redeemed will erupt in music as never before. The gospel says that we will sing a new song. It will sound "like the roar of many waters and like the sound of loud thunder . . . like the sound of harpists playing on their harps" (Revelation 14:2). We have not yet heard that sound—sustained intensity like a waterfall, punctuated bursts like claps of thunder, overwhelming sweetness like an orchestra of harpists, all rolled into one. There is no such sound in all the world. But someday we will be a part of it. Our fully saved hearts will become capable of it. It will pour out of us forever.

Isaiah is echoing the Song of Moses, sung after God rescued Israel through the Red Sea (Exodus 15:2–18). They were weak. But it didn't matter. Why? Here is the confidence of the Biblical gospel from cover to cover: "If God is for us, who can be against us?" (Romans 8:31). His power is made perfect in our weakness (2 Corinthians 12:9). When that assurance enters our hearts, we see that even the frightening experiences of life are leading us more deeply into our salvation. We can stop thinking like victims and start singing even now.

Isaiah describes God in an unusual way. The English Standard Version translates verse 2 "the LORD GOD." The New International Version translates this more literally: "the LORD, the LORD." Isaiah is overusing the Old Testament's personal name for God, because grace enriches us with a strong sense of personal possession in God himself. The text literally reads, "Yah, Yahweh, is my strength and my song, and he has become my salvation." In the triumph of grace we stop standing outside the store, looking in wistfully at the treasures in the window; we walk right in and receive more than we could ask or imagine, because this Owner refuses to do business upon the basis of our payment. Everything is free (cf. Isaiah 55:1, 2). And we will share him all together.

Our Rich Enjoyment

> With joy you [plural] will draw water from the wells of salvation. (Isaiah 12:3)

David said to God, "My soul thirsts for you, my flesh faints for you, as in a dry and weary land where there is no water" (Psalm 63:1). Our prejudices see this world as the satisfaction of our thirst, and sometimes God feels like a dry and weary land. The truth is the opposite. We live in a burning wilderness, and God is all our satisfaction. He opens up to us wells of life-giving fullness, through Jesus Christ, by the Holy Spirit (John 4:13, 14), enough for all of time and eternity.

The prospect of thirsty, weary, dirty people pulling up bucket after bucket of fresh, cool water in endless supply—drinking deeply, pouring it over their heads, dunking their faces into it, splashing one another—that is a vision of God's gifts of salvation widely shared. Joyfully drawing water from the wells of salvation is the very life of God, openly accessible to us all, entering into our actual experience. And the deeper we drink, the greater our praise.

Jesus said, "If anyone thirsts, let him come to me and drink. Whoever believes in me, as the Scripture has said, 'Out of his heart will flow rivers of living water'" (John 7:37, 38). One commentator explains it this way:

> When the believer comes to Christ and drinks he not only slakes his thirst but receives such an abundant supply that veritable rivers flow from him. This stresses the outgoing nature of the Spirit-filled life. . . . There is nothing of the piety of the pond in Christianity.[4]

Stagnant experience—the piety of the pond—is not of God. His salvation flows in endless freshness.

Isaiah says, ". . . *wells* of salvation." How many are there? What different kinds are there? The well of love, the well of delight, the well of healing—wells of every grace and favor. We will enjoy every one. The gospel says, "For the Lamb in the midst of the throne will be their shepherd, and he will guide them to *springs* of living water, and God will wipe away every tear from their eyes" (Revelation 7:17).

Our Universal Mission

And you will say in that day:

"Give thanks to the LORD,
    call upon his name,
make known his deeds among the peoples,
    proclaim that his name is exalted." (Isaiah 12:4)

Isaiah foresees one message spreading over the world, exalting the truth about God, awakening all peoples to the infinite greatness and majesty of God revealed in his saving deeds. As we embrace this mission now, we exalt his name very profoundly.

In 1993 three New Tribes Mission missionaries were kidnapped in Colombia by terrorists. For eight years their families and friends wondered and prayed and worried. Eventually they were informed that the men were dead. Dan Germann was the NTM director in Colombia at that time. In an interview he said that their prayers changed through those long years of uncertainty. They started out praying that God would bring the men home safely. They ended up praying, "God, even if we never know what has become of them, you will still be God." Dan said, "There is a very special sense of awe at who God is and how sufficient he is when the miracle doesn't happen, but the wonder of his sufficiency is still present."[5] This too is the triumph of grace. We come to realize that God is *God*. Our living and our dying take on a very special sense of awe, no matter what price we pay to spread his song. His cause is the one cause on the face of the earth that will finally succeed.

> Sing praises to the LORD, for he has done gloriously;
>   let this be made known in all the earth.
> Shout, and sing for joy, O inhabitant of Zion,
>   for great in your midst is the Holy One of Israel. (vv. 5, 6)

There we are, out in the future kingdom, no longer hanging back but alive with joy in God alone. John Trapp, the Puritan scholar, wrote, "No duty is more pressed in both Testaments than this, of rejoicing in the Lord. It is no less a sin not to rejoice than not to repent."[6] In his great prayer, Jesus asked his Father on our behalf "that they may have my joy fulfilled in themselves" (John 17:13). Paul defined the essence of Christianity as "righteousness and peace and joy in the Holy Spirit" (Romans 14:17). Isaiah foresees "a day yet to be when a restored people will in hilarious celebration delight in their only asset—the Holy One."[7]

The reason why Christian missions will write the last, happy chapter of history is the great presence of God with his people: "Great in your midst is the Holy One of Israel." He is not content to stand off at a distance. From the beginning, God wanted to dwell among his people (Exodus 25:8). He dwelt among us in Jesus (John 1:14). He comes to us through the Holy Spirit (John 14:21, 23). And in the messianic kingdom, his presence will be great among us, uniting the world in holy delight (Zechariah 2:10, 11).

14

The Supremacy of God over the Nations I

ISAIAH 13:1—20:6

IN THESE CHAPTERS ISAIAH'S VISION OF GOD judging the nations is unsparing. Some would say that such talk of national judgments is danger-ous. Some would say that perceiving God as stirring up nations against one another can be used to rationalize brutality. "If God does it, why can't we?"

Miroslav Volf is a Croatian theologian who has wrestled with this problem not in theory but in the face of his nation's being mauled by out-law Serbian forces. He wrote about his struggle in the book *Exclusion and Embrace*. It's easy for us, Volf argues, sitting in our pleasant living rooms in the West, to come up with high-minded theories of nonviolence. Our villages have not been burned, our brothers have not had their throats slit, our sisters have not been assaulted. His had. And he lumps the idea of a noncoercive God in with "many other pleasant captivities of the liberal mind."[1] But there is one thing that can save us from becoming vengeful people. It's a belief in *divine* vengeance. "The certainty of God's just judgment at the end of history is the presupposition for the renunciation of violence in the middle of it."[2] The blood of the innocents still cries out to God from the ground (Genesis 4:10). And when a confidence in God's fierce opposition to all human injustice enters our hearts, we have a reason to forsake our savage impulses and love our enemies.

We should oppose all injustice because God does. But what if we try, and lose? What if wrong stomps on us? What can stabilize us when injustice gloats in triumph over us? If we don't have a just God to trust in, we will have no logical reason not to become violent ourselves. It is Isaiah's vision of God's final justice that moderates our anger and frustration right now. God has scheduled on the human calendar a day of final intervention when *he* will repay all the dirty deals and broken promises and backstabbings of history with a justice clear enough to satisfy no one less than himself.

We long for a true and final justice from beyond ourselves. Human justice is often inadequate. Hitler orchestrated the murder of millions of innocent people. Then he committed suicide. He got off easily. Where is the moral resolution to his monstrosities? Human justice isn't even capable of punishing evil at that level of magnitude. We wonder, is there somewhere a justice worthy of the name, or is that idea just one more of life's mocking disappointments? Isaiah has an answer to our longings. His answer is the day of the Lord (13:6).

God has promised to step in decisively and to punish all wrong with absolute finality. And what the Old Testament calls "the day of the Lord," the New Testament calls "the day of our Lord Jesus Christ" (1 Corinthians 1:8), because Jesus is the one through whom God will judge the world and bring us into eternal peace.[3] *He* is the reason we can live now with redemptive tolerance (Romans 12:14–21).

Here is something else about the day of the Lord that can help us. It's not only a future event; it is also present, if we have eyes to see it. As the prophets observed the unfolding of events in their own day, they realized they were watching previews of the great and final day of the Lord. Look at Isaiah 13. Verse 1 says, "The oracle concerning Babylon." That puts us back in Isaiah's day.[4] In verse 17 God says that he is sending the Medes against Babylon. He did, in 539 B.C. So we know that God is confronting an ancient civilization here. He is announcing a judgment *within* history. But God has still more in mind. In verse 11 he says, "I will punish *the world* for its evil."[5] And verse 13 adds, "I will make *the heavens* tremble, and *the earth* will be shaken out of its place, at the wrath of the LORD of hosts in the day of his fierce anger." This prophecy is about more than historic Babylon. In fact, "Babylon" is Biblical code-language for the entire social construct of human defiance toward God pushing and shoving its way through the length of human history. It began at the Tower of Babel in Genesis 11, and it will go on until the second coming of Christ. This world is one vast "Babylon" from Isaiah's point of view. Therefore, when ancient Babylon finally fell in 539 B.C., that event was crying out, "The end of the whole world will be just as richly deserved and just as real as this."

Isaiah is teaching us that the day of the Lord includes both the final intervention by God at the end of time and each occasion within history when he steps in to enforce his just will. Viewing history this way, we can see that the two world wars of the twentieth century were dress rehearsals for the Grand Finale, as are the tremendous events of our own day. Every shock of history is *a* day of the Lord foreshadowing *the* day of the Lord, because history whispers ultimacy. Along the way we will never win "a war to end all wars." Evil is out of our control. But evil is within God's control. Isaiah is giving us prophetic eyes to see that, so we can live with confidence in God now, whatever happens.

Throughout these judgments pronounced upon the nations in chapters 13—20, Isaiah is making one basic point. The God and Father of our Lord Jesus Christ is not a local deity, not a tribal god, not an American pet. He is the Lord of the nations, they are all accountable to him, their fates and fortunes are in his hands alone, he will have the final word, and he will vindicate the faith of his people.[6] Individuals are judged in eternity, but nations are judged in time. And time is moving inexorably forward, through the tremors of present judgments to the final shaking of all things on the day of the Lord. That certainty helps us to live above the madness and to care for others in their distress.

Isaiah shows us the government of God over all the nations through five representative examples.

1. Babylon (13:1—14:27)
    A¹ The day of the Lord looms over the whole world (13:1–16)
        B¹ God will overthrow the kingdom of Babylon (13:17–22)
            C But God will honor his own people—for the blessing of the whole world (14:1, 2)
        B² God will overthrow the king of Babylon (14:3–23)
    A² God will soon judge Assyria as a token of his final judgment of the whole world (14:24–27)
2. Philistia (14:28–32)
    A The far destiny of Philistia (14:29–30)
        B The near outcome for Philistia (14:31, 32)
3. Moab (15:1—16:14)
    A¹ Moab's ruin is certain (15:1–4)
        B¹ God grieves over Moab's destruction (15:5–9)
            C¹ Moab seeks asylum, but safety is in Messiah alone (16:1–5)
            C² Moab's pride scorns safety in Messiah (16:6–8)
        B² God laments Moab's sufferings (16:9–12)
    A² Moab's ruin is imminent (16:13, 14)
4. The Damascus/Israel alliance (17:1—18:7)
    A Israel's alliance with human power will fail (17:1–3)
        B In that day, only trust in God will survive (17:4–11)
            C The ragings of *all* human power will be humbled (17:12—18:7)
5. Egypt (19:1—20:6)
    A God will undo the strengths of Egypt: social, economic, intellectual (19:1–15)
        B God will heal Egypt—and even Assyria (19:16–25)
            C God will soon strip Egypt as a token of his final judgments (20:1–6)

Isaiah is looking out over the Fertile Crescent, where most of the events in the Old Testament took place, from one end to the other. What does he see out there in the push and shove of human politics? He sees *God*, powerfully at work to bring salvation to us. Let me draw out the three primary truths Isaiah is declaring in these chapters.

God Is Opposed to the Proud

We should not be surprised by now to find Isaiah confronting the mega-sin of human pride.

> We have heard of the pride of Moab—
>   how proud he is!—
> of his arrogance, his pride, and his insolence;
>   in his idle boasting he is not right. (Isaiah 16:6)

What makes Moab's pride so stupid is obvious. In verses 1–5 the prophet envisions refugees from Moab pleading for asylum in Judah. Moab has come under attack. Moab is being ravaged. The people are running for their lives. They beg Judah to open the border and let them in. But there is a problem. Judah is the throne of the Davidic Messiah (16:5). And Moab refuses help on those terms. They would rather take their chances than submit to the throne of the Messiah.

Isaiah looks at that pride with astonishment: "How proud he is!" You can see how Isaiah heaps words upon words to describe this national ego. Why is the prophet gasping in astonishment? The four words for pride in verse 6—"pride" (twice), "arrogance," "insolence," and "boasting"—are matched by four words in verse 5: "steadfast love," "faithfulness," "justice," and "righteousness." Moab could have enjoyed all that. But no. They would have to humble themselves to enter in, and that's too high a price to pay.

Some of us have watched dearly loved family members on their deathbeds cling to their defiance rather than be saved. Something inside us all would rather *die* than bow. What does God see in the heart of the king of Assyria?

> You said in your heart,
>   "I will ascend to heaven . . .
>   I will make myself like the Most High." (Isaiah 14:13a, 14b)

Some interpreters refer this to Satan. And pride *is* a devilish way of thinking (1 Timothy 3:6). But Isaiah is talking about the mentality of the elite of Assyria. And if it *sounds* like the devil, well, what does that imply? But God will never respect human caricatures of deity.

Some people actually have the nerve to say out loud what most others learn to camouflage. Jean-Jacques Rousseau dared to say:

> What could your miseries have in common with mine? My situation is unique, unheard of since the beginning of time. The person who can love me as I can love is still to be born. No one has ever had more talent for loving. I was born to be the best friend that ever existed. I would leave this life with apprehension if I knew a better man than me. Show me a better man than me, a heart more loving, more tender, more sensitive. Posterity will honour me because it is my due. I rejoice in myself. My consolation lies in my self-esteem. If there were a single enlightened government in Europe, it would have erected statues to me.[7]

If we listen to Rousseau carefully, we hear the same self-esteem and moral superiority and exaggerated sense of entitlement that we venerate in our own society today.[8] Haven't you ever resented being overlooked? Haven't you ever thought, *If only those people knew what a wonderful person I really am*? Haven't you ever thought, *I can't be happy until my world is arranged around me in just the pleasant way I want*? I have. Isaiah's point is that pride is not the bizarre eccentricity of a few megalomaniacs; it's the spirit of the world. *Our pride is what's wrong with the whole world.* Arnold Toynbee studied civilizations across the sweep of history, and he concluded that self-worship is *the* religion of mankind, though that self-exaltation takes different forms.[9]

Refusing to humble ourselves before God is the essence of sin. It spawns all the misguided, destructive attempts at self-salvation that make life so rotten. But God is bringing true salvation to us. In her *Magnificat*, Mary, the mother of Jesus, rejoiced that God intervenes to scatter the proud, bring down the mighty, and exalt those of humble estate (Luke 1:51, 52). Jesus put it bluntly: "What is exalted among men is an abomination in the sight of God" (Luke 16:15). The humility of Jesus was God's ultimate statement of contempt for our culture of pride (Philippians 2:1–11). The Bible says that God opposes the proud (James 4:6; 1 Peter 5:5). So if you want Almighty God actively opposing you as your staunchest enemy, just cling to your demands and hurt feelings and outward polish.

The Bible says, "Do not be haughty, but associate with the lowly" (Romans 12:16). Do we want world peace? This is where it begins. It begins with not being ashamed to be seen with lowly people. And if we refuse to obey God in such a simple and obvious way, well within our reach, then we have nothing to say when whole nations step on one another in their guilty national pride. God says through Isaiah, "I will put an end to the pomp of the arrogant, and lay low the pompous pride of the ruthless" (13:11b). God says, "And Babylon, the glory of kingdoms, the splendor and pomp of the Chaldeans, will be like Sodom and Gomorrah when God overthrew them" (13:19). God says, "Your pomp is brought down to Sheol" (14:11), where it belongs. But Jesus said, "Blessed are the meek, for they shall inherit the earth" (Matthew 5:5). If humility is the spirit of Christ, then our pride is the spirit of anti-Christ.

Our God Reigns

Secondly, Isaiah declares that, high above the passing spectacle of human arrogance called history, God reigns in unchallenged sovereignty.

> The Lord of hosts has sworn:
> "As I have planned,
>   so shall it be,
> and as I have purposed,
>   so shall it stand,
> that I will break the Assyrian in my land,
>   and on my mountains trample him underfoot;
> and his yoke shall depart from them,
>   and his burden from their shoulder."
> This is the purpose that is purposed
>   concerning the whole earth,
> and this is the hand that is stretched out
>   over all the nations.
> For the Lord of hosts has purposed,
>   and who will annul it?
> His hand is stretched out,
>   and who will turn it back? (Isaiah 14:24–27)

Dear friends, we are in God's hands. He is *here*, directly involved in our world today. He has a purpose for this world. And his purpose is not an ideal that he hopes might pan out. As you can see in the logic of these verses, the purpose of God is the very *hand* of God at work, and *who can turn it back?* You need to believe that. You have God's word on it: "The Lord of hosts has sworn." He can't be telling the truth *sort of.* Either God is telling us the truth here, or he's lying. Is God sincere when he tells us that his good purpose will prevail in our world? If you believe he's sincere, will you swallow his word whole and trust him, come what may? His final purpose is not judgment but graciously inclusive salvation: "Blessed be Egypt my people, and Assyria the work of my hands, and Israel my inheritance" (19:25). This takes us to Isaiah's third major emphasis in these chapters.

Look to Him

If it's true that the ultimate decisions are not made in Washington or London or Baghdad but in Heaven, then one thing follows. There is no security for us in this world but only in God himself. Therefore, let's not put our trust in man but in God alone.

> In that day man will look to his Maker, and his eyes will look on the Holy One of Israel. He will not look to the altars, the work of his hands, and he will not look on what his own fingers have made, either the Asherim or the altars of incense. (Isaiah 17:7, 8)

God is calling us to look away from the little world we have made to the One who made us. God is calling us to stop putting our hope in what we can do and start putting our hope in the divine Doer. Regard him with desire and glad expectation, and you will discover that he is enough. Reject everything incompatible with him—the idolatrous altars of your heart. If you will suffer the loss of all things to gain Christ, he will make you too happy to care. *That* is faith, and God is calling you to *live* by that faith. Stop trusting in your own altars of incense. Let Christ alone be your sweet incense before a holy God. Reject yourself. Embrace Christ as your offering acceptable to God, and he will accept you without your own works-righteousness. No matter what you lose in order to gain Christ, don't worry about it. He's worth everything.

The Bible speaks of a faith that overcomes the world (1 John 5:4). But too many American Christians have a faith that is more American than Christian. Their faith is not overcoming the world; the world is overcoming their faith. But God is calling us to an overcoming faith in him, because he rules over the nations. That should be enough to stabilize us. What more could we ask for than our God involved in our world?

The Westminster Shorter Catechism of 1648 teaches the strong theology of the Isaianic vision. B. B. Warfield, the Princeton theologian, asked, "What is the indelible mark of the Shorter Catechism?" He answered by recounting this story:

> We have the following bit of personal experience from a general officer of the United States army. He was in a great western city at a time of intense excitement and violent rioting. [Was this the San Francisco earthquake of 1906? Warfield doesn't say.] The streets were overrun daily by a dangerous crowd. One day he observed approaching him a man of singularly combined calmness and firmness of mien, whose very demeanor inspired confidence. So impressed was he with his bearing amid the surrounding uproar that when he had passed he turned to look back at him, only to

find that the stranger had done the same. On observing his turning, the stranger at once came back to him and, touching his chest with his forefinger, demanded without preface: "What is the chief end of man?" On receiving the countersign, "Man's chief end is to glorify God and to enjoy him forever"—"Ah!" said he, "I knew you were a Shorter Catechism boy by your looks!" "Why, that was just what I was thinking of you," was the rejoinder.[10]

People made confident by the truth of God's sovereignty stand out amid the surrounding uproar. And their influence spreads faith to others. As a pastor, my dad received a letter from an Army medic during the war in Vietnam:

> As you have read in the papers, we've had a real busy time with Viet Cong activities lately. The night we were overrun by some 300 Viet Cong was a night I will never forget. We had some forty wounded and twenty killed. In this moment of darkness there was brightness for me and for one of the guys I was treating, for he accepted the Lord in the middle of the battle. Though he left me a few minutes later, I'll never forget the shine that he had on his face. Being wounded about the chest and the legs and arms, the pain had no bearing, for the Lord had come to him and brought him more comfort than any medical man could.[11]

Will you put your trust in God's sovereignty and justice for you right now in the midst of the battle? Let him stabilize you with comforts this world can never give and can never take away. You will stand out.

15

The Supremacy of God
over the Nations II

ISAIAH 21:1—23:18

THE SCARLET LETTER BY NATHANIEL HAWTHORNE is a story of the controlling power of shame. Hawthorne called it a "drama of guilt and sorrow."[1] In Puritan Boston the minister, Mr. Dimmesdale, commits adultery with Hester Prynne. She bears a child, and the community ostracizes her by sentencing her to wear a scarlet A, for "Adulteress," the rest of her life. Her sin is made obvious to all. But Mr. Dimmesdale conceals his sin. He keeps up an appearance of rectitude, but within he is tortured with guilt. After seven years he finally makes a dramatic public confession, tearing open his shirt to reveal his own scarlet A etched into his very flesh, infinitely more painful than Hester's embroidered accusation.

What saddens me when I read *The Scarlet Letter* is that no one in this story understands redemption. No one understands that public disgrace has no benefit and that private hypocrisy only binds us to our sins. No one in this story has hope, because no one sees how God is able to create beauty out of the wreckage we create. The place where sin enters in is where God himself enters in with redeeming grace. When I read this book I wish I could step inside it and say to Mr. Dimmesdale and Hester and everyone there, "It doesn't have to be like this." But I can say to you, "It doesn't have to be like this. You don't have to be controlled by shame and hypocrisy. Your past is unchangeable in fact but beautiful in potential, because there is a Redeemer."

Isaiah is teaching us to see with prophetic eyes. He wants to give us a sense of God as we live in this world. In chapters 13—20 he made five declarations that God rules decisively over the nations. Now in chapters 21—23 he makes five more declarations to the same effect, but with an interesting difference. Now he speaks more allusively, more vaguely, more mysteriously, because he's giving less attention to his immediate surroundings and peering out further into a more remote future. What does he see out ahead? He sees a redeeming God at work in a deeply troubled world. Five civilizations appear before Isaiah, as the structure of the text makes clear.

1. The desert of the sea: Babylon (21:1–10)
    A¹ The oracle received: a stern vision (21:1, 2)
        B¹ The prophet's horror (21:3, 4)
        B² The Babylonians' hedonism (21:5)
            C Babylon's end already visible (21:6–9)
    A² The warning implied: "Babylon is not your hope!" (21:10)
2. Silence: Edom (21:11, 12)
    A Edom: "How much longer?" (21:11)
        B Isaiah: "Too early to tell; come back later." (21:12)
3. At eventide: Arabia (21:13–17)
    A Refugees fleeing into the Arabian desert (21:13–15)
        B Arabia's own imminent fall, by God's decree (21:16, 17)
4. The valley of vision: Jerusalem (22:1–25)
    A¹ The prophet's discerning sorrow (22:1–8a)
        B The root sin: trust in self rather than trust in God (22:8b–11)
    A² The people's undiscerning silliness (22:12–14)
            C¹ No human being self-sufficient (22:15–19)
            C² No human being sufficient for others (22:20–25)
5. Tyre: the prostitute—but someday consecrated to God (23:1–18)
    A The fall of Tyre lamented by the world (23:1–7)
        B The purpose of God commanded against Tyre (23:8–14)
            C Redemption demonstrated in the holiness of Tyre (23:15–18)

Let's take this in two steps. First, what does Isaiah see? Secondly, what is its relevance to us? He wants us to see God, our cultural surroundings, and ourselves with realism. Then he wants to give us hope in the redeeming grace of God.

What Isaiah Sees

Isaiah looks into his prophetic crystal ball, as it were, and sees God out in the future ruling decisively over five cultures. We'll look briefly at each oracle. First, "The oracle concerning the wilderness of the sea" (21:1). Isaiah is talking about Babylon (v. 9). But he doesn't call it Babylon. He calls it "the wilderness of the sea," or "the desert of the sea" (cf. NJPS). That's strange.

Babylon was well inland, not on a seacoast. Why does he give Babylon this improbable title? Remember Isaiah's life mission—to persuade people to stop trusting in their own salvations and start trusting in God's salvation. When he calls Babylon "the desert of the sea," he's being sarcastic. A desert can't sustain human life. And the sea, as Coleridge put it, is "water, water everywhere, but not a drop to drink." The sea can't sustain human life either. "The desert of the sea" is the worst possible scenario—both dry and wet together, but neither condition conducive to human life. In other words, Babylon has *nothing* to offer us. Do not trust Babylon. Do not admire Babylon. Do not invest your hopes there. God has another kingdom for us, another glory, another salvation.

Secondly, "the oracle concerning Dumah" (21:11). Isaiah is talking about the nation Edom. But he calls it "Dumah," which means "silence." He is playing on words: *ᵉdôm* becomes *dûmâh*. Why? He is saying that God has no word of hope, nothing but silence, for Edom. In verse 11 a plaintive Edomite voice is asking, "Watchman, what time of the night?" In other words, "Mr. Watchman, Mr. Prophet, what time of the night is it? How much more darkness and gloom do we still have to endure? How long until the dawn of a new era?" The prophet responds in verse 12, but his answer is vague. And that's the point. God is not giving Edom a clear word. Everything hangs in suspense, but God puts them off: "Come back again."

There is another nation, the people of God, and they have a bright future in his many explicit promises. He is not silent to us. Paul writes in the New Testament that "whatever was written in former days was written for our instruction, that through endurance and through the encouragement of the Scriptures we might have hope" (Romans 15:4).

A friend of mine was enduring a time of deep anguish. He wrote out encouragements from Scripture on slips of paper and placed them all over his house—in the fridge, in the closets, and so forth—so that wherever he went, he was greeted with some promise from God. It got him through. The world has wishful thinking; the believer has a sure word from God. And here is Edom, typifying the whole world, hovering in fearful uncertainty. So why run off to Edom for assurance and comfort and answers? Don't pin your hopes there. God has real answers for you in the gospel.

Thirdly, in 21:13 we find "the oracle concerning Arabia." Isaiah is playing on words again. The Hebrew consonants in the word translated "Arabia" are the same as the Hebrew word for "evening." The prophet is using *double entendre* to portray Arabia slipping into the night.[2] The sun is setting on that nation. It's the twilight of their culture. The net impression Isaiah creates throughout this passage is the civilizations of man in a darkening world. There is no salvation for us in any society of human devising. But—and here is Isaiah's subtext—the sun will never set on the kingdom of God. The

Bible says, "But our citizenship is in heaven, and from it we await a Savior, the Lord Jesus Christ, who will transform our lowly body to be like his glorious body, by the power that enables him even to subject all things to himself. Therefore, my brothers, whom I love and long for, my joy and my crown, *stand firm thus in the Lord*, my beloved" (Philippians 3:20—4:1).

Fourthly, in 22:1 we encounter "the oracle concerning the valley of vision." Don't miss the irony here. Isaiah is referring to Jerusalem (vv. 9, 10). And what was so special about Jerusalem? It was the place where divine revelation shone forth. It was the place where people did have answers— and from God too. But are the people of God clear-sighted in their spiritual vision? Is God so real to them that they see everything in a new way? Verse 11 says, "You did not look to him who did it, or see him who planned it long ago." Their eyes are on all the wrong things. God has spoken, but they don't get it.

When Isaiah calls Jerusalem "the valley of vision," he is hinting that Mount Zion has become a valley, and vision has become blindness. The "valley of vision"? You can't see anything from there. Without a sense of God in their hearts, even the people of God are reduced to a visceral drivenness: "Let us eat and drink, for tomorrow we die" (v. 13). That is the extent of their vision. They're not living for the End; they're living for the weekend. But Jesus said, "You are the light of the world. . . . Let your light shine before others, so that they may see your good works and give glory to your Father who is in heaven" (Matthew 5:14, 16).

Finally, Isaiah records "the oracle concerning Tyre" (23:1). His last prophecy in chapters 21—23 matches his first in chapters 13—20. Isaiah started out with Babylon (13:1); now he concludes with Tyre (23:1). Babylon and Tyre are like bookends around Isaiah's vision of the nations. Why? The New Testament explains. The Revelation of John sees the whole world as one vast Babylon (Revelation 14:8; 16:19; 17:1—19:2). "Fallen, fallen is Babylon the great!" (Revelation 18:2). That's the way John perceives the end of the world culture we live in. It's the fall of *Babylon*. So on the one hand he calls the world Babylon. But on the other hand John also describes our world as an Isaianic Tyre—a prostitute out hustling the nations: "Come, I will show you the judgment of the great prostitute who is seated on many waters, with whom the kings of the earth have committed sexual immorality, and with the wine of whose sexual immorality the dwellers on earth have become drunk" (Revelation 17:1, 2; cf. Isaiah 23:3, 15–17). The prophetic eye merges Babylon and Tyre together into one understanding of our world.

Babylon and Tyre together typify all human societies. Babylon symbolizes ruthless political power, and Tyre symbolizes dishonest commercial success. Babylon was a land power, Tyre a sea power. Babylon used force;

Tyre used seduction. The strategies differ from one culture to the next, but what matters in the one kingdom of man is money and power and ego and visceral pleasure—all the things that belong to time rather than eternity. This is our brilliant, heroic, costly, empty world.

The prophets understood the power of the Babylon-Tyre of this world. They saw that this world is not only the opponent of faith, it's also the seductress of faith. The world not only punishes all who follow Christ; it also panders, tempting believers away from Christ. The devil doesn't much care either way. He'll use harsh intimidation, and he'll use soft seduction—whatever works, as long as we lose sight of Christ, so that our faith no longer overcomes. That is the spiritual battle being fought deep in our hearts every day.

It's into this world and our hearts that the Redeemer comes. He doesn't bully us. He doesn't degrade us. He wants to become so real to us that we gladly turn away from the false security and bogus significance and fading pleasures. He comes to give us clarity and courage as we live in this world, so that our faith joyfully overcomes. But these two kingdoms are in absolute conflict—the kingdom of this world and the kingdom of Jesus Christ. God will humble Tyre (Isaiah 23:9). But he would prefer to re-create our lives out of the secret corruptions we long to keep concealed.

That's the surprising end of chapter 23.[3] Who would have expected it? Speaking of Tyre as a prostitute, Isaiah writes:

> Her merchandise and her wages will be holy to the LORD. It will not be stored or hoarded, but her merchandise will supply abundant food and fine clothing for those who dwell before the LORD. (Isaiah 23:18)

Wait a minute. The law of Moses was clear. Money associated with prostitution could not be given to the Lord (Deuteronomy 23:18). It was dirty money. But God is able to bring redemption into our corruption. Isaiah looks at our "everything has a price" culture, our "anything for money" culture, and he sees it redeemed, made holy to the Lord, devoted to God, for the benefit of all who dwell before him. Therefore (he is implying), why envy Tyre? The future lies with the kingdom of God's redeeming grace. Jesus meant it when he said, "Seek first the kingdom of God and his righteousness, and all these things will be added to you" (Matthew 6:33).

How Isaiah's Vision Is Relevant to Us

Isaiah's vision answers a question that Christians wrestle with: How should believers relate to the world? How should we interact with our cultural surroundings? J. Gresham Machen, the Presbyterian leader from the early twentieth-century, said there are basically three answers to this question.[4]

First, Christianity can be subordinated to culture. In other words, the world should tell Christians what enlightened people can believe today, and the church should adjust to those views. But subjecting Christianity to the world denies the lordship of Christ and destroys Christianity. So that won't work. The second proposal is for Christians to negate the world, or at least treat it as a necessary evil, while they live in their own religious ghetto. But that too denies the lordship of Christ. Withdrawal may feel safe, but it's escapism (1 Corinthians 5:9, 10). The third proposal is consecration. Instead of subordinating Christianity to culture, and instead of running from culture, God wants us to consecrate all things to his glory. God doesn't bow to the world. Neither does he run from the world. He redeems the world, because his glory shines the most brilliantly in his grace.

In the Revelation of John, the apostle sees the holy city, the new Jerusalem, coming down out of heaven from God, prepared as a bride adorned for her husband (Revelation 21:2, 10). The Prostitute will go out of business, and the Bride will come to her wedding day. Evil will be defeated, and purity and joy will go into warp speed forever. This will be God's doing, not ours. It will come down to us. And as God dwells with us in the New Jerusalem, the Bible says that

> . . . the kings of the earth will bring their glory into it, and its gates will never be shut by day—and there will be no night there. They will bring into it the glory and the honor of the nations. But nothing unclean will ever enter it, nor anyone who does what is detestable or false, but only those who are written in the Lamb's book of life. (Revelation 21:24–27)

The holy city is luminous with divine glory, standing with its gates continually open; and the kings of the earth are bringing in their glory, their national and cultural treasures—the fruit of human thought and imagination and effort and skill no longer distorted by evil, the literary and artistic and musical treasures of the human race no longer in tribute to the pride of man but now joyfully consecrated to God. And nothing unclean will enter in. This is redemption.

We've all bought into the prostitution of Tyre. Everyone has something to be ashamed of. But God is a Redeemer. He wants us to become his pure bride in the New Jerusalem. The only thing is, we cannot retain our shame and hypocrisy. No unclean thing enters there. The shame that has defined us must be redeemed. And our stories of despair can be lifted into his story of redemption. Every last petty souvenir of Tyre can be redeemed into something beautiful for God.

The gospel gives us a reason to draw the curtain back, show God everything, and confess every detail. Let's trust him that much and open our hearts to his redemptive love. This is how he saves sinners. And how could it be otherwise? God redeems the dirty, the unwashed, the unworthy, and no one else.

In *Les Miserables*, Javert, the driven legalist, pursues Valjean, the convicted thief whose life is a tale of redemption. At one point Valjean spares Javert when he has the chance to kill him. Later Javert sings:

> Who is this man? What sort of devil is he to have me caught in a trap and choose to let me go free? It was his hour at last to put a seal on my fate, wipe out the past, and wash me clean off the slate! All it would take was a flick of his knife. Vengeance was his, and he gave me back my life! I'll spit his pity right back in his face. There is nothing on earth that we share. It is either Valjean or Javert!

Do you resent God for loving you? Must your ego have the last word? Or will you bow to his redemptive power and authority with no preconditions? Here's what upright but troubled people need to do. Stop treating Christ as your customer, and start treating him as your lover. Stop trying to work a deal, and let him love you freely. The shame and hypocrisy that control you lose their power as you open your heart to a redemption from beyond yourself. Will you?

16

The Supremacy of God over the Nations III

ISAIAH 24:1—27:13

You are surprised that the world is losing its grip, that the world is grown old? Think of a man. He is born, he grows up, he becomes old. Old age has many complaints: coughing, shaking, failing eyesight, anxious, terribly tired. A man grows old; he is full of complaints. The world is old; it is full of pressing tribulations. . . . Do not hold on to the old man, the world. Do not refuse to regain your youth in Christ, who says to you: "The world is passing away, the world is losing its grip, the world is short of breath. Do not fear. 'Your youth shall be renewed as an eagle.'"[1]

AUGUSTINE SAID THAT IN A SERMON after Rome was sacked by the Goths in A.D. 410. It was like Muslim fundamentalists bringing down the World Trade Center in New York. It was the end of an era—the end of security, the beginning of uncertainty. Augustine wrestled with the implications of his crumbling world, and out of his struggle came a book entitled *The City of God*.

He proposed that mankind consists basically of two groups of people—two cities, as it were. There is the city of man. The nations and cultures and businesses and ideas and trends and politics and moralities of this present age, however much they disagree on the surface, are in fact unified at the profoundest level. They are all against God. What is our world really all about? It's a massive social construct, often beautiful and even heroic, rendering plausible life without God at the center. The human race is deeply united in building its own world on its own terms. That construction of reality is passing away. But there is another city, and it can never fall. It wasn't built by human hands; it can't be destroyed by human hands. It's the city of God. And God is inviting us to pick up and move, leave our old lives behind, and build new lives in his city.[2]

We all need a home, a place of our own, a refuge, a community, a loyalty. We don't like being wanderers. We long to be owners. The city of God is the only address that will last forever. Our longings are that large, and God's offer is nothing less.

But how can we tell the difference between these two identities within human society now? We can't see it at the level of mere externals or race or education. These are all superficial. To find the real difference, Augustine probed into the human heart.

> Two cities have been formed by two loves: the earthly by the love of self, even to the contempt of God; the heavenly by the love of God, even to the contempt of self. The former, in a word, glories in itself, the latter in the Lord. For the one seeks glory from men; but the greater glory of the other is God, the witness of conscience. The one lifts up its head in its own glory; the other says to its God, "You are my glory, and the lifter up of my head."[3]

Augustine thought his way back to the beginning and traced out the story of these two cities stemming originally from Cain and Abel—two humanities, traceable through history in parallel tracks, defined by two loves, the city of man and the city of God.

Augustine's metaphor of the city is a good one, because the Bible says that Cain built the first city (Genesis 4:17). God planted a garden, but Cain built a city—Cain, doomed to be a fugitive and a wanderer, always insecure, always on the outside of things. He satisfied his need for belonging and significance by remaking the world his own way, by taking control on his own terms, by constructing an alternative reality to keep the divine curse from having its full impact.[4] A city is not just a collection of buildings. It is a mechanism for living independently of God. It is a device for human self-salvation. It is a denial of human mortality. The city is man establishing his own enduring greatness. But even civilizations are mortal.

If you want to see the grace of God, look where this proud human invention ends up. At the end of the Bible, God's final victory is not just a restored Eden, not just a return to paradise. His final victory is a holy *city*, the New Jerusalem (Revelation 21:1—22:5). God takes the very symbol of our rejection of him and transforms it into *Heaven*. That is what a Redeemer does.

So we aren't surprised when Isaiah concludes his vision of the supremacy of God over the nations with two cities. That's the key to chapters 24—27, where Isaiah looks all the way forward to the end of all things. Particular nations fade completely into the background, and the whole earth emerges as one city plunged into final ruin.

The wasted city is broken down. (24:10)

Desolation is left in the city. (24:12)

You have made the city a heap,
    the fortified city a ruin. (25:2)

For he has humbled
    the inhabitants of the height,
    the lofty city. (26:5)

For the fortified city is solitary,
    a habitation deserted and forsaken, like the wilderness. (27:10)

And so the world will end—the city of man, constructed at such human cost, so impressive, so talented, so evil (Revelation 18:9–13). But the redeemed are able to say, "We have a strong city; he sets up salvation as walls and bulwarks" (Isaiah 26:1). Two cities, two destinies. And two songs can be heard rising from these cities. The city of man is a place of drunken revelry falling silent under the judgment of God (24:7–11), while the city of God will sing on forever about One who is strong for the weak and compassionate toward the needy (26:1–21). But the dominant figure throughout the landscape of these chapters is God himself, judging and saving. *God* is the reason why the city of man cannot endure and why the city of God cannot fall, and God will have the final word in both overwhelming woe and overwhelming joy. That is the vision of Isaiah 24—27.

The structure of this section follows the same fivefold pattern we saw in chapters 13—20 and again in 21—23.

1. "The wasted city" will be broken, the people of God joyful (24:1–20)
    A^1 World desolation: decreed, justified (24:1–6)
        B^1 Joy reduced to frustration in "the wasted city" (24:7–13)
        B^2 Joy increased worldwide among God's people (24:14–16a)
    A^2 World desolation: mourned, described (24:16b–20)
2. Then the Lord alone will be glorified (24:21–23)
    A^1 The divine visitation upon his rivals (24:21)
        B The triumph of final justice (24:22)
    A^2 The divine glory before his friends (24:23)
3. Then the Lord will entertain his people at the eternal banquet of salvation (25:1–12)
    A^1 Individual delight in God's final judgment and salvation (25:1–5)
        B The feast provided, sorrow and death removed (25:6–8)
    A^2 Shared delight in God's final salvation and judgment (25:9–12)
4. Then the Lord will stand forth as the only reason for our deliverance (26:1–21)
    A^1 The believer will be secured within a mighty salvation (26:1–4)

    B¹ The lofty city of man humbled to the dust (26:5, 6)
        C¹ The Godward path of yearning (26:7–9)
            D The human heart impervious to the gospel (26:10, 11)
        C² The God-supported peace of weakness (26:12–15)
    B² The failed people of God risen from the dust (26:16–19)
  A² Believers will be secured from a mighty wrath (26:20, 21)
5. Then the Lord will bring to consummation his purpose for his people (27:1–13)
  A¹ The great sword: demonic forces defeated (27:1)
    B¹ The vineyard people of God lavishly fruitful (27:2–6)
        C¹ Atonement for the disciplined people of God (27:7–9)
        C² Wrath for the deserted city of man (27:10, 11)
    B² The harvest people of God carefully gathered in (27:12)
  A² The great trumpet: lost people worshiping (27:13)

Isaiah is concluding another major section in his book. Chapters 1—12 reveal God's saving purpose for Judah and Israel. Chapters 13—27 reveal his saving purpose for the whole world.

How the World Will End

Isaiah paints the big picture in 24:1–20. Then he sketches in the details throughout the rest of the passage. Seven times in chapters 24—27 Isaiah uses the phrase "on that day" or "in that day" to point back to 24:1–20.[5] What then is Isaiah saying in 24:1–20? The centerpiece is verse 10:

The wasted city is broken down;
    every house is shut up so that none can enter.

Isaiah deploys an unusual expression here. Our English versions translate it variously: "the city of confusion" (KJV), "the city of chaos" (RSV), "the city of emptiness" (JB). Isaiah reaches back to Genesis 1:2—"the earth was without form and void"—and takes the Hebrew word translated "without form" and inserts it here: "The city without form is broken down." His point is that just as the creation in Genesis 1:2 was like a lump of clay without the impress of the Potter's hands, without shape and meaning, so the city of man will finally be seen for what it is—a social construct without transcendent meaning, without enduring purpose, like a lump of clay spinning on the wheel but never really coming to anything.

The city of man is where we live when we refuse the divine order for our lives and jury-rig our own values and definitions and boundaries. But the prophet has eyes to see what so many deny—the regressive power of sin, turning human life back into formlessness. He has eyes to foresee a day when the ever-changing shapes and trends of the city of man, however attractively presented by human fashion, however brilliantly rationalized by human scholarship—all denial of God will finally be seen to amount to nothing more than whimsy, just one thing after another going nowhere.

If we reject God (24:5), if we think that success and happiness can come on our terms, the inherent instability of that overreaching will eventually catch up with us. God is patient. He gives us time to rethink our lives and repent (2 Peter 3:9). But we don't have forever. The Bible speaks of "the fleeting pleasures of sin" (Hebrews 11:25) as opposed to "pleasures forevermore" at God's right hand (Psalm 16:11). Which pleasures are you living for, and which pleasures are you letting go of? That tells you which city you're living in. The rollicking good times in the city of man will someday be replaced by an ominous silence the world over (Isaiah 24:7–9). Instead of the streets full of partying people going from house to house for more drinks, like the Mardi Gras, the second line of verse 10 says that every house will be shut up. People will be terrified as society breaks down, and they will shut each other out. Why? The mythology of human pride always leads to the reality of human desolation.

Back in the 1960s we who are now broken-down, middle-aged has-beens used to speak of our "plastic culture." We used to whine about how phony and unsatisfying and unreal our society was, *and we were right.*[6] In fact, nothing has changed. The only difference now is that somewhere along the way we gave in and joined that plastic culture. We need to be careful what we buy into, what we give even our tacit allegiance to. Isaiah is saying that the city of God will have no room for defiant artificiality. But right now God wants to redeem us out of our precariously phony lives and lead us into the solid joys and lasting treasures of his kingdom. Here's the beautiful thing. His kingdom is *not* "shut up so that none can enter" (v. 10). The gates of the city of God stand wide-open because of the finished work of Christ on the cross. And any God-evading, plastic hypocrite can walk right in, get real with God, and find an eternal welcome in him.

So in 24:1–20 Isaiah projects onto our mental screens his vision of a world in ultimate crisis. On that day we will not worry about the Dow dipping below 10,000. "Behold, the LORD will empty the earth and make it desolate, and he will twist its surface and scatter its inhabitants" (24:1). But that's not the only thing Isaiah foresees. He sketches in details in the other four sections of the passage (24:21—27:13). I will draw out one salient point from each.

The Lord Alone Glorified in That Day

> Then the moon will be confounded,
>   and the sun ashamed,
> for the LORD of hosts reigns

on Mount Zion and in Jerusalem,
and his glory will be before his elders. (Isaiah 24:23)

Right now it's possible to be a skeptic and hold your head high. People can see the absurdities of life, and they wonder, *Where is God?* There are solid answers to that question. Christianity is not a leap of faith; it's the logic of faith. But we all have doubts. And when our faith lacks assurance, the struggles of life knock us off-balance and keep us from living boldly for God. But Isaiah is saying that a day is coming when God will reveal his glory with such brilliance that the sun and moon will hang their heads in shame. Literally, the last line of this verse says, ". . . and before his elders, glory!" His glory will appear before us, as he did before the elders of Israel long ago (Exodus 24:9–11), but in the undimmed brightness of his face forever (Revelation 4:4, 9–11).

How could it be otherwise? After all, what is God driving at in all of history? The open display of his glory before wholehearted worshipers. That is salvation. That is Heaven. Think about it. What will Heaven and Hell have in common? What they'll have in common is that everyone in Heaven and everyone in Hell will be honoring God. The people in Heaven will be a tribute to his grace, and the people in Hell will bear witness to his justice. But everyone will bring honor to God. What then is the difference between Heaven and Hell? The difference is that people in Heaven will be delighting in God's glory, and people in Hell will be raging in shrieking hatred at God's glory. The way we will experience God forever will come out of our own hearts. This is why the most urgent business before us every day is not amassing pleasures in this world but satisfying our hearts with pleasures in the glory of God. That is what this life is for.

The Lord Our Gracious Host in That Day

On this mountain the LORD of hosts will make for all peoples
    a feast of rich food, a feast of well-aged wine,
    of rich food full of marrow, of aged wine well refined. (Isaiah 25:6)

God offers everyone a place at his eternal banquet table, and all peoples will be represented. He serves nothing but the best. There is nothing here to disappoint, nothing the human heart doesn't relish. But the feast will be held "on this mountain," referring to Mount Zion (24:23). It does not belong to the city of man. God's people had to wait all their lives to sit at this table, but it was worth the wait. This is the banquet of true salvation. All the guests are happy, and nothing can ever make them sad again.

How can we find our way there? The gospel says that we can come even now through Jesus Christ (Hebrews 12:22–24). This party is open to one and all, but there is only one location. If you will enter in through God's appointed way, he will reserve a place for *you*, whoever you are.

The banquet God is preparing is so rich, Isaiah is forced to heap terms upon terms to describe it. So do not think of life in the city of God as dreary. Do not think you have to sacrifice anything to gain Christ. We do say good-bye to the world's drunken binge (24:7–9). But as the hymn-writer put it, "The hill of Zion yields a thousand sacred sweets."[7] The gospel leaves no room for self-pity; the future promised is too generous for that. Even Jesus is looking forward to this banquet. The night he instituted his supper, he said, "I will not drink again of this fruit of the vine until that day when I drink it new with you in my Father's kingdom" (Matthew 26:29). That is when he will lift the gloom that now hangs over all human experience, he will swallow up death forever, he will wipe away every tear from our eyes, and we will be so glad finally to be saved by him (Isaiah 25:7–9).

The Lord Our Merciful Savior in That Day

> O LORD, you will ordain peace for us;
>   you have done for us all our works. (Isaiah 26:12)

The center of this section is 26:10, 11, where Isaiah asserts the impenetrable blindness of the human heart. That is why, even at our best, we owe God everything: "You have done for us all our works" (cf. Ephesians 2:1–10). The Christian life is not what we give to God but what God gives to us. And what he gives is peace, wholeness, humanness at its authentic best forever. Moreover, it's not because we happened to catch God in a good mood. He ordained peace for us. Full, beautiful salvation is the settled will of God for weak and stupid people who don't mind being saved.

Is there anything in your life that you are really proud of precisely because it has nothing to do with you? The Bible says, "Let the one who boasts, boast in the Lord" (1 Corinthians 1:31). There is a kind of pride that actually humbles us and satisfies us because it's not about us. The pride of the city of man inflates the ego, yet leaves the self empty. But the boast of the city of God is God himself, because he is enough to enrich us forever (Romans 5:2, 3, 11, NRSV). Everything good that we are and have is his doing, not ours. Our place in the city of God is his gift of grace. He even preserves us in the mentality of faith: "You keep him in perfect peace whose mind is stayed on you" (Isaiah 26:3). God stimulates in our hearts a longing for him: "My soul yearns for you in the night; my spirit within me earnestly seeks you" (v. 9). Faith and longing prove that *God* is at work in our hearts. That yearning he is awakening in you is the most important thing about you. It's the key to your future. Fan that flame, and never let it die.

The Lord Our Only Worship in That Day

> In that day the LORD with his hard and great and strong sword will punish
> Leviathan the fleeing serpent, Leviathan the twisting serpent, and he will
> slay the dragon that is in the sea. (Isaiah 27:1)

"Leviathan" symbolizes the monster of moral chaos that has raged in
our world since the fall of Adam. The evil established in the city of man is
worse than human. It is demonic. Isaiah borrows a mythological image from
the ancient world to describe it.[8] He sees evil as a coiling, wriggling, serpen-
tine monster not because he's a primitive thinker but because nothing less
can tell us the truth about evil. Truth requires imagination, and sometimes
we surrender that prophetic clarity.

> Vice is a monster of so frightful mien,
> As, to be hated, needs but to be seen;
> Yet seen too oft, familiar with her face,
> We first endure, then pity, then embrace.[9]

Our age, Flannery O'Connor said, "has domesticated despair and
learned to live with it happily."[10] But Isaiah wants us to grasp the magnitude
of God's victory over the evil we blithely trivialize.

The victory God has won over everything set against his glory and our
happiness is the greatest truth in the universe. God has not only restrained evil,
he has not only made it serve his good purposes, he will also annihilate evil
at the end of time. His threefold "hard and great and strong sword" will hack
to pieces the threefold "Leviathan the fleeing serpent, Leviathan the twisting
serpent . . . the dragon that is in the sea." No compromise. No mercy. It will be
good versus evil, simple as that, and evil will be destroyed fully and forever.

How does this battle play out? At his cross, Christ triumphed over
demonic powers (Colossians 2:15). That's when the devil lost his power to
manipulate us with fear (Hebrews 2:14, 15). He has no more claim on us,
no advantage over us. We are no longer the devil's victims. "Lo, *his* doom is
sure," as Martin Luther put it. And at Christ's second coming he will oblit-
erate all his enemies with finality.[11] We will even have a role in the victory
(Romans 16:20). For every woe Satan dealt us in this life, we will kick him
into the dust. But all the glory will go to Christ crucified, and we will be
forever safe in his strong presence.

> And in that day a great trumpet will be blown, and those who were lost
> in the land of Assyria and those who were driven out to the land of Egypt
> will come and worship the LORD on the holy mountain at Jerusalem.
> (Isaiah 27:13)

In the book of Leviticus the Year of Jubilee was launched with the blowing of the trumpet (25:8–55). Every fifty years the Jubilee was a yearlong celebration of rest and release and homecoming. The Jubilee was an Old Testament way of saying, "For freedom Christ has set us free" (Galatians 5:1). And we need periodic renewal and refocus and release because we clutter and complicate our lives. But the trumpet of the gospel calls us back to God, and the freedom of worship will be our focus in our eternal home. Out of the oppressive city of man—in Isaiah's categories, Assyria and Egypt—God's lost ones will come home to worship him forever.

Give the love of your heart to God, even to the contempt of self. Believe that he is worth that much. Earthly-mindedness, to use an old Puritan word, will kill your heart for God, or your heart for God will kill your earthly-mindedness.[12] But you cannot have both. Stop trying to.

How can we stop? One thing that helps is to look at the cross of Jesus. If you want to know what the city of man is really committed to, look at the cross. How can you and I kiss up to a system that made its truest statement about God by crucifying him? If you always get along with a world dead set against the glory of God, what does that say about you? Paul was glad to suffer the loss of all things to gain Christ. He considered his old life so much garbage, compared with the surpassing worth of knowing Christ (Philippians 3:7, 8). That is the heartbeat of the city of God. "Whom have I in heaven but you? And there is nothing on earth that I desire besides you" (Psalm 73:25). That passion is clear evidence of citizenship in the city of God. Abraham felt that way. He felt such a sense of possession in the promised kingdom of God that his life became a journey. He was looking forward to a city whose designer and builder is God (Hebrews 11:10). He desired a better country, a heavenly one (Hebrews 11:16). That longing for something better in God—that is what it means to be a Christian. Therefore, stop living like a resident, and learn what it means to live like a pilgrim.

17

Our One Security: God's Sure Foundation

ISAIAH 28:1–29

One word of truth outweighs the whole world.[1]

IF GOD SAVES SINNERS, WHAT IS OUR PART? It could be reduced to two simple words: Trust God. That's what he wants from us. Why does he want trust? Because he's trustworthy. We keep running off to other salvations. But God wants to show us what a great Savior *he* is.

Trusting God is not easy. If we actually live by faith in God, it means we follow him out of our ways into his adventures (cf. Revelation 14:4). That isn't easy for us. It may even be unimaginable. What is there in our culture that encourages us to live on the belief that God's salvation is what we're really longing for? And deep inside ourselves, something whispers that God is a bad risk, that he won't be there for us when we need him, and therefore the past is better than the future. We think small, dark thoughts of God. That's why, after setting our hand to the plow, we keep looking back rather than pressing on. We are too much controlled by fear. But a confident trust is how we experience the all-sufficiency of God.

Here is the question lying at the center of our lives: Do we feel safe, do we feel rich, with God alone? Every one of us struggles to answer that question, and each one of us is making a statement about it by the way we live. And here is the statement God wants us to make: "Yes, Lord, walking in the way of your laws, we wait for you; your name and renown are the desire of our hearts" (Isaiah 26:8, NIV). That is faith. It's a great way to live.

At chapter 28 we enter a new section of the book of Isaiah. In chapters

28—35 God affirms that he has the power to fulfill all the saving purposes
he has declared in chapters 1—27. God looks us right in the eye and claims
that he can and will deliver on every single promise in the gospel. Do we
believe him? Does Jesus rule over the mess called my life, or in unsparing
realism must I despair? May I expect a new work of the Holy Spirit in my
experience, or is my past the measure of my future? Isaiah now prompts us
to rethink our lives with questions like these. They have the potential to help
us break the faith barrier into a new sense of God's power and love.

Isaiah sets up a series of three contrasts. He wants us to see the issues
clearly and to respond decisively.

1. The two crowns: What are we proud of? (28:1–6)
   A The pride of Ephraim trampled by Assyria (28:1–4)
      B The glory of the remnant empowered by God (28:5, 6)
2. The two words: What are we hearing? (28:7–22)
   A¹ Degraded leaders, insensitive to God's word (28:7, 8)
      B¹ God's simple message rejected, man's mockery reversed (28:9–13)
   A² Scoffing leaders, overwhelmed by God's word (28:14–19)
      B² Man's false trust exposed, God's "strange . . . work" activated
         (28:20–22)
3. The two outcomes: Can we trust God's ways with us? (28:23–29)
   A God's work of "plowing" purposeful (28:23–26)
      B God's methods of "crushing" appropriate (28:27–29)

Isaiah 28 invites us to find in God glory for our shame, truth for our lies,
and confidence for our timidity.

What Are We Proud Of?

The key word in verses 1–6 is "crown." It appears three times. Isaiah speaks
of a *crown* because he's probing into what makes us feel important.

> Ah, the proud crown of the drunkards of Ephraim,
>   and the fading flower of its glorious beauty . . . ! (Isaiah 28:1)

> The proud crown of the drunkards of Ephraim
>   will be trodden underfoot. (v. 3)

Isaiah is looking north from Jerusalem to Ephraim, the northern kingdom of Israel, and his prophetic eye notices something. Their capital city,
Samaria, is the crown of the nation. There it is, situated "on the head of the
rich valley" (28:1, 4), luxuriant with gardens and groves and trees and vines.
They have it made. But Isaiah sees in Samaria a living metaphor for the easy-
going decadence soon to become easy pickings for the Assyrian invader,

which is what happened in 722 B.C. (He alludes to this in 28:3, 4.) The very privileges that made Ephraim great, the people turned into a drunken binge.

What Isaiah sees in Ephraim is the script we've played out a thousand times in history. Kingdoms rise and fall; wealth is accumulated and then stolen; ego climbs up onto some pedestal and then falls down into absurdity. Standing back and looking at it, we have to ask:

> Can this really be what life is about, as the media insist? This interminable soap opera going on from century to century, from era to era, whose old discarded sets and props litter the earth? Surely not. Was it to provide a location for so repetitive and ribald a performance that the universe was created and man came into existence? I can't believe it. If this were all, then the cynics, the hedonists and the suicides would be right. The most we can hope for from life is some passing amusement, some gratification of our senses, and death. But it's not all. . . . As Christians we know that here we have no continuing city, that crowns roll in the dust and every earthly kingdom must sometime flounder, whereas we acknowledge a king men did not crown and cannot dethrone, as we are citizens of a city of God they did not build and cannot destroy.[2]

It's a mercy to live in a troubled time like ours, when the world is falling apart and secularism is discredited and we have no clever answers for our needs. We're less likely to be taken in. It's more believable now that our only salvation is in God. The collapse of the city of man is the opportunity of the city of God. It's a good time to be living for God.

Believers in Christ have another crown. It does not fade away. It cannot betray our hopes. We will never look stupid wearing this crown.

> In that day the LORD of hosts will be a crown of glory,
>   and a diadem of beauty, to the remnant of his people,
> and a spirit of justice to him who sits in judgment,
>   and strength to those who turn back the battle at the gate. (Isaiah 28:5, 6)

In the very day that the drinks run out and the lights dim and all false crowns roll in the mud, that is when we turn to God. We come to the end of ourselves, we reach out for him, and we find him to be all we ever longed for. He is "a crown of glory."

When God is our treasure, more delightful than all the world (Matthew 13:44), when we *like* the fact that the last will be first and the weak are strong and the fools are wise (Matthew 19:30; 1 Corinthians 1:18–25; 2 Corinthians 12:9, 10), when we gladly identify with a rejected Savior (Galatians 6:14), that's when we're making contact with reality. And Isaiah is saying that when we see through the world's deception and nothingness, and our hearts prize Christ above all, that's when "a spirit of justice" and "strength" empower us to bring into the world the only true good that exists. God is the least exploited resource in this world. The one we treat as our last resort is in fact our Fountainhead. And he is saying, "Let me prove it to you."

"The fading flower of its glorious beauty"—those words in verse 1 are written by the hand of God across every worldly status symbol. You were not created for this tinsel. You were created for a greatness that comes from beyond this world (2 Thessalonians 2:13, 14). God is your crown of glory. Don't be too proud to be adorned with God.

Isaiah looks north to Ephraim to make that point only as an introduction to his primary message, in verses 7–22. Verse 7 begins "These also." Isaiah turns back to his own nation, to Judah in the south, and he says, "These also . . ." What's happening up in Ephraim is also happening down in Judah. "These also" have lost a sense of God in their hearts. They too have fallen into spiritual drunkenness ("they reel in vision").[3] Isaiah can see that not even the conservatives down in Judah look like God's remnant people. So Isaiah goes right to the heart of the problem. The deal-breaker for Judah is the word of God. Isaiah asks a searching question of us all: What are we hearing?

What Are We Hearing?

Isaiah sets up his scenario, and it isn't pretty: "For all tables are full of filthy vomit, with no space left" (28:8). He sees the priests and the prophets of his generation drunk with their own trendy wisdom. He sees them vomiting up their folly, disgorging their disgusting philosophies. And they mock Isaiah.

"To whom then will he teach knowledge,
    and to whom will he explain the message?
Those who are weaned from the milk,
    those taken from the breast?
For it is precept upon precept, precept upon precept,
    line upon line, line upon line,
    here a little, there a little." (vv. 9, 10)

Isaiah is quoting the priests and the prophets. He is repeating back to them their response to his message. (The "he" in the first line of verse 9 is Isaiah.) There are two things they can't stomach about Isaiah.

First, the content of Isaiah's ministry. That's the point of verse 9. They think his call to faith in God is childish and simplistic. And it is true that at the heart of Isaiah's ministry was the simple appeal, "Trust God." There it is in verse 12: "This is rest; give rest to the weary; and this is repose." Isaiah's mission was to call people to find rest in God by faith.[4] But the experts mock his message. It's beneath them. It isn't sophisticated enough. It isn't deep enough. They don't "feel fed" when Isaiah preaches. Some people never do. Martin Luther said this about his preaching:

> When I preach I regard neither doctors nor magistrates, of whom I have above forty in my congregation; I have all my eyes on the servant maids and on the children. And if the learned men are not well pleased with what they hear, well, the door is open.[5]

The second thing these critics can't tolerate is the style of Isaiah's ministry. That's the point of verse 10, which is difficult to translate. The reason is, the priests and prophets are being derisive and silly. They're using what sounds like singsongy baby talk to heap scorn on Isaiah's way of preaching. Their words in Hebrew are *ṣav lāṣāv ṣav lāṣāv qav lāqāv qav lāqāv*. Maybe it's their way of dismissing Isaiah's brilliance with "Blah, blah, blah, yada, yada, yada!" They have no comprehension of the profundity of his ministry.

So God steps in to defend his Word. The NIV opens verse 11 with "Very well then . . ." That's good. When people refuse the message of God, he still has something to say to them:

> Very well then, by people of strange lips
>   and with a foreign tongue [that is, the Assyrians]
> the LORD will speak to this people,
>   to whom he has said,
> "This is rest;
>   give rest to the weary;
> and this is repose";
>   yet they would not hear.
> And the word of the LORD will be to them
> precept upon precept, precept upon precept,
>   line upon line, line upon line,
>   here a little, there a little,
> that they may go, and fall backward,
>   and be broken, and snared, and taken. (vv. 11–13)

What Isaiah is saying is real. One person is sitting in the pew, hearing the gospel and thinking, *I never knew the Bible had so much to say to me. This is so meaningful. I can't wait until next Sunday*, while the very next person in the pew is thinking, *This is dumb. Why doesn't the Bible say something impressive, something up at my level?* Same message, different impact. So the question is, what are *you* hearing? When the Bible is opened up, are you delighted or are you annoyed? The offer of rest for the weary becomes to you, if you resist it, a message of judgment.[6] Paul quotes this passage to warn us that an incomprehensible message is not the way God speaks to believing people; it's the way he speaks to unbelieving, immature people who ought to know better (1 Corinthians 14:20–22).

In *The Last Battle*, C. S. Lewis illustrates how reality can run on two different tracks for people who are right beside each other. On the one hand, there are Tirian and Peter and Lucy and Jill, all friends of Aslan, the Christ figure. Their world is a summer morning and bright blue skies and friendship and laughter. That is their experience. On the other hand, there is a group of dwarves, sitting huddled together in a circle, shutting others out, and their world is a dark and smelly stable. That's what they are experiencing. Aslan walks up to them, shakes his mane, and

> . . . instantly a glorious feast appeared on the Dwarfs' knees: pies and tongues and pigeons and trifles and ices, and each Dwarf had a goblet of good wine in his right hand. But it wasn't much use. They began eating and drinking greedily enough, but it was clear that they couldn't taste it properly. They thought they were eating and drinking only the sort of things you might find in a stable. One said he was trying to eat hay and another said he had got a bit of an old turnip and a third said he'd found a raw cabbage leaf. And they raised golden goblets of rich red wine to their lips and said "Ugh! Fancy drinking dirty water out of a trough that a donkey's been at! Never thought we'd come to this."[7]

To you, is the ministry of the gospel rich wine or trough water? If it isn't sweet to your taste, there's a reason. You're too cynical to enjoy it. What you must do is humble yourself and ask God to soften your hard heart. He can change what you hear. He can turn your trough water into his rich wine.

Sadly, the leaders of Jerusalem refused. The point at which their faith was being tested was the threat of Assyrian aggression. But they tried to save themselves through a political alliance with Egypt. Egypt was offering them protection, and God was offering them protection. Egypt was saying, "You can count on us," and God was saying, "Let *me* show you how I can care for you." But God wasn't real to their hearts. So they signed a treaty with Egypt rather than with God. "Peace in our time!" But Isaiah says in effect, "You haven't made a covenant with Egypt; you've made a covenant with death" (28:15, 18). Their unbelief sealed their fate. In New Testament categories, God had to remove their lampstand (Revelation 2:5) because in the moment of truth they decided, "We have to be practical and do this our own way."

Isaiah is communicating the tragedy of unreality with God. Any shelter other than God is a "refuge of lies" (Isaiah 28:15, 17). What is the point at which *your* faith is being tested? How is God calling you to surrender control and accept his answers and keep pace with his timing? There's a lot more to God's salvation than deliverance from long-gone powers of the ancient Near East. Our real enemy is sin, and it can enslave us forever. God is saying, "Take refuge in *me*, not in denial, not in pleasant falsehoods. You can face the reality of your guilt, and I will show you how I can forgive a sinner." One of Nietzsche's aphorisms shows how we take refuge in soothing lies:

> "I did this," says my memory. "I cannot have done this," says my pride, remaining inexorable. Eventually, my memory yields.[8]

Isn't that the way we are? But God loves dishonest sinners. He is willing to be our ally through Christ, if only we'll trust him.

> Behold, I am the one who has laid as a foundation in Zion
>   a stone, a tested stone,
> a precious cornerstone, of a sure foundation:
>   "Whoever believes will not be in haste." (Isaiah 28:16)

Isaiah is still thinking of the city of God. He is saying that the "foundation," the major premise, of life in the city of God is trust in Jesus Christ (cf. Romans 9:32, 33; 1 Peter 2:4–6). And this is a solid, valuable insight into life. The church's one foundation is not her institutions or history or traditions. They will all fade away. At best they only point to the foundation. The church's one and only foundation is Jesus Christ her Lord, whom we know by faith alone.

A living sense of *him* works in us with saving power: "Whoever believes will not be in haste." In other words, the mentality of faith will not be all in a flutter, will not be driven, will not freak out, will not be scurrying here and there in frantic self-salvation. Faith in Christ can stand up to anything. But self-trust offers as much rest as a bed that's too short and as much comfort as a blanket that's too narrow (Isaiah 28:20). Our compulsive, restless unbelief always frustrates us. It never works out. The secret to the way life really works is living out the gospel with the openness of faith. We don't have to be geniuses. Just believe the truth and follow it.

But if childlike trust is not the bed we choose to rest in, God doesn't go *poof*. Verses 17–19 show that turning from God cannot succeed. In fact, God is at work even in the lives of people who refuse him.

> For the LORD will rise up as on Mount Perazim;
>   as in the Valley of Gibeon he will be roused;
> to do his deed—strange is his deed!
>   and to work his work—alien is his work! (v. 21)

Isaiah is thinking of two battles in Israel's past when God fought for them—against the Philistines on Mount Perazim (2 Samuel 5:17–21) and against the Amorites in the Valley of Gibeon (Joshua 10:1–11). And God will fight on, as he did before. He always will. He's on the move right now. The question is, who is God fighting *for*? Anyone who trusts him, according to the gospel. And who is God fighting *against*? Anyone who refuses him, including his own covenant people. No one owns God. And yesterday's faith belongs to yesterday. If God doesn't find in us a real faith for today, he's prepared to do something strange. He's prepared to leave his own people out of the loop and move on to those who will listen (Acts 28:23–28). "Now therefore do not scoff, lest your bonds be made strong" (Isaiah 28:22a).

Can We Trust God's Ways with Us?

Isaiah concludes with two encouragements. In verses 23–26 he looks at a peasant farmer—not a scientific farmer of today but just a serf. But this humble man is smart enough to know that the upheaval of plowing is only temporary. Plowing changes to planting. Now, Isaiah wonders, how does Mr. Farmer know that? God taught him (v. 26). Therefore God himself must be smart enough to know that endless upheaval and disruption in our lives would be fruitless. Does God break up the rock-hard soil of our hearts? Yes. Does his work of plowing get rough with us? Yes. But not continually, and only in order to plant new life there. God always has a life-enriching purpose.[9] Yield to him.

In verses 27–29 Isaiah looks at that farmer again. This time he notices the way that simple man threshes and crushes his crops. Each crop requires its own treatment, its own method of refinement. And even a correct method must not be overused. Again it was God who made the farmer savvy to that (v. 29). Therefore, God himself is smart enough to know exactly how to work with each one of us (John 21:20–23). He has just the right touch for you. Trust him.

18

God's Power on God's Terms

ISAIAH 29:1–24

IN THE BIBLE GOD IS SAYING, "You won't always understand me, but you can always trust me. If I surprise you with trouble, I will also surprise you with the joy I'll bring out of that trouble. You may struggle to believe that right now. But what seems so impossible is the very thing I specialize in."

Did you know that your greatest breakthrough might be when you hit a brick wall? Did you know that the most constructive thing that might happen to you is when your world falls apart? Sometimes we Christians need that, because we think we have God figured out. We do know something about God, because he has revealed himself to us. But imperceptibly, unintentionally, we can slide into the feeling that if we know God at all, we should be able to explain everything. But the fact is, we can't explain everything. Sometimes God doesn't make sense, to us. Let's humble ourselves and admit it. If we refuse to accept mystery, we jeopardize what we do know. We risk ending up with nothing. C. S. Lewis put it this way:

> You cannot go on "explaining away" for ever; you will find that you have explained explanation itself away. You cannot go on "seeing through" for ever. The whole point of seeing through something is to see something through it. It is good that the window should be transparent, because the street or garden beyond it is opaque. How if you saw through the garden too? It is no use trying to "see through" first principles. If you see through everything, then everything is transparent. But a wholly transparent world is an invisible world. To "see through" all things is the same as not to see.[1]

When God surprises you so that you can't see through what God is doing in your life into the reason behind it, when he becomes opaque and mysterious, you *are* seeing something. You are seeing that God is God and you are not God. You are encountering him at a new level of profundity. You are discovering what it means to trust God and surrender to God rather than control him. If God never shocked you, you wouldn't really know him, because you wouldn't be able to tell the difference between your notions of God and the reality of God.

Isaiah 28 alerted us to God's "strange work" (28:21). Sometimes God seems to act out of character. Isaiah 29 now tells us more about his strange work—not his absurd work, not his hateful work, but his surprising methods with us.

As we begin, let's remember this: If you are in Christ, God never gives you what you deserve. In grace, he gives you what you need. You need encouragement. He gives it. You need confrontation. He gives it. At all levels of the multilayered complexity of your being, right down to the very roots of what you are, beyond your own self-understanding, God can see how you need victory and how you need defeat. And he enters into your subjectivity with mercies both severe and sweet. The gospel equips us with large under-standings of God, so that we can make large allowances for the full range of his ways and stop resenting him and meekly surrender to the deep work of renewal he wants to accomplish in us.

The structure of the chapter highlights three glories of the God with whom we are dealing in every instance of life.

1. The victory of God over all—his friends and his enemies (29:1–8)
    A The complacent church brought low (29:1–4)
        B The malicious world frustrated (29:5–8)
2. The mystery of God over all—the learned and the unlearned (29:9–14)
    A Willful blindness made blind (29:9, 10)
        B Blasé ignorance made ignorant (29:11, 12)
            C Religious dullness made dull (29:13, 14)
3. The sovereignty of God over all—the ruthless and the meek (29:15–24)
    A Practical atheism discredited (29:15, 16)
        B Moral disorder righted (29:17–21)
            C Spiritual greatness revived (29:22–24)

At this point in the unfolding vision of Isaiah, God is saying, "I will keep my every promise to you. I have the power. And here is how my power enters into your weakness." God is saying, "Deal with me as I am. I will triumph. *Therefore, yield to me*. I will surprise you. *Therefore, be open to me*. I plan to remake the whole human scene. *Therefore, lift up your hearts*." The power of the gospel becomes our experience as we accept defeat at God's hands and respect the mysteries beyond our understanding and embrace the renewal he promises.

The Victory of God

> Ah, Ariel, Ariel,
>> the city where David encamped!
> Add year to year;
>> let the feasts run their round. (Isaiah 29:1)

Isaiah is addressing Jerusalem, the city of David, Mount Zion (29:8). Why does he call it "Ariel"? That word means "altar hearth"—that is, the stone surface of the altar where fire consumed the sacrifices (Ezekiel 43:15, 16). So, why "Ariel"? What Isaiah can see is that Jerusalem itself is an altar, where sinners worship a holy God through substitutionary sacrifice. But then Isaiah says, "Add year to year; let the feasts run their round." This is a sarcastic poke at their annual round of worship events and festivals and celebrations—so elaborate, so beautiful, so empty. He's saying, "Carry on with your religious routine. But it's getting you nowhere."

What is the problem? Jerusalem does not see her privilege and her peril. The God she worships is a fiery personality—not erratic but holy (Hebrews 12:28, 29). For us sinners, God is both high-voltage danger and overflowing salvation. And the only refuge from his holy wrath is his holy love in Christ, our substitute on the altar of his cross. In other words, the only escape *from* God is *in* God. But the worship of these people is impervious both to the heat of his anger and to the warmth of his love. They neither tremble nor rejoice in God's presence. They just go through the motions. So, in his sight they're wasting their time. That's why he goes on to say:

> Yet I will distress Ariel,
>> and there shall be moaning and lamentation,
>> and she shall be to me like an Ariel. (Isaiah 29:2)

Jerusalem will indeed be a place where the fire of God burns! Even so, we face a choice today. Will our worship be consumed *with* God, or will it be consumed *by* God? But worship without reality means nothing to him.

This is when God does his strange work: "I will encamp against you . . . and will besiege you . . . and I will raise siegeworks against you" (v. 3). Our God on the attack against us? How does *that* make sense? It makes sense because we need it more than we know. We need to do serious business with God more than we know. Isaiah doesn't even bother mentioning the Assyrians, the obvious candidates to fit into a scenario of Jerusalem under siege. God himself is so immediately involved, we can look beyond the obvious. If we are under siege, *God* is the one we must reckon with.

When he brings us down into the dust, so low we can barely cry for help (v. 4), that's when, as the gospel reveals, the Holy Spirit enters in to intercede with groanings too deep for words (Romans 8:26, 27).[2] That's when God becomes more meaningful to us than ever before. Yield to the victory of God. Let *him* win. In your defeat, God will lift from your heart that old lust for control, and you will be free.

In verses 5–8 Isaiah turns it around. The One who burns like a fire in Jerusalem will confront the world with "the flame of a devouring fire" (v. 6). But Isaiah is not using future tense verbs here to predict a particular event. He is meditating on the ways of God, actualized many times along the way and brought to final expression at the second coming of Christ. He is showing us what God is like. He is saying that the very forces through which God may afflict his own people—God turns that formidable human power into dust and chaff. He can do it "in an instant, suddenly" (v. 5). All by himself, without our help, he frustrates the schemes of those who oppose his cause and his people.

> As when a hungry man dreams, and behold, he is eating
>   and awakes with his hunger not satisfied,
> or as when a thirsty man dreams, and behold, he is drinking
>   and awakes faint, with his thirst not quenched,
> so shall the multitude of all the nations be
>   that fight against Mount Zion. (v. 8)

How many times have people hostile to God licked their chops prematurely over the demise of the church?[3] In Acts 23 more than forty men bound themselves with an oath that they would neither eat nor drink until they had assassinated Paul. Years later, when Luke wrote that account and Paul was carrying on in full strength, he must have smiled as he wondered whatever became of those men. At the high tide of the Enlightenment, Voltaire claimed that by the early nineteenth century the Bible would have passed "into the limbo of forgotten literature."[4] But the Second Great Awakening replaced Enlightenment arrogance with Christian devotion across American society. Maybe you remember when John Lennon said—and I remind you of this with no contempt for him at all but only with sadness—"Christianity will go. It will vanish and shrink. I needn't argue with that; I am right, and I will be proved right. We're more popular than Jesus now. I don't know which will go first—rock and roll or Christianity."[5] The victory of God— the one who besieges us is also well able to defend both himself and us. He knows just what to do every step of the way. Surrender to him.[6]

The Mystery of God

Isaiah is so frustrated with the spiritual malaise he sees in his generation, he blurts out in verses 9, 10, in essence, "Go ahead and be blind, if that's what you want! You have so offended God that, even as you continue to worship, he'll *darken* your minds from understanding the gospel." This way of thinking doesn't make sense to us. We don't understand how this can work, much less be fair. But we should respect it. This is very real. There is mystery in the ways of God.

The key to this section is the picture of the two men in verses 11, 12. You see a literate man, a learned man, in verse 11. Someone hands him a sealed scroll, like a closed Bible. But he's too lazy to open it up and find out what it says. You see an illiterate man, an unlearned man, in verse 12. Someone hands him a sealed prophetic scroll too. But he can't read, and he has no interest in learning. Isaiah sees both responses among the people of God. Both are symptoms of unbelief. And Isaiah is saying that God hardens a distaste for his truth into spiritual blindness.

The blindness Isaiah is lamenting is not the darkness of a primitive pagan culture out in the bush. The blindness he is so worried about is the tiring, rote worship of the people in covenant with God.

> And the Lord said:
> "Because this people draw near with their mouth
>   and honor me with their lips,
>   while their hearts are far from me,
> and their fear of me is a commandment taught by men,
> therefore, behold, I will again
>   do wonderful things with this people,
>   with wonder upon wonder;
> and the wisdom of their wise men shall perish,
>   and the discernment of their discerning men shall be hidden." (vv. 13, 14)

Jesus applied this text to the Pharisees, who worshiped God punctiliously (Matthew 15:1–9). They were saying all the right things, doing all the right things. They feared God. But their fear of him—even this interior dimension of worship—was only a doctrine taught by human instruction. It was just an idea, a concept in their minds, a catechetical answer, not a Spirit-imparted awareness transforming their hearts. Beneath the beautiful observance, they were using the worship of God as a mechanism for avoiding God, for controlling God, for setting limits on God. They were like Flannery O'Connor's character Haze Motes: "There was already a deep black wordless conviction in him that the way to avoid Jesus was to avoid sin."[7] God-evasion can look good. You can deceive even yourself. In his teaching on repentance, Calvin says that one way to get real with God is "to flee splendor and any sort of trappings."[8] So which do you really prize—tradition or God? You cannot serve two masters. You must choose between authentic worship and pious blasphemy. "Without love in the heart, the seeming gift of worship is but mockery of the Most High."[9]

When form replaces freshness, when rote replaces reality, worship treats God as less than the living God, and he is offended. Isaiah says that God visits such worship with an unlikely miracle.

> . . . therefore, behold, I will again
>   do wonderful things with this people,
>   with wonder upon wonder. (v. 14a)

"Wonderful" and "wonder" are Old Testament words for "miraculous" and "miracle." And the age of miracles is not over today. God is able today to transform head-only religion into empty-headed religion with no answers for our real problems. "The wisdom of their wise men shall perish," Isaiah says (v. 14b; cf. 1 Corinthians 1:19). Truly, God is not mocked.

Outside the Bible itself, no one has explained the urgency of personal reality with God more helpfully than Jonathan Edwards:

> If we are not in good earnest in religion, if our wills and inclinations are not strongly exercised, we are nothing. The things of religion are so great, the responses of our hearts cannot be commensurate unless those responses are lively and powerful. In nothing is vigor in the actings of our inclinations so appropriate as in religion, and in nothing is lukewarmness so odious. True religion is evermore a powerful thing; and its power appears primarily in its inward exercises in the heart, its principal and original seat.[10]

The Bible warns us that some people hold to the form of godliness, but their lives deny its power (2 Timothy 3:5). They attend church dutifully, but their hearts are far from God. Their religion is orthodox, beautiful *nothing*.

Older people need the power of godliness in their hearts because they have little time left to get ready for Heaven. Middle-aged people need the power of godliness in their hearts because they are strongly tempted to coast, to rest on their laurels, to become dull and mediocre. Young families need the power of godliness in their hearts because they are forging the convictions that will shape their home for a lifetime. Singles need the power of godliness in their hearts because they can gain or they can forfeit single-minded devotion to Jesus. Students and teenagers need the power of godliness in their hearts because they are being targeted by the world with brilliant and attractive seductions. Children need the power of godliness in their hearts while they are young and open, to be set apart to God forever. We Presbyterians, for example, need the power of godliness in our hearts because *the* sin of the Presbyterian church is to settle for the *doctrine* of the power of God rather than pressing on by faith into the *experience* of the power of God.

If you have a troubled child, for example, what will be most helpful to your child? Wouldn't it help your child for him or her to see your heart enthralled by a sense of the glory of Jesus? Or would that damage your child somehow? Your child might just think, *If God can change Dad and Mom, maybe he can help me too.*

The mystery of God—if he has poured out upon you "a spirit of deep sleep" (Isaiah 29:10), he can also awaken you (cf. Ephesians 5:14). Bring your emptiness out into the open before him. If you come out of hiding, so will God, and he will do a new miracle of grace in your heart.

The Sovereignty of God

I hope you love the sovereignty of God. You really can, because his sovereignty is his freedom to do whatever he pleases (Psalm 115:3). Aren't you glad that God is free, unbound, supreme in this universe? Our unbelief doesn't neutralize God. Our unbelief is where God starts out with us (Ephesians 2:4, 5). The practical atheism Isaiah exposes in verses 15, 16—this very American way of thinking—cannot stop God.

> Ah, you who hide deep from the LORD your counsel,
> whose deeds are in the dark,
> and who say, "Who sees us? Who knows us?" (v. 15)

In 1983 *Time* magazine published a sixtieth anniversary issue, including an essay entitled, "What Really Mattered?" What really mattered in the world between 1923 and 1983? What idea shaped these crucial years?

> . . . the fundamental idea that America represented corresponded to the values of the times. America was not merely free; it was freed, unshackled.[11]

The spirit of modern times is the spirit of autonomy. "Who sees us? Who knows us?" But this blindness cannot defeat the Sovereign. Human defiance is the madness out of which his grace is creating something new. These are the raw materials he is using to build his kingdom. Its appearing is imminent.

> Is it not yet a very little while
> until Lebanon shall be turned into a fruitful field,

and the fruitful field shall be regarded as a forest?
In that day the deaf shall hear
    the words of a book,
and out of their gloom and darkness
    the eyes of the blind shall see.
The meek shall obtain fresh joy in the LORD,
    and the poor among mankind shall exult in the Holy One of Israel. (vv. 17–19)

Isaiah sees in the forests of Lebanon a picture of human nobility and might. But God will cut it all down and humble it into a common field. And in an ordinary field the prophetic eye discerns such luxuriant growth to come, it will someday be a mighty forest. The values of human society now don't make sense. But God is promising to change things around. "The meek shall obtain fresh joy in the LORD . . . the ruthless shall come to nothing" (vv. 19, 20). Fresh joy in Christ will flood the world.

That beautiful eruption of unpersecuted spiritual vitality will not be a mid-course correction in the plan of God. This "fresh joy" will fulfill God's ancient covenant with Abraham, Isaiah explains in verses 22–24. God has been moving in this direction from the beginning. This *is* salvation. He began it in sovereign grace; he continues it in sovereign grace; he will consummate it in sovereign grace. We should trust him for that, however perplexing his strategies may be along the way.

Our part is meekness. It is the meek and poor alone whom God blesses. In 1971 my dad and mom were ministering to the student body of Taylor University in Indiana. For one week in the dead of winter God visited that campus with fresh joy. I was listening the other day to a recording of my parents' report to their church soon afterward. They said that one night, as the students met in the gym, God gave them the meekness to begin confessing their sins. They began to get real with God and with one another. They yielded to the work he wanted to do. Their confessing went on for hours, because real repentance can't be hurried. Real repentance is not general and vague but detailed and thorough. At one point late into the night, Dad suggested they take a short break to stretch their legs. In my parents' own words,

We were not at all prepared for what was about to happen. When those kids stood up, you would have thought it was the split second after their most crucial basketball game against their toughest opponent, they had just won by a hair and became number one in the nation. They went wild with joy. It was like back in Leviticus, shouting and falling on their faces (Leviticus 9:24). We had never experienced anything like it. They were hugging each other. They would run for somebody and say, "Did you ever think this would happen to us? Praise God! Isn't this beautiful?" We kept trying to start a song to get them to calm down. But for ten minutes you couldn't stop it. It was like taking a Coke bottle and shaking it up and then taking the lid off. They could not be held down. They had to express themselves.

"The meek shall obtain fresh joy in the LORD, and the poor among mankind shall exult in the Holy One of Israel." God wants this for us. It is his ancient covenant purpose. He might have to do a strange work to get us there. Will we trust him and follow him in meekness, wherever he leads?

19

The Counterintuitive Ways of God

ISAIAH 30:1–33

IN 1 CORINTHIANS 2:14 PAUL WRITES, "The natural person does not accept the things of the Spirit of God, for they are folly to him, and he is not able to understand them because they are spiritually discerned." The ways of God are counterintuitive.

There's a lot of talk today about spirituality, which is good. But true spirituality might not be what we think it is.[1] God sent Isaiah to us with an improbable message: Our only hope is in abandoning every other hope, however obvious. Our only truth is in disbelieving every other truth, however widely accepted. Our only safety is in trust; our only stability is in yielding control; our only freedom is in surrender. God is saying that the conventional wisdom of our culture, which magnifies human potential and human virtue and human smarts, is stupid. He is saying that the inner fullness we all desire comes from outside ourselves. He is saying that our initial reaction to real spirituality might be irritation and disbelief. God directs our eyes to a bloodied mass of human flesh, a man beaten beyond recognition, rejected by the elites and the opinion-shapers and the religious gurus, a man suffering on a cross, and God says, "*He* is the Giver of the Spirit. *That cross* is the secret to true spirituality."

Can we receive that? If so, how do we enter into it? For starters, in Colossians 3:2, 3 Paul writes, "Set your minds on things that are above, not on things that are on earth. For you have died, and your life is hidden with Christ in God." Who would have thought that? True spirituality comes when we stop setting our minds on the obvious and the immediate. It comes in union with the Christ who died and was raised again. He is the key to *the life that is hidden*. The Bible is saying that God has stockpiled resources for us that outperform all human techniques and coping strategies and spiritual regimens. The things of the Spirit are hidden *for* us, not *from* us, with Christ in God, and the gospel is the map showing us the way there.

In so much of the Bible God is patiently instructing us in another way to think and live. That's what Isaiah 30 is for. It alerts us to the surprising ways of God. True spirituality is not a lifestyle option we pick up along the way. It goes against the grain of our nature. We never stop learning. Back in Isaiah's day, his generation felt more secure in living by their own wits than by God's wisdom. They saw help where there was no help. They saw a threat where there was no threat. Why? They were forgetting that the best-kept secrets to life are hidden for us with Christ in God.

The structure of the chapter clarifies four questions we need to think about, to access authentic spirituality.

A¹ Who is not a help to us? Egypt (30:1–7)
    1. Human protection obvious but empty (30:1–5)
    2. Human favor costly but worthless (30:6, 7)
  B¹ What should we listen to? Not smooth lies (30:8–17)
    1. Prophetic truth always relevant (30:8)
    2. Pleasant illusions inevitably crushed (30:9–14)
    3. Frantic unbelief relentlessly driven (30:15–17)
  B² What can we look forward to? Not fancy idols (30:18–26)
    1. Divine mercy always ready (30:18)
    2. Personal immediacy vividly real (30:19–22)
    3. Ultimate blessing wonderfully abundant (30:23–26)
A² Who is not a threat to us? Assyria (30:27–33)
    1. Divine wrath overwhelming and just (30:27, 28)
    2. Divine fire terrifying and celebrated (30:29–33)

Isaiah 30 is premised in the faithfulness and power of God. If God is our ally, if the gospel is the truth, if our future is Christ-filled, and if nothing can separate us from the love of God, can't we live out of those resources? If that isn't salvation, what is? As all that God is worth comes home to our hearts, we start off-loading our alliances with the false salvations of this world, and we enter more and more into the life that is hidden for us with Christ in God.

Who Is Not a Help to Us?

"Ah, stubborn children," declares the LORD,
  "who carry out a plan, but not mine,

and who make an alliance, but not of my Spirit,
    that they may add sin to sin;
who set out to go down to Egypt,
    without asking for my direction,
to take refuge in the protection of Pharaoh
    and to seek shelter in the shadow of Egypt!" (Isaiah 30:1, 2)

The key here is "who carry out a plan." God is not primarily concerned here with our beliefs per se. He is concerned with our plans, our strategies for living life, our functional faith. It's possible to believe all the right things but to negotiate everyday life by another wisdom, little different from the world. Isaiah's generation did that. They knew about the exodus and the saving power of God. They knew their Bibles. But in the hard business of daily life, they made their way by other ground rules.

Their practical struggle was the growing pressure of the Assyrian Empire. Judah was being shoved around, and they were terrified. But it was for such a time as this that God had covenanted with them in the first place (Leviticus 26:1–13). He had said, "Let's go through this together. Let me help." And he had proven himself again and again. But there's something deep inside us that diminishes past facts and magnifies present uncertainties. Somehow God's faithfulness in the past doesn't carry weight for long, and pretty soon we start feeling as unloved and alone as ever. It's just the way we are. It's why we need constant renewal. There is always some plausible alternative to trusting in God, something to take our eyes off of God.

The mistake Judah made was to protect herself from Assyria through an alliance with Egypt. But that wasn't God's plan. He had liberated them from Egypt in the first place. Think about it. Judah is going back to the old slave-master, *to ensure her freedom.* At one level it seemed the obvious thing to do. But at the level of the spiritual, it was foolish. Egypt can offer the people of Judah nothing they don't have already in their Lord. The irony of this appears in the word translated "alliance" in verse 1. The Hebrew word there is a pun. It can mean "alliance," obviously; but it can also mean "covering" (Isaiah 28:20) and "[idolatrous] image" (Isaiah 30:22). Here is Isaiah's point. Judah's alliance with Egypt covered them like a warm blanket. It made them feel comfortable against the storm of Assyria. But it was an idol.

God does not bless our plans. He blesses only that which is of himself. And if his salvation does not live in our hearts, we inevitably "add sin to sin" (Isaiah 30:1). The first sin is not seeking a heart filled with God, and the second sin we add to it is to fill our emptiness with our own false comforts. But they never work out: "Therefore shall the protection of Pharaoh turn to your shame, and the shelter in the shadow of Egypt to your humiliation" (v. 3).

What does this mean for us today? Isaiah 30 does not translate into pacifist politics. But it does translate into pacifist spirituality: "If God does not protect me from my guilt and sin, I have no defense at all. His way is my only plan. I will not complicate the finished work of Christ on the cross by justifying myself. If Jesus can't pay for my guilt, I'm damned. If the Holy Spirit isn't enough to fill my heart, I'm empty. But I will not fill myself with plastic substitutes. All I need, all I desire, is the plan of God."

In verses 6, 7 the prophet has some fun. He is thinking of Judah's official caravan traveling south through the Negeb to Egypt. The donkeys and camels are loaded down with money and treasures to buy Egyptian protection. The way Isaiah starts out, "An oracle on the beasts of the Negeb," drips with mocking solemnity. Remember how he introduced his oracles on the nations in chapters 13—23? "The oracle concerning Babylon," for example (13:1). But this is "An oracle *on the beasts of the Negeb*." The officials back in Jerusalem, forging this treaty with Egypt, are wringing their hands and wondering, *How is the embassy to Egypt going? Have they arrived safely with the payment? Any word yet?* But Isaiah derides them with, "Forget the ambassadors and the money. What about the poor pack animals?" He reduces their unspirituality to its true absurdity. The leaders of Judah are not seeking things above. They are not living out of the life hidden for them with Christ in God. By reverting to self-rescue, their arduous journey back to Egypt, from which they had escaped in the first place, is reversing their very salvation. And to gain what? "Rahab the Do-Nothing!" (30:7, NIV).

God is so gracious. His message to all unspiritual nitwits stumbling through life is, "Come to me, all who labor and are heavy laden, and I will give you rest. Take my yoke upon you, and learn from me, for I am gentle and lowly in heart, and you will find rest for your souls" (Matthew 11:28, 29). And how do we do that? By asking new questions like, "Who is *not* a help to me? What false savior has disappointed me again and again and cost me dearly but I keep going back to it?" The reality we long for is *spiritual* in nature, it's hidden for us *with Christ* in God, and it's *free* for the seeking.

What Should We Listen To?

Isaiah's generation has passed the point of no return. He wanted to lead them in the ways of God. But by now, he has to record his ministry for later generations (30:8). His people have rejected God's wisdom for their own intuitive wisdom.

> For they are a rebellious people,
>   lying children,
> children unwilling to hear
>   the instruction of the LORD;
> who say to the seers, "Do not see,"

and to the prophets, "Do not prophesy what is right;
speak to us smooth things,
   prophesy illusions." (vv. 9, 10)

A friend e-mailed me a quote from Flannery O'Connor: "The truth does not change according to our ability to stomach it." But we resent the flinty objectivity of truth. That's why the beginning of true spirituality is openness to whatever the gospel has to say to us. For Isaiah's generation, their treaty with Egypt was only a symptom. The problem was an unteachable impatience with the word of God. They didn't want to hear it. Why? Because God's spiritual remedy seemed at the same time both unhelpful and demanding—a terrible combination. If a certain spiritual path is demanding but the payoff is rich and obvious, that's one thing. But these people could only feel the demand; they couldn't savor the value. So they just got tired of Isaiah's ministry. What they wanted was not an end of preaching. What they wanted was preaching that would agree with their preconceptions and not ruffle their feathers.

I saw a recommendation for a book in which the reviewer said this: "Truths most offensive to the natural man, yet most salutary and essential for him, find expression [in this book] that is both plain and eloquent." True spirituality is a spirituality of truth. We go deep by making our hearts vulnerable to truths most offensive, yet most salutary and essential. And we *can* open our hearts. Why? Because whatever God says to us in the gospel, he speaks with love and grace. Some of his truths will melt in your mouth. Other truths will hit you like a ton of bricks. But everything God says opens up to you the life hidden with Christ in God—if *you* are open. Trust him enough to keep listening. Give his gospel a willing audience in the inmost chamber of your soul, whatever his Word says. Do not listen with detachment, but open your heart wide to God. He will surprise you with how his wisdom really does work.

In verses 12–14 Isaiah turns this around. He shows us what our own native ideas are really worth. They're like a high wall (v. 13). It seems solid. It might protect us. But then a crack slowly forms. Eventually the whole thing caves in suddenly, in an instant. It can't hold. It isn't sustainable. Our own ways are also like a broken potter's vessel, smashed to smithereens (v. 14). Both are too brittle, too delicate, to stand up to the pounding that life inevitably inflicts. Obviously, the smart thing to do is not to hide behind *that* wall and not to put your precious oil in *that* jar. Isaiah is saying that our natural mechanisms for responding to life may seem impressive, but they can't be trusted. Entering into the hidden riches of Christ means going back and relearning everything. We must become like children (Matthew 18:3). Our need is that great.

Isaiah puts the two alternatives before us in verses 15, 16, taking us to the heart of his prophetic message.

> For thus said the Lord GOD, the Holy One of Israel,
> "In returning and rest you shall be saved;
>   in quietness and in trust shall be your strength."
> But you were unwilling, and you said,
> "No! We will flee upon horses";
>   therefore you shall flee away;
> and, "We will ride upon swift steeds";
>   therefore your pursuers shall be swift.

The film *Chariots of Fire* illustrates what this looks like in real life. It tells the story of two men, Harold Abrahams and Eric Liddell. Both are great athletes on the same team, but there is a difference. Abrahams competes out of an inner drivenness. He is deeply insecure. He has a point to prove. It's all about *him*. Liddell also competes to win. But he runs out of a sense of God's goodness. He's not in bondage to himself. He runs for the glory of God. Two men, two motives, two inner lives—Eric Liddell competing in the Holy Spirit, Harold Abrahams running on sheer adrenaline. It's the difference between spirituality, even in athletics, and self-absorption.

When Isaiah says, "In returning and rest you shall be saved; in quietness and in trust shall be your strength" (v. 15), he means that repentance and faith are God's way to fill us with salvation and strength. But whatever else we choose will be our undoing (vv. 16, 17). Any alternative to God plays right into the hands of what we don't want for ourselves.

For example, if your career is about your own self-validation, at what point will you be able to say, "I'm satisfied. I'm finally the human being I've always wanted to be"? You'll never get there. You'll never relax. But if you pursue your career out of a sense of the goodness of God, if you live out of spiritual union with Christ, you will experience the rest and quietness your heart longs for. This is salvation on the job.

What Can We Look Forward To?

> Therefore the LORD waits to be gracious to you,
>   and therefore he exalts himself to show mercy to you.
> For the LORD is a God of justice;
>   blessed are all those who wait for him. (v. 18)

This verse is the hinge on which the chapter turns. Look at the logic of God. "You have been unwilling. *Therefore*, I wait to be gracious to you." What is he saying? "Wait" is the operative word. The Lord waits, and we wait. But the grammar of the Hebrew tells us that the Lord's waiting and our waiting are not quite the same. *We wait* for him in faith, in openness, in humility, confident that his timing is right, his methods are wise, and so forth ("the LORD is a God of justice"). That mentality of trust is the way into spiritual blessedness: "Blessed are all those who wait for him." And for his part, *the Lord waits* to be gracious to us. In other words, he exercises continual patience with us, he puts up with us moment by moment. He doesn't forsake us. He anticipates and compensates for our needs. Nothing will ever separate us from his love. His faithfulness, not ours, is what we can look forward to. So when we find ourselves asking the question, "How long, O Lord?" his answer may be, "Whenever you're ready."

> He will surely be gracious to you at the sound of your cry. As soon as he hears it, he answers you. And though the Lord give you the bread of adversity and the water of affliction, yet your Teacher will not hide himself anymore, but your eyes shall see your Teacher. And your ears shall hear a word behind you, saying, "This is the way, walk in it," when you turn to the right or when you turn to the left. (vv. 19b–21)

Even in affliction, God's greatest gift to us is himself, his presence and immediacy. The eyes of our hearts are enlightened and our ears are opened so that the merest word from him changes the course of our lives. *This is spirituality*, when the Presence of God breaks through and the Word of God acts with authority. We finally see our darling, costly, stupid idols for what they are, and we junk them (v. 22). Christ *alone*, grace *alone*, faith *alone*, Scripture *alone*—in all conditions of life, we are so well off with him.

And our growing enjoyment of him is only a foretaste of what is to come. In verses 23–26, with our idols finally broken in pieces at our feet, Isaiah foresees God fulfilling his purpose of grace. The prophet uses Old Testament language to describe the renewal of all things. "The creation itself will be set free from its bondage to decay and obtain the freedom of the glory of the children of God" (Romans 8:21). Our Teacher showing us the way there (Isaiah 30:20) will also be our Doctor binding up our wounds (v. 26). Isaiah is talking about ultimate grace flowing over us at the second coming of Christ. And if this is what we have to look forward to, nothing can really harm us now.

Who Is Not a Threat to Us?

The key to Isaiah's closing section is "the name of the LORD" in verse 27 matched by "the breath of the LORD" in verse 33.

> Behold, the name of the LORD comes from afar,
>   burning with his anger, and in thick rising smoke. . . .

For a burning place has long been prepared; indeed, for the king it is made ready, its pyre made deep and wide, with fire and wood in abundance; the breath of the LORD, like a stream of sulfur, kindles it.

The Assyrians and their king were no threat. All the powers of evil and oppression and injustice throughout history were no threat. All the powers of sin and death and hell are no threat. Why? Because of the name of the Lord. Isaiah means that God has declared himself to us. We can be sure about him. He has revealed himself to us, supremely in Jesus, as the Archenemy of all evil and the Defender of the broken. He burns with intensity about this. It is simply who he is—so much so that he died on the cross to break the hold of evil on his chosen ones. He is coming again in power and glory to put a stop to it forever, and no power can resist him. The breath of the Lord is so scorching, all he has to do is blow on the evil one and the funeral pyre goes up in flames.

I need the imagination of a J. R. R. Tolkien to help me convey Isaiah's vision of the gladness of God's final victory over all evil (30:29–33). At one point in The Lord of the Rings, the army of Rohan is defeating the evil army of Mordor.

The hosts of Mordor wailed, and terror took them, and they fled, and died, and the hoofs of wrath rode over them. And then all the host of Rohan burst into song, and they sang as they slew, for the joy of battle was on them, and the sound of their singing was fair and terrible.[2]

If we have peace with God through the merit of Christ, we have a strong Ally. Let's not forget him. He doesn't forget us. He is so loyal that, here in the final section of Isaiah's chapter, who shows up again? We do.

You shall have a song as in the night when a holy feast is kept, and gladness of heart, as when one sets out to the sound of the flute to go to the mountain of the LORD, to the Rock of Israel. (v. 29)

With his eye turned to the future, what does Isaiah see out there for us? A feast, with music and song and gladness of heart. The victory will be God's, and the delight will be ours. Right now we don't always treat God as a loyal ally. But he is faithful still. When our hearts are finally and forever drawn away from all false saviors and are endlessly celebrating his all-sufficiency, we will know his name.

You need to follow through in three ways.[3] One: avoid any spiritual path that deviates from the gospel. The Spirit of God is "the Spirit of truth" (John 16:13). If therefore a certain spirituality diminishes the Scriptures, it is at best defective. Two: guard against your own prejudices that take offense at the counterintuitive ways of God. Open yourself to newness. Doesn't God have the right to surprise you? Or do you know all the answers already? Three: as the Holy Spirit speaks to you about the false saviors you're presently allied with, be honest with him, break those alliances, and lean on Christ alone. He is a strong Savior.

20

Our Only True Hope

ISAIAH 31—32

HEARTBROKEN PEOPLE GATHERED IN A FIELD in Pennsylvania where United flight 93 crashed on September 11, 2001. It was a memorial service. Lisa Beamer, widow of one of the men who led a revolt against the hijackers, was among them. She later wrote:

> I couldn't help but compare this service to the one in Cranbury the day before. Todd's memorial service had been so uplifting, so inspiring, because the emphasis had been on hope in the midst of crisis. On Monday, as I listened to the well-intentioned speakers, who were doing their best to comfort but with little if any direct reference to the power of God to sustain us, I felt I was sliding helplessly down a high mountain into a deep crevasse. As much as I appreciated the kindness of the wonderful people who tried to encourage us, that afternoon was actually one of the lowest points in my grieving. It wasn't the people, or even the place. Instead, it struck me how hopeless the world is when God is factored out of the equation.[1]

Sincere clichés are not enough. We need God. If we factor him out of the equation, we strip ourselves bare before the blast of life's cruelties. But if we factor God in as our hope, we can face anything.

God has made commitments to us. "I will counsel you with my eye upon you" (Psalm 32:8). "I will come again and take you to myself, that where I am you may be also" (John 14:3). "My grace is sufficient for you" (2 Corinthians 12:9). "Fear not . . . I am your shield; your reward shall be very great" (Genesis 15:1). What makes us into world-beaters is a sense of God's love for us, a sense on the heart of his promised power on our behalf.

That awakening in the heart is what empowers us to face life not with res-
ignation but with expectancy.

Jonathan Edwards explained how the human being makes contact with
reality. We know things at two levels. We grasp things with conceptual
knowledge in our heads. We also enter into things with the sense of the
heart. It's the difference between reading a recipe for apple pie and actually
putting a piece of hot apple pie à la mode into your mouth. God has made
us to know him at both levels—with the thoughts of our minds and with
a sense in our hearts. And it's the sense of the heart that gives us traction.
When his assurances in the gospel melt into our hearts, we experience the
power of hope.[2]

Isaiah ministered in a day when his people needed the courage of hope,
just as we do today. But they had only a theoretical knowledge of God to get
them through the threat of Assyrian invasion. Their beliefs hadn't penetrated
their hearts. So in their practical struggle, their beliefs kept losing the argument. Expediency was driving them. The prophet understood their need and
our need. He guides us into the spiritual insight that makes a difference in
the heart. This is how his message unfolds:

> A[1] Prologue: The undeniable power of God (31:1–5)
> > B[1] Return to the Fire in Zion! (31:6–9)
> > > C[1] The Messianic King, a new people (32:1–8)
> > B[2] Hear the word of the prophet! (32:9–14)
> > > C[2] The outpoured Spirit, a new people (32:15–18)
> A[2] Epilogue: The undeniable truth of God (32:19, 20)

Isaiah is answering a question: When God feels unreal in our very real
crises, how do we find our way back? His answer is, the grace of God. We
need *the grace of confrontation*. God calls us to repent (B[1]) and to listen (B[2]).
Even more, we need *the grace of provision*. Our King reigns over us (C[1]),
and his Spirit is poured out upon us (C[2]).

> Woe to those who go down to Egypt for help
> > and rely on horses,
> who trust in chariots because they are many
> > and in horsemen because they are very strong,
> but do not look to the Holy One of Israel
> > or consult the LORD! (Isaiah 31:1)

The prologue in 31:1–5 is the key to the whole passage. And the question here is obvious: What's wrong with going down to Egypt for help? Why

is God offended? The Assyrian army was threatening little Judah. Why *not* form an alliance with Egypt?

The first problem is that Judah was *not* looking to their Holy One or consulting the Lord. They believed in him, in their way; but they weren't looking to him. Their real faith was in human power. Isaiah understands that some "helps" are inconsistent with God. If you need money, for example, it isn't wrong to get a job. But it is wrong to steal. You can work and trust God at the same time. But you can't steal and trust God at the same time, because stealing factors God out, as if he doesn't care. And God wants us to trust him in ways that count, so that he can prove himself to us in ways that count. He wants reality with us. But any so-called help that diminishes our experience of God always turns out to be just another Egyptian slave-master.

We can think of "Egypt," then, as a cipher for *anything I think I need outside the promises of God*. And that's why Judah was wrong to go down to Egypt for help. God had declared his commitment to them. Their Biblical creed was, "Some trust in chariots and some in horses, but we trust in the name of the LORD our God" (Psalm 20:7). But now, going down to Egypt for the help God had already promised them, they were going back to the bondage he had saved them from in the first place. They were throwing their salvation into reverse gear and holding God's love in contempt. They expected nothing from him. He was a theory—a beautiful theory—while their *modus operandi* for real life said in effect, "Whatever gain I have in Christ I count as loss for the sake of the world. I have suffered the loss of Christ and count him as rubbish, in order that I may gain the world" (cf. Philippians 3:7, 8).

We all feel vulnerable. But Christ means it when he says, "Let not your hearts be troubled" (John 14:1). He means it when he says, "I will never leave you nor forsake you" (Hebrews 13:5). What do we need to understand to experience his serenity? We need to understand that the "Assyria" threatening us is not our real crisis. Our real crisis is our own unbelief in God. Our real danger is not when we're exposed to the brutalities of life; our real danger is when our hearts are not filled with a sense of God. What we most need is not to find a way to cope with our distress. What we most need is reality with God, so that we can live out of the inner fullness he gives, whatever life may bring.

Judah's first problem, then, is that they weren't living by faith in God. They didn't sense that "the battle is the LORD's" (1 Samuel 17:47). The second problem with Judah's alliance with Egypt is the flip side. They *were* trusting in chariots "because they are many" and in horsemen "because they are very strong" (Isaiah 31:1). In other words, they were impressed with what human minds and human skills can control, manage, and understand.

But trusting in many chariots and strong horsemen never works. It only compounds our feelings of nakedness because we're always left wondering who has *more* chariots and *stronger* horsemen. When we step outside the promises of God, we only find more uncertainty.

We need to stop this whole way of thinking and ask a deeper question: What *is* the real world?

> And yet he is wise and brings disaster;
>   he does not call back his words. (v. 2a)

When we see things going wrong, let's never think, *Poor God! He sure has gotten himself into a tight spot this time. What can he do now?* God is wise. The royal advisers in Jerusalem thought they were so smart, dealing with "things as they are." They thought they were wise enough to avert disaster. But God is wise enough to use their brilliant plans to *bring* disaster. And if *God* is in our troubles, all the Egypts in the world cannot save us. The only way out is *his* way. God's words are the one fixed point in the confusion of life that we can absolutely count on.

> The Egyptians are man, and not God,
>   and their horses are flesh, and not spirit. (v. 3)

That's an odd thing to say. Whoever claimed that the Egyptians *were* God or that their horses *were* spirit? But sometimes we need a closer look at the obvious. Flesh, however great and strong, is no match for spirit, however abstract and elusive (John 3:5–8). After all, "God is spirit" (John 4:24). The Westminster Shorter Catechism of 1648 asks, "What is God?" And the answer is, "God is a spirit, infinite, eternal and unchangeable, in his being, wisdom, power, holiness, justice, goodness and truth." A spiritual ally is our mightiest ally.

But isn't this the very point where our faith sometimes breaks down? Our problems are concrete enough. And God's spiritual remedies can seem weak and irrelevant. The word for "spirit" here in Isaiah is also used in the Old Testament for "wind" (Ecclesiastes 1:6) or even the merest "breeze" (Psalm 78:39, NIV). "Spirit"—what is it? It's airy and insubstantial, just a breath. What kind of help is that in this world? But *God* is spirit. And he's saying that spirit is stronger than flesh. He's saying that an unseen ally is more reliable than a visible ally. He's implying that if we live out of tangible, earthly resources, we are *dis*empowering ourselves.

This is true all the way up at the level of our culture's mythology. The modern view is that there is nothing in the universe greater than man. We factor God out and see ourselves at the top of the evolutionary heap. So the future of the race lies with us. But that myth has only made the world more tragic. Thinking that we are the apex of reality creates despots like Stalin and Hitler and Mao.[3]

This is true at a personal level too. The richness and fullness of life come from what is spiritual, not earthly. Money, for example, can buy a house, but it can't make a home. Money can put food on the table, but it can't put laughter and joy around that table. Money can fly you to Paris, but it can't kindle romance there. What money *can* do is make you an attractive target for thieves and lawsuits. There is no security in money. There is no life for us in any tangible thing. *What makes for life comes not from this world but from the grace of God.* Therefore, a heart at one with God is the secret to life. To have God is to have all things. To trust him is to be saved.

God hides his best gifts in improbable packages. The *spiritual* nature of true life—so frustrating to us—this is not something God failed to foresee. He set it up that way. The foolishness of God is wiser than men, and the weakness of God is stronger than men. And God wants everyone to know it, so that no flesh will boast in his presence (1 Corinthians 1:25, 29). For most of us, this means we humble ourselves like children, start all over again, and relearn everything from the ground up.

In 31:4, 5 Isaiah reinforces his vision of God's effortless, powerful care for us with two similes. God is like a lion in his unperturbed sovereignty. A lion stands astride the body of a sheep it has caught. The shepherds are shouting, to scare it away. But the lion just stands there and purrs. And God is like a bird in his gentle protection, fluttering over its nest. God is like *both*. He is all the salvation we need. And whatever tangible helps God does give us find their meaning only in their derivation from God himself.

So how do we get back on track with our true hope in God? Our part is to return and to listen. God's greater part is his Messiah and his Spirit.

Return to the Fire in Zion!

> Turn to him from whom people have deeply revolted, O children of Israel. For in that day everyone shall cast away his idols of silver and his idols of gold, which your hands have sinfully made for you. (vv. 6, 7)

Isaiah is talking about repentance, turning back to God, and throwing away our costly idols. There is no other way to get beyond theory into experiencing God. When God says, in verse 8, that Assyria will fall by a superhuman sword, he is saying, "Forget about Assyria. Factor *them* out of the equation. *I* am the one you need to think about." Then, in verse 9, the fire and furnace imagery is an Old Testament way of saying, "Aslan isn't safe, but he's good."[4] Our best Friend is also a living Fire. But getting singed by him is one of the best things that can happen to us. The conviction of sin is a fast track back to God.

Have you ever experienced the thrill of renouncing some precious idol, some hard-won token of power or superiority? Isaiah says that when we return to the one from whom we have deeply revolted, something happens. We throw away our idols of silver and gold. We finally see how contemptible is a self-image unsurrendered to Christ. That is what an idol does. It obscures God and magnifies self-idealization. And that's why our idols are so precious to us. We pour so much hope and effort and expense into becoming our dreams. But however precious an idol has become to us, the loss of it is a relief. The heart awakened to the value of Christ doesn't ask what price must be paid to get real with him. And as long as our hearts are wondering if we can afford the loss of self, the price will always seem too high to pay. But Isaiah is saying, "Turn back to him now, *even with your idols*. He will graciously help you suffer the loss of all things in order to gain him. And you won't regret it because he is *life*."

The Messianic King, a New People

Behold, a king will reign in righteousness,
    and princes will rule in justice.
A man[5] will be like a hiding place from the wind,
    a shelter from the storm,
like streams of water in a dry place,
    like the shade of a great rock in a weary land. (Isaiah 32:1, 2)

The "rock" of Assyria in 31:9 is probably their king. But here is our King. And unlike the megalomaniacs of human power, our Messiah reigns in righteousness (32:1). That's the operative word. His *righteous* rule makes him a shelter from the storm. He is a king who comes not to be served but to serve (Mark 10:45). And Isaiah is saying that the Messiah's lordship is what makes us into new people. The newness he brings is the answer to all the failed human ideals littering history. According to 32:3, 4, it's his righteous lordship that takes away our dullness and awakens in us spiritual alertness. He does it through the gospel, as the eyes of our hearts are enlightened, so that we see and sense our hope and riches and power in Christ (Ephesians 1:18, 19).

With these bright new convictions entering our hearts, we are changed, according to verses 5–8. New heroes stand forth as their true worth is recognized. But it's all the effect of the lordship of Christ. It's his nobility that dignifies us. "He . . . plans noble things, and on noble things he stands." We who believe in Jesus should never grovel at the feet of failed human powers. We are dignified by kneeling before the lordship of Christ.

Hear the Word of the Prophet!

> Rise up, you women who are at ease, hear my voice;
>   you complacent daughters, give ear to my speech. (v. 9)

Is Isaiah picking on the women? No. But he is singling them out. As Isaiah writes, it's harvesttime (v. 10), a time of plenty. The houses are joyous, and the city is exultant (v. 13). But Isaiah warns the women that next year the crops will fail (v. 10). They should stop partying and start mourning.

Isaiah sees the women of Jerusalem as blatant illustrations of spiritual complacency. He uses the word "complacent" three times in verses 9–11. There's nothing wrong with a life of quiet pleasantness. We know that from verse 17. But these women were living for the false peace of momentary indulgence.

So here's the situation. The men at the royal court are wringing their hands over Assyria, fretting over a danger that God has already promised to take care of. The women at home can't see beyond the great bargains in the marketplace. They're not worried about anything. They represent the kind of happiness that will kill us—earthly contentment, with no longings for God.

Here's the point. The messianic kingdom is no place for escapist, elitist, selfish materialism. But there is a way back to God. And his way out of our soul-destroying complacency is right here before us. We need to listen to the prophetic gospel with a heart so open that we accept even hard truths calling us to change. God knows our needs so thoroughly that his Word also includes this: "Be wretched and mourn and weep. Let your laughter be turned to mourning and your joy to gloom. Humble yourself before the Lord, *and he will exalt you*" (James 4:9, 10).

The Outpoured Spirit, a New People

> . . . until the Spirit is poured upon us from on high,
>   and the wilderness becomes a fruitful field,
>   and the fruitful field is deemed a forest.
> Then justice will dwell in the wilderness,
>   and righteousness abide in the fruitful field.
> And the effect of righteousness will be peace,
>   and the result of righteousness, quietness and trust forever.
> My people will abide in a peaceful habitation,
>   in secure dwellings, and in quiet resting places. (Isaiah 32:15–18)

The spiritual nature of God reappears as the passage comes full circle. But now we see that *the Spirit of God is super-reality, dominating everything else*. God is promising to pour out his Spirit upon us with life-enriching abundance. This is a major theme in the prophecy of Isaiah. The renewal of God's people is central to his message.[6] He brings it into sharp focus here in chapter 32. And he isn't talking about a little drop of the Spirit here and there. He's talking about God immersing us in a deluge of the Spirit. He's talking about an outpouring that washes all complacency away like a flood, replacing that counterfeit joy with the real joy of peace, quietness, and trust forever.

God is keeping this promise. He's been doing so for 2,000 years, and sometimes with astonishing abundance. He began at Pentecost (Acts 2), and he continues to pour out his Spirit today. He pours his very love into our hearts through the Holy Spirit, so that we boast in our sufferings with an unbeatable hope (Romans 5:3–5). Our part is to be open to the Spirit, to pray for and welcome the outpouring of the Holy Spirit. The lordship of Christ and the outpouring of the Spirit are the secret power of God's people, *and nothing else is.*

The Undeniable Truth of God

> And it will hail when the forest falls down,
>   and the city will be utterly laid low.
> Happy are you who sow beside all waters,
>   who let the feet of the ox and the donkey range free. (Isaiah 32:19, 20)

Isaiah puts two undeniable truths side by side. He has been saying, "You don't need to run off to any Egypt. God will save you." Now he concludes by saying two things. First, in 32:19 the newness that God brings does not leave our familiar world unchanged. The "forest" of Assyria is cut down, and the "city" of Zion is humbled. Whenever God moves, both the world and the church are in for some surprises. The blessing of God does not work around the world and the church as they presently are; the blessing of God remakes all things. But the upheaval of his blessing is worth it.

That is Isaiah's second truth. In 32:20 he paints a picture of a peaceful, richly supplied, pastoral scene, with plenty of water and such a bumper crop that nobody even bothers to chase the animals out of the fields. It's an Old Testament way of saying, "All things are yours, whether . . . the world or life or death or the present or the future—all are yours, and you are Christ's, and Christ is God's" (1 Corinthians 3:21b–23). When our hearts cherish a sense of personal possession in God, we need no more.

God is spirit. Let's not factor him out. The benefits of an intangible ally are endless. But at the end of the day, the most direct way into your heart is the truth that the God who is spirit humbled himself and became flesh for you (John 1:14). The God who is all-powerful became weak for you. The God who is wise became foolish for you, at his cross. Stop treating him as a beautiful theory. Turn to him. Listen to him. Trust him. He promises to save you, very really.

21

Finding God in Failure

ISAIAH 33

C. S. LEWIS WAS AN ATHEIST who became a Christian. He tells us about the very moment of his conversion:

> You must picture me alone in that room in Magdalen, night after night, feeling, whenever my mind lifted even for a second from my work, the steady, unrelenting approach of Him whom I so earnestly desired not to meet. That which I greatly feared had at last come upon me. In the Trinity Term of 1929 I gave in, and admitted that God was God, and knelt and prayed: perhaps, that night, the most dejected and reluctant convert in all England. I did not then see what is now the most shining and obvious thing; the Divine humility which will accept a convert even on such terms. The Prodigal Son at least walked home on his own feet. But who can duly adore that Love which will open the high gates to a prodigal who is brought in kicking, struggling, resentful, and darting his eyes in every direction for a chance to escape?[1]

Lewis is speaking for us all. We come to God reluctantly. We return to God reluctantly. But who can help but adore the divine humility that receives reluctant penitents with joyful enthusiasm (Luke 15:7, 10)? God is more ready to meet us than we are to meet him.

Isaiah 33 came out of a setting where God's people were turning back to him—not as their great Fountain of all good but as their last resort. Repentance was not their way of life. It was a last-ditch effort to stave off disaster. But God humbly received them anyway.

As we have seen, Judah was being threatened by the Assyrian Empire. God had promised to help them. But they went down to Egypt for help, and

Egypt let them down. So Assyria kept on coming—pushing, reaching, grab-bing. King Hezekiah tried to buy the Assyrians off (2 Kings 18:13–16). He withdrew money from the temple treasury and stripped the gold from the doors of the temple and handed these sacred resources over to the king of Assyria to get him to leave them alone.

We can imagine the scene—the hordes of the Assyrian army surround-ing Jerusalem, filling the landscape out to the horizon. The officials of Judah stand there on the city wall, watching nervously as the chests filled with gold and silver are carried on carts out through the city gate to the Assyrian command center off at a distance. It is humiliating to Judah and doubly dis-honoring to God. His people treat him as a worthless ally and then make *him* pay the bill for their disloyalty. But they don't see it that way. Not yet. What they see is hope: "Finally those Assyrians will let up on us! This will all be over soon." So there goes God's money, God's honor, and their integrity in the form of payment to the Assyrian mafia.

But as they watch from the wall, waiting for the foreign army to pack up their weapons and disassemble their battering rams and fold up their tents, the leaders of Judah begin to realize that the Assyrians aren't going any-where. It's a double-cross. Assyria plans to attack anyway. Judah has made a bargain with the devil. As the truth dawns on them, they finally admit, "We've miscalculated. In fact, we've done everything wrong. Our whole strategy has been wrong. We've offended God. We've weakened ourselves and gained nothing in the deal." They finally realize that they have nothing left but the grace of God. Therefore, to God they go. They can't tell him that they value him as the One from whom all blessings flow. They only value him as their backup plan. But God receives them even on those terms.

That is the setting for Isaiah 33. And what Isaiah reveals here is God's answer to overdue human repentance. What does God say to people who have failed him and are only beginning to get it? Isaiah 33 tells us that the mess we've made of our lives is the very place where God meets us afresh. He isn't put off by the disproportion between our paltry repentance and his overflowing grace. He accepts it, at cost to himself.

Isaiah 33, therefore, is for people who haven't been trusting God. It's for people who are seeing in a new way that they can't treat God as a rabbit's foot *and* experience his power; they can't marginalize God *and* live in the flow of his blessing. Isaiah 33 is for people who've given themselves to all the wrong things and are only now seeing that their lives are fast becoming a lost opportunity. And the message of Isaiah 33 is this: It *is* too late to think that you really honor God. But even now, if you'll come to him just as you are, "your eyes will behold the king [God] in his beauty" (v. 17).

The outline shows us the way back to God: trust (33:1–6) and broken-ness (33:7–12), leading to renewal (33:13–24).

1. God makes a difference, when we trust him (33:1–6)
   - A¹ The destroyer destroyed (33:1)
      - B¹ The Savior prized (33:2)
   - A² The nations scattered (33:3, 4)
      - B² The Lord exalted (33:5, 6)
2. When we own our failures, God asserts his glory (33:7–12)
   - A We say, "We have failed" (33:7–9)
      - B God says, "*Now* I will arise" (33:10–12)
3. Listen! The King will save his people (33:13–24)
   - A¹ The renewing power of practical repentance (33:13–16)
      - B¹ The gladdening vision: the King (33:17–19)
         - C The trusting church at rest (33:20)
      - B² The saving presence: the King (33:21–23)
   - A² The healing power of forgiving grace (33:24)

Our repentance is imperfect—itself a reason for even deeper repentance. But still, repentance does take us back to practical trust in God, it pulls his blessing down upon us, and it replaces our chronic impulses toward self-salvation with the peace of full salvation in Christ alone.

Trust

> Ah, you destroyer,
>> who yourself have not been destroyed,
> you traitor,
>> whom none has betrayed! (Isaiah 33:1)

Assyria is the destroying, double-crossing traitor who seems to be getting away with everything. But in fact the tyrant is doomed. This verse is God's cry of judgment. And I want to show you something I haven't pointed out before. I've said that Isaiah chapters 1—12 highlight God's gracious purpose for his covenant people, chapters 13—27 reveal God's gracious purpose for the nations, and chapters 28—35 argue that God is able to fulfill all his purposes. He has both the grace and the power to do everything he has promised. What I haven't shown you is that chapters 28—35 are marked by a key word, appearing six times, here in 33:1 for the sixth and final time:

> Ah, the proud crown of the drunkards of Ephraim! (28:1)

> Ah, Ariel, Ariel, the city where David encamped! (29:1)

> Ah, you who hide deep from the LORD your counsel. (29:15)

Ah, stubborn children. (30:1)

Woe[2] to those who go down to Egypt for help. (31:1)

Ah, you destroyer. (33:1)

Throughout this section, God is speaking his sovereign will into the world. The word "Ah" marks God's spoken intervention in human affairs. But now in 33:1, instead of confronting his own people Judah, as in the first five uses of this word, God addresses the Assyrian enemy. Why? Because his people are entering into repentance. They've always called him their King, but now they're starting to treat him as their King.

What does repentance sound like? The prophet gives voice to the people's newfound feelings for God:

O LORD, be gracious to us; for you we wait.[3]
  Be our arm every morning,
  our salvation in the time of trouble. (33:2)

How the tune has changed! This is how trusting people speak to God. They say, "The only thing between us and disaster is you, Lord. Our only hope is your strength moment by moment. Our needs are both constant and urgent, but by faith we lay hold of your endless grace, promised in the gospel."

In verse 3 the people look up to God in confidence. They see him in a new way—ruling decisively over everything threatening them (Matthew 8:23–27). They see that all he has to do to scatter the nations is just stand up: "peoples flee when you lift yourself up." And in verse 4 they look out to those nations—the "your" there is plural—with boldness. The powers of evil will be stripped bare and enthusiastically looted. And then in verses 5, 6 the people reaffirm that all they need is God. In other words, now they know that *the key to life is miracle, and by faith that miracle is becoming theirs.*

Here's the point: When we really trust God, lo and behold, we find that he's there! When God is all we have, we find that God is all we need. This is how trusting God changes our experience of God. When we respect him enough to let him take control, he becomes "the stability of your times, abundance of salvation, wisdom, and knowledge" (v. 6). And no one else can give those treasures to you—not even yourself. That is our first step back to God—to start trusting him. Now, our second step.

Brokenness

Behold, their heroes cry in the streets;
  the envoys of peace weep bitterly.

The highways lie waste;
    the traveler ceases.
Covenants are broken;
    cities are despised;
        there is no regard for man. (vv. 7, 8)

Desolation and despair—that is what Isaiah portrays as Judah dissolves in panic. Their peace negotiations have failed. The invader is at the gates. Self-salvation makes a lot of sense, *until you try it*. No one anywhere, even under ideal conditions, has ever figured out how to live well without God. That is the point of verse 9. Not trusting God always blights human existence. Always, everywhere.

The countries mentioned in verse 9 are pleasant places. You know the television commercials of some South Sea island, with a handsome young couple strolling down the beach, and for $1999.00 plus tax that can be you? Well, maybe you do need some time off. But more profoundly, if you were there on that beautiful beach, you would still need God. And being there without God would be hell. And being here or anywhere with God can be heaven.

But when we are defeated, downcast, disgraced, broken, and so disappointed with ourselves and what we've done with our lives, *that is when God enters in*.

"Now I will arise," says the LORD,
    "now I will lift myself up;
        now I will be exalted." (v. 10)

God wants to mark your life with his decisive "Now!" He's saying here, "When you sink to your lowest, that's when I will say, '*Now* we're getting somewhere! *Now* I can help you!'" Then God turns to our "Assyria" and all the powers of evil that would destroy us and speaks their doom (vv. 11, 12). But our part is to "cry in the streets" (v. 7), admitting right out in the open that only God can save us now. The Bible is so clear. "A broken and contrite heart . . . [he] will not despise (Psalm 51:17).[4]

So do you see why, in the ways of God, a sense of failure and weakness and need is essential to his favor upon you? Never outgrow the humility of brokenness before God. In becoming a Christian, you admit that your whole life has been wrong. As you grow in Christ, never leave that realism behind. Your failure is God's opportunity. Your sin is God's moment. Jesus said, "Those who are well have no need of a physician, but those who are sick. . . . I came not to call the righteous, but sinners" (Matthew 9:12, 13). Here is a doctor who calls *us* to schedule an appointment! If you will answer his call, he will exalt himself on your behalf, even at the eleventh hour of your overdue repentance.

Renewal

What we're waking up from, under Isaiah's influence, is the dreamy illusion of our own self-sufficiency. We are coming alive to the all-sufficiency of Christ. And now Isaiah holds before us his vision of the peace, freedom, and joy of belonging to Christ. As Paul puts it, "We . . . boast in God" (Romans 5:11, NRSV). That confident delight is the spirit of Isaiah 33:13–24. But interestingly, a part of this is the conviction of sin—sinners becoming alarmed about themselves. The outline shows that a part of renewal is God wounding our consciences (A^1), but also healing us with forgiveness (A^2). A part of renewal is God bringing down to us the presence of Christ in his glory and fullness (B^1, B^2). And that is how he leads us into peace and joy (C). Sin must be exposed and healed. Christ must become beautiful to us. Then it doesn't matter anymore what the world may do to us. We are safe and rich in Christ.

> The sinners in Zion are afraid;
>   trembling has seized the godless:
> "Who among us can dwell with the consuming fire?
>   Who among us can dwell with everlasting burnings?" (v. 14)

Isaiah is saying that God is holy. God is a fire who will burn forever with consuming intensity. *God is unsafe.* Our problem is, we fear the wrong things. We fear the "Assyrias" of our lives. We blame the world for our problems. So we ask all the wrong questions, like, "Why isn't God helping me? What practical good is God for my life?" But when the truth of God's holiness gets ahold of us, we start asking new questions, like, "Why should God care about me at all? How can a life like mine be compatible with someone like him?" That new sense of God is a big step toward renewal.

Reforming our lives in bold and practical ways would, as verse 16 promises, cause us to "dwell on the heights," secure us in "fortresses of rocks," and fill us with all we need. We can never deserve God's favor. Only Christ deserves good from God. But his grace in Christ does create in us an urgency to reshape our lives, because now we belong to a holy God. Jesus said, "Blessed are those who hunger and thirst for righteousness, for they shall be satisfied" (Matthew 5:6).

Jesus also said, "Blessed are the pure in heart, for they shall see God" (Matthew 5:8). That's the logical connection with where Isaiah goes next.

> Your eyes will behold the king in his beauty;
>   they will see a land that stretches afar. (Isaiah 33:17)

Isaiah is talking about a reversal of our whole perception of reality. Before, all Judah could see and all that mattered was the Assyrians. But they're going to see something new. The eyes of their hearts will be enlightened to see their King in his beauty. And they will then see themselves in their land as secured by a wide margin of safety. They will realize that under the protection of their King, they are safe. The enemy that seemed so overwhelming will finally be perceived with new objectivity and detachment.

> Your heart will muse on the terror:
> "Where is he who counted, where is he who weighed the tribute?
> Where is he who counted the towers?" (v. 18)

The old Assyrian enemy, who stood outside Jerusalem and picked out his priority targets, will be just a memory. Where did he go? When our eyes behold the King in his beauty, we see everything else in his light, we break out of our nervous addiction to crisis and self-salvation and start to glorify and enjoy God. The Holy Spirit does this in us. He makes Jesus glorious to our hearts as we behold him in the gospel (2 Corinthians 3:18).

Looking at our lives with our focus on Christ as the only one finally to be reckoned with, the only one whose opinion really matters, we taste something of the peace, rest, and joy of Heaven itself.

> Behold Zion, the city of our appointed feasts!
> Your eyes will see Jerusalem,
> an untroubled habitation, an immovable tent,
> whose stakes will never be plucked up,
> nor will any of its cords be broken. (Isaiah 33:20)[5]

The crisis of life is over. We find rest, not because we can cope with our attackers but because we are at peace with God. Isaiah portrays how delightful it is when we are enjoying God. We *will* do so perfectly in Heaven, and we *can* imperfectly but really right now. Verse 20 takes us to the heart of the message of Isaiah: The church *will* be transformed into gladly, solidly God-trusting people, who can face anything with him as their Savior.[6] That is where God is taking his believing people, and he invites you to be a part of it.

Verses 17–19 describe the King taking us into a *land* with secure borders. Now verses 21–23 match that by describing the presence of our King as creating "broad *rivers* and *streams*"—in other words, no attack by sea. These two opposites, land and sea, argue how fully our King cares for us. We delight ourselves in his greatness.

> For the Lord is our judge; the LORD is our lawgiver;
> the LORD is our king; he will save us. (v. 22)

And what are *we* in this prophetic scenario? According to verse 23, the church is a ship of state, but a drifting hulk, with cords hanging loose and so forth. And this floating disaster wins the victory and takes the spoils. Why? The Lord is our King; he will save us.

Isaiah's final word is what every failure must remember. The God who wounds us over our sins also heals us.

> And no inhabitant shall say, "I am sick";
> the people who dwell there will be forgiven their iniquity. (v. 24)

Isaiah uses a Hebrew idiom that makes forgiveness vividly graphic. It suggests that when God forgives our iniquity, *he bears it away*. The same wording appears in Leviticus 16 about Israel's annual Day of Atonement:

> Aaron shall lay both his hands on the head of the live goat, and confess over it all the iniquities of the people of Israel, and all their transgressions, all their sins. And he shall put them on the head of the goat and send it away into the wilderness. . . . The goat shall bear all their iniquities on itself to a remote area. (vv. 21, 22)

All our happiness depends on this, because the only final crisis in our existence is our guilt before a holy God. Have your sins been forgiven? Has *God* borne them away? Or are you still denying them and thereby clinging to them and reinforcing their power over you? Two thousand years ago, on a cross outside Jerusalem, there was a Goat who bore the guilt of others far away. God says that if we trust him to bear all our guilt away, it's never coming back. And that startling sense of acceptance in Christ is how we become the trusting people we should be, the broken people we should be, and the renewed people we should be. That's when nothing can hold us back from newness of life, not even our own second-rate repentance.

22

The Two Final Outcomes

ISAIAH 34—35

ISAIAH LEADS US NOW TO THE POINT of personal decision. He has been showing us God and ourselves with new clarity. What has Isaiah told us about God? God is our most loyal ally in the struggle of life. He has made promises to us. He has proven himself already. He deserves to be trusted. What has Isaiah told us about ourselves? We barely trust God. God is faithful, but we are guarded. We need to make up our minds. Are we going to live by faith in God or by faith in ourselves? Will God save us, or do we have to save ourselves?

God defends us against our ultimate enemy, our own moral guilt. He rescues us from condemnation by justifying us on the basis of what Christ deserves, not on the basis of what we deserve. God treats us in a way that has nothing to do with what we deserve. But do we allow ourselves to enjoy our acceptance before a holy God? Or are we constantly on edge, wondering how he might punish us next? Martin Luther wrote:

> Let it not be tedious to you if we repeat these things that at other times we teach, preach, sing and set forth in writing. For if we lose the doctrine of justification, we lose everything. . . . It cannot be beaten into our ears too much. Yes, though we learn it and understand it well, still no one takes hold of it perfectly or believes it with all his heart, so frail a thing is our flesh and disobedient to the Spirit.[1]

The default setting in our hearts is to treat God as a shaky person, while we trot off to other saviors for reassurance. We don't think of it that way, because we don't see that the category of "salvation" is the key to everything. Salvation is what we are always looking for, even in the wrong places. But true salvation is simply God entering into our lives with his grace in Christ to meet all our needs. And Isaiah has been urging us to *treat* God as a faithful Savior, so that we look like people who have actually been saved from something. Then our faith will be convincing.

Isaiah now moves us toward closure. Assyria fades from view, and the prophet addresses the whole world (34:1). The one nation he does mention is, surprisingly, Edom (34:5, 6, 9). Why? Because Edom typifies the whole world. When the infant nation of Israel was journeying toward the Promised Land, they requested passage through Edom (Numbers 20:14–21). They even offered to pay for the water they would drink along the way. And why shouldn't Edom be open to Israel? They were related. Jacob and Esau, the forefathers of these two nations, were brothers (Genesis 25:21–26). But Edom held a grudge against Israel (Genesis 27), and they refused to let them through. Edom tried to block the salvation that God was bringing into the world. Edom, then, is the antithesis to God's pilgrim people. That is why Isaiah singles out Edom. The ethos of the Edomite culture is the spirit of the whole world, a spirit that finds its salvation in the resources of this temporal, physical order. We have to get past Edom to be saved by God. And Isaiah is saying to us now, "I want you to listen in to what God has to say to this world about the great and final day of judgment. Is *that* what you want to be a part of? Or will you set your heart on a salvation from outside this world, coming only from God?" Chapter 34 shows us what will become of everyone who buys into this world, and chapter 35 shows us what will become of everyone who banks everything on the promised salvation of God.

In these two chapters Isaiah leads us by the hand all the way out to the brink of future history, where time merges into eternity. He shows us the seamless connection between what we embrace now and what we will have then. He lifts his eyes from his own times in the eighth century B.C. to see how things will finally end up "forever and ever" (34:10). He sees this world order deconstructed (34:11, 12), human existence renewed (35:1, 2), God's people no longer enfeebled by sin (35:5, 6), all tears wiped away from their eyes (35:10). His point is this: The salvation you prefer now, whether earthly or heavenly, is shaping who you are and which direction you will go forever.

You need to understand that Hell or Heaven will be, in one sense, the eternal extension of the deepest, truest you that you become in this life. So here is the most important question of your existence: What are you *becoming*? Whatever you are becoming reveals where you are going. If you are savoring by faith a salvation and fullness from God, you are already on your way to what Isaiah calls Zion in chapter 35. But if you choose not to live by faith in this world, Isaiah 34 is showing you your future.

What if God does leave you to yourself? What if God doesn't intervene to save you from yourself and Isaiah 34 writes your final chapter? What if that itching envy in your heart, that bitterness eating away inside you, that anger raging inside you, your ungrateful self for whom nothing is ever good enough, the you lurking in the fantasy twilight of lust, the you buried alive in the coffin of greed, the you that's too sophisticated for childlike delight in God—*what if God does not save you?* The you that you are becoming now is what you will be forever. Unless God saves you, you will eventually find that you cannot stop anymore. And the grumbling and blaming and all the rest will take over and churn on forever like a machine, and you won't be able to stop and rest. That hell is when you become the photographic negative of what you were meant to be when God made you.[2] God says, "I have no pleasure in the death of the wicked, but that the wicked turn from his way and live; turn back, turn back from your evil ways, for why will you die, O house of Israel?" (Ezekiel 33:11).

And God *can* save you. He *wants* you to be a part of the Isaiah 35 scenario. If you will turn to him, he will make the difference, all by himself. Salvation is God liberating the soul from the habits of self-focus. Salvation is God clearing away this tangled undergrowth of self-absorption forever. Salvation is God replacing all this dark complication with something new and simple and beautiful, flooding the human soul with a sense of his glory. That is how we obtain gladness and joy. That is how sorrow and sighing flee away. So, let God save you. Your heavenly joy will begin even now (1 Peter 1:8, 9).

Isaiah structures his text to make the alternatives unmistakably clear. We need it that way.

1. Judgment: God, not this world, is the one to fear (34:1–17)
    A[1] Listen to what God has planned! (34:1)
        B[1] The resources of the Lord (34:2–10)
        B[2] The unmaking of this world (34:11–15)
    A[2] Read what God has determined! (34:16, 17)
2. Salvation: God, not this world, is the one to hope in (35:1–10)
    A[1] The desert blossoms with joyful song (35:1, 2)
        B[1] Encourage one another with this hope! (35:3, 4)
            C God's people *will* sing for joy (35:5, 6a)
        B[2] God can do the impossible! (35:6b, 7)
    A[2] The way home leads to joyful song (35:8–10)

It's clear. There is judgment (chapter 34), there is salvation (chapter 35), and you must choose God's salvation to avoid God's judgment.

Judgment

> Draw near, O nations, to hear,
>   and give attention, O peoples!
> Let the world hear, and all that fills it;
>   the world, and all that comes from it. (Isaiah 34:1)

It is not abusive to tell people about the judgment of God. God *wants* everyone to know. Francis Schaeffer used to say that if he had one hour to explain the gospel to someone, he would spend the first fifty minutes on the bad news of judgment and then the last ten minutes on the good news of salvation, because without the context of judgment we don't appreciate or even understand salvation.

God wants us to stop and think. What does it mean to live in a universe where God judges evil? We fear the wrong things. We fear looking bad in the eyes of people. But what do they matter? The God who will either judge us or save us has four resources, according to 34:2–10:

> For the LORD has rage against all the nations.[3] (v. 2)

> The LORD has a sword; it is sated with blood. (v. 6)

> For the LORD has a sacrifice in Bozrah. (v. 6)

> For the LORD has a day of vengeance. (v. 8)

The God with whom we have to deal has four things going for him: "rage," "a sword," "a sacrifice," and "a day of vengeance." What does that tell us?

First, on that great and final day, the wrath of God will explode upon the world like the bursting of a dam, with the mountains dissolving in mudslides of human blood (v. 3). God is patient with human evil, more patient than we would be. He is giving everyone a chance. But his patience will have an end, because he is also just, more just than we are, more just than we wish he would be. Secondly, the sword of God will descend from Heaven. And how can we run from that? What canopy of defense can deflect the tip of the sword of God? Thirdly, there will be a final sacrifice. All the moral guilt not paid for by the sacrifice of Christ will be paid for by the guilty themselves. *Someone* will be sacrificed for your sins, either Christ as your substitute or you yourself. But God *will* balance out the scales of justice in your case. Fourthly, all this terrible finality has actually been scheduled on the calendar of this human history in which we are living. The Lord has a day. It is coming. God will not leave things hanging forever. He will vindicate the faith of everyone who trusts him ("for the cause of Zion," v. 8). And the social order we see around us right now, so impressive, so formidable, will melt into a volcanic wasteland (vv. 9, 10). If this is who God is, what kind of people should we be (2 Peter 3:11–13)?

But Isaiah doesn't let up on us yet. In 34:11–15 he does something we don't expect. We look at the smoking ruins of verses 9, 10 and think it can't get any worse. It's not a picture of Sodom and Gomorrah under fire and brimstone, but this time the whole world. *What next?* There is more, because the judgment of God is not merely extinction. The judgment of God not only reduces stylish and powerful evil to smoking ash; his judgment also turns self-salvation into a kind of tragic parody of its former self. In verses 11–15 the prophetic eye sees this world of human pride devolving into the haunt of creepy animals and overgrown with thorns. It is made unfit for human habitation, like a rat-infested, condemned building. And the most chilling thing about it is the precision with which God will unmake the world-culture we live in now.

> He shall stretch the line of confusion over it,
>   and the plumb line of emptiness. (v. 11b)

Isaiah is not condemning God's good creation. He is thinking of the human social order, the doomed Edom of verses 5, 6, 9, the human kingdom of verse 12 that comes to nothing. What does God intend to do about that social order? The prophet sees God busily at work as a construction worker—or, better, a *de*construction worker. God puts on his hard hat, bends over the society that man is assembling with such effort and brilliance, this massive project minimizing dependence on God, and instead of building it up further he reverses it to nothingness. The words "confusion" and "emptiness" appear also in the creation account: "The earth was *without form* and *void*" (Genesis 1:2). Isaiah borrows those words from Genesis and loads them into his vision here, as God hits the rewind button to reverse into disorder the system that has so long distorted God's good order for our lives and has so long disregarded Christ. God will destroy it with a precision that overlooks nothing. He will never make peace with human society outside of Christ. It's too corrupt.

Isaiah looks us straight in the eye, reads our minds, and says, "Don't hold out for God to change his mind. Don't think God might lose his nerve. It won't happen. There is no Plan B. You *must* reckon with the finality and the detail of the judgment of God."

> Seek and read from the book of the LORD:
>   Not one of these shall be missing;

none shall be without her mate.
For the mouth of the LORD has commanded,
    and his Spirit has gathered them. (v. 16)

You can choose not to live by faith in God, but you cannot choose to evade the consequences. Lance Armstrong is a great athlete, a seven-time winner of the Tour de France, and a courageous survivor of cancer. We all admire him. But when his life was in danger, he rated his chances this way:

> Quite simply, I believed I had a responsibility to be a good person, and that meant fair, honest, hardworking, and honorable. If I did that, if I was good to my family, true to my friends, if I gave back to my community or to some cause, if I wasn't a liar, a cheat, or a thief, then I believed that should be enough. At the end of the day, if there was indeed some Body or presence standing there to judge me, I hope I would be judged on whether I had lived a true life, not on whether I believed in a certain book, or whether I'd been baptized. If there was indeed a God at the end of my days, I hoped he didn't say, "But you were never a Christian, so you're going the other way from heaven." If so, I was going to reply, "You know what? You're right. Fine."[4]

Do we know who we are? Do we know who God is? Nobody will get the last word in on God.

"The good life" turning into an eternally barren desert—that is where God-neglect takes us (Isaiah 34). But if you will put your trust in God, your desert will be transformed into a garden. That is what the grace of God can do (Isaiah 35). Each one of us is moving in one of these two directions, either into judgment or into salvation. What God *wants* is to save you.

Salvation

The wilderness and the dry land shall be glad;
    the desert shall rejoice and blossom like the crocus;
it shall blossom abundantly
    and rejoice with joy and singing.
The glory of Lebanon shall be given to it,
    the majesty of Carmel and Sharon.
They shall see the glory of the LORD,
    the majesty of our God. (Isaiah 35:1, 2)

God starts his renewing work of grace in the desert of our real lives. How could it be otherwise? A dreary desert is what we are. But God is able to give lush growth and life and joyful song. Joy pervades chapter 35, because salvation is not just when we stop being bad; salvation is when we delight in God's glory and majesty. What must he be, if the mere sight of him transforms us from death into life? It is so foolish to hold God at arm's length. He himself is the desire of your heart. And he wants you to see his glory, both now by faith and in Heaven face to face.

How does God show himself now? Through the ministry of the gospel: "For God, who said, 'Let light shine out of darkness,' has shone in our hearts to give the light of the knowledge of the glory of God in the face of Jesus Christ" (2 Corinthians 4:6). We see God's glory in the face of Jesus. And we see the face of Jesus as the Holy Spirit makes him real to us through his Word—how Christ is an overflowing fountain for thirsty sinners, how Christ is their wealth and honor and wisdom and happiness, how Christ's righteousness covers all their guilt, how he is a power to conquer all their sins, a purity to wash away all their filth, and their spring of eternal freshness. They see in Christ a fullness to satisfy them forever. And the believing heart thrives in this new awareness of Jesus Christ.

We should help one another to seek him, to go hard after him, to live as confident people because of his promises.

> Strengthen the weak hands,
>   and make firm the feeble knees.
> Say to those who have an anxious heart,
>   "Be strong; fear not!
> Behold, your God
>   will come with vengeance,
> with the recompense of God.
>   He will come and save you." (Isaiah 35:3, 4)

Encouragement is one of the most important ways God spreads his goodness in our direction (2 Corinthians 1:3–7). And he wants us to encourage one another to look for new blessing from God. If what we've experienced thus far is all we can expect, that would be demoralizing. But God's great goodness is what puts the thrill into life. There is more for us in Christ than we have yet apprehended—always. Following Christ, we are never at a dead end, but always at a threshold. Isaiah is calling us to create that atmosphere of expectancy, because God is coming to us with fullness of salvation.

> Then the eyes of the blind shall be opened,
>   and the ears of the deaf unstopped;
> then shall the lame man leap like a deer,
>   and the tongue of the mute sing for joy. (Isaiah 35:5, 6a)

What do we contribute to this beautiful outcome? Blindness, deafness, lameness, and silence. What does God contribute? Sight, sound, agility, and joyful song. Maybe you know how Charles Wesley described the impact of the gospel: "Hear him, ye deaf; his praise, ye dumb, your loosened tongues employ; ye blind, behold your Savior come; and leap, ye lame, for joy." This is what God does. It is his professional business to make spiritual cripples into world-beaters. And his motivating power is joy.

Not only will he renew you, if you will trust him, he also promises a new, life-enriching environment.

> For waters break forth in the wilderness,
>   and streams in the desert;
> the burning sand shall become a pool,
>   and the thirsty ground springs of water. (vv. 6b, 7a)

We should never give up, no matter what we or others have done. "The way of man is to make the inhabited uninhabitable; the way of God is to take the barren and make it abundant."[5] In other words, what we spoil, God renews. He does it through the Holy Spirit, *breaking forth* into our hearts with saving, satisfying fullness. In fact, God will restore nature itself.

> And a highway shall be there,
>   and it shall be called the Way of Holiness;
> the unclean shall not pass over it.
>   It shall belong to those who walk on the way;
>   even if they are fools, they shall not go astray.
> No lion shall be there,
>   nor shall any ravenous beast come up on it;
> they shall not be found there,
>   but the redeemed shall walk there. (vv. 8, 9)

Isaiah is thinking of a raised causeway, literally a *high* way, clearly visible. God makes it so obvious that even fools can find their way. But "the unclean," however brilliant, will find no place there, because the way into this new order that God is creating is holiness. Nor will any "ravenous beast" wander along. Think of rats scurrying off a ship, spreading their fleas and infectious diseases to the port city. In our present world we have to hold our breath and get inoculations and lock our doors. But God has a better world for "the redeemed," the people he has taken on as his personal responsibility. That is what it means to be redeemed. Christ pays the price *for* you. You get in free. That's the deal. Where does it get you?

And the ransomed of the LORD shall return
   and come to Zion with singing;
everlasting joy shall be upon their heads;
   they shall obtain gladness and joy,
   and sorrow and sighing shall flee away. (v. 10)

The ESV reads, "they shall obtain gladness and joy." But the NIV may be closer to Isaiah's intent with "gladness and joy will overtake them." The Hebrew verb carries this force in Deuteronomy 28:2, where the blessings of God "overtake" his people.[6] Isaiah is saying that, on the one hand, intense joy will come over us. On the other hand, all our sadness will hightail it forever.

All our lives we've just wanted to be happy. But all our lives something has always spoiled it. God is saying, "Trust me enough to follow me, and I will bring you home with singing. I will overwhelm you with a joy unbroken and unbreakable, and your sorrow and sighing will run for it!"

Some people are content with the self-importance and pettiness and materialism of this present evil age. They fill their bellies, their bank accounts, and their egos with the salvations of this world. They will go on forever discovering how empty such fullness really is. There are others whose hearts yearn for something more. They long for God's salvation. And they will receive it, not because they deserve it but because Jesus lived and died for them. And though the pursuit of their joy in Christ may cost them everything here in this world, they don't mind. They gladly leave it behind and press on toward a joy that can never end.

Two kinds of people, two destinations. Who are you? What are you *becoming*?

23

In Whom Do You
Now Trust?

ISAIAH 36:1—37:7

HERE IS THE CHRISTIAN LIFE in just six words: "Not knowing where" (Hebrews 11:8), "I know whom" (2 Timothy 1:12). Abraham didn't know where God was leading him, but he didn't need to know where. Like Paul, he knew whom he had believed. And so it is with us. We don't know where, but we know whom, and that's enough.

If you always have to know where and what and when and how and so forth, all in advance, before you obey God, then you are not living by faith in God. Living by faith in God accepts ambiguity without getting nervous, because God is the one in charge. "Not knowing where, I know whom"— that's Christianity.

The key to Isaiah 36:1—37:7 is the taunt "In whom do you now trust?" (36:5). We always live on the cutting edge of faith, either faith in God or faith in something else. And yesterday's faith in God belongs to yesterday. In whom do you *now* trust? In the struggle you are facing *now*, in whom do you trust?

We come inevitably to those moments in life when nothing will suffice but what is directly and immediately of God. After we've done all we can and should, and life demands of us still more, nothing but God himself will suffice. Whatever your challenge may be right now, God is with you in it. Trust him. Look for him. He will not fail you.

We need to keep our heads because other forces cloud our vision of God and complicate our thinking and pressure us not to take him at his word but to shave the radical edge off our faith. There is always some voice whispering to us that God is not a resource, he is a problem. So the question before us is both profound and urgent. Whose voice will we believe, whose wisdom will we follow, whose hope will we cherish and live for? In whom do we now trust?

Right now "two worlds exist simultaneously, unblendable but also inseparable"[1]—this world dominated by man, and the higher world of the Creator, the eternal world. These two worlds are in conflict. Everyone is caught up in this spiritual tension, whether they know it or not. This present age tells us that this life is our only chance for happiness, that human power is the only reality that counts, that we can bank on only what we can see right before us. But that way of thinking is ruinous. It kills our sense of higher purpose. It quenches the Holy Spirit. It reduces us to mediocrity. It has an appearance of wisdom, but inevitably it lets us down.

Christians understand that there is another way to live, drawing strength from that higher world. We call it living by faith. What do we mean by that? We mean living as if God really exists and really rewards those who seek him (Hebrews 11:6). We mean living by God's promises as the bedrock under our feet while everything else is shifting around us. But sometimes Christians have vague ideas about how that works out. Sometimes Christians live by a creedal faith rather than a daring faith. And Isaiah is talking about an audacious faith that the world cannot understand.

A creedal faith says, "I believe in God the Father Almighty" and so forth. That's good. What if we *didn't* believe that? We'd really be in trouble. But a creedal faith is a beginning point only. After all, if people who do *not* believe in God the Father Almighty often live like people who do believe in God the Father Almighty, then living by faith must be more profound than a creed. God is calling us to live by a daring faith because the world is daring us to live by faith in God. That is what Isaiah shows us—human skepticism throwing down the gauntlet before believers in God.

Isaiah is beginning a new section of his book. We can tell just by looking at the page of our Bibles. For the most part, chapters 1—35 are Hebrew poetry, with its parallel structure: an A-line, then a B-line, and sometimes a C-line, over and over again. Chapters 40—66 are also poetic in form. But chapters 36—39 are framed in historical narrative. This is prose, for the most part. These historical chapters form a bridge between the first and second major sections of the book. What we are reading here is the dramatization of truth in the theater of human events. That is why I have outlined the passage in terms of Acts and Scenes. Our lives are telling a story. We are acting out our beliefs, whatever they may be. Isaiah is calling us to live out a daring faith in God, whatever the opposition. The structure of the text is this:

Act One: The Ultimatum (36:1–21)
    Scene One: The bullying challenge (36:1–10)
        Point One: The inescapable necessity of a daring trust (36:1–3)
        Point Two: The worldly assault on a daring trust (36:4–10)
    Scene Two: The feeble response (36:11, 12)
    Scene Three: The intensified challenge (36:13–21)
        Point One: A counterfeit deliverance offered as real (36:13–17)
        Point Two: A real deliverance mocked as futile (36:18–21)
Act Two: The Promise (36:22—37:7)
    Scene One: The God with whom we always have to deal (36:22—37:4)
    Scene Two: The God who will defend his own cause (37:5–7)

Isaiah has been urging us, in chapters 28—35, to trust God. Now in chapters 36—39 he answers an objection. Does faith work right here, right now, or is faith just a remote vindication at the End Times when Christ returns? Is faith in God a smart policy for real life in the here and now? Does God intervene in our experience? Is God the King of this world we live in today? And the answer is, yes, God is with us even now. We have a reason to stand up with a bold faith in God. In fact, he expects us to.

Act One: The Ultimatum

It is the year 701 B.C. The army of Sennacherib is swarming over Judah like a horde of Tolkienian Orcs, and only Jerusalem remains (Isaiah 8:8). Here is the setting:

> And the king of Assyria sent the Rabshakeh[2] from Lachish to King Hezekiah at Jerusalem, with a great army. And he stood by the conduit of the upper pool on the highway to the Washer's Field. (Isaiah 36:2)

That location has a familiar ring to it, doesn't it? Where have we seen that before? It takes us back to an earlier episode in Isaiah's prophecy:

> And the Lord said to Isaiah, "Go out to meet Ahaz, you and Shear-jashub your son, at the end of the conduit of the upper pool on the highway to the Washer's Field." (7:3)

Thirty-four years earlier, Isaiah had met King Ahaz, the father of King Hezekiah, at this same place, at another moment when faith was being tested. Same place, same crisis. And Ahaz, in his day, decided not to trust God. But his unbelief didn't make God go away. It only intensified the crisis when it resurfaced later. Now God visits his people again with the question that always lies before us: "In whom do you now trust?"

Obviously, the Rabshakeh doesn't intend to frame the question so helpfully. He's waging psychological warfare against Judah. But his speech in 36:4–10 uses the word "trust" seven times,[3] making it the key word. The Arabic cognate to this Hebrew word means to throw oneself down on one's face, to lie extended on the ground.[4] Trust is a deep and entire dependence.

The Rabshakeh asks a revealing question: "Do you think that mere words are strategy and power for war?" (v. 5). "Mere words" stands in contrast with "a great army" (v. 2). Is Hezekiah so crazy as to confront a great army with mere words? That takes us to the heart of the matter. Is the gospel a safe place to take your stand amid the brutal realities of this world? Are God's promises "strategy and power for war," or are they "mere words"? Is the secret to life money, good looks, health, brains, acceptance in the right circles, degrees from the right schools, and all the other mechanisms of self-empowerment we use to get a jump on others, or is God our strong ally? When the human props are kicked out from beneath us, do we have anything left to stand on? That is *the* question of the book of Isaiah and of our lives.

The answer depends on who God is. The Bible says he is "the God . . . who gives life to the dead and calls into existence the things that do not exist" (Romans 4:17). If that is who God is, we can turn the Rabshakeh's question right around: Do you think that mere human empowerment, without God, is a realistic strategy for the challenge of life?

The answer also depends on who God's rivals are. The king of Assyria asks, "In whom do you now trust, that you have rebelled against me?" (36:5). Trust and loyalty always go together. We obey whoever or whatever we trust. Trust is more than creedal; it is practical. It stirs up controversy and conflict, because we yield to the one we trust, and we resist the one we don't trust. Again, the king of Assyria doesn't intend to be helpful by his arrogant questions. He has such a low view of God and such an inflated view of himself, he can't imagine anyone so brash as to defy him. But he does end up defining the source of daring Christian rebellion—a conviction that God is the best ally anyone can find.

In 36:6–10 the swashbuckling Rabshakeh brags on with a mixture of half-truths, spin, and intimidation. There are always arguments against living by faith in God. They can be effective too. In verses 11, 12 the officials of Judah plead with the Rabshakeh to stop speaking in Hebrew and to use Aramaic, the language of diplomatic protocol. They don't want the common people to know how bad the situation really is. Now the Assyrian knows he has them on the run! He presses his advantage by hinting at the hellish conditions of a full siege—the people doomed "to eat their own dung and drink their own urine" (v. 12). He hopes the people of Jerusalem have heard enough. Maybe now they'll rise up against their leaders and demand an immediate surrender.

Next the Rabshakeh turns up the volume (vv. 13–21). The key word in this scene is "deliver," which also occurs seven times. To "deliver" means to extract, to draw out, to snatch away from danger. What Isaiah wants us to see is how the Rabshakeh parodies God's promises of deliverance. Verse 14: "Thus says the king." Verse 16: "Thus says the king of Assyria." The Rabshakeh speaks in the form of a royal decree. But there is another royal decree: "Thus says the LORD" (37:6). Two kings, two decrees, both offering deliverance. The Rabshakeh is a false prophet, offering a false peace. He's saying, in 36:13–17, "You know what living under siege is like. But you don't have to eat your own dung and drink your own urine. This can all be over so soon, so easily. Just give in, and my king will give you peace and security and your own land." Do you see the devilish logic in that? God had promised his people peace and security and their own land. But a counterfeit deliverance is being dangled in front of God's people. "Thus says the king of Assyria: Make your peace with me and come out to me" (36:16). One of the devil's tactics is to offer us what seems a lot like the blessing of God. All he asks is that we make peace with evil and surrender.

But when, in 36:18–21, the Rabshakeh mocks the Lord as just another idol, he seals his own fate.

> "Beware lest Hezekiah mislead you by saying, 'The Lord will deliver us.'
> Has any of the gods of the nations delivered his land out of the hand of the
> king of Assyria?" (v. 18)

Evil eventually overplays its hand. The human arrogance blindly challenging God may appear powerful, but it cannot succeed here in God's world. The Lord is not one more idol. He is not even the greatest of this world's gods. He is of another order entirely. He is from beyond this world, and he will have the whole world know it. Our part is to honor him by trusting him as the true God that he is. And he enters in with real deliverance through our bold faith.

Act Two: The Promise

This is one of the turning points in the history of God's people. They are at their end, surrounded by an overwhelmingly superior force. The enemy is gloating over royal Jerusalem, saying "Checkmate!" What move will Judah make next? All they have left is God. Will they try to rescue their pride and negotiate their own way out of this? Or, for the first time in a long time, will they stop faking it and go deeper with God?

To his lasting credit, Hezekiah gets real with God, unlike his father Ahaz. He goes into the house of the Lord (37:1). He understands that what really matters is not his relationship with the king of Assyria but his relationship with the King of Heaven. He can see that nothing will suffice but what is directly and immediately of God. His faith is no facile optimism. We know that because he tears his clothes and puts on sackcloth. He is soberly realistic about what is happening. He disregards appearances. He turns to God in deep need.

King Hezekiah wants a word from God. So he sends for Isaiah with a message of humble honesty.

> "This day is a day of distress, of rebuke, and of disgrace; children have come
> to the point of birth, and there is no strength to bring them forth." (v. 3)

In other words, "We admit it. We've failed. We are not living proof of the reality of God. We've produced nothing but exhaustion. We must be delivered, but we have no strength to do it ourselves."

Hezekiah's first concern is the honor of God in the world. The king of Assyria is "mock[ing] the living God" (v. 4). *And Judah is the reason for it.* Hezekiah's heart is breaking for the right reason. That's when God comes with a word of promise.

> "Thus says the Lord: Do not be afraid because of the words that you have
> heard, with which the young men of the king of Assyria have reviled me.
> Behold, I will put a spirit in him, so that he shall hear a rumor and return
> to his own land, and I will make him fall by the sword in his own land."
> (vv. 6, 7)

"The great king, the king of Assyria" (36:4)—to little Judah, this man was "as if Nature had intended to make a gorilla, and had changed its mind at the last moment."[5] But how does God handle him? Not by meeting his force with force. God is subtle. He flies in under this man's radar, enters into his psyche, and changes his mood. God sends him a rumor, a mere whisper, that gets him worried. And Mr. Bigshot picks up, goes home, and is killed in his own place of safety (v. 38). The people of Judah don't go out and whip the Assyrians by their own force of arms. God does it for them with a spiritual, irresistible strategy. That is how God dispatches the blasphemer who had boasted, "Do you think that mere words are strategy and power for war?" (36:5). The "mere words" of a rumor did him in!

There's the story. Why is it in the Bible? Why is this in the permanent, public record of God's Word? Because unbelief still sneers at faith in God, we still lose our nerve, and God is still there to deliver us if we'll get real with him. He only wants us to trust him with a daring faith.

If no one ever thinks we're crazy for the way we stick our necks out in trusting the promises of God, are we really living by faith? If no one ever asks us to explain the hope that is in us (1 Peter 3:15), is our hope any different from their hope? Is our Christianity so audacious that it requires nothing less than a religious conversion to enter in? One reason we see so few conversions today is that our Christianity isn't an alternative to convert *to*. It's padded, safe, predictable worldliness with occasional stop-offs at church. We think it's God's job to ensure our undisturbed routines. God thinks it's our job to prove how real he is in the real world today.

We are often weak. But to get fresh courage, we don't have to look inside ourselves and ask, "How much faith do I have?" We should look to God and ask, "What new step of audacious obedience do you want me to take right now? How can my life be a prophetic statement to my generation that you are a reliable Savior, as you've promised?" Thinking in terms of *God first*, we will find new courage.[6]

A passage like this raises searching questions. For example, do our committees and boards at church make decisions by a bold faith? In our homes, do we raise our children to live with boldness? Personally, when was the last time you made a major decision that was so clearly of God and so clearly not of yourself that your conclusion actually surprised you? Are we shocking anybody by our faith? If God were to show us in one instant the full meaning of living by faith, we might all gasp and say, "Nobody can live that way, not in this world." That's why he keeps throwing our lives into upheaval. He wants us to experience what it's like for him to come through when the only thing that will suffice is what is directly and immediately of God. He wants us to be living proof that he is real, as we dare to treat him as the greatest ally in the universe.

During a time when God was doing a deep work of renewal in the life of Francis Schaeffer, he asked his wife,

> "Edith, I wonder what would happen to most churches and Christian work if we awakened tomorrow, and everything concerning the reality and work of the Holy Spirit, and everything concerning prayer, were removed from the Bible. I don't mean just ignored, but actually cut out—disappeared. I wonder how much difference it would make?" We concluded it would not make much difference in many board meetings, committee meetings, decisions and activities.[7]

When God led the Schaeffers to begin the L'Abri ministry in Switzerland, they trusted him to be God to them in specific ways. Mrs. Schaeffer writes:

> This is what we felt we were being led to do: to ask God that our work, and our lives, be a demonstration that he does exist. . . . We wanted a

demonstration of the fact that God is able in the twentieth century to give a plan that is fresh and unique, that it is not necessary to follow along in the ruts of "the way it has always been done." Among other things, we were sure that in this way the work would be prepared for the needs of the future, and not just be meeting the needs of the past.[8]

The Schaeffers were discovering what it means to live by faith. And God met them very profoundly. It's what God wants for you and me too.

Whatever your challenge is today, it's a gift of God. He wants you to see his deliverance for his glory. Realize the drama you're a part of. Realize the meaning of what's happening to you. *God is in your crisis.* Maybe you haven't been trusting him. Maybe you feel deeply disappointed in yourself and tired of your life. Maybe you've squandered years of opportunity. How do you get going again? The Bible says that God has made Christ Jesus our wisdom, righteousness, sanctification, and redemption (1 Corinthians 1:30). He is enough for all your needs. Begin by trusting him to forgive you even for your lost opportunities. Start there. He is a deliverer. Trust him for that—*now.*

24

That All the Kingdoms of the Earth May Know

ISAIAH 37:8–38

"I don't like anything here at all," said Frodo, "step or stone, breath or bone. Earth, air and water all seem accursed. But so our path is laid." "Yes, that's so," said Sam. "And we shouldn't be here at all, if we'd known more about it before we started. But I suppose it's often that way. The brave things in the old tales and songs, Mr. Frodo: adventures, as I used to call them. I used to think that they were things the wonderful folk of the stories went out and looked for, because they wanted them, because they were exciting and life was a bit dull, a kind of a sport, as you might say. But that's not the way of it with the tales that really mattered, or the ones that stay in the mind. Folk seem to have been just landed in them, usually—their paths were laid that way, as you put it. But I expect they had lots of chances, like us, of turning back, only they didn't. And if they had, we shouldn't know, because they'd have been forgotten. We hear about those as just went on—and not all to a good end, mind you; at least not to what folk inside a story and not outside it call a good end. You know, coming home, and finding things all right, though not quite the same—like old Mr. Bilbo. But those aren't always the best tales to hear, though they may be the best tales to get landed in! I wonder what sort of tale we've fallen into?"[1]

WHAT SORT OF TALE HAVE YOU FALLEN INTO? One thing's for sure—it will demand your all, and then still more. You need courage.

The Bible says that Christian faith has the power to "overcome the world" (1 John 5:4). What does that mean? It means that this present evil age does *not* have to squeeze us into its mold. It means that the ocean of God-denial we swim in every day does *not* have to drown us. Trusting in God gives us the courage to overcome the world.

Faith gives us a sense of God, such a sense of God that he becomes more important than life itself (Psalm 63:3). It's when we die to our plans and our claims and our comfort and our control and come alive to God that his power enters in. If Jesus is the most important thing in your life, you won't make it. What do I mean? He is not the most important thing in your life; he *is* your life. And when faith awakens in your heart a sense of his glory, greater than life itself, you become unstoppable.

Pastor Tim Keller in New York City faced tremendous ministry demands after September 11, 2001. On top of that, he was diagnosed with cancer. He kept going. But by his own account it was not the courage of faith; he was just numb. There's a difference between coping and overcoming. Then God gave him the insight we all need: "With God there is hope. Your own fate ceases to be the reason for your courage."[2]

The impulse of self-preservation kills courage. But when your personal fate is no longer what you're living for, when your own ideal life scenario of perfect health and a perfect marriage and perfect children and a perfect job and a perfect church and perfect control—when that's no longer what you're clinging to and demanding of life, when all you want is the glory of God to be put on display through your existence, that's when God fills you with overcoming courage.

The crucible you find yourself in right now is where God is deepening your faith. What he is accomplishing in you is more significant than any passing mood of your own. So look beyond yourself. God is giving you a sense of his glory. He is setting you apart to himself. He is awakening your faith, to make you living proof that his salvation is worth anything. Heroic people in the past may inspire you.[3] But their greatness can also make you feel inadequate. Their stories can even have the effect of saying, "Don't stand up for anything! Look how *they* took hits." God is saying to you, "Look to Jesus, the founder and perfecter of your faith, who for the joy that was set before him endured the cross, despising the shame, and is seated at the right hand of the throne of God" (Hebrews 12:2). Jesus overcame *for us* (John 16:33). And he is able to help us in our weakness today (Hebrews 4:14–16).

God is positioning us to play a role in a great spiritual drama. He is deploying us in a battle between forces we dimly comprehend (Ephesians 6:12). And this world-culture we live in every day is where we encounter ultimate evil. We're being told, "You have no lasting significance. Grab what you can while you can. God won't come through for you. You have to make your own way by your own rules." That's a demoralizing lie. Those who live by that wisdom end up with emptiness. But others stake everything on God and his salvation. They are called Christians. I hope God is making you a Christian. I hope your greatest success in life is in losing your perfect, self-centered world in order to gain Christ (Philippians 3:4–11). That's your part in the drama. That's *how* you overcome the evil that would grind you into nothing.

Isaiah tells the story of a man who found courage in the crucible because all he wanted was for God to be glorified. Here is the structure of the text:

Act One: The king of Assyria against King Hezekiah (37:8–13)
> Point: Will you stake your life on the truthfulness of God?

Act Two: Hezekiah with the King of the Universe (37:14–35)
> Scene One: Hezekiah's prayer (37:14–20)
>> Point: That all the nations may know the one true God
> Scene Two: The King's sovereignty (37:21–29)
>> Point: God is opposed to the proud . . .
> Scene Three: The King's sign (37:30–32)
>> Point: . . . but he gives grace to the humble
> Scene Four: The King's decree (37:33–35)
>> Point: The cause of God defended by God for the sake of God

Act Three: The King of the Universe against the king of Assyria (37:36–38)
> Point: Who can survive the attack of God?

When you are opposed for the Lord's sake, remember that you're not really the one being attacked. Christ is. And he will defend his cause. Therefore, if your cause is his cause, he will defend you. If the glory of Christ is what you're living for, he will defend you against everything.

Act One: The King of Assyria against King Hezekiah

The king of Assyria continues his war of nerves against Hezekiah. With a rumor that a hostile army from Egypt is heading Assyria's way, he doesn't want Hezekiah back in Jerusalem to think he's getting off the hook. So even as the king of Assyria braces himself for a possible Egyptian attack, he sends a threatening letter to Hezekiah to keep him on the defensive (37:8–13).

The king of Assyria is brash enough to identify exactly what's at stake in all this maneuvering: "Do not let your God in whom you trust deceive you" (v. 10). God had assured Hezekiah that he would get rid of the king of Assyria: "I will make him fall by the sword in his own land" (v. 7). But now the Assyrian king is saying, "Don't buy it. Don't believe any messages you're getting from God. You're still in my clutches. And I'll get around to you when I feel like it. Has any other nation matched my power? Has any other god defeated me? Has any other king resisted me? Think about it, Hezekiah." In his own perverse way, Sennacherib is being helpful. He objectifies *the* question at the heart of our struggles: *Will we stake our lives on the truthfulness of God?* It's *his* integrity that's on the line in what becomes of us, if we're living for him. Do we believe that God will defend himself by defending us? Are we so allied with God that we know he is allied with us?

The threat in verse 13 would be the most effective if Hezekiah had known these kings personally. He could then picture in his mind's eye each one being taken prisoner, impaled, butchered. That's what the Assyrians did to their victims.[4] Is the king of Judah next? But by faith Hezekiah doesn't let the Assyrian king change the subject. He is not intimidated into thinking that this struggle is about his own personal fate. What is uppermost in Hezekiah's thinking is the reputation of God in the world. So to God he goes.

Act Two: Hezekiah with the King of the Universe

Hezekiah goes up to the house of the Lord, spreads the Assyrian letter before the Lord, and prays it through (vv. 14–20). That's significant. Hezekiah responded to the first threat from Assyria by going into the house of the Lord and by asking Isaiah for a word from God (vv. 1, 2). That was good. His faith was coming alive. But now Hezekiah is going deeper with God. Back in 36:6, 7, the Rabshakeh could see that Hezekiah was trusting both Egypt and the Lord. But this time when the king of Assyria mocks Hezekiah's faith, he doesn't even mention Egypt. Why? Because by now Hezekiah is trusting in God alone. His faith is less complicated, more straightforward. Now his passion is the glory of God.

> O Lord of hosts, God of Israel, who is enthroned above the cherubim, you are the God, you alone, of all the kingdoms of the earth; you have made heaven and earth. Incline your ear, O Lord, and hear; open your eyes, O Lord, and see; and hear all the words of Sennacherib, which he has sent to mock the living God. (Isaiah 37:16, 17)

Hezekiah is saying, "Lord, this isn't about me. This is a direct attack on *you*. You can't let this letter go unanswered. What the king of Assyria says here is true. He really has beaten up on everyone and discredited all their gods. But *that* is why I am asking you to save us—'*that all the kingdoms of the earth may know that you alone are the* Lord'" (v. 20).

That's a different way of praying. What inspires it? Hezekiah understands the meaning of his life. His existence is a platform for the display of God's glory in the world. He is not treating God as a means to his own ends but as the worthy end of all things. He is not praying, "Lord, why are you allowing this to happen to me?" He is praying, "Lord, will you not glorify yourself in this?" His own personal fate is not his concern. He's released from that prison. He has become a God-centered man, and he is courageously undaunted because of it.

We need to pray this way. We need to see our lives this way. *Why are we here?* Not to play in some sandbox of our own making, but to be living proof that God saves sinners. *Why is God there?* Not to service our convenience and our selfish dreams, but to display his glory in our salvation. And when his glory becomes our passion, we are not robbed, we are not diminished. Rather, we are dignified, we overcome evil. Evil is secondary, derivative, parasitic, and temporary. Only God is ultimate. Let his ultimacy change the whole agenda of your life.

Hezekiah finally sees what Isaiah has been saying all along. It is not this world with whom we have to deal, primarily; it is always God. The nations and powers and ideas and fashions of human making are not ultimate and definitional of us; God is. It is not human power that we need; what we need is God. He has allied himself with us not to serve our will but to defend his own glory as we serve his will.

Have you come to realize how the God-centeredness of God is good news for *you*? For one thing, it means that your unworthiness is irrelevant to God's readiness to save you. He is not responding to what you deserve; he is proving what a good Savior he is. Don't you see? This opens up a new definition of happiness. Happiness is God being God to you. Stop praying, "Lord, I want you to make my life better." Stop praying, "Lord, I want you to make my husband or my wife better. I want my children to behave. I want an ideal job." When you pray that way, you can only end up frustrated, because God will not subordinate himself to any human agenda. Start praying, "Lord, I just want you to be *God* to me. I want my life, with my problems, to show the world that you save sinners." Learn what it means to say with Paul, "It is my eager expectation and hope that I will not be at all ashamed, but that with full courage now as always Christ will be honored in my body, whether by life or by death" (Philippians 1:20). That is Christianity. If you'll trust God's goodness enough to pray for *his* triumph, he'll give you everything you long for in your own deepest intentions.

The way we respond to our challenges determines whether we will confirm the world's suspicions that Christianity is just another selfish power trip or whether we will surprise them by proving that Christianity is about finding in the glory of Christ everything desirable, though it means we remove self from the center and erect his cross there.

The next three scenes in Act Two go together, because God is speaking in all three. In verses 21–29, the divine King puts the king of Assyria in his place.

> Whom have you mocked and reviled?
>   Against whom have you raised your voice
> and lifted your eyes to the heights?
>   Against the Holy One of Israel! (v. 23)

Sennacherib has no idea whom he has picked a fight with. And what most offends the Holy One is the pride with which Sennacherib has strutted from one victory to the next (vv. 24, 25). The Assyrian tells himself, "Nothing can stop me!" He sees himself doing whatever he wants, whenever, wherever. That pride is the sin of sins. Pride is the perfect blasphemy, because it denies the perfect God.

So in verses 26–29 God asserts his ultimacy. The string of victories the Assyrian army chalked up were all the plan of God.

> Have you not heard
>   that I determined it long ago?
> I planned from days of old
>   what now I [not you, Sennacherib!] bring to pass,
> that you should make fortified cities
>   crash into heaps of ruins. (v. 26)

Look how the Bible unites human initiative with divine sovereignty. In verse 21 God says to Hezekiah, "Because you have prayed to me . . ." What if Hezekiah had not prayed to God? Human responsibility is real. What we do and don't do matters. Then in verse 26 God asserts his ultimacy over human actions. Sennacherib has been scoring victory after victory, but God was the one who planned it and accomplished it. Divine sovereignty is real. The purpose of God is what explains the twists and turns of history. And we see in Isaiah's prophetic reasoning that *both* human responsibility *and* divine sovereignty are real and compatible. God doesn't hesitate to say it. And Isaiah doesn't hesitate to record it. Why do we hesitate to believe it? Let's take the Bible *straight*, with no spin, lest we end up belittling God in our thoughts.

From his position of sovereignty, God opposes the human pride scarring the face of human history.

> Because you have raged against me
>   and your complacency has come to my ears,
> I will put my hook in your nose,
>   and my bit in your mouth,
> and I will turn you back on the way
>   by which you came. (v. 29)

Isaiah comes close to explaining the mystery of God's sovereignty interfacing with human responsibility. In some sense at least, it must be like a man riding a horse: "I will put my bit in your mouth." The Lord rides the horse of history, with all its restless energy, but all the while he is fully in control. Human pride cannot throw him off.

But God "gives grace to the humble." This is axiomatic (James 4:6; 1 Peter 5:5). That's what Isaiah 37:30–32 is saying. Hezekiah has turned to God in absolute trust, and God never lets faith go unmet. By this time Judah has lost many opportunities by not trusting God, and the nation is diminished as a result. They've paid a price for being allergic to God for so long. But this time Hezekiah turns back to God on God's terms, and God honors his faith. God promises to sustain a remnant through the Assyrian invasion and its aftermath. It will be a "sign," revealing that what gets us through is not our zeal for God but his zeal for us (v. 32). Even when we lose sight of him, God remains eager for us. Even a belated faith—he doesn't scold us, saying, "It's about time!"—even a belated faith finds him ready to come down with help.

But still more ultimately, verses 33–35 reveal what motivates God in all his ways with us. "I will defend this city to save it, for my own sake and for the sake of my servant David" (v. 35). Why does God put up with us? Why does God defend us? Not because of anything in us but for his own sake and for the sake of the ultimate David, Jesus Christ. He is committed to us not because of us but because of our Substitute. That is our strong position with God.

Act Three: The King of the Universe against the King of Assyria

In a matter-of-fact way, almost as an afterthought, Isaiah tells us how it all turned out (vv. 36–38). The angel of the Lord struck down 185,000 Assyrian troops—one against 185,000, and the victory was absolute. The shocking scene is depicted in only three verses, with little detail. Why? Because the real drama was back in verses 14–35, when Hezekiah and God were doing serious business together.

So there goes Sennacherib, slinking off to his home back in Nineveh. And the perfect irony is this: Just as Hezekiah went into the house of his God and got help, Sennacherib goes into the house of his god and gets killed (vv. 14, 38). The final blow fell in 681 B.C., twenty years later. Maybe during those twenty years people back in Judah wondered if God's word would ever come true: "I will make him fall by the sword in his own land" (v. 7). Thomas Hardy wrote a poem ("The Convergence of the Twain") about the loss of the *Titanic* in 1912, including these verses:

And as the smart ship grew
In stature, grace, and hue,
In shadowy silent distance grew the Iceberg too.

Alien they seemed to be:
No mortal eye could see
The intimate welding of their later history.

Assyria was the *Titanic* of antiquity. But God kept all his promises. He brought together unlikely turns of events. He seems to enjoy surprising outcomes.

One last point: The Assyrians bragged about their exploits. But interestingly, their national archives do not record their defeats. Sennacherib wrote the story of his siege of Jerusalem this way: "Hezekiah I made a prisoner in Jerusalem, his royal residence, like a bird in a cage."[5] In other words, "I had him trapped!" But he passed in silence over the rest of the story. The Old Testament tells us the truth. It puts right out in the open Israel's slowness to believe and Assyria's humiliating defeat. Why? Because the Bible is not about man's glory. It's about God's glory. So is your life.

There are two ways you can live. You can hide the ugly details and try to get God to collude with you in assembling a little personal world of make-believe for your own reputation and comfort. Or you can let God tell *his* story in your life. You can bow to his will and promote his glory, whatever adjustments that may require, because his glory is your salvation. If you choose the first way, you will be endlessly frustrated. God will always seem to be against you, and you will have no fortitude. But if you choose God's way, he will draw near with empowering mercies, and you will become living proof, against the odds, that God is the true Savior.

Every one of us wants the last sentence in the last chapter of his life to read, "And he lived happily ever after." But sometimes courage demands that you jeopardize that happy ending. What you decide at that pivotal moment depends on how you define happiness. The world says, "Oh, what a beautiful mornin'! Oh, what a beautiful day! I've got a beautiful feelin', everything's goin' my way."[6] If you embrace that ideal, your happiness will be forever brittle and insecure. You will have no courage to risk anything. But there is another happiness. Jesus said, "Seek first the kingdom of God and his righteousness, and all these things will be added to you" (Matthew 6:33). Do you see how he arranges things both for his glory and your joy? Will you trust him with an audacious faith and live for his glory? If you will, your happiness will be as secure as his glory.

25

Peace and Security in Our Days?

ISAIAH 38:1—39:8

THOMAS CRANMER IS A NAME you might not know offhand. Maybe you've heard his voice echoing in *The Book of Common Prayer*:

> Almighty God, Father of our Lord Jesus Christ, Maker of all things, Judge of all men, we acknowledge and bewail our manifold sins and wickedness. . . . The remembrance of them is grievous unto us, the burden of them is intolerable. Have mercy upon us, have mercy upon us, most merciful Father.

As Archbishop of Canterbury, Cranmer bravely advanced the gospel during the English Reformation. But when Mary became Queen in 1553, she had him arrested. From his prison window, he watched his fellow-reformers Hugh Latimer and Nicholas Ridley burn at the stake. It was unforgettable, with Latimer encouraging Ridley, "Be of good comfort, Master Ridley, and play the man; we shall on this day light such a candle, by God's grace, in England, as I trust shall never be put out."

Cranmer did not play the man. He caved in. Government agents brainwashed him into recanting the gospel. He was set free and for several weeks enjoyed a comfortable life again. But they put him back in prison, and he signed more recantations. But when he realized that they were going to kill him anyway, his old courage returned.

On the day of his execution in Oxford, he sat through a two-hour sermon at the Church of St. Mary denouncing him as a heretic. Then he was expected publicly to admit the error of his ways. But he stood firm:

And now I come to the great thing, which so much troubleth my conscience, more than anything that ever I did or said in my whole life, and
that is the setting forth of a writing contrary to the truth. . . . And forasmuch
as my hand offended, writing contrary to my heart, my hand shall first be
punished.[1]

The remembrance of his sins was grievous to him and the burden intolerable. In fact, he walked from the church to the stake so quickly, his guards
could hardly keep up with him. An eyewitness described his death:

Fire being now put to him, he stretched out his right hand and thrust it into
the fire, and held it there a good space, before the fire came to any part of
his body, where his hand was seen of every man sensibly burning, crying
with a loud voice, "This hand hath offended." As soon as the fire was got
up, he was very soon dead, never stirring or crying all the while.[2]

Thomas Cranmer was a martyr, but he was no superman. He was like us.
Sometimes he lost his nerve. What is it that empowers us to live well for the
Lord and to die well for the Lord? What is it that keeps us steady in life and
in death? A living sense of the living God in our hearts. With that radiance
within, we can face anything. Without it, we're defeated already.

Hezekiah, like Thomas Cranmer, like us, wavered. In Isaiah 36—37
he stood up to the whole Assyrian army. God was so real to him that God
was all he cared about. Now, in chapters 38—39, he's in trouble again. This
time it isn't a national emergency. It's only personal. He gets sick. But his
courage fails him, he becomes shortsighted and irresponsible, and he doesn't
end well. Why? He loses his sense of God. Instead of praying for God's
will and glory alone, now he's saying, "All I want is my own comfort and
peace." The contrast between Hezekiah's anguish over his own illness at the
beginning of chapter 38 and his blasé contentment with the captivity of his
nation at the end of chapter 39 is striking. When his own life is on the line,
he's devastated. But if a later generation is doomed, no problem!

What is Isaiah accomplishing in chapters 36—39? He's forming a
bridge from one major section of his book into the next. The first two chapters, 36—37, look back. They validate what Isaiah has been saying. Trusting
God is a smart policy for life. The second two chapters, 38—39, look forward. They prepare us for what follows by showing us the failure of human
faith. In the next major section of his book, beginning in chapter 40, Isaiah
is going to take us beyond our own faith, because our faith is unsteady. Our
sense of God comes and goes. We need constant renewal. We can't trust in
our trust in God. We must rest in God himself. He himself is the only bedrock under our feet, and his promises and his grace alone secure our future.
That's where Isaiah is going next.

Sometimes we sin so badly, we wonder if trusting God is even possible again. But God meets us even there. When our faith crashes and burns, is that the end of everything? No. It can be a new beginning. Our failure is God's opportunity.

The passage falls out in three acts. Act One sets the scene, Act Two reveals the tension, and Act Three tells us the sad ending.

Act One: The Sickness—"Hezekiah wept bitterly" (38:1–8)
    The point: God gives the king added opportunity
Act Two: The Double Mind—devotion with doubt (38:9–22)
    A¹ Superscription (38:9)
      B¹ Crisis: banished to Sheol (38:10, 11)
        C¹ Lament: the God who afflicts (38:12–14)
        C² Hope: the God who restores (38:15–17)
      B² Resolution: restored to the house of the Lord (38:18–20)
    A² Postscript (38:21, 22)
Act Three: The Betrayal—"peace and security in my days" (39:1–8)
    The point: The king bungles his opportunity

Isaiah is warning us that our weakness of faith has a costly impact on others. But he's also preparing us to see God bringing beauty out of the wreckage we create.

Act One: The Sickness

In those days[3] Hezekiah became sick and was at the point of death. And Isaiah the prophet the son of Amoz came to him, and said to him, "Thus says the LORD: Set your house in order, for you shall die, you shall not recover." Then Hezekiah turned his face to the wall and prayed to the LORD, and said, "Please, O LORD, remember how I have walked before you in faithfulness and with a whole heart, and have done what is good in your sight." And Hezekiah wept bitterly. (Isaiah 38:1–3)

On the face of it, this seems straightforward enough. Hezekiah becomes seriously ill, God tells him to get ready to die, and Hezekiah cries out for mercy. But it's more complex. We know from 2 Kings 18:5 that trust in God was the lasting statement Hezekiah's life made. But we also know from 2 Chronicles 32:25 that his pride seduced him at this critical moment. We further know from the end of this story in Isaiah 39 that Hezekiah made poor use of his new lease on life. And how a story ends sheds light on what came before. So when he says here, "Remember how I have walked before you in faithfulness and with a whole heart, and have done what is good in your sight," that is neither entirely wrong nor entirely convincing. But God blesses him anyway.

> Then the word of the LORD came to Isaiah: "Go and say to Hezekiah, Thus says the LORD, the God of David your father: I have heard your prayer; I have seen your tears. Behold, I will add fifteen years to your life. I will deliver you and this city out of the hand of the king of Assyria, and will defend this city." (Isaiah 38:4–6)

God is generous with second chances because what motivates him is his commitment to Christ, our ultimate David. And he wants us to *know* that he is committed to us at that level. So he gives Hezekiah a sign of his favor.

> "This shall be the sign to you from the LORD, that the LORD will do this thing that he has promised: Behold, I will make the shadow cast by the declining sun on the dial of Ahaz turn back ten steps." So the sun turned back on the dial the ten steps by which it had declined. (vv. 7, 8)

How did God do this? We don't know. We know something about how light works, and it doesn't work this way. But the anomaly in this passage is not a problem; it's the whole point. A miracle is persuasive as a sign from God precisely because we can't explain it. It can't be a human stunt. It must be of God. That's the point. Apparently, in this case God temporarily bent the sunlight. And why not? He created it. He controls it. He can do whatever he wants with it (Psalm 115:3). And the shadow went backwards, at least long enough for the sign to make its point. What we see in Act One is God both saying and showing that he is turning the clock back on Hezekiah's life.

Act Two: The Double Mind

Why do I call Act Two, in verses 9–22, "The Double Mind—devotion with doubt"? The Bible says that "a double-minded man [is] unstable in all his ways" (James 1:8). But where is the double mind here in Isaiah 38? Hezekiah's prayer is meaningful. Think it through with me.

In verses 10, 11 he savors the fellowship with God and man he has enjoyed so long. He doesn't want to lose it. After all, the best thing about this life is closeness to God and to one another, isn't it? So Hezekiah dreads being "consigned to the gates of Sheol" (v. 10). In verses 12–14 he laments the cost of death. He uses four similes here, marked by the word "like," to describe the anguish of death. In verses 15–17 he looks by faith to the Lord. He says in effect, "This difficulty has taught me a lesson. I'm going to watch my step from now on. Other people will learn from my restoration and take heart." In fact, Hezekiah's very name means something like "The Lord has strengthened me." His name and his experience join together as a statement of God's saving power. We know from what follows that Hezekiah's sense of God is weakening. But for now, in verses 18–20, he looks forward to more years of joyful worship in the house of the Lord, reversing the gloomy prospects of verses 10, 11. He sees that the essence of life is enjoying the presence of God in worship. Worship is what it means to really live! And Hezekiah is so glad to know that God has promised him more of this joy.

So where is the double mind? The clue is in the postscript Isaiah places strategically at the end of Act Two:[4]

> Now Isaiah had said, "Let them take a cake of figs and apply it to the boil, that he may recover." (v. 21)

Not only does God give Hezekiah a promise of divine healing (v. 5), but here God gives him a felt token of his care, a simple remedy for the infection. It's an acted-out prophecy of the kindness of God. He goes so far as to apply his loving care to Hezekiah with a literal touch on his body. That is God's gracious heart. But what is Hezekiah's state of mind?

> Hezekiah also had said, "What is the sign that I shall go up to the house of the LORD?" (v. 22)

This looks like trouble. Hezekiah's father, Ahaz, had refused a sign when one was offered him (Isaiah 7:10–12). That was proud unbelief. Now Hezekiah asks for a sign because the promise of God isn't good enough for him. That too is proud unbelief. Do you see? Hezekiah trusts in God—*sort of*. He's a double-minded man, unstable in all his ways. His sense of God is weak. And that's going to hurt him for the rest of his life. What is Hezekiah going to do with the privilege of his added years?

Act Three: The Betrayal

> At that time Merodach-baladan the son of Baladan, king of Babylon, sent envoys with letters and a present to Hezekiah, for he heard that he had been sick and had recovered. And Hezekiah welcomed them gladly. And he showed them his treasure house, the silver, the gold, the spices, the precious oil, his whole armory, all that was found in his storehouses. There was nothing in his house or in all his realm that Hezekiah did not show them. (Isaiah 39:1, 2)

The book of Revelation portrays the evil arrayed against us in two forms: the great Beast to intimidate us and the great Whore to seduce us (Revelation

13:1; 17:1). In some parts of the world today, persecution is the dominant strategy of the devil. In our part of the world, seduction is his usual method. But Satan doesn't care one way or the other, as long he wins. He may savage us, or he may flatter us. We see both here in Isaiah. In chapters 36, 37 the army of Assyria surrounds Jerusalem like muggers on the street surrounding a defenseless girl. But Hezekiah's sense of God makes him brave, and the girl mocks her fleeing attackers (Isaiah 37:22). Now in chapters 38, 39 the Babylonians appear in Jerusalem with congratulations and smiles, and Hezekiah melts. He's putty in their hands. He overcomes the Beast, only to fall into the arms of the Whore (cf. James 4:4).

> Then Isaiah the prophet came to King Hezekiah, and said to him, "What did these men say? And from where did they come to you?" Hezekiah said, "They have come to me from a far country, from Babylon." (Isaiah 39:3)

Hezekiah feels flattered, and flattery is hard to resist. His sense of self-importance is clouding his sense of God's importance. "These envoys have come such a long way, from such an important country, to gush over me!" He is blind to their true intent. Babylon is no friend. Throughout the Bible, *Babylon* is a cipher for everything wrong with the world, everything against God. But instead of asking himself what these Babylonians really want, Hezekiah opens up to them.

What's happening here? This man is a significant leader among God's people. How are we to understand him? The erosion of his sense of God deep within is finally showing. His insecure need for worldly recognition is ruining him. He throws open the doors and draws back the curtains and unlocks his vaults and brags to the Babylonians about what a big deal he is. Poor, naive Hezekiah! He wants to be "a player" in international politics. He wants to be up in the big leagues, even if God isn't there. (He doesn't consult God before he commits himself here.) But these Babylonians don't respect him. In their eyes, he's just another petty kinglet out in the boondocks. As they walk with him from room to room in his palace, politely smiling, oohing and ah-ing as he shows off, they've seen wealth many times greater in their own kingdom. They're just making a mental inventory of what they'll someday carry back to Babylon.

A sense of the glory of Jesus Christ is the only thing that can deliver us from making fools of ourselves before condescending powers of evil. Let those powers play their own game. You and I are better off with Jesus the crucified Savior.

> Then Isaiah said to Hezekiah, "Hear the word of the LORD of hosts: Behold, the days are coming, when all that is in your house, and that which your

fathers have stored up till this day, shall be carried to Babylon. Nothing shall be left, says the LORD. And some of your own sons, who will come from you, whom you will father, shall be taken away, and they shall be eunuchs in the palace of the king of Babylon." Then Hezekiah said to Isaiah, "The word of the LORD that you have spoken is good." For he thought, "There will be peace and security in my days." (vv. 5–8)

Some Christians live too long. It's better to die prematurely and honorably than to live long enough to betray the cause of God in our generation. Hezekiah would have been better off dying in chapter 38. His faith, his honor, his responsibility—now they all lie in ruins at his feet, and the disaster is his own doing. W. S. Plumer, the nineteenth-century Presbyterian pastor, warned us well:

> All those affections, sentiments and practices, whose nature is to beget carelessness and unguarded conduct, are unscriptural. If even our joys and hopes make us heedless, we are better without them. If we have so conceived of the gospel as to judge that its fullness and promises render watchfulness unnecessary, we quite mistake its true nature.[5]

In Isaiah's Hebrew text, the word translated "good" is emphatic: "*Good* is the word the LORD has spoken!" In other words, "Isaiah, you had me worried there for a minute, with your talk of Babylonian invasion. But what a relief! The collapse of everything I've lived for, the ruin of the kingdom of God, my descendents as servile bootlickers in Babylon—it's all okay, because *I'll* die peacefully in my bed." And Hezekiah was one of the *good* kings of Judah!

Malcolm Muggeridge went to the Soviet Union in the 1930s as a good Socialist, expecting to find a worker's paradise. The reality he found was betrayal.

> In Kiev, where I found myself on a Sunday morning, on an impulse I turned into a church where a service was in progress. It was packed tight, but I managed to squeeze myself against a pillar whence I could survey the congregation and look up at the altar. Young and old, peasants and townsmen, parents and children, even a few in uniform—it was a variegated assembly. The bearded priests, swinging their incense, intoning their prayers, seemed very remote and far away. Never before or since have I participated in such worship; the sense conveyed of turning to God in great affliction was overpowering. Though I could not, of course, follow the service, I knew from Klavdia Lvovna little bits of it; for instance, where the congregation say there is no help for them save from God. What intense feeling they put into these words! In their minds, I knew, as in mine, was

a picture of those desolate abandoned villages, of the hunger and the hopelessness, of the cattle trucks being loaded with humans in the dawn light.
Where were they to turn for help? Not to the Kremlin, and the Dictatorship
of the Proletariat, certainly; nor to the forces of progress and democracy
and enlightenment in the West. . . . Every possible human agency found
wanting. So, only God remained, and to God they turned with a passion, a
dedication, a humility, impossible to convey. They took me with them; I
felt closer to God then than I ever had before, or am likely to again.[6]

In this world of weakness in the good and malice in the evil, with every
possible human agency found wanting, only God remains. May we turn to
him with a passion that will bring many others with us.

There we are, at the end of Isaiah 1—39. The people of God have heard
the truth. But they haven't received it into their hearts, where it could make
a difference, and now they're headed for exile. Every human agency is found
wanting. Only God remains. And therefore God alone will restore his people
by his own grace and power, according to Isaiah 40—66.

How does this story help us today? When we see Hezekiah healed by
God in chapter 38 and dazzled by all the wrong things in chapter 39, it
doesn't make sense. But that's who we are. *We* don't make sense. We need
constant renewal. And God has a way.

In 1841 Octavius Winslow wrote a book entitled *Personal Declension
and Revival of Religion in the Soul*, to help people like us who so easily
lose clarity and drift away from God. The Bible says, "He restores my soul"
(Psalm 23:3). So Winslow has a chapter on "The Lord, the Restorer of his
People."[7] How does God restore vacillating people to himself?

First, if you're a believer, remember that your sanctification is incomplete, and every single day you need your Lord afresh. The world is dis-
tracting you. Satan is condemning you. Temptations are whispering to you.
Familiar sins don't easily go away. Is it any wonder that sometimes we
buckle? Let's remember how weak—how bad—we still are. The Bible
warns us, "Take care, brothers, lest there be in any of you an evil, unbelieving heart, leading you to fall away from the living God" (Hebrews 3:12).
Let's be realistic. We're more evil than we know. We're spring-loaded to
fall away from God. It is a *sin* to fall out of love with God. It is a sin of the
greatest magnitude, and it isn't hard to do.

But, secondly, let's be realistic about him as well. Christ loves empty,
ungrateful, waffling, confused sinners. *He* restores our souls. When the
shepherd finds his lost sheep, he lays it on his shoulders and carries it home,
rejoicing (Luke 15:5). He awakens our repentance by his kindness.

"Return, faithless Israel, declares the LORD. I will not look on you in
anger, for I am merciful, declares the LORD" (Jeremiah 3:12). If Satan dis-
courages you, if your sins hold you back, if your shame tells you to hide,

if your conscience says you've gone too far, *God* says, "Return, for I am merciful." The God whom you've offended tells you to return to his mercies. And God's word overrules every objection. Remember that. Remember that the cross of Christ was the gushing forth of the ocean of God's mercies for stupid sinners. It's the costly display of the love of God at the cross of Christ that restores our souls. *When your faith is weak, his love is strong.* That's the gospel. Believe it.

26

God's Glory, Our Comfort

ISAIAH 40:1–11

We are entirely alone, without help from outside. Hitler has left us in the lurch. If the airfield is still in our possession, this letter may still get out. . . . So this is what the end looks like. Hannes and I will not surrender; yesterday, after our infantry had retaken a position, I saw four men who had been taken prisoner by the Russians. No, we shall not go into captivity. When Stalingrad has fallen, you'll hear and read it. And then you'll know that I shall not come back.

. . . The Führer made a firm promise to bail us out of here; they read it to us and we believed in it firmly. Even now I still believe it, because I have to believe in something. If it is not true, what else could I believe in? I would no longer need spring, summer, or anything that gives pleasure. So leave me my faith, dear Greta; all my life, at least eight years of it, I believed in the Führer and his word. It is terrible how they doubt here, and shameful to listen to what they say without being able to reply, because they have the facts on their side.[1]

THE LAST GERMAN PLANE OUT OF STALINGRAD in January 1943 carried those letters. But they were never delivered. The German high command intercepted them, to assess troop morale. On the other side of the battle line was a regime of equal brutality and betrayal, with its vast network of concentration camps. The Leninist program was epitomized in a sign at the main camp at Solovki: "With an Iron Fist, We Will Lead Humanity to Happiness."[2] And what about us Americans? On May 8, 1945, the night of the Allied victory in Europe, my mother went with her parents to downtown Washington to celebrate. No one stayed home that night. They had all suffered together, and they wanted to enjoy the victory together. But when Mom came home later that evening, she just wanted to take a bath. The triumph of democracy had dissolved into a pretext for public vulgarity. Did Washington represent the triumph of good over evil?

When we see how far we have fallen and how broken the world is, it explains something. It explains why disappointment pervades our experience. As we see more and more of life, we are confronted with disappointment so persistently and so convincingly, hope starts to look just plain stupid. We become disappointed in our ideals, disappointed in romance, disappointed in our careers, disappointed in the people we trust, disappointed in ourselves. When all human hopes have let us down, we might be ready for the only real salvation that exists.

In chapter 39 Isaiah predicted that Judah would go into exile in Babylon. They did, in 586 B.C., just over a century later. The Babylonian army overwhelmed Jerusalem and led the survivors off to captivity at the other end of the Fertile Crescent—a far cry from what God had wanted for them! He had said that Abraham would become a mighty nation, blessing the whole world (Genesis 18:18). But the people of God failed their high calling, and paid heavily for it.

Now, in Babylonian exile, God's people are defeated, bitter, disillusioned. In fact, they think *God* has failed them (Isaiah 40:27). That's what we typically do—blame God. And for his part, what does God do? He comes down to comfort us. He comes down with a promise, with a hope that doesn't depend on us but only on himself. He promises to display his glory before the whole world. And as we savor his promised salvation, he strengthens us to face anything while we wait.

Isaiah 40 begins a major new section of the book. Isaiah is no longer addressing Judah in his own day. He is being projected by the Holy Spirit out into the future, like the Apostle John in the Revelation. He is looking into his prophetic crystal ball, so to speak, seeing a future day and declaring the gospel to the Jews languishing in Babylonian exile. He is saying to them and to us, "God has not abandoned you. Your best days are still ahead. God has a purpose of grace for you better than ever. He is coming to save you. Believe it, and let this hope fill your sails."

On an aside, you may have been exposed to a different view of the book of Isaiah in your college Intro to Civ course or on The Discovery Channel or wherever. Some scholars say there is more than one author behind this book. They propose that, beginning here in chapter 40, we are reading the work not of Isaiah but of an anonymous prophet living during the Babylonian exile. They call him "Second Isaiah." Some even propose that, with chapters 56—66, we are reading yet another, still later anonymous prophet, "Third Isaiah."

By now I don't know how many more Isaiahs to expect. It depends on which scholar I read. But at latest count, we have at least three—one who wrote chapters 1—39, a second who wrote chapters 40—55, and a third who wrote chapters 56—66. But the logic of literary fragmentation can't stop there. It must, and it does, tend toward an ever-expanding galaxy of authors, editors, supplementers, and Isaianic disciples. We end up with as many Isaiahs as there are theories, and the whole project starts to break down.

Why would anyone come up with the idea of multiple authors for this book? Because dividing the books of the Old Testament into many hands writing over long periods of time has become an established tradition in some academic circles. And in the book of Isaiah, we do see the style and tone changing along the way. Reading Isaiah 40, we sense the change from 1—39 instantly. The scene has shifted from Judah facing the Assyrians in the eighth century B.C. to the exiles in Babylon in the sixth century B.C. And some cannot accept that Isaiah saw beyond his own day to speak into a later historical situation, especially in view of the detailed predictions in this section of the book.[3]

But not all Biblical scholars agree that we should break this book apart into multiple authors spread across the centuries. Why? Primarily because the Bible itself identifies only one author for this book. The heading that stands over all sixty-six chapters is, "The vision of Isaiah the son of Amoz" (1:1). And the New Testament refers to passages throughout this book as the word of Isaiah the prophet.[4] If we accept the testimony of Jesus and the apostles on other matters, why would we reject their word on this? If we say that their confidence in the unity of Isaiah was a function of their times—nobody questioned it back then—couldn't we also say that today's confidence in the partition of Isaiah is a function of our own times? Let's remember that Jesus and the apostles didn't walk in lockstep with received opinion in their day. What's most remarkable about them is how *unlike* their times they were. They were competent thinkers for all times and seasons. They demonstrated an objectivity that, if we recovered it today, would advance our understanding on all the most important fronts. We who profess to be Christians must accept their view of the Bible not because we've proved it by our own methods but because we can't be faithful Christians without accepting it. It isn't a matter of weighing theoretical options; it's a matter of conscience and authority—our only escape from captivity to every dominant cultural construct.

It's also worth noting that the text of Isaiah has come down to us through history as a unified whole. In the Great Isaiah Scroll from Qumran—one of the Dead Sea Scrolls you can see on display in Jerusalem—chapter 39 flows into chapter 40 as a seamless unity. A partitioned book of Isaiah is nowhere found in the manuscripts.

A two- or three-Isaiah theory is driven not by proofs but by an unproven assumption that a prophet's range of vision could not be extended into the unknown future by God. If we can't accept a mini-miracle like this, how can we swallow the mega-miracle of God's grace in Christ? This theory also assumes that a prophet was basically a morally sensitive person, a genius of ethical insight. But a true prophet was more than a moralistic nag. His vision was filled with nearly unbelievable divine grace for sinners. He was, above all, a herald of good news for bad people from a surprising God. The gospel is miraculous throughout. Take the improbable out of it, and you have nothing left worth having. Grace has implications for higher criticism.

But why does this question of the authorship of Isaiah matter? Because we must receive the message of God on his terms or we won't hear him at all. The Word of God has the right to explain itself to us. How could it be otherwise? There is no independently available "real world" against which we can test the truthfulness of what God says. The Bible's prophetic vision *is* the most penetrating way of seeing reality. We might not like it, but we may not redefine it.

What then can we say about the unity of this book? Chapters 1—39 address Isaiah's own generation with a message primarily of confrontation. Chapters 40—55 address the Jews of the Babylonian exile with a message primarily of consolation. Chapters 56—66 seem to be omni-temporal, urging all readers to apply the truths of chapters 1—55 to their own times with reviving power. Within that simple framework, nuances abound. But this multifaceted book has one author, Isaiah, the son of Amoz, as the Bible itself says. End of aside.

Chapter 40, then, changes the subject. Its structure is threefold. In verses 1–11, the introduction, God comes with his comforting promise of worldwide salvation. In verses 12–26, the body, he argues that he is able to keep his promise. And in verses 27–31, the conclusion, he explains how his promise can energize us to live above despondency right now. This chapter is so important, we will devote three studies to it. Verses 1–11 tell us four things about God's promise:

1. The occasion of his comforting promise (40:1, 2)
2. The content of his comforting promise (40:3–5)
3. The certainty of his comforting promise (40:6–8)
4. The spreading of his comforting promise (40:9–11)

We brood over the bitterness of life. We think God is against us. But he wants to breathe new life into us. Will we give ourselves permission to stop resenting him and start delighting in him, according to the promises of his gospel?

The Occasion

Comfort, comfort my people, says your God.
Speak tenderly to Jerusalem,
   and cry to her,
for[5] her servitude[6] is ended,
   for her iniquity is pardoned,
for she has received from the LORD's hand
   double for all her sins. (Isaiah 40:1, 2)

There is an end to the disciplines of God. Faith is not all struggle. It is also release and hope and new beginnings. God's deepest intention toward us is comfort. How could it be otherwise? If the focus of Christianity were our sins, our future would shut down. But in fact Christianity is all about the saving grace of God. He overrules our stupidity with his own absolute pardon through the finished work of Christ on the cross. Do we sin? Yes. Do we suffer for it? Yes. Is that where God leaves us? No. When his discipline has done its good work, God comes back to us with overflowing comfort. See in God not a frown but a smile, not distance but nearness. Even when we don't act like the people of God, he still identifies with us: ". . . my people . . . your God." He stills calls us "Jerusalem," even when we're far away in exile.

Do you have glad expectations of God? You may, even as a sinner. Do you see God as coming down to you as you are, with your mission still unfulfilled, but with his renewing mercies? You may and you must see God that way, or you'll get no traction for holiness. The Bible says that God's *kindness* leads us to repentance (Romans 2:4). John Calvin explains that "no one will ever reverence God but he who is confident that God is favorable toward him."[7]

The occasion of God's renewing comfort is our failure. It's as if Isaiah had fallen asleep at the end of chapter 39. While he slept, Judah was taken into exile. And it's as if, in a prophetic dream, Isaiah was lifted into God's heavenly court to hear Judah's predicament being discussed (cf. 1 Kings 22:19–23). But now in chapter 40, Rip Van Winkle-like, Isaiah wakes up in (to him) a new historical situation. He reveals to the Jews what he heard in the heavenly throne room. God has summoned his prophets to take a message of hope to his demoralized people.

The Content

A voice cries:
"In the wilderness prepare the way of the LORD;
   make straight in the desert a highway for our God.

> Every valley shall be lifted up,
>   and every mountain and hill be made low;
> the uneven ground shall become level,
>   and the rough places a plain.
> And the glory of the LORD shall be revealed,
>   and all flesh shall see it together,
>   for the mouth of the LORD Has spoken." (Isaiah 40:3–5)

Isaiah hears a voice! God has commanded his servants, still unidentified, to bring a message of comfort to his people. ("Comfort" in verse 1 is plural in the Hebrew text.) Now Isaiah hears one of those prophetic voices. He hears the content of the comforting message. What is God saying? Three things.

One: the King *is* coming. He comes to us as we are, where we are, in the wilderness and desert of our real lives. He wants us to get ready to receive him, because right now we aren't ready. We know from Luke 3:1–18 that Jesus is the coming King and that the readiness we need is newness of life. We can't hide behind denominational labels, however correct ("We have Abraham as our father," Luke 3:8). What we need is new selves. Prepare the way of the Lord!

Two: God *will* accomplish his purpose. Every valley *shall* be lifted up, and so forth. Isaiah is not talking about literal, topographical change. He is talking about the upheaval of true repentance. He is talking about a new moral topography, a new social landscape. He is talking about the disruptive advance of salvation. He is saying that lifting and lowering and leveling and smoothing are necessary to the kingdom of Christ. He is talking about depression being relieved, pride being flattened, troubled personalities becoming placid, and difficult people becoming easy to get along with. And he is also implying that if we cling to the status quo and refuse God's upsetting but constructive salvation, we risk having no part with Christ.[8]

Three: the glory of the Lord Jesus will be revealed to the whole world. We can be certain of it. God has decreed it: ". . . for the mouth of the LORD has spoken." His glory *will* be admired and delighted in and trembled at everywhere. The great sin of our race is to diminish God, but he has resolved to overcome all God-trivializing obstacles and magnify himself in our eyes through Jesus Christ the Lord.

We Presbyterians (and others) talk a lot about the glory of God, and so we should. Do we understand what we're talking about? John Piper's assessment seems accurate:

> In the church, our view of God is so small instead of huge, so marginal instead of crucial, so vague instead of clear, so impotent instead of all determining, and so uninspiring instead of ravishing that the responsibil-

ity to live to the glory of God is a thought without content. The words can come out of our mouths, but ask the average Christian to tell what they know about the glory of this God that they are going to live for, and the answer will not be long.[9]

What is the glory of the Lord? His glory is the fiery radiance of his very nature.[10] It is his blazing beauty. At Mount Sinai "the appearance of the glory of the LORD was like a devouring fire" (Exodus 24:17). Ezekiel saw the glory of the Lord in the form of a supercharged war chariot coming down from Heaven to establish the rule of God on earth (Ezekiel 1:4–28). When Jesus was born, the glory of the Lord shone around the shepherds, and they were terrified (Luke 2:9). The Bible also says that Jesus himself is the ultimate display of the glory of God (John 1:14). His transfiguration unveiled his glory (Luke 9:28–36). But also—this is the irony of the gospel—when Jesus hung on the cross in shame, we were seeing the glory of God (John 13:31).

Our ideas of God's glory have to adjust to his beautiful willingness to humble himself all the way to a wretched death for us. Paul taught us that in this arrogant world only a weak and foolish gospel can reveal "the Lord of glory" (1 Corinthians 2:8). The cross of glory shames all human pride. But when Christ returns, how different it will be! He will appear in overwhelming glory (Titus 2:13). And God has called us to share in that glory of Christ (2 Thessalonians 2:14). Believers stand to inherit "an eternal weight of glory" (2 Corinthians 4:17). And throughout eternity the New Jerusalem will need no sun or moon, for "the glory of God gives it light, and its lamp is the Lamb" (Revelation 21:23).

The glory of the Lord, therefore, is God himself becoming visible, God bringing his presence down to us, God displaying his beauty before us, the true answer to our deepest longings. And he *promises* to do this for us. It is *the* central promise of the gospel.

God kept his promise in the hidden glory of Christ's first coming. He continues to keep his promise as the Holy Spirit awakens us to the glory of Christ in the gospel (2 Corinthians 3:18—4:6). He will consummate his promise at the second coming of Christ. All this is contained in seed form in Isaiah 40:5. Our part is to have the courage to welcome him with a bold restructuring of our lives. Nothing could be greater for us than to be wonderfully disrupted by the power of this hope. He's worth the upheaval.

The Certainty

A voice says, "Cry!"
    And I said, "What shall I cry?"
All flesh is grass,

and all its constancy[11] is like the flower of the field.
The grass withers, the flower fades
  when the breath of the Lord blows on it;
  surely the people are grass.
The grass withers, the flower fades,
  but the word of our God will stand forever. (Isaiah 40:6–8)

Isaiah hears another voice, giving him a message to declare. It's a strange message. Isaiah is told to tell us that we are unreliable. God's promise is infallible, we are not, and that must be said. Remember King Hezekiah in chapter 39: "My people, even my own sons, will someday be slaves in Babylon? No problem, as long as *I* die comfortably in bed" (v. 8). Even our good intentions are inconstant, like the flower of the field. We blossom only under ideal conditions, not under the blasts of real life. That's why Christianity is not about what we can do; it's about what God promises to do for us. Christianity is not fundamentally challenge; fundamentally it is assurance. It must be. Only God qualifies for our final trust. And he does because no human power or condition can stop him. We are the merest grass and flowers, but the word of our God will stand forever. Human failure is costly, but it's not the end of our happiness. God's promise of salvation is final. He is committed to his own glory and our joy in his glory. And in that certainty our hopes come to rest.

The Spreading

Go on up to a high mountain,
  O Zion, herald of good news;
lift up your voice with strength,
  O Jerusalem, herald of good news;
  lift it up, fear not;
say to the cities of Judah,
  "Behold your God!"
Behold, the Lord God comes with might,
  and his arm rules for him;
behold, his reward is with him,
  and his recompense before him.
He will tend his flock like a shepherd;
  he will gather the lambs in his arms;
he will carry them in his bosom,
  and gently lead those that are with young. (Isaiah 40:9–11)

Isaiah calls all who cherish this hope to spread their enthusiasm for God's coming glory. He's saying in verse 9, "Get way up on a conspicuous location, turn up the volume, don't let your fears keep you silent, and draw attention to God. Say to everyone around, 'Look! It's your God!'" Our God doesn't work at arm's length or only through church programs or just by handing down decrees from on high. *He comes.* He brings his presence. And his presence is our joy. This is a simple message to spread around. You don't need to know much. You only need the courage of faith.

What is "your God" worth to us all? He is a conquering king (v. 10a). He is a wealthy benefactor (v. 10b). He is a tender shepherd (v. 11). This is Jesus. What more could you hope for? The Geneva Bible of 1560 comments at verse 9: "He shows in one word the perfection of all man's happiness, which is to have God's presence."

Spreading this glad expectation to others is the best way to amplify our own joy in it. Paul organized his whole life this way: "I do all things for the sake of the gospel, so that I may become a fellow partaker of it" (1 Corinthians 9:23, NASB). C. S. Lewis explains how this works:

> The world rings with praise—lovers praising their mistresses, readers their favourite poet, walkers praising the countryside, players praising their favourite game—praise of weather, wines, dishes, actors, motors, horses, colleges, countries, historical personages, children, flowers, mountains, rare stamps, rare beetles, even sometimes politicians and scholars. . . . Just as men spontaneously praise whatever they value, so they spontaneously urge us to join them in praising it: "Isn't she lovely? Wasn't it glorious? Don't you think that magnificent?" . . . I think we delight to praise what we enjoy because the praise not merely expresses but completes the enjoyment; it is its appointed consummation.[12]

God's purpose is not only that you and I enjoy the comfort of the gospel, but that we increase our enjoyment of it by spreading that joy to others, all to the glory of God.

God had told Judah to trust him and no one else. They refused and suffered for it. But God does not forsake people who forsake him. His promise, his initiative, his imagination, his grace and glory are our comfort in our failure. *You can trust this God even more than you trust yourself. You can trust this God absolutely.*

27

God's Uniqueness,
Our Assurance

Isaiah 40:12–26

GOD HAS PROMISED TO COME DOWN TO US in overwhelming glory and remake the whole world. That's the force of Isaiah 40:5, and God always keeps his promises. This world is in for a surprise.

Right now two idols dominate our world. One idol is enormous. The other is smaller but influential. The big idol is secularism. I mean not only naturalism as a technical philosophy but also a general outlook that makes man the measure of all things. Our social atmosphere esteems skepticism as the mature point of view and reduces God to an object of sentimental indulgence, if he has any place at all.[1]

The other rival to God, the smaller idol, is alternative spiritualities. Naturalism leaves us so unsatisfied, we shouldn't be surprised that pagan spirituality has resurfaced as a serious option. But how can anyone tell if a certain spiritual path is mind over matter or demonic or just plain bogus?

Secularism and superstition—despite their obvious differences, they're both allied against the God who loves rationalists and pagans and is inviting them into his glorious kingdom with open arms. The door stands open to both atheists and witches and everyone in between.

The open display of the glory of the Lord will be an adjustment for the church too. One of our theological leaders describes the church of our time as a place where God is "weightless."[2] What is the weightlessness of God? It's the opposite of his glory. If God makes little impact on the lives of Christians, if our churches are not wonderfully heavy with the felt presence of God, is God being glorified in us? We need to start over again. We need to rediscover God. The adjustments would be more than worth it, because his glory is all our happiness.

Why does the glory of God sit lightly on believers today? It may be the fault of those of us who are preachers. Is our constant message to the people, "Behold your God"? Or have we changed the subject? We seem to have sunk to the level of quick-stop churches where God is expected to lubricate the vehicle of American selfishness. Many churches have never known what it's like for God to come down and dwell among them in glory. Charles Misner commented on Albert Einstein's view of Christian preaching:

> [The design of the universe is] very magnificent and shouldn't be taken for granted. In fact, I believe that is why Einstein had so little use for organized religion . . . . He must have looked at what the preachers said about God and felt that they were blaspheming. He had seen much more majesty than they had ever imagined, and they were just not talking about the real thing.[3]

God helping me, I want to talk about the real thing. People must see and sense that God is beautiful with a beauty they have never known. But who is sufficient for these things? As a preacher, I know why Paul asked the church in Ephesus to pray that utterance would be given to him (Ephesians 6:19). How can *I* describe *God*? J. I. Packer, one of our best theological minds, begins his book *Knowing God* by saying, "As clowns yearn to play Hamlet, so I have wanted to write a treatise on God."[4] Augustine prayed:

> O God most high, most good, most powerful . . . most tender-hearted and most just, most remote and most present, most beautiful and most vigorous, stable and ungraspable, unchanging yet changing all things, never new yet never old, renewing all things . . . And what have we said, my God, my Life, my holy Delight? Or what can anyone say when he speaks of you? And alas for those who are silent about you . . . ![5]

Isaiah helps us end our guilty silence by showing us more of God. Standing at the edge of the Grand Canyon, with the work of the Creator displayed before us, our hearts sing to God, "How great thou art!" But that view of his glory isn't enough. We need more than seeing God through our own eyes. Isaiah shows us God *through God's eyes*. If we see God through our own eyes, we diminish him without meaning to or even realizing it. But if we see God through God's eyes, it changes how we see everything else. Isaiah understands that. In this passage he shows us the whole universe through God's eyes.

In Isaiah 40:1–11, God promises to come to us, to make his glory the unavoidable center of everything in this world. Now, in verses 12–26, God anticipates an objection. It's this: Making a promise is one thing; keeping it is another. Can God really do this? When he destroyed the Assyrian army (Isaiah 37), was that just a lucky shot, or can God handle the Babylonians too? Can God overcome the obstacles in our world today? Can God handle any and all opposition the human race throws at him? When God promises a massive reordering of human society around his glory, can we really believe it with an audacious faith? Isaiah's answer echoes the words of the psalmist: "Our God is in the heavens; he does all that he pleases" (Psalm 115:3).

The structure of the passage focuses on the one and only incomparable God, transcending all his rivals.

> A¹ God is the wise Creator (40:12–14)
> > B¹ God is the immense Lord over the nations (40:15–17)
> > > C God alone is God (40:18–20)
> > B² God is the active Lord over world leaders (40:21–24)
> A² God is the watchful Creator (40:25, 26)

God is able to keep every promise he has given us because he is the Creator, he is the Lord of history, and he alone is God.

The Wise Creator

> Who has measured the waters in the hollow of his hand
> > and marked off the heavens with a span,
> enclosed the dust of the earth in a measure
> > and weighed the mountains in scales
> > and the hills in a balance? (Isaiah 40:12)

The waters of all the oceans, lakes, and rivers held as one little pool in God's cupped hand, the heavens marked off by the span between God's outstretched thumb and pinkie, plus the earth, the mountains and the hills— Isaiah takes in the whole creation at a glance and asks in essence, "Who else but God can weigh it, measure it, and determine it with perfect precision and ease?" To us, it's massive. To God, it's easily manageable.

> Who has measured the Spirit of the LORD,
> > or what man shows him his counsel?
> Whom did he consult,
> > and who made him understand?
> Who taught him the path of order,[6]
> > and taught him knowledge,
> > and showed him the way of understanding? (vv. 13, 14)

When God created everything, he needed nothing. All the ideas, all the genius, were his alone. God imagined every tropical fish. He established every function of gravity. He shaped galaxies as irregular, spiral, and elliptical. He came up with it all, by himself alone, out of his own super-intelligence. In Babylonian religion the creator god Marduk had to consult with "Ea, the all-wise." The pagan gods worked by committee.[7] God the Creator needs no one else, including you and me.

The Immense Lord

> Behold, the nations are like a drop from a bucket,
>> and are accounted as the dust on the scales;
>> behold, he takes up the coastlands like fine dust. (v. 15)

If you were carrying a bucketful of water across your backyard and jostled it so that a drop sloshed out and rolled down the outside of the bucket and fell kerplunk to the ground, would you go back and refill the bucket? Of course not. One drop just doesn't matter. And so it is with God's deployment of the nations in his plan for history. He does not despise the nations; he loves them. They are not worthless. *But they derive their worth from him alone.* Sadly, the nations are blind to God's glory, pursuing their own self-exaltation and resisting his kingdom. But this isn't a problem that God has to work around somehow. It doesn't matter. As God governs this world, he has no problems.

> Lebanon would not suffice for fuel,
>> nor are its beasts enough for a burnt offering. (v. 16)

Isaiah moves from the nations in general to one nation in particular. Lebanon was famous for its cedar forests. What if you could cut down all those trees, collect all that timber in one massive pile, and then top it off with the bodies of all of Lebanon's animals as a burnt offering to God? Would it be enough? Would it be worthy of God? Not at all. How much less, then, our little worship.

We should worship God as well as we can. But let's remember that to God a fugue by J. S. Bach is like playing "Chopsticks." Don't let "the greatness of the God we worship" slip in our thinking into "the greatness of our worship of God." When Solomon dedicated the temple in Jerusalem, he prayed, "Behold, heaven and the highest heaven cannot contain you; how much less this house that I have built!" (1 Kings 8:27). There is only one sacrifice worthy of God. It was offered 2,000 years ago on a cross. Everything else is, at best, "Chopsticks."

All the nations are as nothing before him,
   they are accounted by him as less than nothing
   and emptiness. (Isaiah 40:17)

Isaiah shifts back again from a particular nation to all the nations. His point is that when God created man, he didn't dig his own grave. He didn't create an unforeseen difficulty. All human opposition is, to God, a minus factor in the equation of reality. Why are we impressed with it? When we begin to see God through God's eyes, we see the promises of God as more real, more weighty, more solid than anything else in all of life. And that's thrilling.

The Only God

To whom then will you liken God,
   or what likeness compare with him? (v. 18)

Isaiah is a wise pastor. He knows our most urgent need. He knows that the human heart is driven with a compulsive desire to make God controllable by reducing him to our own categories. That's why he insists that God is unique. The Bible often describes God with comparisons from within the creation.[8] He's like a lion, a fountain, a tower, a husband, a father, a soldier, and so forth. But verses like Isaiah 40:18 remind us that no analogy within the creation can say it all. When we see God through God's eyes, he doesn't fit into any box of created size. He goes beyond our categories of experience and therefore deserves our trust.

An idol! A craftsman casts it,
   and a goldsmith overlays it with gold
   and casts for it silver chains.
He who is too impoverished for an offering
   chooses wood that will not rot;
he seeks out a skilled craftsman
   to set up an idol that will not move. (vv. 19, 20)

Isaiah doesn't criticize idol-making; he just describes it. Look closely. He might as well be writing a caption for a *National Geographic* photograph of idol manufacture. But description is all he has to do. Idol-making is too stupid to require comment. His serious tones and careful observations are dripping with sarcasm. Idols may be decked out impressively, they might even inspire awe and mystery, but all they are is what they are. And that's why we must never derive our sense of worth from anything within the creation. *It will rot.* That's why we must delight that God alone is God. *His incomparability is our salvation.*

The Active Lord

Do you not know? Do you not hear?
  Has it not been told you from the beginning?
  Have you not understood from the foundations of the earth? (v. 21)

Isaiah argues with us because what we know to be true doesn't always make an impact on us. But it helps when we stop seeing the glory of God through our own eyes and begin to see him through his own eyes. What difference does that make as we look out on the political realities and social constructs of our world today?

It is he who sits above the circle of the earth,
  and its inhabitants are like grasshoppers;
who stretches out the heavens like a curtain,
  and spreads them like a tent to dwell in;
who brings princes to nothing,
  and makes the rulers of the earth as emptiness.
Scarcely are they planted, scarcely sown,
  scarcely has their stem taken root in the earth,
when he blows on them, and they wither,
  and the tempest carries them off like stubble. (vv. 22–24)

God is at work in the world today. It is he who raises up leaders and brings them down again, according to his own purpose and for his own glory. The power brokers who seem so formidable to us, with their monumental egos and pretentious ambitions, are to God like little seedlings—scarcely planted—and God merely blows on them, with zero effort on his part, and to them his mere puff of air is a raging tempest driving them into oblivion. And that makes God himself the only world-figure really to fear, doesn't it?

The Watchful Creator

To whom then will you compare me,
  that I should be like him? says the Holy One. (v. 25)

We can love the holiness of God because his holiness means he's in a category all his own. We need Someone who is *not* like us. Only a holy, incomparable God can save us. So Isaiah drives his point home with one final question:

Lift up your eyes on high and see:
  who created these?

> He who brings out their host by number,
>> calling them all by name,
> by the greatness of his might,
>> and because he is strong in power
>> not one is missing. (v. 26)

Go outside on a clear night. Look overhead. Don't take it all for granted. Think about who created those stars. There is a God in Heaven who brings them out every night, one by one. He calls each by name. This vast universe we live in is sustained, moment by moment, by the greatness of his might. And nothing, not the smallest star, falls through the cracks.

The Babylonians were astrologers. That's why Isaiah concludes by directing our eyes to the stars. The heavenly bodies the Babylonians worshiped are in fact the display of *God's* glory. The constellations the Babylonians believed were controlling the destinies of man are themselves controlled by *God.*

We today, with a scientific outlook, should be even more awestruck at the greatness of God displayed in the heavens. Here we are on tiny Planet Earth. The closest star to us is, of course, the sun. The sun generates energy with the same explosiveness as a hydrogen bomb—its own continuous internal nuclear fission. The surface of the sun is a relatively cool 10,000 degrees Fahrenheit, while the center is a toasty 27,000,000 degrees. The diameter of the sun is 870,000 miles, 109 times larger than the earth, and its volume could contain 1,000,000 earths. Its luminosity is equal to four million trillion 100-watt lightbulbs—more than you'll find even at Home Depot. And the sun is just an average star.

Our solar system is inside the galaxy called the Milky Way. And this galaxy we live in is shaped like a spiral, a gigantic pinwheel spinning in the open expanse of space, with our solar system rotating around the center once every million years or so. We lie about two-thirds of the way out from the center of the galaxy, in what might be considered the boondocks. The Milky Way is 104,000 light-years across, containing over 100 billion stars. To count them one by one would take us over 3,000 years. And according to the latest probings of the Hubble Space Telescope, there are hundreds of billions of galaxies in God's universe!

But so what? Is all this just a big stunt? No. God wants us to see something about himself. The God who brings out their host by number every night, who calls them all by name so that not one of them is missing—this God has made a promise to us about this fifth-rate little world we live in. *He has promised us himself in all his glory.* Do you think this God deserves your confidence? Do you think this God who manages the universe, right down to the faintest star, will lose track of you?

In this passage Isaiah is speaking to people whose mood is like that of many today. They may say the right things, but deep inside they don't really believe anymore—not with a faith that overcomes the world. They're looking at things through their own eyes. So the promises of God do not put a spring in their step and a sparkle in their eye and steel in their backbone. Why? God just doesn't look big enough for the risk-taking audacity of true faith. But God is inviting us to turn our perceptions around and see everything from his point of view. He understands that the struggle of faith is won or lost in the way we perceive reality. Yes, we are dwarfed by the creation; but the creation is dwarfed by God. See it that way. See him that way. When you feel threatened by world events and overwhelmed by your own problems, there's another way to perceive it all. God is opening up to you a prophetic vision. And the Biblical gospel is his way of calling to us, "Behold your God!" (Isaiah 40:9).

Will you repent of the sin of diminishing God in your thoughts? It is a hidden idolatry.

> Let us beware lest we in our pride accept the erroneous notion that idolatry consists only in kneeling before visible objects of adoration, and that civilized peoples are therefore free from it. The essence of idolatry is the entertainment of thoughts about God that are unworthy of Him.[9]

Will you dethrone your idols and rediscover God? Look at God, and everything else, through *his* eyes.

28

God's Greatness,
Our Renewal

ISAIAH 40:27–31

VIKTOR FRANKL WAS ONE OF EUROPE'S leading psychiatrists. But from 1942–1945 he endured imprisonment in Auschwitz and three other Nazi concentration camps. He saw what made the difference between the survivors and the dead, and it wasn't a matter of physical health and strength. What made the difference between the living and the dead was hope—something to live for beyond the barbed wire, something to look forward to, something to go home to after the war. He wrote about it in *Man's Search for Meaning*:

> The prisoner who had lost faith in the future—his future—was doomed. With his loss of belief in the future, he also lost his spiritual hold; he let himself decline and became subject to mental and physical decay. Usually this happened quite suddenly, in the form of a crisis, the symptoms of which were familiar to the experienced camp inmate. . . . Usually it began with the prisoner refusing one morning to get dressed and wash or to go out on the parade grounds. No entreaties, no blows, no threats had any effect. He just lay there, hardly moving. If this crisis was brought about by an illness, he refused to be taken to the sick-bay or to do anything to help himself. He simply gave up. There he remained, lying in his own excreta, and nothing bothered him any more.[1]

Neither will we survive without something to live for beyond the barbed wire of this life. We'll give up and just lie here. It's a common condition, called despair.

We look out on the shopping malls and hamburger joints and freeways—is that what we have to settle for? If the best we can expect is next summer's vacation in Hawaii or even just next weekend's outing at the lake, if our hope is a comfortable, successful existence until we die, we'll inevitably fall into the lifestyle Pascal called "licking the earth"—ego, carnality, and materialism. But if we have something beyond the barbed wire to look forward to, something beautiful that's ours, something to live for that can never be taken away from us, we can face anything.

We live our lives right now out of a vital connection with the future.[2] That's why hope makes us invincible. In Isaiah 40:27–31 God is saying, "My promises can give you liftoff, so that you rise up on eagle's wings. Let me show you how."

Isaiah is prophesying to the Jews exiled in Babylon. By this time they've been in captivity for some decades and are teetering on the edge of despair. They would have understood a line in Jackson Browne's song "The Pretender." He speaks of lovers watching "the ships bearing their dreams sail out of sight." We've all thought, *There goes my life. There goes my happiness. All I can look forward to now is one long death sentence.* When our thoughts fall that way, what does God do? He comes with an infusion of hope. He hasn't abandoned us. He's bringing us the display of his glory (Isaiah 40:5). That's the future of the whole world. So reality is more than this prison camp, and better too. There's something beyond the barbed wire—God himself. And he is coming.

In three simple movements, Isaiah points the way out of our despair toward renewal in hope.

> A[1] Our despair (40:27)
>   B God's greatness (40:28, 29)
> A[2] Our renewal (40:30, 31)

The prophet's certainty is God himself, the centerpiece of the brief paragraph. God is not too great to bother with us; he's too great to overlook us.

Our Despair

> Why do you say, O Jacob,
>   and speak, O Israel,
> "My way is hidden from the LORD,
>   and my right is disregarded by my God"? (Isaiah 40:27)

The Jewish exiles living under a kind of mass house arrest in Babylon felt abandoned by God: "The direction my life has taken—I might as well have fallen off the edge of the earth. The justice due to me completely escapes God's notice." Haven't we all asked, "Where is God when I need him? He demands so much but doesn't lift a finger to help. And this happens time after time"? This way of thinking is not new. John Knox, the Scottish reformer, wrote:

> By what means Satan first drew mankind from the obedience of God, the Scripture doth witness: To wit, by pouring into their hearts that poison, that God did not love them.[3]

Isaiah articulates for us our poisonous thoughts, but not to coddle us. He challenges us: "*Why* do you say, O Jacob?" Isaiah reminds me of a letter Martin Luther wrote to his fellow-reformer Philipp Melanchthon, whose faith was faltering:

> I pray for you very earnestly, and I am deeply pained that you keep sucking up cares like a leech and thus rendering my prayers vain. Christ knows whether it comes from stupidity or the Spirit, but I for my part am not very much troubled about our cause. Indeed, I am more hopeful than I expected to be. God who is able to raise the dead is also able to uphold his cause when it is falling or to raise it up again when it has fallen or to move it forward when it is standing. If we are not worthy instruments to accomplish his purpose, he will find others. If we are not strengthened by his promises, where in all the world are the people to whom these promises apply? But more of this another time. After all, my writing this is like pouring water into the sea.[4]

No one lives with an unwavering faith. But Isaiah, like Luther, reasons with us, challenging the irrationality of our unbelief, to help us get back on track.

He understands that there are two kinds of doubt. One kind of doubt *struggles to believe* in view of "the slings and arrows of outrageous fortune." This kind of doubt is open to God's answers. It's willing to listen. The other kind of doubt *resists belief.* Even when good and sufficient reasons are offered, this kind of doubt folds its arms in defiance and says, "Nah! I *still* doubt it. And nothing you can say will satisfy me." That kind of doubt isn't even able to hear what God has to say.

The Jewish exiles seem to have been floating somewhere between a struggling faith and a cynical defiance. So what does God do? He goes the second mile with them. He has already shown them his own incomparability over the entire creation (Isaiah 40:12–26). If not even the faintest star escapes God's attention, the exiles should be confident that God's eye is on them. But now he reminds them of something about themselves. They are "Jacob/Israel." However they may see themselves, God sees them as under his covenant of grace. They still have a place in his heart.

What do these names, "Jacob" and "Israel," evoke? Long before, in *the* crisis of his life, the patriarch Jacob wrestled with God. He was desperate for God's blessing, and God did bless him. God always blesses people who are desperate enough to wrestle with him. As a token of the new beginning in Jacob's life, God changed his name to Israel, "for you have striven with God and with men, and have prevailed" (Genesis 32:28). Now Isaiah is reminding this generation of Israel's descendants, during *the* crisis of their lives, that successful striving with God is their heritage. Their forefather prevailed with God, and so can they. So can we. With the finished work of Christ on the cross guaranteeing even to the most meager faith all of God's promises, he sees us not as victims but as more than conquerors.

Some years ago I felt abandoned by God. I needed help. I began to correspond with Rev. William Still, an older friend in the Church of Scotland. We interacted at length in a series of letters. At one point, in his fatherly way, he wrote, "I do see that a great deal of this has to do with your own sense of worthlessness; but, dear brother, it is quite irrational." I had to throw my head back and laugh when I read that. Of course! Part of the reason I had lost contact with God's love was that my own sense of worth had been hollowed out, for reasons I won't go into right now. I had lost a sense of who I was in Christ, which darkened my view of Christ himself. God says to us all, "Not only do I want you to know how great I am for you, I also want you to know how significant you are to me. Even with your imperfect faith, you have striven with me and have prevailed. And I will never back out on my promises to you."

God's Greatness

> Have you not known? Have you not heard?
> The LORD is the everlasting God,
>   the Creator of the ends of the earth.
> He does not faint or grow weary;
>   his understanding is unsearchable. (Isaiah 40:28)

Everything that matters in life hangs on who God is. What does Isaiah say? Four things. First, *God is eternal, everlasting*. You and I are locked inside a narrow little slot called "right now." The present moment is all we experience. And the urgency of this moment can squeeze us with its pressures, so that we make costly mistakes out of our own exaggerated sense of emergency. We always sin too soon. But God is not confined to time. In his sweeping eternity God is equally present to all points of time at once. He is always out ahead of us. So we should never panic if things aren't falling together according to our deadlines. God is working his purpose out in his own way, at his own pace, without our hurried, nervous desperation.

Secondly, *God is the Creator of everything*, all the way to the very "ends of the earth." There is not a single square inch on this earth unknown to God or lying beyond the range of his presence. Anywhere life may take us, whether Babylonian exile or a lonely hotel room or an intensive care unit, God will already be there for us. We lie in his grace and power at all times, everywhere.

Thirdly, *God is always at work*. We tire daily. We need nourishment and rest every day. We spend about a third of our lives asleep in bed, recouping our strength, and then we die. God does not need restoration. He is an eternally inexhaustible fountain of exuberance and joy. In any given event in your life, he is actively accomplishing about 10,000 things you aren't even aware of. And he never grows tired or weary but is forever fresh, always alert, always able.

Fourthly, *God is wise, and "his understanding is unsearchable."* In other words, we can't figure God out. We often try to find a deepened insight into the meaning and purpose of events. And it is striking when we can trace the movements of his hand. But for every event that we can interpret, aren't there dozens of mysteries as well? That's what the Bible is affirming here. Life is often bewildering to us, but it isn't bewildering to God. There are depths to God's wisdom we can't access. If our lives are not exactly the way we would like them to be, we can be sure they are precisely the way God wants them to be. He knows what he's doing. So we don't live by explanations; we live by promises. We don't figure God out by our brains; we submit to him by faith.

God is always right now, always right here, always at work and always wise. And that changes everything, doesn't it? Why? Because God is not only glorious in himself; he also shares his strength with us in our weakness.

> He gives power to the faint,
>   and to him who has no might he increases strength. (Isaiah 40:29)

God wants to get involved in our subjectivity by making his power perfect in our weakness. The word group "faint" and "be/grow weary" is the key to this passage, occurring seven times. God is speaking to weak, tired, discouraged people. Who are "the faint" in verse 29? They're the complainers quoted in verse 27. So, *how* are these people faint and weak and weary? They're weak in faith. Their fatigue is spiritual. They're weak in courage. They feel like quitting. And it's weaklings like them (and like us) who receive the power of God to live with our heads held high and with a lively confidence in a big God, because we can see in his promise a bright future for us out there beyond the barbed wire. People who find their reasons for living in *God* have an uncanny resilience about them. They live in ongoing renewal. How does God do this?

Our Renewal

> Even youths shall faint and be weary,
>   and young men shall fall exhausted;
> but they who wait for the LORD shall renew their strength;
>   they shall mount up with wings like eagles;
> they shall run and not be weary;
>   they shall walk and not faint. (Isaiah 40:30, 31)

Isaiah's point in verse 30 is blunt. Human strength at its best, in its prime, will inevitably fail. We're no match for the demands of life. But we're not doomed to our own potential. There is a power beyond ourselves, and we can experience it.

In verse 31 Isaiah is not merely saying, "God enables those who draw strength from his promise." He is saying, "God enables those who draw strength from his promise *to do the impossible*." The weak soar like eagles and run without tiring and walk without quitting. Their confidence in God will not let them lie down and give up. It's not a matter of willpower but of expectancy.

The key is the word "wait." What does it mean? To wait for the Lord means to live in confident, eager suspense. It means to live with the tension of promises revealed but not yet fulfilled.[5] This waiting is not killing time. It isn't sitting around, drumming your fingers. It is waiting on tip-toe, waiting with eager longing. It is forgetting what lies behind, straining forward to what lies ahead, and pressing on toward the goal (Philippians 3:13, 14). It isn't erratic bursts of hyperactivity within a general pattern of boredom. It is steady, rugged progress, sustained by the conviction that the display of God's glory in Christ is *yours*.

Some translations of the Bible say that our part is to "hope" in the Lord. That isn't wrong. But the ESV is wise to use the word "wait," because waiting is an important part of our faith. Waiting is what faith does *before* God's answer shows up. God gives us great and precious promises, and then he calls us to wait. And Isaiah's point is that such bright expectancy is the psychological leverage God uses to empower us. The "how" question is answered in this word "wait." Are you willing to wait? Are you willing to let God set the pace? Or are you such a controller you can't live on God's terms? Is the prospect of having the glory of the Lord as your eternal delight out beyond the barbed wire—does your heart prize him as *worth* the wait?

If so, your heart will be endlessly renewed until that great day. If not, you're on your own.

We sometimes look for hope in the wrong places. We look for reasons to live here inside the barbed wire rather than out there in the promised glory of God. But you and I don't need a quick fix. What we need is a clearer vision of God and a keener passion for his glory. What we need is to find rest in his faithfulness and energy in his desirability. Christianity is not a way to cut a deal with God for an easier life now. Christianity is what renews us to live for our real payoff in the future that God has promised.

How can we experience more of what Isaiah is offering? We have to ask ourselves two questions. First: Do I believe that God can take a quitter like me and make him into a hero? We might gulp before we answer that question, but most of us would probably agree that Almighty God in Heaven can do even that. But then we need to ask the second question: Have I deliberately shifted the loyalty of my heart from the false glory of this world to the coming glory of the Lord? God has promised that Christ will bring us salvation with his overwhelming glory. Is that where I have staked my happiness?

It will not do to put my faith in God while I keep my heart on this world. God will not underwrite my worldliness with his power. He never promised the soaring strength of eagles so I could go on grunting in the sty of Babylon. Waiting for the Lord means not only that I trust him to be true (the "rock" of Isaiah 26:4), but also that I admire him as stunning (the "glory" of Isaiah 40:5). Some Christians live defeated lives because God allows them to. He will not support our carnality. But he will renew the heart that says to him, "Whom have I in heaven but you? And there is nothing on earth that I desire besides you" (Psalm 73:25).

On Saturday morning, January 12, 1723, Jonathan Edwards wrote these words in his journal:

> I have been before God, and have given myself, all that I am and have, to God, so that I am not in any respect my own. . . . I have given myself clear away, and have not retained anything as my own. . . . I have this morning told him that I did take him for my whole portion and felicity, looking upon nothing else as any part of my happiness, nor acting as if it were. . . .[6]

In other words, "All I want out of my life, what I'll be happy to walk away with, is God and God alone. Whatever other gifts he gives me I will enjoy with thanks to him and for his sake. But God is my salvation, and everything else in my existence will find its meaning in reference to God, or it will have no meaning for me at all." Paul charted his course that way, and God brought him all the way through. At the end Paul wrote: "I have fought the good fight, I have finished the race, I have kept the faith. Henceforth there is laid up for me the crown of righteousness, which the Lord, the righteous judge, will award to me on that Day, and not only to me but also to all who have *loved* his appearing" (2 Timothy 4:7, 8).

We're all weak. But we don't have to be supermen. God simply calls us to believe what we believe and to set our hearts on things above. If we will, that longing for God is the channel through which his power will lift us and renew us and cheer us all the way there.

29

The Reality of God in an Unreal World

ISAIAH 41:1–20

THERE WAS A TIME WHEN THE BIG CHALLENGE to Christianity in the college classroom was Biology 101. But by now the theory of evolution is being intelligently scrutinized.[1] The real challenge today is in the humanities. It's a bigger challenge because it's more than academic. The atmosphere we swim in every day is corrosive of meaning.

The growing consensus today is that truth is a hoax. What people used to call truth is really just a matter of perception and even politics. In literature, for example, interpretation is no longer a matter of submitting to a text to draw out the meaning intended by the author. Interpretation is when meanings are sparked by the reader's own response to a text. That way, even the Bible can mean anything. As for history, "the facts" are no longer freestanding objects of inquiry. Now the record of history is how some privileged class has told *its* version of events. So Christopher Columbus wasn't an explorer. Now we know he was a Eurocentric oppressor. The challenge of our times is the denial of objectivity, and all that's left is political advocacy.

Today truth really is blowin' in the wind. But when we deny truth, we empty our own lives of significance. Dorothy Sayers put it this way:

> In the world it is called Tolerance, but in hell it is called Despair . . . the sin that believes in nothing, cares for nothing, seeks to know nothing, interferes with nothing, enjoys nothing, hates nothing, finds purpose in nothing, lives for nothing, and remains alive because there is nothing for which it will die.[2]

That is our hollowed-out world, the world God wants to befriend and persuade.

The skepticism of our age isn't completely wrong. Bogus claims to authority have been taking advantage of people and excluding people and reinforcing unfair privilege for ages. It's right to expose all high-sounding pretense. But there is one claim to truth that does deserve our all—the gospel of Jesus Christ. Why? Because at the center of his message is a cross. The cross is God's deconstruction of worldly power. The cross declares that weakness is power and loss is gain and servanthood is greatness. The cross proves that this world does suppress the truth and does oppose what's right. But God himself was willing to take that abuse from us. He suffered unspeakably, in order to love us absolutely and to tell us the truth. The dying love of Jesus is the only truth-claim that deserves our trust.

Isaiah is a prophet of this gospel. He writes with a clear sense of truth. He sees one true God meaningfully at work in history. He denies all counter-explanations of reality. But this God doesn't exploit us; he bears our burdens for us. And Isaiah doesn't just assert that. He reasons with us. In fact, he shows God himself coming down to persuade us, equipping us with a decisive faith in a world of confusion.

Isaiah's thought moves in two directions—God's exclusive sovereignty over history (41:1–7) and God's gracious eagerness to bear our burdens along the way (41:8–20).

1. God alone activates history (41:1–7)
    A¹ God invites the nations to settle a question (41:1)
        B Who controls history? "I, the LORD" (41:2–4)
    A² The nations flee to their idols (41:5–7)
2. God alone emboldens us (41:8–20)
    A He upholds his fearful servant (41:8–13)
        B He transforms his worm into a threshing sledge (41:14–16)
        C He refreshes his thirsty pilgrims (41:17–20)

Isaiah wants to win the glad consent of our hearts that one true God exists, he is involved in history and our lives, and he can carry us through everything.

God Alone Activates History

Listen to me in silence, O coastlands;
    let the peoples renew their strength;
let them approach, then let them speak;
    let us together draw near for judgment. (Isaiah 41:1)

God is speaking. He turns his eye to the Gentile nations, including the distant coastlands, and invites them to a debate. The "judgment" in the last line is not condemnation but decision. The NIV reads, "Let us meet together *at the place of judgment*," that is, in a court of law. God is challenging the nations to decide something on the basis of a proper consideration of the evidences. He wants us to listen to him. He invites us to speak. He wants us to make up our minds.

But what do we stand to gain from engaging thoughtfully with God? There's a clue in the second line: "Let the peoples renew their strength." That sounds familiar. Where have we seen that language before? At the end of the preceding chapter: "They who wait for the LORD shall renew their strength" (40:31). God said that to his covenant people. So do you see? Here in chapter 41 God is offering the whole world the same power of the Holy Spirit to live in buoyant hope. It isn't just for insiders. God wants *the nations* to enjoy the promise of his glory. Didn't he say that all flesh shall see it together (40:5)? From the beginning, the fullest expression of God's purpose has been one multi-ethnic community of redemption in Jesus Christ (Ephesians 2:11—3:12). So the very challenge God lays down here has an offer of inclusion. He's not out just to win the argument; he wants to refresh all of us with hope.

But something has to be settled first. A widespread misconception of God has to be cleared away—the idea that God is uninvolved in our world today and therefore our lives have no meaning. We have to make up our minds about that.

> Who stirred up one from the east
>   whom victory meets at every step?
> He gives up nations before him,
>   so that he tramples kings underfoot;
> he makes them like dust with his sword,
>   like driven stubble with his bow.
> He pursues them and passes on safely,
>   by paths his feet have not trod. (Isaiah 41:2, 3)

Two things here—first, the question, secondly, the answer. The question is not what? but who? That's important. Isaiah is no secularist. When he looks at the movements sweeping across history, he does not ask about class economics, for example. He asks about a Person. And we need to learn to ask Isaianic questions about our world today. It makes a difference.

Do things just happen, or is God at work? Are we involved in chance or Providence? Is history cyclical, with events recurring on a seasonal pattern, or is history taking us toward a final consummation? Are we part of a larger story, or is the meaning of our lives up to us alone? And if all we have is the bits and pieces of our own subjectivity to work with, who can say what's right and wrong, true and false, beautiful and ugly, meaningful and stupid? Dostoevsky articulated the implications of banning God from the questions of life: "Immortality of the soul does not exist, therefore there is no virtue, therefore everything is permitted."[3] But by asking who?, by taking God seriously into account, Isaiah's Biblical way of thinking leads us forward, inevitably if not immediately, toward the question of all questions: *Who was Jesus?* How do we account for this man who changed the course of history not by conquering but by suffering?

As the Holy Spirit awakens in you a new awareness of Christ, he floods your life with transcendent meaning. You see your life as a meaningful sub-plot in the divine drama. You see the cross as God coming down in love to take upon himself the guilt of human rebels bent on ignoring him. And now he is wooing out of the nations a people for himself, because he longs for multitudes to be drawn up into his own mega-joy. God is glorifying himself by communicating to us the wonders of his redemptive love. This outpouring of divine fullness through Christ—*that* is the meaning of human history. And you can be a part of it. Therefore, your first step toward God might be to look again at your life and stop asking what? and start asking who? You'll see things in a new way.

Secondly, the answer. The "He" in "*He* gives up nations before him" is God. That's clear. But what isn't as clear is that the "him" is Cyrus the Great, the founder of the Persian empire. Cyrus is "one from the east." Isaiah is saying that God is activating human history, including the conquerors who rock the world scene. In fact, the towering figures of history like Cyrus are so incidental in terms of historical causation that Isaiah doesn't even bother to name Cyrus—not yet, anyway. He will later (44:28). But for now, it's enough for us to see God as the great Stirrer of events in history. Not by remote control but by direct "stirring," moment by moment, God is accomplishing his redemptive will in this world in which we live.

But why Cyrus, of all people? Because Isaiah is writing to the Jews exiled in Babylon in the sixth century B.C. As the decades of that century wore on and the exiles became increasingly discouraged, Cyrus leaped into historical prominence, conquered Babylon in 539, liberated the peoples held captive there, including the Jews, and repatriated them in their homelands.[4] But as Cyrus rides triumphantly toward world dominion, Isaiah wants everyone to see *God* at work.

> Who has performed and done this,
>   calling the generations from the beginning?
> I, the LORD, the first,
>   and with the last; I am he. (Isaiah 41:4)

This is why the Westminster Confession of Faith affirms, "God from all eternity did, by the most wise and holy counsel of his own will, freely and unchangeably ordain whatsoever comes to pass" (III:1). But not only did God set human events in motion at the beginning, his hand is on the helm all along the way: "I, the LORD, the first, and with the last." When God launched history, he did not unleash independent forces. He was the first cause, he will be with the last effect at the final nanosecond of time, and he is with us right now. Neither Cyrus in 539 B.C. nor your life today is a fluke. Every event within time, including your life, is yet one more demonstration of "I am he." That's how significant you are.

God is inviting the whole world to think that through. And he proves his sovereign presence in this case by predicting the rise of Cyrus over a century in advance. Prophecy is a good argument for God's sovereignty over this world. But as Cyrus appears, going from strength to strength, how do the nations respond?

> The coastlands have seen and are afraid;
>> the ends of the earth tremble;
>> they have drawn near and come.
> Everyone helps his neighbor
>> and says to his brother, "Be strong!"
> The craftsman strengthens the goldsmith,
>> and he who smooths with the hammer him who strikes the anvil,
> saying of the soldering, "It is good";
>> and they strengthen it with nails so that it cannot be moved. (Isaiah 41:5–7)

God moves in history. He invites the nations to take a close look. What do they do? They only reinforce their idols. They long for stability amid the buffetings of life. But their blindness leaves them with no recourse but to manufacture their own gods to help them. God is on the move right out in the open for all to see, but people feel the effects of his presence with dread. So they cheer one another up with their own impotent, man-made ideologies.

I think it was G. K. Chesterton who said, "When people stop believing in God, they don't believe in nothing; they believe in anything." That's true. When fearful people lose their sense of God, what do they do? They join together to construct their own meanings, their own myths. And the artificiality of it all is the world's guilty secret (Romans 1:18–32).

When the craftsman says in verse 7, "It is good," Isaiah hears a parody of the creation account. In Genesis 1, didn't God declare his creation "good"?[5] But here a frightened little created being looks with hopeful longing at the welding on his metallic god and pronounces it "good." That's what we're reduced to, in some way or other, if we don't delight in the

Sovereign of history as our Mighty Fortress. We're left with shoring up our own idols rather than resting in the arms of God.

So the first thing Isaiah does is point us to the God who is with us in this troubled world. He is at work. His glorious salvation is coming. He's moving everything toward that goal. Fortified with a clear awareness of God, we can face anything. Isaiah develops that point next.

God Alone Emboldens Us

> But you, Israel, my servant,
>   Jacob, whom I have chosen,
>   the offspring of Abraham, my friend;
> you whom I took from the ends of the earth,
>   and called from its farthest corners,
> saying to you, "You are my servant,
>   I have chosen you and not cast you off";
> fear not, for I am with you;
>   be not dismayed, for I am your God;
> I will strengthen you, I will help you,
>   I will uphold you with my righteous right hand. (Isaiah 41:8–10)

God longs for us to draw strength from his greatness. Do you see here how he lingers over his commitments to his people? He chose us. He called us. He's committed to us. People who have a sense of that in their hearts are unstoppable.

The word "but" at the beginning of these verses is important. Isaiah is drawing a contrast. On the one hand, the nations nervously prop up their helpless, homemade saviors. On the other hand, the Sovereign of the universe chooses us and upholds us by his unerringly righteous right hand. God is saying, "I want you to *know* what you can expect from me: my presence, my strength, my help, my perfect support." And when he calls us his servant, he's not putting us down. He's saying we're his responsibility, and he will act responsibly.

We need that assurance. When we live for God in this world, we stand out in an awkward way. We even draw fire. But totally apart from any imagined strength of our own, God is our Shield and Defender. So let's not chicken out. After we have demonstrated the value of God by our suffering, he knows what to do with all who have tormented us. They will so utterly disappear, we'll look around for them in vain (vv. 11, 12). The gospel says, "Do not be frightened in anything by your opponents. This is a clear sign to them of their destruction, but of your salvation, and that from God. For it has been granted to you that for the sake of Christ you should not only believe in him but also suffer for his sake" (Philippians 1:28, 29). In the meantime, God will be there for us.

> For I, the LORD your God,
>> hold your right hand;
> it is I who say to you, "Fear not,
>> I am the one who helps you." (Isaiah 41:13)

Are you a fearful person? Do you gravitate toward the path of least resistance? Maybe it's because you're relying on the weakness of idols. God understands that. So he is assuring you in the most emphatic way: "I am not like the idols. I will prop *you* up. Fear not. Live for me with an audacious faith. I am the one who helps you."

That is the first of three strong assurances in verses 8–20. We are important to God. And when we are opposed, he will uphold us. The second assurance is in verses 14–16. Isaiah is heaping reason upon reason for us to live right out loud for God.

> Fear not, you worm Jacob,
>> you men of Israel!
> I am the one who helps you, declares the LORD;
>> your Redeemer is the Holy One of Israel.
> Behold, I make of you a threshing sledge,
>> new, sharp, and having teeth;
> you shall thresh the mountains and crush them,
>> and you shall make the hills like chaff;
> you shall winnow them, and the wind shall carry them away,
>> and the tempest shall scatter them.
> And you shall rejoice in the LORD;
>> in the Holy One of Israel you shall glory.

The way to make sense of this laughable scenario is to think back to chapter 40. God said there that the moral topography of the whole world would be reordered to make way for the glory of the Lord (vv. 3–5). The world as it is now isn't suitable for the display of God. Everything is going to change. Every valley shall be lifted up and every mountain and hill made low, and so forth. Now in chapter 41 God is saying that he intends to use *us* to do it. We're totally inadequate. But God makes a worm into a threshing sledge—and not an old, worn-out thresher but a sharp, new one that gets the job done.

Isaiah is not talking about Christian political power taking over. He's talking about the gospel of human weakness triumphing over opposition and our timid faith overcoming the world. That prepares the way of the Lord. If you know Christians, you'll probably agree with me that it's a miracle the church accomplishes anything at all. But he makes us more than conquerors, for his glory. The Bible says, "We have this treasure in jars of clay, to show that the surpassing power belongs to God and not to us" (2 Corinthians 4:7). And in his strength alone, our privilege is to thresh into smithereens every obstacle to rejoicing in the Lord (Isaiah 41:16). That's our job. Let's get on with it, in the power of the Holy Spirit.

The final emboldening assurance is in verses 17–20, the most thrilling of all to me personally. God is a life-giving person.

> When the poor and needy seek water,
>   and there is none,
>   and their tongue is parched with thirst,
> I the LORD will answer them;
>   I the God of Israel will not forsake them.
> I will open rivers on the bare heights,
>   and fountains in the midst of the valleys.
> I will make the wilderness a pool of water,
>   and the dry land springs of water. (Isaiah 41:17, 18)

Are we poor and needy and parched with thirst? Or are we all perfectly complete? God is presenting himself to us as our refreshment.[6] Jesus said, "If anyone thirsts, let him come to me and drink. Whoever believes in me, as the Scripture has said, 'Out of his heart will flow rivers of living water'" (John 7:37, 38). And what is God's ultimate purpose in lavishing himself upon us so richly?

> . . . that men may see and know,
>   may consider and understand together,
> that the hand of the LORD has done this,
>   the Holy One of Israel has created it. (Isaiah 41:20)

We get the mercy, and God gets the glory. So the answer to the question "Who?" back in verse 2 is grander than we might have thought. The One stirring up the turbulence of history is not someone to dread; by his sovereign greatness he also pours life-giving refreshment upon dry people.

Water outpoured symbolizes bountiful salvation overflowing with the Holy Spirit. When thirsty people "seek water" in prayer, God answers with the greatest gift in the universe: *himself* in his immediacy and fullness (Luke 11:11–13). And he promises not just a morning dew or a light sprinkling but rivers and fountains and pools and springs. We need that much of God.

Life is exhausting, and we are often dry. But God more than compensates with himself.

By refreshing us, God increases his own glory. The outflowings of his renewing grace open people's minds to see, know, consider, and understand how good he really is (1 Corinthians 2:12–14). That's *why* he pours out refreshment from Heaven. And we serve his purpose by enjoying his abundant goodness in the sight of the nations. Therefore, seek this outpouring. Embrace this fullness. Experience God. The most convincing witness in a truth-denying world is not an apologetic argument of our own brilliance; the most convincing answer to our times is the manifest presence of God in our midst. Stake your life, your very survival, on the reality of the Holy Spirit. Live on John 14—16 and Romans 8 and 1 Corinthians 1—2 and other passages on the Spirit. Think of God and treat God and pray to God in keeping with his own self-revelation in his Word. Believe that the sovereign Spirit can uphold you, strengthen you, refresh you. He will make you invincible.

Is your faith self-defined? Have you made yourself what you are? Or are you living proof of what God can do? If you've gone no further than your own legs can carry you and seen no more than your own eyes can show you and tasted no more than your own thoughts can convey to you, you are lost. No wonder you don't live boldly for God. You have no meaning beyond yourself. May the Holy Spirit lead you into some private room today to weep and repent and look to Christ alone, because authentic Christianity is miracle, not management. May you give up on yourself and delight in the sovereign Christ as all the Savior you need. He will fill your life with meaning, and you will make a difference for his glory in the world today.

30

A Delusion, a Servant, a New Song

ISAIAH 41:21—42:17

ISAIAH DOESN'T RESPECT IDOLS. That's obvious. What's less obvious is whether his message is relevant to us today. Didn't modern civilization leave idols behind a long time ago? Doesn't idolatry belong to primitive cultures? That depends.

If idols were only images and figurines and fertility charms and so forth, Isaiah's message would be of antiquarian interest only. But the Bible is smarter than that. Even the Old Testament speaks of people taking idols *into their hearts* (Ezekiel 14:1–11). Idols don't have to be actual images to work their spell on the human psyche. They can be internalized in our hearts. If we understand that an idol is any heart-level substitute for God, then we can see that the modern world is infested with idols. In fact, John Calvin said that the human heart is a perpetual idol-factory.[1]

Idolatry, therefore, is more than a pagan problem. It's a human problem. It's a modern problem. In fact, it's a Christian problem. The Old Testament repeatedly warns the covenant community against idolatry, beginning with the story of the golden calf (Exodus 32). We know that warning applies to us today because the New Testament says it does (1 Corinthians 10:1–12). The New Testament says to us, "Therefore, my beloved, flee from idolatry" (1 Corinthians 10:14). "Little children, keep yourselves from idols" (1 John 5:21). And the flip side of that warning is the gospel's glad announcement that "Christ . . . is your life" (Colossians 3:4).

This is why the Bible attacks idols so aggressively. Christ is serious about being our happiness. His salvation is not a pious slogan; it is our life.

The problem is, we have a hard time believing that. We waffle. He can seem more obligatory than satisfying. And we inevitably gravitate toward whatever we believe will make us happy. So, this category *idolatry* really explains something about us. It explains why we all struggle with persistent, enslaving sins that hold us back. The sin itself is only the surface problem, and mere willpower can't get rid of it. The real problem causing the sinful behavior is some idol or other captivating our hearts by promising to make us happy, and we fall for it. We tell ourselves that our joy and freedom and significance and security require something more than Christ. Our faith in him is so unimaginative. Our expectations of him are so low. We run from him to stuff ourselves full of counterfeit pleasures and empty salvations. What we need every day is to taste the goodness of the Lord all over again.

The first commandment is, "You shall have no other gods before me" (Exodus 20:3). Why is that one the first? Because if we can give ourselves to God alone, it's easier to obey the other nine commandments. But if we reverse that, if we open our hearts to idolatrous substitutes, we unleash all kinds of sinful impulses. This is why the Bible says, "Keep yourselves in the love of God" (Jude 21). Any source of life, any explanation of reality, any strength for living that robs Christ of his exclusive glory in our hearts is an idol and will inevitably degrade us.

But an idol is not a bad thing in itself. It is some good, God-created thing, some gift of God that we use as a substitute for God himself (Romans 1:23, 25). An idol is anything other than God that we absolutize as essential to our peace, our self-image, our contentment, our sense of control, our acceptability. Augustine explained how this worked in his own life and how God liberated him:

> Late have I loved you, Beauty so old and so new; late have I loved you. And see, you were within and I was in the external world and sought you there, and in my unlovely state I plunged into those lovely created things which you made. You were with me, and I was not with you. The lovely things kept me far from you, though if they did not have their existence in you, they had no existence at all. You called and cried out loud and shattered my deafness. You were radiant and resplendent, you put to flight my blindness. You were fragrant, and I drew in my breath and now pant after you. I tasted you, and I feel but hunger and thirst for you. You touched me, and I am set on fire to attain the peace which is yours.[2]

Martin Luther's catechism on the First Commandment helps us all identify with the realities of idolatry:

> What is it to have a god? What is God? Answer: A god is that to which we look for all good and in which we find refuge in every time of need.

> To have a god is nothing else than to trust and believe him with our whole
> heart. As I have often said, the trust and faith of the heart alone make both
> God and an idol. If your faith and trust are right, then your God is the true
> God. On the other hand, if your trust is false and wrong, then you have not
> the true God. For these two belong together, faith and God. That to which
> your heart clings and entrusts itself is, I say, really your God.[3]

Our root problem is not social or intellectual or even moral, as we usually think of it. Our root problem in all of life is that we keep going to false
gods for their false salvations. More than we realize, our hearts complicate
the profound simplicity of faith in God. And then we wonder why we're
disappointed with life. Here's what we need to see with clarity: There is only
one salvation, it belongs to Christ alone, we receive it on his terms, and no
one has ever trusted him in vain.

The Bible says that Israel brought foreign idols into the temple of the
Lord (2 Kings 21:1–9). God had filled it with his very presence (1 Kings
8:10, 11). Then Israel filled it with idols. We read that Biblical story, shake
our heads, and think, "What a bunch of morons." But is it really that far-
fetched? Several years ago the Episcopal Church confirmed a declared
homosexual in the office of Bishop. God loves homosexuals as much as he
loves anyone else. But that decision was wrong. Why? It sanctified within
the church an alien ideal—a worldly ideal of self-defined sexuality in defiance of God's design for human sexuality. It brought a foreign idol into the
temple. But idolatry can cast its spell on any church, even a conservative
church. In Galatians 4:8–10 Paul writes:

> Formerly, when you did not know God, you were enslaved to those that
> by nature are not gods [idols]. But now that you have come to know God
> . . . how can you turn back again to the weak and worthless elementary
> principles of the world, whose slaves you want to be once more? You
> observe days and months and seasons and years!

These legalistic believers were re-enslaving themselves to their old idols
of self-defined righteousness in defiance of Christ's righteousness. They too
were bringing an alien ideal into the church—"the weak and worthless ele-
mentary principles of the world." It was the idol of works-righteousness. So
whether you come from a progressive background or a conservative background, if Jesus Christ is not the defining confidence of your heart, you have
a problem with idols.

But God loves us idolaters and wants us to experience his salvation,
the way Augustine did. And we can. God's whole purpose for human history is to establish his glory as our highest joy and deepest resource. In this
passage Isaiah shows us three things: a delusion, a servant, and a new song.

He shows us how stupid our idols are, how worthy God's alternative is, and how desirable it is to dump our idols and embrace his alternative with all our hearts.

1. "Behold, they are all a delusion" (41:21–29)
    A God sues the idols for false advertising (41:21–24)
        B God proves his own ability to activate history (41:25–27)
            C God dismisses the idols as a delusion (41:28, 29)
2. "Behold my servant" (42:1–9)
    A The servant will bring perfection to the nations (42:1–4)
        B God will discredit the idols through his servant (42:5–9)
3. "Sing to the LORD a new song" (42:10–17)
    A The whole world is invited to worship God (42:10–12)
        B God will rid the world of all idol-worship (42:13–17)

God deliberately embarrasses the idols. He draws our admiring attention to Jesus and invites us to glorify and enjoy him forever.

A Delusion

> Set forth your case, says the LORD;
> > bring your proofs, says the King of Jacob.
> Let them bring them, and tell us
> > what is to happen.
> Tell us the former things, what they are,
> > that we may consider them,
> that we may know their outcome;
> > or declare to us the things to come.
> Tell us what is to come hereafter,
> > that we may know that you are gods;
> do good, or do harm,
> > that we may be dismayed and terrified. (Isaiah 41:21–23)

Verse 1 of this chapter challenged the nations to reflect upon God's sovereignty over history. Now God renews his challenge. What is he saying? He's daring the idols to prove their reality. Is he really expecting the gods of the nations to make a convincing case, or any case at all? No. He denies their very existence. That's the whole point. Really, God is speaking to us. He's appealing to our rationality. In fact, he's *demanding* our rationality. Into a world that had lived by pagan mumbo jumbo from time immemorial, God introduces reason. He dares us to think by daring the idols to act. God isn't afraid of clear thinking; he provokes it. Idolatry flourishes in the fog of our confusion. So God helps us by daring the idols to do something God-like, to prove that they really are in charge of things and to be taken seriously. As the NIV paraphrases verse 22, "Bring in [your idols] to tell us what is going to happen." God is exposing the unreality of every salvation outside himself.

His dare is reasonable. It isn't unfair or even arbitrary. The Jews to whom Isaiah wrote this were exiled in Babylon. And in Mesopotamian culture, fortune-telling was a well-established tradition and a major preoccupation.[4] The Babylonians consulted their gods to interpret events and to foretell the future. For example, they would cut open a sheep, and the priests would interpret the significance of how its intestines were coiled. They saw a message from the gods in that sort of thing. So the Lord is picking a fair fight here, because the pagan gods *claimed* to reveal truth and predict the future. But God is taking them to court for false advertising. It's the court of human opinion. He is saying to every rival god, "Okay, you have the floor. Go ahead and embarrass me. I dare you. But don't just sit there. Do something, do *anything*, to shock us. Here's your chance to prove that you're not dead weight!"

A theological trend is emerging in the church today that one might think Isaiah had foreseen when he wrote this. This new line of thought is called "the openness of God." Some scholars who say they follow the Bible are teaching that "God does not control everything that happens . . . the future is not yet settled."[5] But Isaiah's whole point here is that sovereign foreknowledge and control over human events is an essential mark of deity. If God is not the Lord of the future, then by Isaiah's logic he is not God at all but just another idol. The gospel denies the so-called "openness of God" and delights in the supremacy of God over all things. We need to understand how empty all idolatry is, how inadequate for life, and we need to make up our minds.

> Behold, you are nothing,
>   and your work is less than nothing;
> an abomination is he who chooses you. (v. 24)

Idols are nothing. But they still matter, because choosing a cheap substitute for the living God cheapens us (Psalm 115:2–8). "An abomination is he who chooses you."

In verses 25–27 God predicts the rise of Cyrus the Great of Persia as proof of his sovereign deity, the way he did back in verse 2. The meteoric rise of Cyrus on the human scene proclaimed God's name in history (v. 25). No one saw it coming (v. 26). God alone predicted it (v. 27). And in verses 28, 29 God summarizes his point: There is no divine revelation outside the prophetic tradition culminating in Jesus Christ. The idols of our imaginations don't know what's going on. "Behold, they are *all* a delusion" (v. 29)—all of them without exception. "More than three thousand names of deities have been recovered from Mesopotamia alone."[6] But numbers do not establish truth. Cultural consensus does not establish truth. Reality does. And there is only one real God. How do we know? One way is this: Non-Christian religions do not hold prophecy conferences, but believers in Jesus Christ do.

Verse 24 (*"Behold*, you are nothing") and verse 29 (*"Behold*, they are all a delusion") prepare us for *"Behold* my servant" in 42:1. God's alternative to our idols is his servant.

A Servant

> Behold my servant, whom I uphold,
>   my chosen, in whom my soul delights;
> I have put my Spirit upon him;
>   he will bring forth justice to the nations.
> He will not cry aloud or lift up his voice,
>   or make it heard in the street;
> a bruised reed he will not break,
>   and a faintly burning wick he will not quench;
>   he will faithfully bring forth justice.
> He will not grow faint or be discouraged
>   till he has established justice in the earth;
>   and the coastlands wait for his law. (Isaiah 42:1–4)

Suddenly the atmosphere changes. Instead of controversy, necessary though it is, we enter into peace and delight and gorgeous understatement. This is the first of Isaiah's four Servant Songs, fulfilled in Christ. He is the servant of the Lord. He is God's alternative to our idols. He is not an abomination; he is a delight. But he also stands in contrast with Cyrus the conqueror who "shall trample on rulers as on mortar, as the potter treads clay" (41:25). Cyrus stepped on people. But when Jesus rose in history, he did not break a bruised reed or quench a faintly burning wick. When Matthew quotes this text in the New Testament, he says it was fulfilled when Jesus was healing sick people, and Jesus was quiet about it (Matthew 12:15–21). He gave suffering people their lives back, and he didn't use his success with them to take advantage of them or promote himself. No destructive swagger. No brutal grasping. A gentle servant brings forth justice to the nations.

The key word in Isaiah 42:1–4 is "justice." It appears three times. What does Isaiah mean by this word translated "justice"? He's thinking of more than legal correctness. This word is used in Exodus 26:30 of the plan for the tabernacle, the blueprint God revealed from Heaven. In an analogous way, God has a blueprint for human existence. He knows how human beings and human society can be at their best. He knows how to make us happy and fulfilled. And through his servant Jesus he's bringing his plan down from Heaven, to reorder human civilization in a beautiful way. God's kingdom *will* come, and his will *will* be done on earth as it is in Heaven, and we were made for it.

This word translated "justice" includes within its scope all our longings for a better life and a better world. A just world, to Isaiah, is human society as God means it to be, with no corrupting idolatries. When we see slums and poverty and oppression and illiteracy and pollution and human misery in all its forms, do we have the prophetic eyes to discern the meaning of it? These massive disorders prove that we are arranging human life according to idolatrous ideals. *That's* why we always end up shoving each other into the ground.

Injustice is more than a political dysfunction. It is a spiritual evil, a denial of God. And by now the mess we've made is so far advanced, so systemic, so overwhelming, it's beyond our powers of correction. Should we work for a better society? Yes. God himself tells us to (Amos 5:24). But at the same time, let's have the humility to face the facts. In the whole sorry length of human history, we have failed to assemble even one human society as we ourselves would really like it to be. There are flashes of brilliance here and there, but they never last. Why? Our social constructs are fundamentally *un*just. It is wrong when children are begging on the streets. It is wrong when old people are shivering in the cold. It is wrong when people have only filthy water to drink and sickening food to eat. But the more we try to force our societies into a more human shape by our own schemes, the worse it gets, because every human plan for salvation unwittingly asserts our own idolatrous self-idealization.

Our salvation will never come from our own self-assertion; it will only come from the gentle servant of the Lord. Our idolatries can do nothing but corrupt, because they're the magnification of our proud self-salvation. That's why our good intentions end up unleashing more evil. Everything we do is laced with poisons we cannot detect in time. Isaiah has eyes to see this. He also sees God's alternative—the servant whose salvation will prove how beautiful human life can be, to the glory of God. Jesus will succeed with his gentle servanthood where we have failed with our coercive pride.

Therefore, the hope of the world lies in the servant of the Lord, the delight of God, the quiet healer, the man for others who wields the only true power that exists—the power to reorder human civilization not by bullying but by suffering, not by imposing demands on us but by absorbing our sins and miseries into himself. And the furthest coastlands will not dread his approach; they will wait eagerly for his law. This is Jesus.

In verses 1–4, then, God presents his servant to us. In doing so, he is asking us to step over a line. On this side of the line we might appreciate Christ, but we'll deal with him only on our own terms. We don't delight in him as the Savior of the world and our Savior. More than we want to admit, we trivialize and evade him. We exalt our own potential and wisdom. On the other side of that line, we humble ourselves. We set no preconditions. We say to Jesus Christ, "Lord, you are the only hope of the world, and you are my only hope. I admit my share of responsibility for the world as it is. Forgive my injustice. Destroy my idols. Make me the kind of human being that lives up to the name. You alone are my salvation, and I give my allegiance entirely to you." God wants every one of us to step over that line right now, from pride to worship. Will you do that? Or will you refuse Jesus Christ? Which will it be?

In verses 5–9 God speaks to his servant. God is saying that his very reputation as God stands or falls on the success of Jesus. The servant is doing the work of God on earth. What is that work? To be "a covenant for the people, a light for the nations" (v. 6). God proves that he is God as Jesus Christ delivers us from the darkness of our idolatries, opens our eyes to his glory, and brings us out of our self-created dungeons (v. 7). Have you ever thought, *Can I change, or am I stuck with this forever? Is this it? It this me forever?* You and I are living dungeons. But through Christ God is showing how committed he is to us idolaters by leading us into newness. He will not withdraw his covenant of grace, though we often break it by our emotional attachment to other gods. God *will* make his love known to us. He will give his glory to no other, nor his praise to our carved idols (v. 8). He will love us until we finally get it. He stakes his honor on that. Therefore, we are not confined to our abominations and prisons. God saves us not by telling us to lose ourselves in some vaguely defined cosmic All but by taking upon himself at his cross all the wrongs we've done and by giving back to us our truest selves that we lost so long ago. That is how God proves that he really is God.

We should believe this. In verse 9 God says, "Behold, the former things have come to pass, and new things I now declare." What is he saying? God is proving himself here by prophecies. He gives us a verifiable short-term prediction by foretelling the coming of Cyrus. That happened, as a public event in our human history. This gives God instant credibility. But he does that to get us believing his long-term prediction of worldwide perfection through Christ. God is saying, "If I kept my word about Cyrus, and I did, and you know I did, then you can believe that I'll keep my word about my servant. In fact, I launched his mission 2,000 years ago. It's already underway. So dump your idols and trust *me*. I want you to be a part of my new world." This is exciting. This calls for music!

A New Song

> Sing to the LORD a new song,
>> his praise from the end of the earth. . . .
> Let them give glory to the LORD,
>> and declare his praise in the coastlands. (Isaiah 42:10a, 12)

The prophet calls the whole world to join him in worshiping God for Jesus Christ. The greatest work of grace is when unbelief falls away and our hearts melt into gladness in God. He wants *everyone* to be released into true worship. This is why Christian churches have public, not private, worship services. We welcome the whole world. But we aren't the ones extending the invitation; God is. He has opened the door to idolaters from all cultures, so they can experience something new, worthy of praise in "a new song."

Isaiah tells us in verses 10, 11 that God wants to include diverse peoples, for his glory (cf. Galatians 3:28; Colossians 3:11). Idols divide. That's why the world is a place of anger and hostility today. Whenever you see people divided, it's because they're worshiping their vicious idols. But true worship unites people. There is nothing greater for us than to glorify and enjoy God together. Right now the church is singing this eternally new song, and we're calling the nations to join with us. In Heaven we'll sing forever over the victory of God, and it will never get old (Revelation 5:9; 14:3).

God is determined to put a new song in our hearts. Look how strongly he feels about it. He pursues his goal with the intensity of a soldier psyching himself up for battle (Isaiah 42:13). When a sinner steps over the line from the idolatry of God-plus-whatever to the true worship of God alone, God has fought a battle and won. God is also like a woman crying out in labor (v. 14).[7] He gives life to something new. What do these two similes teach us—God like a soldier going into battle and like a woman going into labor? They teach us that God's grace is more than a lenient niceness. The grace of God is his resolve that will settle for nothing less than our eternal joy in him alone, no matter what the cost to himself. He's willing to fight for our salvation. He's willing to suffer for it.

> And I will lead the blind
>> in a way that they do not know,
> in paths that they have not known
>> I will guide them.
> I will turn the darkness before them into light,
>> the rough places into level ground.
> These are the things I do,
>> and I do not forsake them. (Isaiah 42:16)

If we can get around in our routines without deep dependence on God, that doesn't mean we have sight. Even blind people can be self-sufficient in familiar surroundings. God wants to take us where we're helpless without him. To live free of idols is a new experience for us. It's a path we have not known. God is saying, "Trust me enough to follow me. I want to show you a whole new way to live. As I lead you forward, I will not forsake you. I will be God to you." But look what happens to people who are unwilling to step over that line.

> They are turned back and utterly put to shame,
>   who trust in carved idols,
> who say to metal images,
>   "You are our gods." (v. 17)

The greatest miracle in the universe is not when God hung the planets in space. The greatest miracle in the universe is when God transforms a compulsive idolater into a glad worshiper of himself alone. That's a miracle we urgently need—to love the Giver more than his gifts, to see in God our only ultimate delight and every other joy he gives as just one more reason to glorify and enjoy *him*. That way, we don't have to cling selfishly to his gifts. If he takes them away, we're not devastated, because we have him. That is worship—to be so rich in Christ, so filled with a sense of privilege, that we actually become *happy* on God's terms. Will you open your heart to receive that miracle?

> God is the highest good of the reasonable creature; and the enjoyment of him is the only happiness with which our souls can be satisfied. To go to heaven, fully to enjoy God, is infinitely better than the most pleasant accommodations here. Fathers and mothers, husbands, wives or children or the company of earthly friends are but shadows; but the enjoyment of God is the substance. These are but scattered beams; but God is the sun. These are but streams; but God is the fountain. These are but drops; but God is the ocean.[8]

If you will trust him enough to dive into the Ocean, he will make your life a story of overflowing salvation.

31

God's Way to Reformation

ISAIAH 42:18—43:21

At dinner recently with a group of Christian high school and college students, I asked whether they had any heroes. There was silence. They looked at each other, then looked blankly back at me. Heroes? What is a hero?[1]

FOR AGES PEOPLE HAVE DRAWN INSPIRATION from greatness—from Horatio at the bridge to William Tell to George Washington. But heroism is out of fashion in our time. We don't even believe in it. Our cynicism is so pervasive that the extent of our disillusionment is taken as the measure of our maturity. Marilynne Robinson describes this turn of mind:

> When a good man or woman stumbles, we say, "I knew it all along," and when a bad one has a gracious moment, we sneer at the hypocrisy. It is as if there is nothing to mourn or to admire, only a hidden narrative now and then apparent through the false, surface narrative. And the hidden narrative, because it is ugly and sinister, is therefore true.[2]

What has happened to us is that we've lost our sense of God. And when we lose God, we don't just lose religion; we lose everything worth living for. But God wants to give it all back. He has a purpose for us yet, even in our brokenness. He says, "I created you for my glory. And I want to fill your life with an inspiring new sense of destiny."

God intends to renew the whole universe (Isaiah 65:17; 66:22). That's his goal. Do you know where he begins? Right here with us, at two levels. Isaiah shows us the God who *reforms* people who have lost their purpose (Isaiah 42:18—43:21). Next he'll show us the God who *revives* people who have lost their vitality (43:22—44:23). The renovation of the universe begins with us in reformation and revival. Reformation is the recovery of God's *purpose* for us. Revival is the recovery of God's *life* in us. God loves to renew confused and tired people.

Reformation means a lot to those of us Christians who are Presbyterians (and other believers as well). Our roots go deep into the Protestant Reformation of the sixteenth century. John Calvin influenced John Knox in Geneva. Then Knox took the reformation back to Scotland, and what emerged was a worldwide Presbyterian movement. What was God accomplishing back then? I think of it this way. He hauled the ship that we call the church into dry dock, scraped away 1,500 years' worth of encrusted human traditions that were slowing it down, refitted that ship with fresh gospel understandings, and relaunched a seaworthy vessel that is still going strong. But reformation must never stop. Our constant tendency is toward rudderless inconsequentiality, and God is constantly getting us back on course to our true destiny.

What then is reformation? Reformation is God renewing in our hearts a passionate clarity about his purpose for us. It is God reawakening in us a love for his truth and his standards. It is God preparing us for the display of his glorious salvation as we reshape every aspect of our lives and our churches to that end.

In this passage Isaiah guides us toward personal and corporate reformation. We need it. Every generation needs reformation and not just revival. A. W. Tozer put it bluntly:

> A revival of the kind of Christianity which we have had in America the
> last 50 years would be the greatest tragedy of this century, a tragedy which
> would take the church a hundred years to get over.[3]

What's the point of reviving the wrong kind of Christianity? It's not just more power that we need, though we do need that. We also need a new *kind* of Christianity, reformed according to God's great purpose for us. Too many churches can talk about "the chief end of man" as glorifying and enjoying God, but the meaning of that has never sunk in enough for those churches to pursue their chief end with glad intentionality. They just drift, little realizing how much more God has for them. We need reformation today.

Isaiah's reforming message has four points—the problem God confronts, the remedy his grace provides, the reason for his intervention, and the outcome in our experience.

1. The problem: our guilty insensitivity (42:18–25)
   A Who is spiritually disabled, forfeiting God's purpose? (42:18–22)
      B Who is spiritually backward, dulled to God's disciplines? (42:23–25)
2. The remedy: God's purposeful intervention (43:1–7)
   A¹ He redeems our every experience (43:1, 2)
      B¹ He paid a price for us (43:3)
      B² He will move history for us (43:4)
   A² He gathers in his every adopted child (43:5–7)
3. The reason: the exclusive reality of God (43:8–13)
   A¹ He challenges all rivals (43:8, 9)
      B He appoints us as his witnesses (43:10a)
   A² He claims exclusive deity (43:10b–13)
4. The outcome: personal and corporate newness (43:14–21)
   A His promise: our conquerors conquered (43:14, 15)
      B His pattern: our exodus renewed (43:16–21)

Let's admit our need, let's delight in God's remedy, let's humble ourselves before his purpose, and let's give ourselves permission to experience his newness.

The Problem

> Hear, you deaf,
>   and look, you blind, that you may see!
> Who is blind but my servant,
>   or deaf as my messenger whom I send?
> Who is blind as my dedicated one,
>   or blind as the servant of the LORD? (Isaiah 42:18, 19)

Isaiah has just been talking about leading the blind nations out of their darkness into the light of God (42:16, 17). So who would we expect the deaf and blind to be here? "Who is blind but . . . ?" The idolatrous nations, right? Wrong. "Who is blind but *my servant*?" Wait a minute. At the beginning of this chapter "the servant of the LORD" brings salvation to the nations (42:1–4). But now the Lord's servant is blind and deaf. God's messenger can't hear the message himself. In verses 1–4 the servant of the Lord brings perfection to the world; in verses 18–25 the servant fails. How do we make sense of this?

There's a clue in verse 24: "Who gave up *Jacob* to the looter, and *Israel* to the plunderers?" The nation of Israel was the servant of the Lord (41:8). But they were blind to God's purpose and deaf to God's Word. They failed in their mission. So God sent the ideal servant in Jesus Christ. Verses 1–4 are looking forward to Jesus. Verses 18–25 of Isaiah 42 are looking around at Israel, who is as blind as the pagan nations.

But what does clueless Israel fail to see? What was God's purpose for them that they never understood?

> The LORD was pleased, for his righteousness' sake,
>   to magnify his law and make it glorious. (v. 21)

Israel's life mission was to make God's law glorious to the world around. How? By showing how beautiful it is to live for God according to his word. Israel didn't do that. But Jesus did. His whole life embodied God's law. And people noticed. They flocked to him.[4] That is the church's mission too. When we're like Jesus, people sense that something beautiful has come to them. Francis Schaeffer tells us how this can happen:

> One of the nicest compliments I have ever heard about L'Abri was from a young architect who made a profession of faith at L'Abri, a young architect from Zurich. He was saying goodbye one day. I do not know if you know the Swiss, they often shake hands twice or three times when they are saying goodbye. Thus, when he came back the second time to shake my hand I thought he was only following the Swiss custom. But he said, "I want to tell you, every time I have been here and I go away, I feel like a human being," and we shook hands. I've never heard anything nicer than that in my whole life.[5]

When our life together makes the way of God glorious in human life, people can see it's what they want. And that strategy is not our own self-flattering ambition; it is the purpose of God for us.

But back in Isaiah's day God's people so forfeited his purpose that they invited his discipline.

> Who gave up Jacob to the looter,
>   and Israel to the plunderers?
> Was it not the LORD, against whom we have sinned,
>   in whose ways they would not walk,
>   and whose law they would not obey?
> So he poured on him the heat of his anger
>   and the might of battle;
> it set him on fire all around, but he did not understand;
>   it burned him up, but he did not take it to heart. (vv. 24, 25)

We're not very good at paying attention. Even when the disciplines of God set us on fire, we don't necessarily feel it enough to take it to heart. We think *God* is unfeeling. But he is not the problem. The problem is that our lives bear little relation to his purpose. That's why Judah went into national exile. That's why churches today go into institutional exile. That's why we need reformation, as individuals and as churches. How does God do it?

The Remedy

> But now thus says the LORD,
>   he who created you, O Jacob,
>   he who formed you, O Israel:
> "Fear not, for I have redeemed you;
>   I have called you by name, you are mine.
> When you pass through the waters, I will be with you;
>   and through the rivers, they shall not overwhelm you;
> when you walk through fire you shall not be burned,
>   and the flame shall not consume you. (Isaiah 43:1, 2)

"But now" are welcome words. Do you see how abruptly Isaiah transitions from our problem to God's remedy? The "Jacob" and "Israel" here in verse 1 are just as blind and deaf as the Jacob and Israel in 42:18, 19. "But now" does not signal any change in us. It declares the grace of God. The reason for the "but now" is not even our repentance, but only God himself.

> For I am the LORD your God,
>   the Holy One of Israel, your Savior. (43:3)

If we force him to it, God will put us through "waters" and "rivers," "fire" and "flame." But he still says, "Fear not." Why? Because we feel deeply insecure with God and fearful that he will deal with us as we deserve. But he says, "I am the LORD *your* God, the Holy One *of Israel*, *your* Savior." Do we belong to him? Yes. But even more deeply, he belongs to us. A Savior has given himself to us.

Look at his commitments: "I created you, I formed you, I have redeemed you, I have called you by name, you are mine, I will be with you." In other words, "What matters most about you is not *what you deserve* but *whose you are*." The disciplines of God are real. But they are not his last word to his people; salvation is. Whatever life throws at you, including the tough love of God himself, he will go with you into it.

Let's not think that God is aloof when we go through the fires and floods of life. The truth is, he is "[giving] peoples in exchange for your life" (43:4). When we think about how boldly God orders events for our benefit, it's downright embarrassing. God saved Israel at Egypt's expense back in Moses' day. God handed Babylon over to Cyrus to release the Jews from exile. God has loving intentions toward you, and he uses other people to fulfill them. Why does God care so actively for his people? There is only one reason.

> Because you are precious in my eyes,
>   and honored, and I love you . . . (v. 4a)

Don't let the simplicity of this fool you. God is saying that he orchestrates history to benefit his blind and deaf servants because we are precious in his eyes and honored and he loves us. It's all about God, not us. His is a grace so great, it shuts our mouths in wonder.

But is there an even deeper explanation for God's grace than this? He has given himself to us. He will go with us through affliction. We are precious to him. He loves us. In the cross of Christ, God proved that he would rather die than lose even one of us. *But why?* Isaiah pushes our thinking all the way to ultimacy. In verses 5–7 we see God's ultimate purpose for loving us so.

> ". . . everyone who is called by my name,
>   whom I created for my glory,
>   whom I formed and made." (v. 7)

God loves us "to the praise of his glorious grace" (Ephesians 1:3–6). Our destiny is to be a living advertisement of how good God is to people who deserve the opposite. Don't think of God as playing a supporting role in a movie that features you and me as the big stars. His purpose is to bring the glory of his salvation down into our experience, despite what we deserve, so that he is admired and delighted in. And when this prophetic vision gets into our hearts, other things fall away, and we get traction for reformation.

The Reason

> "You are my witnesses," declares the LORD,
>   "and my servant whom I have chosen,
> that you may know and believe me
>   and understand that I am he.
> Before me no god was formed,
>   nor shall there be any after me.
> I, I am the LORD,
>   and besides me there is no savior." (Isaiah 43:10, 11)

The purpose of God is the glory of God, to the exclusion of all rival glories. There is no room in the gospel for the idea that Jesus is only one of many spiritual paths. Jesus isn't even the *best* way. He is the only way. Do you see? The ultimate reason why God loves us is for us to be his witnesses, for us to be living proof that he alone is the all-sufficient Savior God.

Other religions and worldviews, if they intersect meaningfully with reality at all, have something to say. But their deepest intention is not to glorify God on God's terms. The only truth is the one that glorifies God *as God*. Everything else is compromised with idolatry. And God intends to put all rival glories out of business, because the idols of the modern world are life-depleting, joy-killing disappointments. God says in verse 11, "Besides me there is no savior." Every idol, if you don't toe the line, demands its pound of flesh. If you're serving the idol of career, for example, and you don't sacrifice to that idol as it demands, your career is over. If your idol is political utopianism, and you don't sacrifice to that idol as it demands, your hoped-for world is shattered. If your idol is a perfect body, and you don't sacrifice to that idol as it demands, your self-image is devastated. But when we have defied the one true God, what does he do? He saves us. Why? To make us witnesses that he is not just good; he is the only goodness anyone will ever experience.

Throughout this section God claims, "I am he. I, I am the LORD. I am God." Can you receive that? C. S. Lewis lays out the alternatives:

> It is always shocking to meet life where we thought we were alone. "Look out!" we cry, "it's *alive*." And therefore this is the very point at which so many draw back—I would have done so myself if I could—and proceed no further with Christianity. An "impersonal" God—well and good. A subjective God of beauty, truth and goodness, inside our own heads—better still. A formless life-force surging through us, a vast power which we can tap—best of all. But God himself, alive, pulling at the other end of the cord, perhaps approaching at an infinite speed, the hunter, king, husband—that is quite another matter. There comes a moment when the children who have been playing at burglars hush suddenly: was that a *real* footstep in the hall? There comes a moment when people who have been dabbling in religion ("Man's search for God"!) suddenly draw back. Supposing we really found him? We never meant it to come to *that*! Worse still, supposing he had found us?[26]

I heard a friend say, "In our world it's cool to search for God, but uncool to find him." Are you willing to be uncool enough to find and embrace your only Savior?

The Outcome

Thus says the LORD,
    your Redeemer, the Holy One of Israel:
"For your sake I send to Babylon

and bring them all down as fugitives,
    even the Chaldeans, in the ships in which they rejoice.
I am the LORD, your Holy One,
    the Creator of Israel, your King." (Isaiah 43:14, 15)

The intervention of God is ongoing. The living God came down into the experience of the Jewish exiles long ago, and the same living God comes down into our captivities today. He proves all over again, where it counts for us, that he is real—and not because of what we deserve but because of who he is.

Isaiah is saying that for the sake of a dumpy, fifth-rate, little nation named Judah that most Babylonians had probably never heard of, God is going to turn those proud Babylonians into fugitives rushing down to their ships to escape their conquerors. Why does God do that? Because his people are a big deal? No. It's only because of who he is. He is our Redeemer, taking us on as his personal responsibility. And he will release his own from every bondage they suffer.

Thus says the LORD,
    who makes a way in the sea,
    a path in the mighty waters,
who brings forth chariot and horse,
    army and warrior;
they lie down, they cannot rise,
    they are extinguished, quenched like a wick:
"Remember not the former things,
    nor consider the things of old.
Behold, I am doing a new thing;
    now it springs forth, do you not perceive it?
I will make a way in the wilderness
    and rivers in the desert." (vv. 16–19)

The great exodus out of Egypt, in the days of Moses, was not a one-time event; it was a pattern. In the ways of God, the exodus is repeatable. It is his standard *modus operandi* with us, through the finished work of Christ on the cross.[7] And here he is saying that we shouldn't so concentrate on his mercies in our past that we miss the new things he is doing today. God never acts out of character, but a part of his character is that he never runs out of new ideas. And he is able in amazing new ways to reenact the exodus in your life and to lead you through some Red Sea barrier confronting you today. In fact, he will, if you'll trust him enough to follow him. And what does he get out of it? Verse 21: ". . . that they might declare my praise."

That is the purpose of God, and he will never surrender it. He is the true God, the only Savior, and he will have it known. His ultimate purpose is to magnify himself for the glory of his grace in our everlasting joy. As his glory grips our hearts right now, we are reformed and renewed to live heroic lives in a God-trivializing world. Greatness comes upon *us*, according to the purpose of *God*. And it's not a burden; it's a thrill. On January 15, 1951, Jim Elliot wrote in his diary:

> I walked out to the hill just now. It is exalting, delicious. To stand embraced by the shadows of a friendly tree with the wind tugging at your coat tail and the heavens hailing your heart—to gaze and glory and give oneself again to God, what more could a man ask? Oh the fullness, pleasure, sheer excitement of knowing God on earth. I care not if I never raise my voice again for Him, if only I may love Him, please Him. Perhaps in mercy He shall give me a host of children that I may lead them through the vast star fields to explore His delicacies whose finger ends set them to burning. But if not, if only I may see Him, smell His garments and smile into my Lover's eyes—ah then, not stars nor children shall matter, only Himself.[8]

What really matters to *you*?

32

God's Way to Revival

ISAIAH 43:22—44:23

ISAIAH HAS SHOWN US THE WAY to reformation, as God realigns us with his purpose. Now the prophet shows us the way to revival, as God reinvigorates us with his life. And the point of it all is that we would become living proof that God outperforms all the idols, that he really is as good as he says he is.

The structure of this passage mirrors the four points embedded in the previous text. Isaiah helps us to think through what revival means with the same fourfold line of reasoning:

1. The problem: our guilty boredom (43:22–28)
    A¹ "You have been weary of me" (43:22)
        B¹ "I have not wearied you" (43:23)
    A² "You have wearied me" (43:24)
        B² "I blot out your transgressions" (43:25–28)
2. The remedy: God's spiritual refreshment (44:1–5)
    A Refreshment by God's Spirit alone (44:1–3)
    B Enthusiasm for God's name alone (44:4, 5)
3. The reason: the exclusive reality of God (44:6–20)
    A The Lord and his people (44:6–8)
    B The idols and their people (44:9–20)
        1. Idols cannot rise above their makers (44:9–13)
        2. Idols cannot rise above their materials (44:14–17)
        3. Idols cannot undeceive human hearts (44:18–20)
4. The outcome: universal awakening (44:21–23)
    A "Remember" (44:21)
    B "Return" (44:22)
        C "Sing" (44:23)

The heart of this passage is God's promise to pour his Spirit upon us, and God never makes us a promise just to be sensational. We *need* nothing less than the outpouring of the Holy Spirit of God. Why?

The Problem

> It was not me that you called upon, O Jacob;[1]
>   but you have been weary of me, O Israel!
> You have not brought me your sheep for burnt offerings,
>   or honored me with your sacrifices.
> I have not burdened you with offerings,
>   or wearied you with frankincense.
> You have not bought me sweet cane with money,
>   or satisfied me with the fat of your sacrifices.
> But you have burdened me with your sins;
>   you have wearied me with your iniquities. (Isaiah 43:22–24)

God was not saying that his people were not worshiping. He was saying that their worship wasn't really about him. He was saying that the very sacrifices they were bringing, far from removing sin, were themselves sins and iniquities. God searched the inner reality of their worship. What did he find there? Weariness. And to God, that's a problem.

God did tell Israel how to worship him. The book of Leviticus was their God-given manual for worship, with elaborate instructions. They could follow the script. In fact, on special occasions their worship was down-right lavish. One time they sacrificed 22,000 oxen and 120,000 sheep (2 Chronicles 7:5). That wasn't wrong. But if the worship of God, however extravagant outwardly, sinks to the level of joyless duty, it isn't God's will. He says here, "You have not . . . satisfied me with the fat of your sacrifices" (Isaiah 43:24)! If God wasn't satisfied with the fat of 142,000 sacrifices, what more could he want? What he wants is for worship to *unburden* sinners. That's what the sacrificial system was for. God never meant it to be a wearying imposition. He says here, "I have not burdened you" (v. 23). But throughout Israel's history they treated worship as a mechanism for controlling God and putting God in their debt. And, naturally enough, it became wearisome. How could it be otherwise? Lugging sacrifice after sacrifice to the temple to obligate God—there's no release for us in that. And Isaiah is saying that God himself doesn't enjoy it. The very worship Judah thought put them above reproach was itself, in God's sight, a reproach, because it was weariness and heaviness rather than a lifting of the human spirit.

What does this say about God? Is he being more demanding than ever? Is he saying, "Give me the 142,000 sacrifices *and smile about it*"? No. God wants his worship to set hearts free. Again, how could it be otherwise? The sacrificial system back in the Old Testament prefigured the cross of Christ, who said, "The Son of Man came not to be served but to serve, and to give his life as a ransom for many" (Mark 10:45).

What then are we learning here about worship? Simply this. We violate worship when we turn a means of grace into a means of weariness. And we enter into true worship when our hearts are revived through the finished work of Christ on the cross. That kind of worship pleases God, our burden-bearer.

One would think that such a God would be irresistible. But here's the depth of our problem: We long to save ourselves. We want, with a compulsive craving, to deserve the good we get. The logic of reciprocity runs deep in our moral psychology. For example, when the Disabled American Veterans mail out requests for donations, the appeal draws out of the public a 19 percent response. But when the mailing includes free personalized address labels, the response rate jumps to 35 percent.[2] Why? The logic of reciprocity, of giving in order to get, really works in our minds. It's how we relate to one another all the time. And we drag that way of thinking into our relationship with God. We give in order to get. Our natural drift is to worship God not to unburden ourselves but to obligate him. That denies the very being of God.

> I, I am he,
>> who blots out your transgressions for my own sake,
>> and I will not remember your sins.
> Put me in remembrance; let us argue together;
>> set forth your case, that you may be proved right.
> Your first father sinned,
>> and your mediators transgressed against me.
> Therefore, I will profane the princes of the sanctuary,
>> and deliver Jacob to utter destruction
>> and Israel to reviling. (Isaiah 43:25–28)

God locates his very identity in blotting out our sins and remembering them no more. Satan, the accuser, comes before God and says, "Look at that Christian down there. Why do you still love him? Don't you remember what he did to you last week, and again on Tuesday, and then again yesterday?" And God says, if you'll allow me to put it this way, "No, I don't remember. Gabriel, where does that believer stand with us? Check the database." Gabriel logs on, but the only information that comes up on the screen is the righteousness of Christ freely credited to that sinner, because that's how God honors himself as God. "I blot out your transgressions, I splice your bad plays out of my game film, *for my own sake*." So God says back to Satan, "I'm not saying your facts are wrong, but you're not telling the *whole* story about that Christian. What matters most to me, *for my own sake*, is not that person's record but Christ's record for him." That is grace. That is God. That is the way to revival.

Something inside us doesn't want grace. We want to justify ourselves, at least a little. That's why, with great irony, God invites us to come up with something in ourselves that deserves his mercy (v. 26). When we blame God for the way he treats us, where does that hostility come from? It comes from our own demanding self-righteousness that says we deserve better. And God says, "Okay, make your case." But the fact is, we have nothing to be proud of, right down to our roots (v. 27). What we all deserve is this: "I will . . . deliver Jacob to utter destruction" (v. 28). Do we really want to get justice? Wouldn't we rather get grace? The word translated "utter destruction" is the same word used in the Bible for God's total judgment of Canaanite culture (Joshua 6:17). Turning the grace of worship into the drudgery of penance turns Israel into Canaan. But in the mercy of God, that's not the end of the passage. It's only the beginning. It's not where God leaves us. It's where he starts with us.

The Remedy

> But now hear, O Jacob my servant,
>> Israel whom I have chosen!
> Thus says the LORD who made you,
>> who formed you from the womb and will help you:
> "Fear not, O Jacob my servant,
>> Jeshurun whom I have chosen." (Isaiah 44:1, 2)

Look how he goes out of his way to reassure us. We are his servants, he chose us, he made us, he formed us, he will help us. It's all of grace. God doesn't want us to be insecure with him. His remedy for our violations of his grace is more grace, and he wants us to know it. Our sins do discredit us and do free God of all obligation to us. We can demand nothing of him. But that doesn't mean God quits on us. What does he do? He turns "I will profane" (43:28) into "I will pour":

> "For I will pour water on the thirsty land,
>> and streams on the dry ground;
> I will pour my Spirit upon your offspring,
>> and my blessing on your descendants." (Isaiah 44:3)

It is the way of God to come down to us, even us, with his manifest presence, so that we burst into life. He is promising to pour himself out with such generosity that we become, as one author puts it, "a people saturated with God."[3] Are you thirsty and dry? God has a special tenderness for you. Jesus said, "If anyone thirsts, let him come to me and drink" (John 7:37). What he has for you is full satisfaction. But it comes only from him.

On July 1, 1838, Robert Murray M'Cheyne preached on this verse in Isaiah and said to his congregation in Dundee,

> When two travelers are going through the wilderness, you may know which of them is thirsty by his always looking out for wells. . . . So it is with thirsty believers; they love the Word, read and preached—they thirst for it more and more. Is it so with you, dear believing brethren? In Scotland, long ago, it used to be so. Often, after the blessing was pronounced, the people would not go away till they heard more. Ah! children of God, it is a fearful sign to see little thirst in you. I do not wonder much when the world stays away from our meetings for the Word and prayer; but ah! when you do, I am dumb—my soul will weep in secret places for your pride.[4]

But God is keeping his promise, for his own glory. We are privileged to live now during that era within God's great plan for history when the Holy Spirit *is* being poured out. Two thousand years ago, on the Day of Pentecost, God unleashed the mighty river of the Holy Spirit upon a guilty world. And he continues to pour out his Spirit in wave after wave of reviving grace. Sometimes the tide of the Spirit may ebb. But then God visits us again with his living presence, and we come alive.[5]

What is God saying here? He's not promising just to make church services more fun—although there is no greater joy than a church awash in the Spirit. But understand what God is saying. He will renew all things, and he is beginning the new heavens and the new earth here among us. How? Through new supplies of the Holy Spirit, new life, new growth, new surges forward toward his appointed goal. The remedy God brings is nothing less than himself, his Spirit. We have tasted "the powers of the age to come" (Hebrews 6:5). What greater gift could God give (Luke 11:11–13)?

Under the influences of the Spirit, instead of people sitting on the fence, they line up to identify with the Lord. It's as if they go into a bidding war to convert to Christ.

> "This one will say, 'I am the Lord's,'
>   another will call on the name of Jacob,
> and another will write on his hand, 'The Lord's,'
>   and name himself by the name of Israel." (Isaiah 44:5)

Notorious sinners become notorious believers. *That* is what God does as the magnitude of his grace breaks upon us with reviving power.

Isaiah 44:1–5 is God's way of saying, "Here's the future of the world. I will create new realities by the sheer force of my grace. Your part is not to deny your thirst but to let me quench it. And *why* do I do all this?"

The Reason

> Thus says the LORD, the King of Israel
>   and his Redeemer, the LORD of hosts:
> "I am the first and I am the last;
>   besides me there is no god." (v. 6)

The reason God gives himself to us so much is to prove that he is God. And because his goodness is of a spreading nature, he denies all other gods— not to diminish our joy but to intensify our joy in him as our Redeemer. If we can get past our prejudices and accept him as our self-existent, all-sufficient *God*, we are not robbed, we are enriched. It's perfect. He gets the glory, we taste the joy. Jesus described the ultimate human experience this way: "Enter into *the joy of your master*" (Matthew 25:21, 23).

The exclusive reality of God is an offense in our pluralistic ethos today. But it has always been a stumbling block. Why? We want to range free. We are deeply uncertain that God alone will save us. But we've always been like this. Gerhard von Rad, in his *Old Testament Theology*, explains:

> This intolerant claim to exclusive worship is something unique in the his-
> tory of religion, for in antiquity the cults [the various temples] were on
> easy terms with one another and left devotees a free hand to ensure a
> blessing for themselves from other gods as well.[6]

It was laissez-faire religion back then, and it still is today. But this stub-born insistence of the prophets that there is only one Savior just will not go away, because *he* will not go away. And in every generation he pours out the reality of himself upon idolaters who get thirsty enough to give him a serious chance. Our role is to be fearless witnesses, living proof that God alone is enough to satisfy thirsty people.

> Fear not, nor be afraid;
>   have I not told you from of old and declared it?
>   And you are my witnesses!
> Is there a God besides me?
>   There is no Rock; I know not any. (Isaiah 44:8)

That is the meaning of our lives. That is the church's mission in the world. Nietzsche explained why he rejected Christianity: "I never saw the members of my father's church enjoying themselves."[7]

The flip side is verses 9–20, where Isaiah mocks the absurdity of idols. We see in the ESV how he throttles back to mere prose. The prophet sees no exaltedness here. It's idolatry, not God, that's wearisome. But why does Isaiah keep coming back to the problem of idols? Because idols *are* the problem. "The central theological principle of the Bible [is] the rejection of idolatry."[8] Think about it. If there is only one God, and if we are *not* experiencing his reviving fullness, there is a reason. The reason is, idols are clogging the inflow of his refreshment. The exclusive reality of God forces the question of idolatry. We need to think about this because our world is crowded with idols.

These Jews exiled in Babylon long ago were immersed in a social construct intended to make false worship plausible. For example, as they entered Babylon through the Ishtar Gate and walked onto the great Processional Way, every step they took was on slabs of imported limestone, each one three and a half feet square, and along the beveled edge of each slab was inscribed "To the honor of Marduk," the patron god of the city. Everywhere they stepped, "To the honor of Marduk, to the honor of Marduk." In fact, the name Babylon, *Bab-ilu*, means "gate of gods."[9] Babylon was the way to heaven-on-earth. It was the meaning of their culture. It's the meaning of our culture. The message today is, "God is not your life. Okay, he may have a place. But you'll access the real stuff of life in whatever makes you feel passionate and significant and in control, and the possibilities are endless." Everywhere we step, "To the honor of Marduk, to the honor of Marduk." This is absurd. Whatever derives from the creation for its value can have no ultimate value for us. Who has ever suffered the loss of all things to gain the world and come away a completed human being? Name *one*.

Here's how idolatry goes wrong. In verses 9–17, Isaiah describes how idols are manufactured. He concludes this way: "And the rest of [the worker's piece of wood] he makes into a god, his idol, and falls down to it and worships it. He prays to it and says, 'Deliver me, for you are my god!'" (v. 17). What's wrong with that picture? The man has cut down a tree. Nothing wrong with that. God gave us trees. The man warms himself with a fire from that wood. No problem. He bakes bread over the fire. Good idea. Then he stands up the leftover piece of wood and asks it to save him. *There* is the absurdity. It's absurd to try to derive an ultimate experience from a less-than-ultimate resource. That's false worship.

For example, I have a Ph.D. God gave it to me. It's a good thing. I thank him for it. But if I rely on that to save me emotionally from my deep sense of insignificance, if I derive my sense of myself from a thing, as at times I have, I'm an idolater. *God* is my salvation. But for us all, trying to squeeze life out of objects is the most natural thing in the world.[10] We are constantly turning to created things for the uncreated life without which we die. We don't perceive our roving desires that way, because we limit "salvation" to narrowly religious referents. We must understand that the life that is truly life, in every respect, comes from beyond anything created. God is our salvation, and he is able to make himself real to us, more real than the creation. Bow before him, and enter into true worship. Here's how:

The Outcome

Remember these things, O Jacob,
    and Israel, for you are my servant; . . .
return to me, for I have redeemed you.
Sing, O heavens, for the LORD has done it;
    shout, O depths of the earth;
break forth into singing, O mountains,
    O forest, and every tree in it!
For the LORD has redeemed Jacob,
    and will be glorified in Israel. (Isaiah 44:21–23)

Look at the magnitude of the gospel. What God has promised goes so far beyond what we can ask or think, it will take nothing less than a renovated creation to celebrate it properly. Our part right now is to remember that God alone is the Redeemer. Our part is to return to him.

Let go of your idols, and launch out into God alone. The life you most deeply long for comes only from God in Jesus Christ through the outpouring of the Holy Spirit. You don't have to deserve it. You can't control it. He pours it out freely into the empty hands of faith. That's the deal. That's the way to revival.

Why lose so much of yourself, to get God? Because he's worth it. He gives himself to sinners with overflowing salvation.

The man who has God for his treasure has all things in One. Many ordinary treasures may be denied him, or if he is allowed to have them, the enjoyment of them will be so tempered that they will never be necessary to his happiness. Or if he must see them go, one after one, he will scarcely feel a sense of loss, for having the Source of all things he has in One all satisfaction, all pleasure, all delight. Whatever he may lose he has actually lost nothing, for he now has it all in One, and he has it purely, legitimately, forever.[11]

33

God's Surprising Strategies

ISAIAH 44:24—45:25

J. B. PHILLIPS, whose paraphrase of the New Testament has helped many, also wrote a provocative little book entitled *Your God Is Too Small*. He wanted to help people think of God in new ways.

> Many men and women today are living, often with inner dissatisfaction, without any faith in God at all. This is not because they are particularly wicked or selfish or, as the old-fashioned would say, "godless," but because they have not found with their adult minds a God big enough to "account for" life, big enough to "fit in with" the new scientific age, big enough to command their highest admiration and respect, and consequently their willing cooperation.[1]

It's possible, as our awareness of reality expands with adulthood, for our knowledge of God to remain at a juvenile level. If we let that happen, we end up having to choose between the facts as we see them and loyalty to an inadequate God. We end up secretly fearful that some new discovery in human knowledge might overturn our beliefs. We end up worshiping God not with glad confidence but only as a duty. That is a defeatist faith. Nowhere does the Bible teach us to think that way.

The prophetic faith of the Bible brings all of reality, including the perplexities of life, under the command of God. The Bible doesn't shrink from problems; it deliberately creates more problems for us. Why? Because we do settle for superficial answers. But God wants to lift us to a mature confidence in him as the one true God who is wisely managing reality toward a goal that deserves our all.

Isaiah foresees the glory of the Lord revealed to the whole world (40:5).

The Lord is not coming down just to patch things up a bit. He intends nothing less than a new heavens and a new earth (65:17; 66:22), and he's starting that newness with us. Isaiah envisions the ongoing reformation and revival of the people of God (42:18—44:23), until we are completely remade.

Now, *how* does God work out his great plan? What strategies is he using? Does the history we see unfolding around us look like the emergence of a renewed human race in a renovated universe? Is that the lead story on CNN today? If not, what do we need to understand to be confident in the promises of God? Isaiah shows us the improbable methods God is using. The structure of his message is threefold. First, God accepts final responsibility for everything that happens. Secondly, God warns us not to take offense at that. Thirdly, God calls us to embrace him as *God*.

1. God's greatness: "I am the LORD, who does all these things" (44:24—45:8)
    A God overrules, to fulfill his word (44:24–28)
        B God acts, to make his reality felt (45:1–7)
            C God delights in the good he creates (45:8)
2. Our arrogance: "Woe to him who strives with his Maker" (45:9–13)
    A God alone has the right to be God (45:9, 10)
        B God's will for us is better than we think (45:11–13)
3. God's invitation: "Turn to me and be saved, all the ends of the earth" (45:14–25)
    A God enlarges his people (45:14–17)
        B God reasons with idolaters (45:18–22)
            C God will be our Savior or our Judge (45:23–25)

Isaiah wants to help us accept God not as the God we expect but as the God who does things his own way. God is "a stone of offense and a rock of stumbling" (Isaiah 8:14). But if we'll get past our prejudices and trust him with a new openness, we'll find him to be better than we expected.

God's Greatness

Thus says the LORD, your Redeemer,
  who formed you from the womb:
"I am the LORD, who made all things. . . .
  I am the LORD, who does all these things." (Isaiah 44:24a; 45:7b)

This section is framed within "I am the LORD, who made all things" and "I am the LORD, who does all these things." In fact, the wording in the Hebrew is the same in both lines. God is claiming final responsibility for everything that happens in history.

The whole of creation belongs to God. He "stretched out the heavens" and "spread out the earth" by himself (44:24). As the Creator, God is free to interrupt the processes of history and bend events any way he wants them to go, while the prognosticators of worldly wisdom have nothing but past patterns and present trends from which to extrapolate (44:25). But God can hit rewind, fast-forward, whatever he wants, no matter what anyone else says. In fact, here's one of his improbable strategies. He plans to raise up a man named Cyrus—God is calling him *by name* over a century in advance, to prove his own sovereignty over human events. God plans to raise up Cyrus the Great, the Persian conqueror, to defeat Babylon, set the Jewish people free, and send them home to rebuild Jerusalem and the temple (44:26–28). And why does God bother to do that? Because the promised Messiah, Jesus Christ, will not appear in Babylon. The prophetic word was, "Say to the cities of *Judah*, 'Behold your God!'" (Isaiah 40:9). God's people have to get home to prepare the way of the Lord. So God is shaping all of history, including what we regard as secular events, to advance his purpose centered in the kingdom of Jesus Christ.

You can well imagine Isaiah's original Jewish readers loving his assertions of God's greatness. But there's a problem:

> . . . who says of Cyrus, 'He is my shepherd. . . .
> Thus says the Lord to his anointed, to Cyrus . . . (Isaiah 44:28a; 45:1a)

Isaiah has been arguing that idols and idol-worshipers are stupid. But Cyrus was an idolater. He did give credit to the God of Israel for his victory over Babylon, and he did free the Jews to go home and rebuild the temple in Jerusalem (Ezra 1:1–4), but that was just Cyrus's way of being diplomatic. He freed *all* the foreign peoples enslaved in Babylon and rebuilt all their temples. That was his general policy because he wanted the favor of all the gods. We have a record of this in his own words.[2] But God calls this pagan politician "my shepherd" and speaks to him as an "anointed" messiah-figure. We can feel how bracing this is by looking at the Septuagint, the ancient Greek translation of the Old Testament. Isaiah 45:1 calls the pagan Cyrus χριστός, a "christ."

Shepherd and Anointed One were titles of the royal line of David. Now God is transferring those titles over to a Gentile conqueror? It must have seemed to the Jews that God was not just washing his hands of them but was overthrowing the whole moral order of the universe. And God says here, "I am the Lord, who does all these things."

What does Isaiah see? He sees that the sovereignty of God is big enough to include offense. In his mastery of all things, God uses whatever persons and methods he wants to, whether we like them or not. He is not defeated by the gritty realities of human history; he is using them for a redemptive purpose, so that even a Cyrus can foreshadow the true Shepherd and Messiah, Jesus Christ.

If God is sovereign, then all of history, not just church history, is his plan. All events have one ultimate cause, fit into one great purpose, and find their significance in one final victory. That means we can't box God in. It means we can't think piecemeal. It means making room for the improbable ways of God.

If our God were only a local, tribal deity, life would be simpler. For example, when the going gets tough and you pray and then it only gets worse, you could see that as your god being overwhelmed by some superior force. But if God really is the King of everything, then the bigger questions of life get simpler even as the smaller questions get harder. What do I mean? The smaller questions are: Why do *I* have cancer? Will my boyfriend get home safely from Iraq? Will there be enough money in my retirement plan to see me through? These are not small questions. They're weighty. But they're smaller than questions like: Does my life have any meaning at all? Do I have any enduring hope at all? Am I on my own in an empty universe, or is my experience part of a larger drama with God as the Author? Those are the bigger questions. And the gospel leaves many of our urgent but smaller questions unanswered, even as it assures us of God's redemptive purpose up at the level of our bigger questions. Whatever happens, the greatest thing we can know is this: "I am the LORD, who does all these things." Whatever God does, he is taking us more deeply into his love, and he asks us to trust him enough not to take offense but to follow him.

God has promised that his glorious salvation is the future of the world, and he's bending all of history around in that direction. Isaiah affirms that in 45:1–7. God made his presence felt by handing the known world over to Cyrus on a silver platter. In that very human struggle, God was working his plan. Three times Isaiah uses a Hebrew particle of purpose, *lᵉmaᶜan*:

. . . that [Cyrus] may know that it is I, the LORD. (v. 3)

For the sake of my servant Jacob,
    and Israel my chosen . . . (v. 4)

. . . that people, may know from the rising of the sun
    and from the west. (v. 6)

Do you see how the purpose of God spreads out ever more widely, from Cyrus to Israel to the nations? What is God accomplishing with his ever-expanding reach? He is proving that "I am the LORD, and there is no other" (vv. 5, 6). And in his perfect maturity, if I may put it that way, he accepts full responsibility for his actions.

I form light and create darkness,
    I make well-being and create calamity,
    I am the LORD, who does all these things. (v. 7)

God does not just allow darkness and calamity and then blame someone
else. He creates the problems of human history. How could it be otherwise
with the Sovereign of the universe? Isaiah is not saying that God sins. That's
our problem. But the strategies of God include within their scope *everything*
that happens as God pursues his redemptive purpose in this world. Evil is not
outside God's control. He uses it without being dirtied by it. Therefore, nothing, however evil, deprives God of one particle of his intended outcomes.
Again, how could it be otherwise? What's the most vicious evil perpetrated
in history thus far? The murder of God's own Son by our guilty hands. But
Isaiah says, "It was the will of the LORD to crush him" (53:10). The Apostle
Peter preached that Jesus was "delivered up according to the definite plan
and foreknowledge of God" (Acts 2:23; cf. 4:27, 28). When Peter said that,
he was not excusing himself for denying Jesus. He was saying that the worst
evil we have ever committed God turned into his fountain of salvation. "I am
the LORD, who does all these things."

Let's stop trying to rescue God from a problem he created for himself
by claiming full mastery over all things. Let's not relieve God of his responsibilities as King of the universe. The very thing we perceive as a problem,
God perceives as his glory, namely, God owns the dark moments of life.
He bends everything around for a saving purpose. When Isaiah wrote this
so long ago, he did not overlook a difficulty that we brainy modern people
happened to notice. Isaiah 45:7 is not an embarrassment. It's what we love
about God. Not even evil can frustrate him. And his surprising strategies are
our assurance.

They are also a delight to God himself. See what he's doing by his
sovereign power:

Shower, O heavens, from above;
    and let the clouds rain down righteousness;
let the earth open, that salvation and righteousness may bear fruit;
    let the earth cause them both to sprout;
    I, the LORD, have created it. (v. 8)

If you are in Christ, this is a picture of what God promises to do for
you—fresh, new life springing up out of the natural deadness that you are
without his sovereign grace. Do not insist on what we call miracles. God will
use many methods to do great things. And whatever his strategy may be at
any given moment, he looks at what he's doing and rejoices in it. You should
too. You can be happy that God is God, because he's better qualified for it

than you are. The reason we chafe under God's providences is not God; the reason is our arrogant demands of God.

Our Arrogance

"Woe to him who strives with him who formed him,
  a pot among earthen pots!
Does the clay say to him who forms it, 'What are you making?'
  or 'Your work has no handles'?
Woe to him who says to a father, 'What are you begetting?'
  or to a woman, 'With what are you in labor?'" (vv. 9, 10)

God is not offended by our honest questions. But he is offended when we accuse him of bungling our lives. We just weren't made to sit in judgment on God. We are as far beneath God as clay is beneath a potter. But when we're brooding over how God has ruined everything for us, what does he say? He says, "Woe!" That is a cry of lament. God is saying, "I'm so sorry you feel that way about me. You won't let me be God to you. You keep insisting that I do things your way. But I want to be your God, not your puppet, and I want you to be my people, not my judge and jury. How can you experience the love of *God* without letting me *be* God?"[3]

Isaiah is too wise to imply that faith in God is always easy. Think of the Jews. They had a glorious past in the kingdom of Solomon—national independence, a standing army, and so forth. They had been in control. But now their liberator from exile is a pagan Gentile? Now they'll reoccupy their own land by *his* permission? And *he* will pay for the rebuilding of their temple? The dream is over, and in a humiliating way too. They had a hard time accepting what God was doing. And if you're struggling in your own life—well, who doesn't? But surprising us is just one of the things God does, and we have to come to terms with that. The Incarnation was a shock. The virgin conception of Jesus was a scandal. The cross was an embarrassment. God is too independent for faith in him always to be easy. But whatever your struggle is, God is saying to you today what he was saying to the Jews back then: "My plan is better than you think."

"I have stirred [Cyrus] up in righteousness,
  and I will make all his ways level;
he shall build my city
  and set my exiles free,
not for price or reward,"
  says the LORD of hosts. (v. 13)

In other words, "Cyrus is not a threat to my plan. He *is* my plan, and it's the *right* plan. I want you to share my enthusiasm with me." That's the kind of faith God is asking us for—which leads us to Isaiah's final point.

God's Invitation

Thus says the LORD:
"The wealth of Egypt and the merchandise of Cush,
    and the Sabeans, men of stature,
shall come over to you and be yours;
    they shall follow you;
    they shall come over in chains and bow down to you.
They will plead with you, saying:
    'Surely God is in you, and there is no other,
    no god besides him.'" (v. 14)

Is Isaiah endorsing cultural imperialism? No. He's saying what Jesus said: "The meek . . . shall inherit the earth" (Matthew 5:5). Right now the wrong people are admired. The wrong ideals are promoted. But it won't always be so. The meek *shall* inherit the earth. Fools and rascals will no longer be sought after. They will humble themselves in admiration for saintly people. And why is Isaiah making that point? Because his Jewish people felt that, because they were defeated, God was defeated. But God is declaring that he has not withdrawn his promise of salvation. Far from it. He's including all the nations in his gracious purpose.

Isn't that what God has been doing for more than 2,000 years? It started when the Magi came from the east to worship Jesus (Matthew 2:1–12). And we worship God today because of his inclusive love spreading out over the world, creating worship where there'd been nothing but idolatry. His goal is one world, rid of all idols, enjoying his salvation in Christ. And one of his strategies to that end is to make his presence in his people so real, so beautiful, that even the strong and the privileged find themselves saying, "God is in those people, and I will pay any price to be a part of that."

The strategies of God are surprising. No one less than Isaiah himself marveled at how God pursues his plan.

Truly, you are a God who hides himself,4
    O God of Israel, the Savior. (Isaiah 45:15)

No one watching the Jews struggling to rebuild Jerusalem back then and no one watching Christians struggling to serve God today would think that the future lies with the gospel. Do people look at the church and think, "If only those Christians were running the world"? But God hides his greatness in our commonness. He hides his wisdom and power in the fool-

ishness and weakness of the gospel (1 Corinthians 1:18—2:16). Frederick
William Faber, the nineteenth-century hymn-writer, understood how God
works:

Workman of God, O lose not heart,
But learn what God is like,
And in the darkest battlefield
Thou shalt know where to strike.

Thrice blest is he to whom is given
The instinct that can tell
That God is on the field when He
Is most invisible.

He hides himself so wondrously,
As though there were no God;
He is least seen when all the powers
Of ill are most abroad.

Ah, God is other than we think;
His ways are far above,
Far beyond reason's height and reached
Only by childlike love.

Then learn to scorn the praise of men
And learn to lose with God,
For Jesus won the world through shame,
And beckons thee his road.[5]

It's hard to see the beginning of the new heavens and the new earth in
Christian believers today. But it's here, because God has put the power of
the resurrection of Christ within us (Ephesians 1:15–23). The truth hidden
from natural eyes is, "Israel is saved by the LORD with everlasting salvation;
you shall not be put to shame or confounded to all eternity" (Isaiah 45:17).

If you have difficulty believing this gospel, Martin Luther might be able
to help. He used to speak of "the hidden God" versus "the revealed God."
His counsel was this: "If you accept the God who is revealed, the hidden
God will be given to you at the same time."[6] In other words, if you accept
what is clear to you from the gospel, God will give you more understanding of what is unclear. Accept as much of the offense as you can, and in his
mercy God will help you take the next step into fuller assurance. No one has
ever trusted God without benefiting from it.

"Assemble yourselves and come;
　　draw near together,
　　you survivors of the nations!
They have no knowledge
　　who carry about their wooden idols,
　　and keep on praying to a god that cannot save. . . .
Turn to me and be saved,
　　all the ends of the earth!
　　For I am God, and there is no other." (Isaiah 45:20, 22)

Look how God reasons with us. Look at the way he invites us to rethink our lives. The problem with our idols is not that they break down now and then, like home appliances. The problem is, they're completely useless. When they seem to be helping us, we are in fact experiencing the goodness of God, but without thanking him (Romans 1:21). There is no life, no salvation, no hope at all except in God alone. Our part is to turn away from our worthless idols and turn to the living God. If we will, we can't help but experience salvation because God cannot fail to be God to us. The whole point of creation and history is for God to glorify himself by saving us. Your salvation is not ultimately about you; it's about God. He is both perplexing and faithful because he is *God*, and we should accept that.

"By myself I have sworn;
　　from my mouth has gone out in righteousness
　　a word that shall not return:
'To me every knee shall bow,
　　every tongue shall swear allegiance.'
Only in the LORD, it shall be said of me,
　　are righteousness and strength;
to him shall come and be ashamed
　　all who were incensed against him.
In the LORD all the offspring of Israel
　　shall be justified and shall glory." (vv. 23–25)

Don't be incensed against God. He is glorifying himself by being himself. And his being God is our salvation—if we'll have him. Someday each one of us will bow before Jesus Christ crucified as God's Ultimate Surprise (Philippians 2:9–11). If you'll look past his unimpressive followers now, if you'll trust him enough to join him in the way of his cross, you will bow then in the deepest joy forever. But if you cling to your hurt feelings and dashed expectations and broken dreams and stubborn pride, and if you insist on sulking and having things your own way, you will bow unwillingly then, to your eternal exclusion and regret. And the saddest part will be, you will deserve it. *This is his ultimatum, and the moment to decide is now.*

C. S. Lewis wrote a series of children's stories in which the Christ figure is a lion. In one scene a girl named Jill bursts into an opening in a forest. She's thirsty. She spies a stream not far away, but she doesn't rush forward to throw her face into its refreshing current. Instead she freezes in fear because a lion is resting in the sun right beside the stream.

> "Are you not thirsty?" said the Lion.
>
> "I'm *dying* of thirst," said Jill.
>
> "Then drink," said the Lion.
>
> "May I—could I—would you mind going away while I do?" said Jill.
>
> The Lion answered this only by a look and a very low growl. And as Jill gazed at its motionless bulk, she realized that she might as well have asked the whole mountain to move aside for her convenience. The delicious rippling noise of the stream was driving her nearly frantic.
>
> "Will you promise not to—do anything to me, if I do come?" said Jill.
>
> "I make no promise," said the Lion.
>
> Jill was so thirsty now that, without noticing it, she had come a step nearer. "*Do* you eat girls?" she said.
>
> "I have swallowed up girls and boys, women and men, kings and emperors, cities and realms," said the Lion. It didn't say this as if it were boasting, nor as if it were sorry, nor as if it were angry. It just said it.
>
> "I daren't come and drink," said Jill.
>
> "Then you will die of thirst," said the Lion.
>
> "Oh, dear!" said Jill, coming another step nearer. "I suppose I must go and look for another stream then."
>
> "There is no other stream," said the Lion.[7]

34

Gods That Fail and the
Collapse of Their Cultures

ISAIAH 46:1—47:15

THE PROPHET HOSEA, a contemporary of Isaiah, gives us an insight into idolatry: "With their silver and gold they made idols for their own destruction" (Hosea 8:4b). That's interesting in at least two ways. First, they made idols with *their silver and gold*. Silver and gold are good things, beautiful things, valuable things. An idol is not in essence a smelly monstrosity. It's a good thing God created for us. So how does a good thing go bad? We corrupt it by the way we perceive it and feel about it. Not in our formal, conscious commitments, but in our functional, emotional commitments we exchange the Creator for something created (Romans 1:22–25). We trade down because the gift seems more real and more rewarding than the Giver. That is idolatry. It's a matter of the heart. The prophet Ezekiel said, "Their heart went after their idols" (Ezekiel 20:16b). Whatever good thing your heart goes after, if you prefer it to God himself, it's an idol.

What impact did their gold and silver idols have on Hosea's people? That's the second thing. They made their idols of gold and silver *for their own destruction*. Idols distort and twist and kill. However refined, however impressive outwardly, idols *destroy*. How could it be otherwise? Life is in Christ alone (John 1:4). Life comes to us on his terms, and no other way (John 3:36). We can try to wring life out of created things, but it won't work. If we use this good, God-created world apart from the lordship of Christ, it becomes a destructive power. Even God's creation can become a dark, sinister thing by the way we treat it.

That's what Isaiah shows us in chapters 46—47. Chapter 46 is about the *idols* of Babylon, and chapter 47 is about the *destruction* of Babylon. Idolatry and destruction go together. If Babylon had turned to God, she would have lived. But she clung to her idols, and they weighed her down into the dust.

Henrik Ibsen was not a Christian. But in his play *Ghosts* he feels his way intuitively toward what the Bible is saying here.

> Ghosts . . . But then I'm inclined to think that we are all ghosts, Pastor Manders, every one of us. It's not just what we inherit from our mothers and fathers that haunts us. It's all kinds of old defunct theories, all sorts of old defunct beliefs, and things like that. It's not that they actually *live* on in us; they are simply lodged there, and we cannot get rid of them. I've only to pick up a newspaper and I seem to see ghosts gliding between the lines. Over the whole country there must be ghosts, as numerous as the sands of the sea. And here we are, all of us, abysmally afraid of the light.[1]

Ibsen called them ghosts. The prophets called them idols—these old, dead, obsolete ideas and theories and customs and self-images that feel to us like silver and gold we can't live without but that in fact destroy us because they have no place under the lordship of the living Christ. And we are so afraid of the light.

God is inviting us to trust him so freely and esteem him so highly and prize him so richly that we turn to him alone and enter into the salvation for which we're all groping. God has hidden everything delightful in Jesus Christ, and everything outside him destroys us. The hymn-writer had prophetic eyes: "In the cross of Christ I glory, towering o'er the wrecks of time." Where is Marxism today? It's one of the wrecks of time—an old, defunct idol. Where is secular humanism today? Where is utopian socialism today? Have you listened carefully to John Lennon's song "Imagine"? Who can believe that anymore? The omni-explanatory claims that once compelled the attention of the world are looking more and more dated and tired and dusty in our post-everything age.[2] There is a growing weariness with all grand ideologies today. The idols are bowing down and stooping over, like Bel and Nebo so long ago. Why? Why do we see this repeated pattern of man-centered hopes passionately pursued only to accelerate our misery? The prophets knew why. They knew that our salvation is not anywhere in the creation but only in the Creator. God is there, making sure that the cross of Christ towers over the wrecks of time.

As we think this through, remember that Babylon is not just a culture of a bygone era. In the Bible, *Babylon* is a cipher for the whole of world-culture outside of Christ. The Bible is showing us the essence of the world in our day and in all days until the end.

1. The failure of the false gods versus the success of the true God (46:1–13)
    A The failed gods: "these things you carry" (46:1–7)
       B The successful God: "My counsel shall stand" (46:8–13)
2. The collapse of an idolatrous culture (47:1–15)
    A The fall of Babylon (47:1–7)
          1. Their disgrace: decreed by God (47:1–4)
          2. Their downfall: explained by God (47:5–7)
       B The pride of Babylon (47:8–11)
          1. Their mentality: superior to all (47:8, 9)
          2. Their policy: answerable to none (47:10, 11)
      C The helplessness of Babylon (47:12–15)
          1. Their religion: no answers (47:12, 13)
          2. Their commerce: no refuge (47:14, 15)

Isaiah has lingered over the problem of idols. He doesn't want to move on until we understand that idols are basic to our daily lives. They're so obvious to us, we don't see them. We don't see our culture; our culture is what we see *with*.[3] We're influenced in ways we don't notice. We have problems and never understand their real cause. So Isaiah wants us think about this until we see with new clarity that the salvation God offers is our only hope.

The Failed Gods, the Successful God

Bel bows down; Nebo stoops;
    their idols are on beasts and livestock;
these things you carry are borne
    as burdens on weary beasts.
They stoop; they bow down together;
    they cannot save the burden,
    but themselves go into captivity. (Isaiah 46:1, 2)

Who are Bel and Nebo? Bel was the patron-god of Babylon, the king of the gods and determiner of the destinies of nations. Nebo was his eldest son, the secretary of the council of gods and custodian of the Tablets of Destiny. (The Bible has already introduced us to them indirectly through the Babylonian names Belshazzar and Nebuchadnezzar.) These gods represented the ideals of Babylonia. In the official view of things, it was the authority of these gods that validated Babylon as the lead culture of the world. This was acted out annually at their New Year Festival. The images of Bel and Nebo were carried in grand procession through the city as tokens of good fortune for the coming year.

But Isaiah looks at the same procession and what does he see? He doesn't see Bel and Nebo triumphantly leading the way into the future. He sees them wearying the poor pack animals that have to lug these big, heavy idols through town. He isn't dazzled by the official line. He sees the obvious. What's that? If a god has to be carried, how can it carry you? If a god can't help itself, how can it help you? If a god needs your strength, how can it strengthen you?

The word Isaiah uses for "idols" in verse 1 echoes the Old Testament word for pain and hurt and strain. Idols promise everything, but they take everything from us and leave us fatally wounded in their trail of destruction. Why didn't Babylonian culture endure? Don't take the rise and fall of civilizations for granted. Human achievement wasn't meant to fade away. God meant us to be significant and lasting. Why do human societies collapse, as they all do? Our idols fail us. Who even remembers Bel and Nebo today except as two props on the stage of the Biblical drama? If I have to explain to you who Bel and Nebo used to be, if I have to find an interesting way to describe them to keep your attention, even as the name of Jesus is adored more and more the world over, what does that imply about the pretenses of our culture today? Idolatry, however impressive at the moment, is unsustainable. And all who cling to unreality are going into painful captivity.

By the way, do you see that Isaiah does *not* believe that Bel and Nebo are just different names for the same God everyone worships? Some people tell us, "We're all worshiping the same God. The various religions are just different paths up the same mountain, different ways to the same goal." Would Isaiah say that? He's saying that the gods of the nations are no gods at all; they're pathetic burdens. They have nothing to offer us but weariness. But who is God?

> "Listen to me, O house of Jacob,
>   all the remnant of the house of Israel,
> who have been borne by me from before your birth,
>   carried from the womb;
> even to your old age I am he,
>   and to your gray hairs I will carry you.
> I have made, and I will bear;
>   I will carry and I will save." (Isaiah 46:3, 4)

There is not one moment when God is not carrying you and me along. There will never come a time when we'll have to help poor old doddering God along in his latter years. The reality is, he has taken us on as his responsibility all the days of our lives. Humble yourself to realize that God is bearing you up, moment by moment, by his grace alone. To God, you will always be a child, always dependent, and that's okay with him. Believe his promise that he'll bring you all the way home, and enjoy the ride. The gospel says, "Cast your burden on the LORD, and he will sustain you" (Psalm 55:22).

"Blessed be the Lord, who daily bears us up" (Psalm 68:19). "Casting all your anxieties on him, because he cares for you" (1 Peter 5:7). This is God, and he wants to prove it by bearing your burden for you today.

"To whom then will you liken me and make me equal,
    and compare me, that we may be alike?" (Isaiah 46:5)

We do compare, all the time, don't we? For example, what is the comfort of the gospel worth to me compared with the comfort of Internet pornography? What is my sanctification worth to me compared with a slim, young figure? What is the evangelization of my city worth to me compared with my professional success? *What is the Creator worth to me compared with the creation?* We need to think about that and pray about that until our emotions lock onto God himself. And when our hearts do find that God is what we really long for, then we're released from idolatry and are caught up into the true worship that will never end throughout time and eternity.

Isaiah pokes his finger in the eye of idol worship one more time. He shows us the absurd contrast between gods that have to be made (46:6, 7) and the God who determines all things (46:8–11).

"Remember this and stand firm,
    recall it to mind, you rebels,[4]
    remember the former things of old;
for I am God, and there is no other;
    I am God, and there is none like me,
declaring the end from the beginning
    and from ancient times things not yet done,
saying, 'My counsel shall stand,
    and I will accomplish all my purpose,'
calling a bird of prey [Cyrus] from the east,
    the man of my counsel from a far country.
I have spoken, and I will bring it to pass;
    I have purposed, and I will do it.
Listen to me, you stubborn of heart,
    you who are far from righteousness:
I bring near my righteousness; it is not far off,
    and my salvation will not delay;
I will put salvation in Zion,
    for Israel my glory." (Isaiah 46:8–13)

That's surprising. After his assurances that God will prove that he is God by bearing us faithfully along, why does God confront us now as "rebels," "stubborn of heart," and "far from righteousness"? Because we are. God's people resist God's blessing. He bears us up not because of us but in spite of us. We like his promises, but we don't like his methods. We don't like any "bird of prey" swooping down on us, destabilizing our world, even if it is fulfilling the good purpose of God. William Cowper wrote:

> God moves in a mysterious way his wonders to perform;
> He plants his footsteps in the sea and rides upon the storm.
>
> You fearful saints, fresh courage take; the clouds you so much dread
> Are big with mercy and shall break in blessings on your head.
>
> Judge not the Lord by feeble sense but trust him for his grace;
> Behind a frowning providence he hides a smiling face.[5]

That is what we barely believe. Even as the idols of our age are bowing down and stooping in massive failure, we still struggle to trust in God. But what is his answer to our rebellion? More grace. In the very troubles we fear, God is bringing his righteousness near. He would have to stop being God before he could fail to keep the least of his promises to us. John Newton wrote:

> Begone, unbelief, my Savior is near,
> And for my relief will surely appear;
> By prayer let me wrestle, and he will perform;
> With Christ in the vessel I smile at the storm.
>
> Determined to save, he watched o'er my path,
> When, Satan's blind slave, I sported with death;
> And can he have taught me to trust in his name,
> And thus far have brought me, to put me to shame?[6]

That's a good question. Let's make up our minds about it and live confidently in the promises of God.

The Collapse of an Idolatrous Culture

> Come down and sit in the dust,
>   O virgin daughter of Babylon;
> sit on the ground without a throne,
>   O daughter of the Chaldeans!
> For you shall no more be called
>   tender and delicate. (Isaiah 47:1)

When Isaiah addresses the "virgin daughter of Babylon," he isn't think-ing of an individual person but of the whole city, the way we say "the city of Nashville." The city *is* Nashville. The virgin daughter *is* Babylon. But Isaiah sees Babylon as a pampered, self-indulgent, spoiled girl who has always gotten her own way. But now she suffers the shock of exile and slavery and abuse. Again, this is a picture not only of an ancient culture overrun by Cyrus; it's a prophetic vision of our world coming under the judgment of God (Revelation 18). The virgin daughter of Babylon symbolizes success and ease and cool. But she has forgotten God. That's a significant oversight.

> Vengeance will I take,[7]
>   and I will spare no one.
> Our Redeemer—the LORD of hosts is his name—
>   is the Holy One of Israel. (vv. 3b, 4)

Isaiah makes two back-to-back declarations here. First, God's unspar-ing vengeance is coming to Babylon. We feel tremors of the final shaking of all things even now in the mini-judgments of history, such as the fall of ancient Babylon and every other social collapse along the way. In the upheavals of history, we're hearing whispers of the final shout of triumph: "Fallen, fallen is Babylon the great" (Revelation 18:2). The judgment of God is not theoretical; it is before our eyes. The final reckoning will be as real as the history you and I are experiencing right now. And God will spare no one. Babylon is doomed.

Isaiah's second declaration is that there is another city. God says, "I will put salvation in Zion" (Isaiah 46:13). Vengeance passes over this city, and salvation enters into it because of God himself. He is "our Redeemer," Isaiah says. In New Testament terms, God's holy wrath fell on Jesus, our substitute at the cross. If we take refuge in him now, then for us the final Day of Judgment is already over, the sentence of "righteous" has already been pronounced upon us, our crisis is past, and we have an eternal place in the New Jerusalem. But God's judgment touches everyone—either personally in ourselves on that future day, or substitutionally through Christ crucified in the past. But until that final day, God is offering himself to every one of us as a Redeemer.

The reason why God will never make peace with our world is the human pride lying at the root of all its cruelties (47:5–7). Those who choose a redemption from beyond this world are misunderstood and trampled on. The worldly mind doesn't stop to think about it, and that is its undoing.

> Now therefore hear this, you lover of pleasures,
>   who sit securely,
> who say in your heart,

> "I am, and there is no one besides me;
> I shall not sit as a widow
>   or know the loss of children." (v. 8)

Do you see where the fall of Babylon began? It wasn't when the armies of Cyrus appeared on the horizon. It began in their thoughts. They said something in their hearts, and God heard every word. What did they say? "I am, and there is no one besides me." That sounds ominously familiar. God himself has been saying that all along. For example, "I am God, and there is no other" (46:9). But here in Isaiah 47:8, 10 the corporate mind of world culture declares its own God-like autonomy: "I am, and there is no one besides me." That way of thinking is blasphemy. It is the world's downfall.

Pride distorts judgment. Once pride enters in, we lose our bearings and start overreaching. We become capable of any evil once we lose a sense of our sinfulness. It's the difference, for example, between the Humanist Manifesto and the Passion Band. The American Humanist Association published their second manifesto in 1973. Among other things, it says:

> We affirm that moral values derive their source from human experience. Ethics is *autonomous* and *situational*, needing no theological or ideological sanction. . . . Human life has meaning because we create and develop our futures.[8]

That document was written by brilliant, highly credentialed people. But God says, "Your wisdom and your knowledge led you astray, and you said in your heart, 'I am, and there is no one besides me'" (47:10). The Passion Band has no worldly status to boast of, like the American Humanist Association. But they're saying something we all need to hear. They're a voice from Zion:

> It's all about you, Jesus,
> and all this is for you, for your glory and your fame.
> It's not about me, as if you should do things my way.
> You alone are God, and I surrender to your ways.

Which of those two radically opposing viewpoints do you believe is true to reality, and which is a lie? Which one will bring you to destruction, and which one will bring you to salvation?

In verses 12–15 Isaiah foresees the supports of religion and business failing Babylon when she needs relief the most. "You are wearied with your many counsels," he says in verse 13. As Babylonian society goes into meltdown, many proposals are offered as "the answer," but each one only makes the situation worse. It's what we see today—the exhaustion of our culture under the weight of one failed remedy after another. "This is the way the world ends, not with a bang but a whimper."[9]

Idols destroy through the way we think. However sophisticated our Christ-denying ideas may be, they weary us. That's why we should never be ashamed of the gospel. Many gifted people don't respect it or even understand it, because they've never experienced it. But the gospel remains the power of God for salvation to every one who believes (Romans 1:16), and even believers have only begun to explore its life-giving potentialities.

Isaiah's last line puts it bluntly: "There is no one to save you." That could be translated, "Your savior does not exist." Everyone needs to be saved, and every one of us is trusting in some savior or other. Does your savior exist? What do you really have going for you? Will anything about you last? Does anything about you deserve to? If you define yourself by idols, they'll make you as artificial as they are (Psalm 115:4–8). But there is a real Savior. He has no standing in the eyes of this present age, but this is what he offers: "Come to me, all who labor and are heavy laden, and I will give you rest" (Matthew 11:28). No one has ever come to him and not been saved.

In a letter to a friend, C. S. Lewis stated with his usual clarity what we all need to understand:

> I think one may be quite rid of the old haunting suspicion—which raises its head in every temptation—that there is something *else* than God— some other country . . . into which He forbids us to trespass—some kind of delight which He "doesn't appreciate" or just chooses to forbid, but which would be real delight if only we were allowed to get it. The thing *just isn't there*. Whatever we desire is either what God is trying to give us as quickly as He can, or else a false picture of what He is trying to give us. . . . He knows what we want, even in our vilest acts: He is longing to give it to us. . . . The truth is that evil is not a real *thing* at all, like God. It is simply good *spoiled*. That is why I say there can be good without evil, but no evil without good. You know what the biologists mean by a parasite— an animal that lives on another animal. Evil is a *parasite*. It is there only because good is there for it to spoil and confuse. . . . This is why we must be prepared to find God implacably and immovably forbidding what may seem to us very small and trivial things. But He knows whether they are really small and trivial. How small some of the things that doctors forbid would seem to an ignoramus.[10]

God has real remedies for your real needs. At the very point where you are most weary, he wants to bear your burden for you by his strong grace. Won't you let him? It's the next step toward a whole new world.

35

God's Commitment to God
Is His Assurance to Us

ISAIAH 48:1–22

WE'VE ALL HEARD THE OBJECTION, "Christianity *can't* be true. Look at the people in the church. They're sinners like everyone else." The shoddy lives of Christians do cast doubt on the gospel. The prophet Nathan said to David, "You have given great occasion to the enemies of the LORD to blaspheme" (2 Samuel 12:14, NKJV). But Isaiah 48 goes deeper. How does God think? "Christianity *must* be true. Look at the people in the church. They're sinners like everyone else."

What's the difference between these two lines of reasoning? The logic of each is impeccable in its own way. But each is grounded in a different premise. The skeptical objection to the gospel is premised in works-righteousness. But the logic of God is premised in grace: Christianity must be true, because only God would save sinners. God proves that he is God by his grace to sinners.

The grace of God is not an afterthought. His grace is not Plan B in view of our failures. Grace is the very nature of God. When Moses prayed, "Show me *your glory*," God answered, "I will make all *my goodness* pass before you" (Exodus 33:18, 19). Does it seem obvious to us that God would judge sinners? Yes. Does it seem obvious that God would welcome sinners into the fiery love of the Trinitarian Godhead? That's breathtaking. But God is out to prove that he is God not by nuking us but by embracing us forever. That is his glory.

If you are in Christ, whatever God is doing in your life right now is not an experiment that he might abandon if he gets fed up with you. You need to know that God would have to stop being God before he'd quit on you. And *why* is God devoted to you? It's not because you risk looking like a failure. You already do. So do I. It's because God will never let his purpose fail. The defeat of grace to sinners would be the defeat of God.

The message of God to us all is this: "For my own sake, I love failures and fools and spiritual nitwits, for how could my name be profaned? My glory I will not give to another." God's commitment to God is his assurance to us. If that assurance does not melt your heart, it doesn't belong to you. But if that assurance ignites within you a flame of hope, then he has set you apart to himself forever. The throne of God is a throne of grace (Hebrews 4:16). Here in Isaiah 48 the prophet reveals the way God rules and overrules, to the praise of the glory of his grace.

Isaiah 48 looks back to all of chapters 40—47. Chapter 40 began, "Comfort, comfort my people." God comforted his ancient people with a promise to release them from Babylonian captivity, bring them home, and show them his glory. The problem was, he planned to use a pagan conqueror named Cyrus the Great to set those events in motion. The Jewish exiles choked on that. In fact, the actual appearing of the glory of the Lord was even more problematic. The glory came down in an ordinary man named Jesus of Nazareth who didn't throw off the yoke of Roman tyranny but died on a Roman cross. That was a problem too—"a stumbling block to Jews and folly to Gentiles" (1 Corinthians 1:23). And so it is today. Every culture has its prejudices against God. And here in chapter 48 Isaiah is frank about our bias against God, but for a redemptive purpose. He wants us to know that God displays his grace toward backward people like us, for his own glory. Therefore, nothing can keep him from fulfilling his promises to us.

The passage answers the question, what may we sinners expect of God? The structure breaks that question down into two parts.

1. Why does God put up with us? (48:1–11)
   - A¹ Who we are (48:1, 2)
     - B¹ "The former things" (48:3–5)
     - B² "New things" (48:6–8)
   - A² Why God acts (48:9–11)
2. How does God work with us? (48:12–22)
   - A¹ Who God is (48:12, 13)
     - B¹ "The LORD loves him" (48:14–16)
     - B² "The way you should go" (48:17–19)
   - A² How God acts (48:20–22)

Isaiah's pastoral intention is so to honor God and so to humble us that a new, settled confidence in his grace frees us to say back to him, "Your will be done, *however you want to do it*."

Why Does God Put Up with Us?

> Hear this, O house of Jacob,
>   who are called by the name of Israel,
>   and who came from the waters of Judah,
> who swear by the name of the LORD
>   and confess the God of Israel,
>   but not in truth or right.
> For they call themselves after the holy city,
>   and stay themselves on the God of Israel;
>   the LORD of hosts is his name. (Isaiah 48:1, 2)

The first word of verse 1 is the key: "Hear." Isaiah uses that Hebrew verb ten times in this chapter.[1] He understands that at the heart of faith is listening to God (Romans 10:17). A clear word from God is our only escape from the prison of self and culture out into the open spaces of truth. Our part is to *listen*.

But the centerpiece of these first two verses is the last line of verse 1: ". . . but not in truth or right." The Jewish exiles really were God's people. They had a lot going for them, as Isaiah says here. But something was wrong. Their profession of faith was "not in truth or right." They weren't really listening to God—not with the follow-through that reaches out for the implications of the gospel. They were, in the true sense of the word, nominal. They were not open to the surprising ways of God. They were limiting him to the narrowness of the idols. The idols were predictable. The idols were locked inside the annual cycle of the seasons and were a part of nature. But the transcendent Creator is free to do whatever he pleases (Psalm 115:3). He never acts out of character, but neither is he controllable. That means that true faith is always a cutting-edge adventure. True faith humbly admits, "Oh, the depth of the riches and wisdom and knowledge of God! How unsearchable are his judgments and how inscrutable his ways!" (Romans 11:33). That spirit of wonder keeps us low before God, so that we hold our lives with open hands before him. It keeps us willing to let God be God. Faith says, "Your will be done, in your way, at your pace, by your grace, for your glory."

But God isn't defeated when his people don't live by real faith. He has everything figured out. That's what the next two paragraphs are about. In verses 3–5 God looks back to "the former things." At every step along the way, he has been faithful to his promises—in spite of us, not because of us.

> "Because I know that you are obstinate,
>   and your neck is an iron sinew
>   and your forehead brass,

I declared them to you from of old,
  before they came to pass I announced them to you,
lest you should say, 'My idol did them,
  my carved image and my metal image commanded them.'" (vv. 4, 5)

As God's blessings break upon us, we tend to think in terms of secondary causes and especially our own good sense and hard work. Instead of seeing God everywhere, our perceptions fill the landscape of life with idols.

Why are we like this? Isaiah walks right up to us, looks closely at us, and says, "Yes, I see the problem. Your neck is an iron sinew, and your forehead is brass" (v. 4). In other words, we are opinionated, self-assured know-it-alls. The truth of "Praise God from whom all blessings flow" doesn't make the impact it should. Isaiah is saying, "This is not only the problem with the world; this is the problem with the church." And why is he making that point at all? When the coach of the local high school football team schedules a game against the Green Bay Packers, puts his second string onto the field, and scores a touchdown, there is only one explanation. He is a *great* coach. That is God's strategy. He schedules great things for us, and then he does them, so that we're compelled to say, "He's a *great* God."

In verses 6–8 God looks ahead to "new things," future outpourings of grace. But he'll accomplish them in creative, new ways we can't foresee. He intends to keep on surprising us, because we can't be trusted with full disclosure of his plans. We'd end up saying, "Oh sure, I saw it coming" (v. 7). Isn't that the way we are? We don't like uncertainty. We don't like feeling helpless. If only we could see into the future! But would that really be good for us? What if God did tell us everything in advance? What would we do with it? We wouldn't lean on him moment by moment. We'd soon think we could take control. And Isaiah calls that bent in our hearts rebellion (v. 8). So God tells us enough in advance here in the Bible so that we have something to trust him for, but not so much that we can ignore him along the way. He keeps leading us along, even when our thoughts treat him more like a problem than a joy. *Why does God love us so much? Why does he put up with us?*

"For my name's sake I defer my anger,
  for the sake of my praise I restrain it for you,
  that I may not cut you off.
Behold, I have refined you, but not as silver;
  I have tried you in the furnace of affliction.
For my own sake, for my own sake, I do it,
  for how should my name be profaned?
  My glory I will not give to another." (vv. 9–11)

This is one of the great statements in the Bible. It reveals God's ultimate motive in all his loving ways. He put up with so much from Israel. Even when he sent them into the refining fire of exile, he limited their affliction. And he puts up with us. God is always giving us better than we deserve. The ultimate reason why God treats us so well is for the sake of his own name (Ezekiel 36:22–32). He will not give the glory of his grace to any idol of our moral logic.

Not only does our performance not secure us in God's favor, it's our lousy performance that God uses to display his favor. He loves us for reasons that make sense only within the logic of the divine nature. He loves us with what seems to us like one windfall of mercy after another. God must love his kind of love, because he calls it his glory. His mercy to sinners through Jesus Christ is what sets him apart most impressively from the idols. It takes no one less than the one true God sacrificially and eternally to disconnect what we deserve from what we get.

Do not think of God as a frustrated deity scratching his head as we checkmate one divine move after another. We do grieve his loving heart, but we do not defeat him. Take all our sins and gather them together into one vast stinking pile of garbage, and God is still the King of an infinitely greater realm. He is, in himself, "at home in the land of the Trinity."[2] He has no need that we could satisfy. He is a personal vastness who rejoices to give. For from his fullness we all receive grace upon grace (John 1:16).

This gospel is the only message true to the glory of God. He still confronts us with our sinfulness. The most striking feature of Isaiah 48 is its confrontational tone. All the commentators mention it. But what sets God apart from the vengeful idols of our minds that demand everything and forgive nothing is the dying love of Christ for sinners who don't even listen to him carefully. God will never give that glory away, whatever it takes—even death on a cross.

How Does God Work with Us?

"Listen to me, O Jacob,
    and Israel, whom I called!
I am he; I am the first,
    and I am the last.
My hand laid the foundation of the earth,
    and my right hand spread out the heavens;
when I call to them,
    they stand forth together." (Isaiah 48:12, 13)

In the second half of the chapter Isaiah applies the truth of the first half. If God's grace reveals his unique glory, what are the implications? Isaiah leaves us with four assurances. *First, God will never fail to be God*. He is "the first" and "the last." In other words, he is never forced into anything, he succeeds over all opposition, he is free to carry things forward any way he thinks best, and his final outcome is the pure gold of his triumphant glory. The display of God's redemptive love in Christ is *the* wraparound explanation for *everything*. He is the first and the last.

> "Assemble, all of you, and listen!
>   who among them [the idols] has declared these things?
> The LORD loves him [Cyrus];
>   he shall perform his purpose on Babylon,
>   and his arm shall be against the Chaldeans.
> I, even I, have spoken and called him;
>   I have brought him, and he will prosper in his way.
> Draw near to me, hear this:
>   from the beginning I have not spoken in secret,
>   from the time it came to be I have been there." (vv. 14–16a)

God favors Cyrus as the conqueror of Babylon. And God is unembarrassed by his plan, whatever anyone else may think. He even says that he loves this Persian warlord. God is asking us to look beyond the surface of events into his presence within them: "From the time it came to be I have been there." In the same way, your story is a story of God's surprising presence. Your life is better than you think. And God's greatest involvement with you is hinted at in the last line of verse 16:

> And now the Lord GOD has sent me, and his Spirit.

Who is speaking here? Not Isaiah. What would be the point? Is Cyrus speaking here? Maybe. But could the speaker also be that shadowy figure we have already encountered, the servant of the Lord (Isaiah 42:1–9)? That's a better fit. He is about to reappear in chapter 49. Isaiah looks beyond Cyrus to the perfect conqueror and the true Messiah, Jesus Christ, who is empowered not with a sword but with the Spirit. Therefore, what you and I are experiencing in our lives—if we can receive this—is not some alien intrusion but the very presence and profile of Jesus. That's the meaning of your life and mine. This is the second assurance Isaiah leaves with us: *Even in our unwelcome experiences, Christ is present behind the obvious.*

> Thus says the LORD,
>   your Redeemer, the Holy One of Israel:
> "I am the LORD your God,

> who teaches you to profit,
> who leads you in the way you should go." (Isaiah 48:17)

The third assurance is this: *In all the turbulence of life, God is teaching us and leading us forward*. What does he teach us? Where is he leading us? He teaches us to "profit." In other words, he teaches us what really matters. He opens up to us the real treasures of life. He awakens in us a willingness gladly to suffer the loss of all things in order to gain Christ. And that's the way we should go. Only a Redeemer, the Holy One, would take us there.

But it isn't automatic. For convinced idolaters like us, these can be hard lessons to learn. And when we say no to God, it makes a difference.

> "Oh that you had paid attention to my commandments!
> Then your peace would have been like a river,
> and your righteousness like the waves of the sea;
> your offspring would have been like the sand,
> and your descendants like its grains;
> their name would never be cut off
> or destroyed before me." (vv. 18, 19)

The love of God does not shield us from the immediate impact of our sins. This generation of God's people long ago broke his heart. What he longed for was their peace and righteousness flowing in abundance. But they wouldn't listen. They didn't defeat God. But he did withhold from them the fullness of covenant blessing. He wrote them off (Luke 19:41–44). We would be fools not to take this warning to heart (1 Corinthians 10:1–14).

What is our path forward if we *will* listen?

> Go out from Babylon, flee from Chaldea,
> declare this with a shout of joy, proclaim it,
> send it out to the end of the earth;
> say, "The LORD has redeemed his servant Jacob!"
> They did not thirst when he led them through the deserts;
> he made water flow for them from the rock;
> he split the rock and the water gushed out. (Isaiah 48:20, 21)

These verses bring chapters 40—48 to a climax. What is God saying? There comes the moment when every one of us must decide. Will we settle down in the Babylon of this world or venture out into redemption in Christ? As in the exodus out of Egypt, God is calling us to the adventure of faith. He promises to satisfy our thirst all along the way. He can split a rock so that water gushes out. In fact, he even knows how to nail a perfect man to a cross so that mercy gushes out. That's something to shout about, Isaiah says.

But you have to make up your mind. Will God coax you out into a life of pilgrimage, only to abandon you? Or can God make blessing gush out upon you anywhere he leads? That's the fourth assurance: *God is a good Savior, wherever and however he leads.*

But here's the deal-breaker. The only ultimate wickedness is to refuse the grace of God, because that refusal denies the very nature of God.

> "There is no peace," says the LORD, "for the wicked." (v. 22)

"No peace" is not an arbitrary punishment. It's the inevitable result of rejecting God. Will you let God be God to *you* in his out-gushing grace in Christ? Will you step over the line from resistance to trust, from refusing to listening, from delaying to following?

36

Not with Swords' Loud Clashing

ISAIAH 49:1— 50:3

AS ISAIAH LEADS US ALONG, increasingly he lifts our thoughts beyond our immediate problems to more distant, more luxurious certainties. He opened the second major section of his book with "Comfort, comfort my people" (40:1). Now we read, "Listen to me, O coastlands, and give attention, you peoples from afar" (49:1). The prophetic horizon is broadening.

Isaiah now presents the second of his four Servant Songs. The suffering Jews needed more than release from Babylon. They needed a savior greater than Cyrus. We all need a spiritual liberation and an everlasting Savior. Isaiah is deepening our awareness of this. In chapter 42 he introduced to us the servant of the Lord. This mysterious hero now reappears, along with our hostile response to him.

A¹ The glorious servant of the Lord: a light for the nations (49:1–6)
    1. A new beginning, a discouraging effort (49:1–4)
    2. A divine purpose, worldwide impact (49:5, 6)
A² The despised servant of rulers: a covenant to the people (49:7–13)
    1. Worldly rejection reversed by divine choice (49:7)
    2. Divine favor through worldwide ingathering (49:8–12)
    3. Cosmic delight unleashed by divine comfort (49:13)
  B The despondent people: kept by the power of God (49:14—50:3)
    1. The despondent people (49:14)
    2. The mindful Lord (49:15–21)
    3. The triumphant Lord (49:22–26)
    4. The powerful Lord (50:1–3)

Isaiah wants to fix our attention on the servant of the Lord, who embodies God's loving intentions toward us. We should melt in delighted wonder that he gives us such a gift as his servant.

The Glorious Servant of the Lord

> Listen to me, O coastlands,
>   and give attention, you peoples from afar.
> The LORD called me from the womb,
>   from the body of my mother he named my name.
> He made my mouth like a sharp sword;
>   in the shadow of his hand he hid me;
> he made me a polished arrow;
>   in his quiver he hid me away.
> And he said to me, "You are my servant,
>   Israel, in whom I will be glorified."
> But I said, "I have labored in vain;
>   I have spent my strength for nothing and vanity;
> yet surely my right is with the LORD,
>   and my recompense with my God." (Isaiah 49:1–4)

The servant of the Lord, set apart from birth and uniquely equipped for his mission, is a prophet. He is the voice of God on earth, and he demands a hearing from the entire world. But unlike Cyrus, the weapons of his warfare are not of the flesh but have divine power to destroy strongholds (2 Corinthians 10:4). His word is a sharp sword. He himself is a polished arrow. He is a dread weapon in the hand of God. But he compels the attention of the world by God's improbable gospel strategies. Hidden until the time is right, he emerges in history to conquer not by military might or cultural imperialism but by the force of truth. This is Jesus.

But there's a problem here. In verse 3 the servant is identified as "Israel, in whom I [God] will be glorified." Then in verses 5, 6, as we'll see, this same servant is the one who restores Israel to God. How can Israel restore Israel?

A clue appeared already in 48:1 where Isaiah confronted the "house of Jacob, who are called by the name of Israel . . . but not in truth or right." Isaiah understood that these demoralized Jews in exile, whose failed historic mission was obvious to the nations, no longer lived up to their name. God's purpose was so to bless them that the world would be drawn to him (Psalm 67). But Israel failed, and by now their failure makes a mockery of their ancient identity as the Israel of God. Is the purpose of God therefore defeated? No. God provides a substitute Israel, who does live up to the name. Jesus Christ is our substitute not only in his death but also in his life. He is everything to us (1 Corinthians 1:30, 31). His only failure was our failure, and our only success is his success.

So the Israel of verse 3 is Messiah, the servant who embodies all that historic Israel should have been. He is the Israel *in whom God will be glorified*. We can't make sense of the Old Testament without Christ. He's the one on whom all lines converge. All the persons, events, and institutions of the Old Testament, including the nation of Israel itself, find their truest meaning in Christ. The Old Testament has obsolescence built into it. It points beyond itself, both because of the human failure its story tells and also because, even at their best, the figures moving through the pages of the Old Testament were only meant to prepare for something greater. The incompleteness of the Old Testament demands resolution, a breakthrough. On every page it cries out for Christ. So we shouldn't be surprised when the Old Testament uses the name Israel for the Messiah. We should expect it, because *the whole Bible is all about Christ*. If we understand the signals the Old Testament itself is sending us, we'll read it that way. Why shouldn't we? The apostles did, and they were good theologians. Better than we are.

Verse 4 reveals something of the psychology of Messiah. Jesus Christ, the very center of God's purpose unfolding in history, struggled at times with feelings of failure: "I have labored in vain." Does that surprise us? It shouldn't. His earthly mission 2,000 years ago did not come across as one continual triumph. Unlike the human conquerors strutting across the stage of history, adored by the envious, Jesus was despised and rejected. At times he felt frustrated (Matthew 17:17). In the end he was abandoned: "My God, my God, why have you forsaken me?" (Matthew 27:46). But unlike historic Israel, this true Israel did not turn away from God in cynical unbelief. In all his setbacks he trusted God: "Yet surely my right is with the LORD, and my recompense with my God." Jesus saw the joy set before him, he clung to it by faith, and that faith preserved him in his arduous mission.

Far from failing to renew historic Israel, Christ has been given an even greater task. He is the divinely appointed Savior of the whole world.

And now the LORD says,
    he who formed me from the womb to be his servant,
to bring Jacob back to him;
    and that Israel might be gathered to him—
for I am honored in the eyes of the LORD,
    and my God has become my strength—
he says:
"It is too light a thing that you should be my servant
    to raise up the tribes of Jacob

and to bring back the preserved of Israel;
I will make you as a light for the nations,
    to be my salvation unto the end of the earth."[1] (Isaiah 49:5, 6)

Jesus Christ is the Savior of the world, and there is no other. He is God's appointed "light for the nations." Every wisdom and philosophy and moral code outside Christ lies in the deepest, outermost darkness as to salvation. But to enter into the light of Christ is to have your gloom lifted and your confusion replaced with truth and delight. He is your breakthrough to seeing everything in a new light. And his God-appointed mission, to bring the light of God into our natural darkness, will succeed with worldwide impact. Jesus himself said, "I am the light of the world. Whoever follows me will not walk in darkness, but will have the light of life" (John 8:12).

The Despised Servant of Rulers

Thus says the LORD,
    the Redeemer of Israel and his Holy One,
to one deeply despised, abhorred by the nation,
    the servant of rulers:
"Kings shall see and arise;
    princes, and they shall prostrate themselves;
because of the LORD, who is faithful,
    the Holy One of Israel, who has chosen you." (Isaiah 49:7)

The ways of God are so strange. Christ's strategy is not to overwhelm the arrogance of the world with even more formidable arrogance, like every other conqueror, but to empty himself and take the form of a servant.

The servanthood of Christ can make it easy for us to dismiss him with contempt. Even professing believers treat him as an optional add-on, enhancing their lifestyle, rather than as the Lord of all. Why? For one thing, the human heart is endlessly self-exalting and Christ-despising, more than we realize. But for another thing—and this is Isaiah's point—Christ approaches us not like a Cyrus fuming with rage, cracking the whip, jerking our chain; he approaches us as a servant (Matthew 11:28–30). He is more than a servant, but not above servanthood. His meekness is so real, he *can* be misunderstood and "deeply despised," as Isaiah puts it. But God has resolved that even the great ones of this earth, kings and princes, will put their pride away to honor the servant of the Lord, to the glory of God the Father (Philippians 2:11). This is the way of God—humiliation, then vindication.

The true worth of the servant of the Lord shines forth in his influence on people. They joyfully flock to him from around the world. God addresses his servant:

Thus says the LORD:
"In a time of favor I have answered you;
    in a day of salvation I have helped you;
I will keep you and give you
    as a covenant to the people,
to establish the land,
    to apportion the desolate heritages,
saying to the prisoners, 'Come out,'
    to those who are in darkness, 'Appear.'
They shall feed along the ways;
    on all bare heights shall be their pasture;
they shall not hunger or thirst,
    neither scorching wind nor sun shall strike them,
for he who has pity on them will lead them,
    and by springs of water will guide them.
And I will make all my mountains a road,
    and my highways shall be raised up.
Behold, these shall come from afar,
    and behold, these from the north and from the west,
    and these from the land of Syene." (Isaiah 49:8–12)

The way to understand this is to view it against the backdrop of Cyrus liberating the Jewish exiles in the sixth century B.C. That event fills Isaiah's mental landscape throughout this section of his book, because his prophetic eye discerns in it how Jesus saves us today. Isaiah would have loved Charles Wesley's hymn "And Can It Be":

Long my imprisoned spirit lay fast-bound in sin and nature's night;
Thine eye diffused a quickening ray; I rose, the dungeon flamed with light.
My chains fell off, my heart was free; I rose, went forth, and followed thee.
Amazing love! How can it be that thou, my God, shouldst die for me?

Isaiah perceives in the historic liberation of God's people by Cyrus a model of a greater liberation by the servant of the Lord in this age of gospel fulfillment. We're no longer waiting for something better. *Now* is the time to be liberated from the sins that tyrannize us (2 Corinthians 6:2)!

Think of what Christ is worth to us. He is "a covenant to the people," Isaiah says (49:8). In other words, he is himself the very embodiment of God's pledge of grace to us. He is how God pours out favor upon us and how we are bound to God in return. From the beginning, God has given himself to us through covenants, through formal agreements we can bank on (e.g., Genesis 15). God is not ad-libbing his way along. He has a plan. He is not casual or offhanded in his dealings with us. He is a serious person who takes us seriously but who also knows how weak our faith is. He knows we need the strong assurance that he has given himself to us by oath. This is the way of God. And now Isaiah shows us that Christ is himself God's covenant with weak people who have failed to keep their end of the bargain. Jesus said at his last supper with his disciples, "This cup is the new covenant in my blood" (1 Corinthians 11:25). Can we imagine a more solemn declaration of God's grace toward us? Is it conceivable that God could finally forsake us? The whole story of the human race is God's way of staging the outpouring of his redemptive love in Christ. He is in earnest with you. Be in earnest with him!

Isaiah's prophetic vision sweeps across the history of salvation. He sees God, through the covenant man Jesus Christ, restoring the ruins that sin has made of us. He sets us free from our self-imposed prisons. He leads us forward into a new way of life, caring for us moment by moment, providing for us fully, overcoming the obstacles, getting us all the way home to his eternal presence (Revelation 7:9–17). And this liberation gathers in not only the Jews of ancient Babylon, not just the isolated straggler along the way, but masses of people from all over the world as history rushes toward The End. Can you see what Isaiah sees? God is doing something new and constructive and lasting in our messy human scene, and anyone can be a part of it. God is out to prove how kind he can be through Jesus Christ. And there is room there for *you*.

> Sing for joy, O heavens, and exult, O earth;
>   break forth, O mountains, into singing!
> For the LORD has comforted his people
>   and will have compassion on his afflicted. (Isaiah 49:13)

Worldwide redemption calls for cosmic celebration. The people of God, now from all the nations, are so richly comforted and loved, it takes nothing less than the heavens, the earth, and the mountains to shout their hurrahs to God. In fact, they will (Romans 8:19–21).

The Despondent People

> But Zion said, "The LORD has forsaken me;
>   my Lord has forgotten me." (Isaiah 49:14)

What a letdown! The prophet has just told us that nothing will ever separate us from the love of God in Christ Jesus our Lord. But then we look around at our problems and mumble, "No, the Lord has forsaken me. He has forgotten me." The people of God, even as they're being carried in the everlasting arms toward Heaven, can be gloomy, sour, impossible-to-please people. How hard it is for some Christians to be happy! Shouldn't the good news make people smile?

Here is ultimate joy, drawing praise from the heavens, the earth, and the mountains, pouring down out of Heaven into our lives with solid hope, and yet our emotions can be *dead*. How exasperating! What should be done to hearts impervious to such goodness? What *does* God do? He goes on and on, proving himself as no one less than God.

Isaiah argues this point by reminding us of three things about God. First, in 49:15–21, *he is the mindful Lord*. God has not forgotten us; it is we who forget him.

> "Can a woman forget her nursing child,
>   that she should have no compassion on the son of her womb?
> Even these may forget,
>   yet I will not forget you.
> Behold, I have engraved you on the palms of my hands;
>   your walls are continually before me." (vv. 15, 16)

God is addressing Zion. In Isaiah's culture, a city was thought of in the feminine gender. That's why this final section of the passage (49:15—50:3) is filled with images of Lady Zion and her children—in our terms today, the church and her members. And God is saying that he will never abandon his family. *Never.* His love is more mindful than even the love of a tenderly nursing mother. God *is* love (1 John 4:8–10).

The imagery of verse 16 suggests a vision of God spreading out his hands before us, so that we can see our very names engraved there. Have we thought through how profoundly we're loved by God? If his assurances do not move us, what more are we holding out for? Isn't the love of *God* enough?

Far from neglecting us, God swears by his very life to surprise us with the expansion and growth of his church. Isaiah imagines it like a childless woman delightedly astonished at the multitude of happy children gathering around her as their mother, replacing her devastation with fullness (49:17–21). This is the future of the church, by God's decree. His people will someday look around and blink with amazement: "Can it be? All these multitudes gathered into the bosom of the church, even in our barrenness and futility? What on earth has happened?" The growth of the church will be too vast to be explainable by any human plan, too massive to be accommodated by any human program. It won't be our faith that grows the church but only God's deep resolve to show mercy to more and more sinners. In the final triumph of grace, we won't congratulate ourselves on a job well done; we'll stutter in amazement, "Behold, I was left alone; from where have these come?" (v. 21b).

Isaiah is displaying the endless love of God to all who are slow to believe what the prophets have spoken (Luke 24:25). Secondly, in 49:22–26, *our God is the triumphant Lord.*

> Can the prey be taken from the mighty,
>   or the captives of a tyrant be rescued?
> For thus says the LORD:
> "Even the captives of the mighty shall be taken,
>   and the prey of the tyrant be rescued,
> for I will contend with those who contend with you,
>   and I will save your children.
> I will make your oppressors eat their own flesh,
>   and they shall be drunk with their own blood as with wine.
> Then all flesh shall know
>   that I am the LORD your Savior,
>   and your Redeemer, the Mighty One of Jacob." (vv. 24–26)

Isaiah's bold language in this paragraph should not be misunderstood. With the gospel expanding the whole world over, with more and more people reverencing the church as their spiritual mother, is this powerful movement the tedious imposition of just another religious colonialism? No. The prestige given to the growing church of the latter days is the willing expression of spiritual indebtedness. In fact, it's happening all around the world today through Christian missions. And as history draws closer to the return of Christ, gospel breakthroughs will accelerate. Middle walls of partition will break down, and new bonds of spiritual affection will bring former enemies together as one in Christ, filling Mother Church with many happy children. Far from religious bondage, the gospel-driven triumph of the church is God himself putting an end to long-standing oppressions.

Those who oppose the onrush of Joy end up consuming themselves as they hold out in their psychological and cultural bastions against Christ (v. 26). The victory of Christ will be so glorious that all flesh will admit God has stepped into history with a mighty salvation.

Isaiah is heaping assurance upon assurance because when God's people are too demoralized to believe his promises of grace, they need more grace. In 50:1–3, then, *our God is the powerful Lord.*

> Thus says the LORD:
> "Where is your mother's certificate of divorce,
>   with which I sent her away?
> Or which of my creditors is it
>   to whom I have sold you?

Behold, for your iniquities you were sold,
> and for your transgressions your mother was sent away.
Why, when I came, was there no man;
> why, when I called, was there no one to answer?
Is my hand shortened, that it cannot redeem?
> Or have I no power to deliver?" (vv. 1, 2a)

God is challenging his exiled people to think. They feel abandoned (49:14). And yes, they had been disciplined—but not abandoned. So God says, "Okay, pull your mother's divorce certificate out of the file. What does it say? What are the charges there? Was it my failure as a husband that ruined the marriage, or was it your mother's? Is it really fair to me, is it even helpful to you, for you to keep blaming me for your captivity in Babylon? Or if you feel like property that's been sold off because my creditors were putting pressure on me, think that one through too. Do I even have creditors? To whom do *I* owe anything? *What are you thinking?*" What explains their exile is not the failure of God. The truth is this: "Behold, for your iniquities you were sold, and for your transgressions your mother was sent away." When we are under God's discipline, we never have a reason to find fault with him.

God presses the point. In his many approaches to his people and his many offers of help, why was there no clear and glad answer from them? When his outstretched hand provided everything helpful, relevant, and encouraging, why was his hand not grasped? Is his hand shortened, that it cannot redeem? Or has he no power to deliver? He is the powerful Lord. If we aren't experiencing that power, it isn't because of weakness or reluctance in him. God is both ready and willing to meet us with saving power, if only we'll stop hanging back in sullen reluctance and haughty fault-finding and step forward in the eagerness of repentance and faith.

> Luther was right: the root behind all other manifestations of sin is compulsive unbelief—our voluntary darkness concerning God, ourselves, his relationship to the fallen world and his redemptive purpose.[2]

The faith God wants to find in us is childlike, uncomplicated by our calculating grudges against God. How could it be otherwise? Isaiah has shown us that we are mere children in God's family, loved beyond calculation. And if God is our Father, isn't the greatness of his love enough for our faith to become simple? Jonathan Edwards expressed the beauty of this spirit of faith: "I very often think with sweetness and longings and pantings of soul of being a little child, taking hold of Christ, to be led by him through the wilderness of this world."[3]

If Isaiah's vision of God is true, and it is, why do we cling to our resentments and anger? Isn't this a way of passing the buck and excusing our own mediocrity? Doesn't that sourness bind us further to what we are? But God has given his servant Jesus Christ as a light for the nations and a covenant to the people. He loves you more than you love yourself. Let go of your self-pity, and rest in his mighty arms.

37

Why Do We Have Ears on the *Outside* of Our Heads?

ISAIAH 50:4—51:8

WHY DO WE HAVE EARS ON THE OUTSIDE OF OUR HEADS? Why not on the inside? Because we're not supposed to listen to ourselves. I wonder how much of our misery stems from our almost religious devotion to our own thoughts and feelings. But that inner personal world where you and I live constantly—what relation does it bear to the atmosphere that the gospel creates? We spend every moment of our entire lives within a mental universe. The quality of that environment matters. Are our ears open to the in-flowing blessing of God? Do we understand what it means to *listen* to God?

In the New Testament we are told, "He who has ears, let him hear."[1] If the Bible urges us to use our ears, they must be important. Think of the frequent prophetic summons: "Hear the word of the LORD" (e.g., Jeremiah 2:4). Go all the way back to the foundation of Israel's faith: "Hear, O Israel" (Deuteronomy 6:4). At least 394 times the Old Testament refers to the word of God coming to us.[2]

Why does this matter? Malcolm Muggeridge framed the question in his typically delightful way some years ago in his London Lectures in Contemporary Christianity. What if, instead of the Dead Sea Scrolls, we'd found the Dead Sea Videotapes? Would the difference matter? Would it matter if Biblical faith had been handed down to us in images rather than in words? Does the camera make the same impact as the pen? And Muggeridge argued that the camera deceives us. It makes us think we are seeing reality. But television, especially, brainwashes us with carefully edited fantasies. God encounters us meaningfully through words—words that illuminate, words that last, words that undeceive our confusion.

The Christian faith has come to us in words, not images; I find that passage in the first chapter of the Gospel according to St. John—the Word becoming flesh, and dwelling among us full of grace and truth—one of the most beautiful and profound things ever written. If it had come to us in images instead of words, it would not have lived as it has.[3]

If God's way of getting through to us is the word, then we need to learn what it means to listen.

Isaiah brings us to the third of his four Servant Songs. It's about listening. The nation of Israel had a hearing problem, and it was their undoing (48:8). But the servant of the Lord was a good listener. He had an ear constantly open to God (50:4, 5). The one who fears the Lord also listens obediently to the servant (50:10).[4] All who seek righteousness are good listeners (51:1, 4, 7). Dr. Isaiah is calling us in for a hearing check. He wants to retune our ears so we can hear the word of God again. That alone is how we escape our fantasies and enter into reality with God.

The Lord's servant appears first (50:4–9). Only he can ease our defensiveness and open our ears. Then everything pivots on the question of how bravely we're willing to listen to the servant (50:10, 11). Finally Isaiah equips us with three incentives for listening to the Lord's servant even when our courage is failing (51:1–8).

A[1] The suffering scholar: defended by God (50:4–9)
      1. The learned servant (50:4)
      2. The suffering servant (50:5, 6)
      3. The confident servant (50:7, 8)
      4. The vindicated servant (50:9)
  B Our choice: to follow Christ or ourselves? (50:10, 11)
A[2] The attentive listeners: reassured by God (51:1–8)
      1. God's comfort is life-giving (51:1–3)
      2. God's power is world-transforming (51:4–6)
      3. God's righteousness is courage-inspiring (51:7, 8)

Isaiah shows us the sustaining ministry of the servant of the Lord. Sustained by his word, we'll find the strength to follow him all the way.

The Suffering Scholar: Defended by God

The Lord GOD has given me
    the tongue of those who are taught,
that I may know how to sustain with a word
    him who is weary.
Morning by morning he awakens;

he awakens my ear
to hear as those who are taught. (Isaiah 50:4)

Each section of this Servant Song is marked by "the Lord GOD"—the sovereign Yahweh (50:4, 5, 7, 9). The initiative of the Sovereign lies behind everything in the passage. What does he do with all his power? He sends us encouragement through his servant. How different this vision of God is from the understanding of some Christians. Listening to them, we might think that God the Father is a difficult personality, nearly impossible to please, while God the Son is the gracious intermediary, winning over the reluctant Judge. Is that fair to God? John 3:16, the most famous verse in the Bible, says, "For God so loved the world, that he gave his only Son. . . ." Sovereign love is the true motive behind the whole drama of redemption. Isaiah was clear about that.

Interestingly, Isaiah presents Messiah to us as a well-taught disciple, a learned person, a scholar who has given himself devotedly to the word of God. How unlike Cyrus and other conquerors. The world has seen few philosopher-kings. But the servant of the Lord is given "the tongue of those who are taught," "an instructed tongue" (NIV). The point is that the servant of the Lord is a sage, well-schooled in the ways of God. Jesus Christ is not just loving; he is competent. He is wise enough to know how to help weak people. When everyone else fails us, he can "sustain with a word him who is weary"—weary with sin, weary with life. As we listen to the gospel, we find that Jesus is a wonderful counselor.

A sustaining ministry, a gospel ministry, requires more thought, more study, more insight than a condemning ministry. A finger-pointing ministry is easy. Moralism is the default setting of our minds. But it takes divine wisdom to understand God's grace in a new way, so we can sustain weary people. Jesus gave himself fully to that ministry.

Isaiah also presents the servant of the Lord as a sufferer. Christ's learning and his suffering went together (Hebrews 5:8).

The Lord GOD has opened my ear,
   and I was not rebellious;
    I turned not backward.
I gave my back to those who strike,
   and my cheeks to those who pull out the beard;
I hid not my face
   from disgrace and spitting. (Isaiah 50:5, 6)

It was with an open ear that Christ became obedient to the point of death, even death on a cross. He didn't suffer as a secondary result of his commitments; he *chose* the way of suffering. He *gave* his back to those who strike and his cheeks to those who pull out the beard. He walked into opposition with eyes wide-open. There was no place Jesus wouldn't go, nothing he wouldn't do, to care for weary people with the truth of God's grace. Those who hated God, even as they thought they honored him, were threatened by such radical love and tormented Jesus for it. The human heart naturally responds to truth not with honest inquiry or even rational rebuttal but with shrieking, spitting hatred, as Isaiah foresaw. In such a world as this, the Word-become-flesh *had* to suffer. And so will we, especially those of us who are pastors, if we listen to him with the openness of heart that will set our feet in his path.

Martin Luther was given an instructed tongue to sustain many weary people, and his sufferings were essential to his competence. Looking back on the opposition he had endured, Luther wrote:

> For as soon as God's Word becomes known through you, the devil will afflict you, will make a real [theologian] of you, and will teach you by his temptations to seek and to love God's Word. For I myself . . . owe my [Roman Catholic opponents] many thanks for so beating, pressing and frightening me through the devil's raging that they have turned me into a fairly good theologian, driving me to the goal I should never have reached.[5]

One reason we see widespread breakdowns in our own wisdom and even integrity today is that we seem to have forgotten that God calls us to follow Christ into suffering. What sustains us is not selfish predictability but the unchanging word of the Lord. That's what we need above all else and, in the end, all we have to offer others. Isaiah shows us the servant of the Lord suffering. And the servant was not rebellious; he did not turn back. When we turn away from God-ordained hardship, we are rebelling against God and diminishing our own capacity to breathe life into others.

The servant of the Lord knew that obedience to God is always a winning move (50:7, 8). It kept him going all the way, undaunted (Luke 9:51). Others misjudged him, but God helped him (Isaiah 50:9). And his opponents, who seemed so powerful at the time, proved as durable as a garment being eaten by a moth. The victories and defeats of this life are not at all what they seem. In the experience of Jesus—the paradigm for us—his faith was vindicated by an unexpected but unstoppable resurrection. And in his dazzling, immortal body, forever scarred but forever alive, Jesus Christ will never suffer again.

Our Choice: To Follow Christ or Ourselves?

Who among you fears the LORD
    and obeys the voice of his servant?
Let him who walks in darkness

and has no light
trust in the name of the LORD
    and rely on his God.
Behold, all you who kindle a fire,
    who equip yourselves with burning torches!
Walk by the light of your fire,
    and by the torches that you have kindled!
This you have from my hand:
    you shall lie down in torment. (Isaiah 50:10, 11)

The reference to the Lord's servant in verse 10 confirms that verses 4–9 are indeed a Servant Song. Now Isaiah challenges us to follow the servant with trust like his. Who is really listening to the servant's voice? There's a way to know.

Isaiah builds a contrast into these verses. The person listening to the voice of Christ "walks in darkness," with not a glimmer of light around him (v. 10). Yesterday morning before dawn I was deer hunting in the Georgia woods. The darkness was impenetrable, disorienting. There was nothing to do but wait for sunrise. Isn't that the life of Christian faith? We often live in perplexity, with no way out. That doesn't mean we aren't obeying God. We might be there in the darkness because we *are* obeying God. But here's a great truth: *Faith offsets darkness.* Darkness is what faith is for. It's there that we "trust in the name of the LORD."

When nothing else in our experience makes sense, when we have no visible path forward and everything seems to be closing in around us, what should we do? We should take our stand on the revealed character of God and keep going in his will, one step at a time. We should announce to ourselves again and again the promises of the gospel. The bare word of God has the power to stabilize our panicky hearts. In this simple, profound way, our lives will declare that God is a good Savior. And it's how we show that we really are listening to Christ.

Before we look at the other side of the contrast, there's a problem here. Maybe you've thought of it already. Jesus said, "I am the light of the world. Whoever follows me will not walk in darkness, but will have the light of life" (John 8:12). How is that consistent with Isaiah 50:10? The "darkness" in Isaiah 50:10 is not the same as the "darkness" in John 8:12. The darkness of Isaiah 50:10 is the courageous, hard path of obedience to the Lord, while the darkness of John 8:12 is abandonment by God, his face turned away, eternal death.

But setting Isaiah 50:10 and John 8:12 side by side is helpful. It suggests that walking through a dark season in this life, faithful to Christ, has more light to it than walking in the shining brilliance of our own brainstorms. It suggests that the darkness of obedience is better than the light of disobedience. God did not promise that we would never be confused and distraught; he did promise that he would never leave us or forsake us (Hebrews 13:5). Even when we can't see him, he does surround us and guard us and lead us forward. We can expect moments in this pilgrimage when the only way into "the light of life" of John 8:12 is the "walking in darkness" of Isaiah 50:10. And which would we rather have—the "darkness" of faithful obedience leading to our vindication, or the "light" of self-will leading to endless miseries? This is *the* question of our existence.

Listening to Christ rather than to ourselves is a startling way to live. No one likes darkness, and there are so many "lights" out there to live by. That's the other side of the contrast, in verse 11. There are ways to shave the radical edge off of Christian obedience. People light their own fires, to use Isaiah's metaphor. They have their own ideas to live by. Why listen to Christ when there are plausible, and certainly easier, ways to live? Some people sit through sermons, but are they listening? Their lives are not set apart from the convenient, soft ways of the world. Why? They don't feel in their hearts that Christ can be counted on when it matters. They are making their own way. But remember the drawback to that approach to life: "There is a way that seems right to a man, but its end is the way to death" (Proverbs 16:25).

So then, the Bible says that faith comes through hearing, and hearing through the word of Christ (Romans 10:17). That bold faith, urged upon us in verses 10, 11, is now reinforced with three incentives for a full-hearted Yes!

The Attentive Listeners: Reassured by God

> Listen to me, you who pursue righteousness,
> you who seek the LORD:
> look to the rock from which you were hewn,
> and to the quarry from which you were dug.
> Look to Abraham your father
> and to Sarah who bore you;
> for he was but one when I called him,
> that I might bless him and multiply him. (Isaiah 51:1, 2)

Why listen to the voice of the servant when doing so will inevitably take us into moments of darkness? When we feel like saying no to him, how can we talk ourselves back into saying yes? In the final section of the passage, Isaiah offers three encouragements that can keep us listening. "Listen to me" appears in verses 1 and 7, with "Give attention to me" in verse 4. That's where God wants to keep us—in a *listening* frame of mind—because that's where courage is found. And the prize that makes real listening worth the struggle is "righteousness," seen in verses 1, 5, 6, 7, and 8. Jesus said, "Blessed are those who hunger and thirst for righteousness, for they shall be satisfied" (Matthew 5:6). The promise of satisfying righteousness as our peace with God and as the very core of our beings draws us on with brave openness to the gospel.

The first incentive to keep listening, in verses 1–3, is that *God is a life-giver*. If he touched old Abraham and barren Sarah with new life and out of that unpromising beginning created a mighty nation to bless the world, why can't God do something new with you and me? If we have the faith of Abraham—not the adequacy, but the need, matched with the openness, of Abraham—then even in our weakness our lives become a part of that larger Abrahamic saga. What God did with Abraham was not an anomaly; for every believer, it is a pattern. God "gives life to the dead and calls into existence the things that do not exist" (Romans 4:17). God makes our waste places like Eden, like the garden of the Lord; he spreads joy and gladness, thanksgiving and the voice of song (Isaiah 51:3). The secret to your existence is the life-giving God who purposes your everlasting comfort. Keep going in the way he has ordained for you.

> Give attention to me, my people,
>   and give ear to me, my nation;
> for a law will go out from me,
>   and I will set my justice for a light to the peoples. (Isaiah 51:4)

The second incentive to keep listening is that *God is a world-changer*. We don't like the way the world is now. Neither does God. The difference is that he can change it. Through the gospel he is sending out his "law" and his "light," Isaiah says, for all peoples everywhere. And his spreading salvation creates a welcoming response in human hearts the world over (v. 5). To quote one commentator:

> The power of self-denial, the power of self-sacrifice, the power of innocence, the power of faithfulness, the power of holy love—this is the power for which all the world waits in breathless anticipation. Does it always know that it so waits? Hardly! Yet when the Servant/Messiah, the "arm of the Lord," is revealed to them, there is frequently that immediate sense of recognition, that satisfying click of a key fitting a lock, of a vague memory suddenly coming to full consciousness.[6]

This gospel expansion out into the world—we are a part of it today—will outlast every brilliant human project (v. 6). The heavens and the earth themselves will endure for the merest flicker of a moment, compared with

God's salvation that will last forever and never diminish at all. The cause of the gospel has the power of God upon it. Live for it.

> "Listen to me, you who know righteousness,
>   the people in whose heart is my law;
> fear not the reproach of man,
>   nor be dismayed at their revilings.
> For the moth will eat them up like a garment,
>   and the worm will eat them like wool;
> but my righteousness will be forever,
>   and my salvation to all generations." (vv. 7, 8)

The third incentive to keep listening is that *God is a courage-inspirer*. No one has ever listened to God without reward, without benefit. The love of righteousness he puts in our hearts will be satisfied forever, and no one can take it away from us. We might talk ourselves out of it and quit. That's our only real danger—our own unbelief and timidity. We should fear nothing else.

In this world, if our hearts relish God's law, we will be persecuted (2 Timothy 3:12). We must accept it. We must not be above it. Our faith can go the distance, as we look beyond this world to the eternal salvation of God. There is God, preparing a place for us. There is God, welcoming us home. There is God, offering us the courage we need right now, moment by moment. "Fear not the reproach of man." "If God is for us, who can be against us?" (Romans 8:31).

Jesus came from God to sustain us in our weariness by his Word. What is his message? "Take heart; I have overcome the world" (John 16:33). His power enables him "to subject all things to himself" (Philippians 3:21). Therefore, like sailors on a stormy sea, being lured to our destruction by the Siren calls all around, let's *lash* ourselves to the reality of Christ.[7]

38

Wachet Auf

ISAIAH 51:9—52:12

IN 1731 J. S. BACH WROTE his cantata *Wachet auf*. We know it as "Sleepers, Awake!" The gospel reading in the service when *Wachet auf* was first performed was Matthew 25, the parable of the wise and foolish virgins. Five of the virgins were ready for the bridegroom's arrival, but five others fell asleep and were excluded from the marriage feast. Bach was saying, "Christ is coming. Get ready." The cantata sings,

> "Awake!" calls the voice of the watchman to us,
> Very high up on the battlements.
> "Awake, you city of Jerusalem!
> This is the hour of midnight,"
> Calling us with clear voice:
> "Where are your wise virgins?
> Prepare! The Bridegroom is coming;
> Arise and take your lamps! Alleluia!
> Make yourselves ready for the wedding,
> You must go forth to meet him!"
>
> Zion hears the watchmen singing.
> Her heart leaps with joy,
> She wakes and rises in haste.
> Her Friend comes from heaven in splendor,
> Strong in mercy, mighty in truth;
> Her light burns bright, her star rises.
> Now come, you worthy crown,
> Lord Jesus, God's Son! Hosanna!

We all follow to the hall of joy
And join the Lord's Supper.

Bach was inspired by a hymn written by a German pastor, Philipp Nicolai, during a plague in 1597. More than 1,400 people died. Pastor Nicolai lived in a world of death. But he looked beyond his surroundings, found in the gospel a transcendent hope, and gave it to his people in a hymn entitled *Wachet auf*. It was this hymn that Bach developed into his own cantata—a song of hope, even joy, in suffering.

Sometimes we feel like telling God to wake up. But we are the ones who fall asleep, and it's high time for us to come alive to the gospel. Isaiah's tone in this passage is urgency. We see it in the four double-imperatives marking the main sections of his text:

> A¹ Awake, awake! God's comfort is invincible (51:9–16)
>   1. His ancient power will be renewed (51:9–11)
>   2. His comfort is as secure as his existence (51:12–16)
>   B Wake yourself, wake yourself! God's wrath is past (51:17–23)
>   1. The only escape from the wrath of God . . . (51:17–20)
>   2. . . . is the mercy of God (51:21–23)
> A² Awake, awake! God's salvation is spreading (52:1–10)
>   1. Enter into the reality of your ideals (52:1, 2)
>   2. God is extending his grace to you (52:3–6)
>   3. Expect the victorious homecoming of God (52:7–10)
>   C Depart, depart! The life of pilgrimage has begun (52:11, 12)

Isaiah is urging us: "Awake, O sleeper, and arise from the dead, and Christ will shine on you" (Ephesians 5:14). No more dreamy, drifting, half-way Christianity! The life of pilgrimage has begun.

Awake, Awake!

Awake, awake, put on strength,
    O arm of the LORD;
awake, as in days of old,
    the generations of long ago. (Isaiah 51:9a)

God's strength is always fresh. The past is not the limit of his power but the pattern of its ongoing expression: ". . . *as* in days of old." Sometimes it feels to us as though God has dozed off. After all, we do. Suddenly we remember what we have forgotten, drop everything, and rush off to make amends. But God never fails. He has, however, built waiting into our experience of him. So this bold prayer does not offend him. Jesus himself taught us to pray with "impudence" that God would take action (Luke 11:5–10). The cutting edge of salvation is always *now*. We can pray that way.

> Was it not you who cut Rahab in pieces,
>> that pierced the dragon?
> Was it not you who dried up the sea,
>> the waters of the great deep,
> who made the depths of the sea a way
>> for the redeemed to pass over? (Isaiah 51:9b, 10)

This is prayer that clings to God in the worst of life, with confidence that he makes obstacles into "a way." Isaiah is thinking of the exodus of God's people from Egyptian bondage as the original breakthrough salvation event. But the way he describes it illuminates the historical fact with spiritual insight. "Rahab" is Egypt (Isaiah 30:7). In it Isaiah perceives an evil of mythical monstrosity. The literature of ancient Canaan told tales of a sea dragon, an evil force of watery chaos, slain in combat by the hero-god.[1] Isaiah has the imagination to use that Canaanite imagery for his own purpose. He merges pagan legend into covenant history to say that the evils oppressing us are more hideous than we know, that all our hope lies in the Hero-God of the exodus, that our pagan story can become a part of his sacred story, and that the forces we so deeply fear have already been defeated by Christ: "Was it not *you* . . . ?"

The secularized West has still not awakened from the so-called Enlightenment. If we lived elsewhere in the world today, we might not be so blind to the demonic powers hiding behind human tyrannies. Our dismissive attitude is not a function of maturity but of cultural conditioning and even satanic intent (2 Corinthians 4:3, 4).[2] But at the cross of Jesus the devil went down in humiliating defeat (Colossians 2:15). Christ will destroy his spiritual enemies (1 Corinthians 15:24, 25). He warns us to be alert (1 Peter 5:8), and he equips us for battle (Ephesians 6:10–18). But if you must, go ahead and smile condescendingly at the Biblical view of demonic involvement in the world. Believe in *Christ*, and you will have his victory as your safety, even in your incomprehension. When you are asleep, he is awake.

> And the ransomed of the LORD shall return
>> and come to Zion with singing;
> everlasting joy shall be upon their heads;
>> they shall obtain gladness and joy,
>> and sorrow and sighing shall flee away. (Isaiah 51:11)

Isaiah evoked the historical exodus from Egypt, from his vantage point already "long ago," in order to portray our future hope. He is saying that the final homecoming of those ransomed by the cross will be an unforeseeable, exodus-like breakout, but better. This time our joy will be "everlasting" and unmixed.

As in Isaiah 35:10, another translation is "gladness and joy will overtake them," even as our depression runs for cover. How could it be otherwise? For God to hold out the prospect of joy, but forever mingled with sorrow and sighing, would be too much like the present to thrill us as a *hope*. God wants us to know that he will allow no place in his coming kingdom for even a trace of our present sorrows. They will flee before the onrush of a formidable joy, worthy of all our hope now.

> "I, I am he who comforts you;
>> who are you that you are afraid of man who dies,
>> of the son of man who is made like grass,
> and have forgotten the LORD, your Maker,
>> who stretched out the heavens
>> and laid the foundations of the earth,
> and you fear continually all the day
>> because of the wrath of the oppressor,
> when he sets himself to destroy?
>> And where is the wrath of the oppressor?" (Isaiah 51:12, 13)

God meets the "Awake, awake" of verse 9 with "I, I" in verse 12. He is not asleep; he hears the cry of our hearts, and he is all the answer we need: "I am he who comforts you." He is able to breathe life into despairing people like us. He admonishes us for being fearfully overimpressed with the human factor in the way reality unfolds. "Where is the wrath of the oppressor?" is asking us, "Honestly, how much does human malice count for, when *God* has given you his promises?" Timidity is the default setting of our minds, but the fear of man is a denial of God. His promises should make us bold.

Armando Valladares was a prisoner of Castro for twenty-two years. In prison his faith in Christ came alive.

> I had come to prison with some religious feeling; my beliefs were genuine but no doubt superficial at that time, since they had never been submitted to hard trial. I held to the religion I had learned at home and at school, but it was very much like a man who has acquired good manners or who carries along the lessons of the things he first learns to read, without examining them. But very quickly I began to experience a substantial change in the nature of my beliefs. . . . There came a moment when, seeing those young men full of courage depart to die before the firing squad and shout *"Viva Cristo Rey!"* at the fateful instant, I not only understood instantly, as

though by a sudden revelation, that Christ was indeed there for me at the moments when I prayed not to be killed, but realized as well that he served to give my life, and my death if it came to that, ethical meaning. Both my life and my death would be dignified by my belief in him. . . . Because of my situation, it seemed my life would necessarily be a life of resistance, but I would be sustained in it by a soul filled with love and hope.

Those cries of the executed patriots—"Long live Christ the King! Down with Communism!"—had wakened me to a new life as they echoed through the two-hundred-year-old moats of the fortress. The cries became such a potent and stirring symbol that by 1963 the men condemned to death were gagged before being carried down to be shot. The jailers feared those shouts.[3]

The gospel inspires awesome courage. "The LORD is on my side; I will not fear. What can man do to me?" (Psalm 118:6). Christ can even turn the fear around. "Don't be intimidated in any way by your enemies. This will be a sign to them that they are going to be destroyed, but that you are going to be saved, even by God himself" (Philippians 1:28, NLT). We conquer as we suffer. "This is the true grace of God. Stand firm in it" (1 Peter 5:12).

True courage comes not from our own bravado but from the promises of God. If we have to fend for ourselves, however strong we may be, we are doomed. But if God is watching over us, we can face anything, even with quiet good cheer. Isaiah is putting steel in our backbones by arguing that our hope is as secure as the existence of God: "I, I am he who comforts you." This is what God most wants us to grasp:

"I am the LORD your God . . .
    saying to Zion, 'You are my people.'" (Isaiah 51:15a, 16b)

God forms an unbreakable bond with his people and gives them firm promises. The conversation goes like this. *God:* "I am your God. You are my people. I will bless you." *Sinners:* "But at our best, we barely believe you." *God:* "True. But I will bless you." *Sinners:* "But we don't deserve you." *God:* "More than you know! But I will bless you." *Sinners:* "But we don't live up to this. We're cowards." *God:* "You are. But I will bless you." *Sinners:* "But we're so entrenched in this world, we'll never change." *God:* "Not true. You are Zion, the eternal city of God. I will bless you accordingly, and everything will change."

Wake Yourself, Wake Yourself!

Wake yourself, wake yourself,
    stand up, O Jerusalem,
you who have drunk from the hand of the LORD

> the cup of his wrath,
> who have drunk to the dregs
> the bowl, the cup of staggering. (Isaiah 51:17)

Isaiah sees the people of God lying in a drunken stupor, having been force-fed the bitter cup of his wrath in Babylonian captivity. That liquor was more than their faith could handle. They reeled and collapsed in despair. No human defense or comfort could help (51:18–20). Judah hadn't understood that it was God, not the Assyrians or Babylonians or any human power—it was God alone they had to reckon with. And if God is against you, what escape is there? Now Isaiah reveals the good news inside that bad news. The God who put that cup to their lips can also take it away. He can even refill it with his most potent, 100-proof judgment and shove it down the throats of the Babylonians—which is what he promises to do (51:21–23).

God, the Jewish exiles must see, has fulfilled his disciplinary purpose. A new day of grace has dawned. For the Jews in Babylon, this meant getting up and returning to the Promised Land. For us today, it means getting up and entering into the promises of Christ. Isaiah is saying to us all, "It isn't God who needs to be aroused. You do. Wake up to what God has done. His salvation is ready and waiting. Come on!"

Awake, Awake!

> Awake, awake,
>   put on your strength, O Zion;
> put on your beautiful garments,
>   O Jerusalem, the holy city;
> for there shall no more come into you
>   the uncircumcised and the unclean.
> Shake yourself from the dust and arise;
>   be seated, O Jerusalem;
> loose the bonds from your neck,
>   O captive daughter of Zion. (Isaiah 52:1, 2)

God wants Lady Zion to stop feeling sorry for herself, throw off her chains, and put on the beautiful garments laid out for her. A throne awaits: "Arise, sit, O Jerusalem, on the throne of glory."[4] There was a time when the faithful city had fallen to the level of a whore (Isaiah 1:21). But now she is a queen—by the power of God's grace.

The Jewish exiles didn't see themselves in any remarkable way. They felt neither the magnitude of their guilt nor the majesty of God's grace. And true, they were the "*captive* daughter of Zion." Their sufferings were real. But when they lost their sense of God, they could only feel victimhood

(Isaiah 40:27). This is why we all need to hear the gospel again and again. Martin Luther wisely said, "It cannot be beaten into our ears enough or too much. Yes, though we learn it and understand it well, yet there is none that takes hold of it perfectly or believes it with all his heart. So frail a thing is our flesh, and disobedient to the Spirit."[5]

The truth we scarcely believe is that through Christ we have a new dignity and distinction, a new freshness and freedom, as Isaiah says. He is urging us to enter into the experience of our new position. "For freedom Christ has set us free" (Galatians 5:1a). Not for the theory but for the *enjoyment* of freedom Christ has set us free. "Stand firm therefore, and do not submit again to a yoke of slavery" (Galatians 5:1b).

The new identity we receive from Christ does not oppress others. Isaiah says, "There shall no more come into you the uncircumcised and the unclean." Imagine Tolkienian Orcs overrunning fair Lothlórien. But, as the New Testament makes clear, God's definition of who is clean and who is unclean surprises us. God calls anyone clean who has been washed in Christ (Acts 10:1—11:18; 1 Corinthians 6:11). Isaiah's point is that the glory of Zion will never again be taken away, because it isn't worldly prestige, not even religious prestige—always a cruel game of winners and losers.[6] What sets the people of God apart is the beauty of holiness: "Put on your *beautiful* garments, O Jerusalem, the *holy* city." Anyone can come into that.

But how? How can the city of God be open to everyone, even as "the uncircumcised and the unclean" will never come in? The inner logic of the gospel is, "You shall be redeemed without money" (Isaiah 52:3). The community of redemption is open to all alike because God refuses every penny of our self-righteous moral currency (Philippians 3:3–9). Every one of us has nothing to offer God. *Nothing.* What all of us admire about ourselves and the way we preen ourselves in the mirrors of our proud self-awareness—it's all unclean to God and oppressive to others. But to all overbearing self-flatterers God is offering true worth by sheer grace. Christ pays our way in advance, in full, by his own merit—or the deal's off. God has no "pay as you go" plan, though we wish he did. Then we could retain our pride. It is humiliating for accomplished people to be given free entry. But what is the alternative? "The Assyrian oppressed them" (Isaiah 52:4). It's either grace or oppression, and face-saving always suckers us into stylish oppression. We must overcome our dread of being loved.

God intends to display the glory of his grace to all who are willing to become his people (v. 6). His eager heart sends messengers into the world to awaken their faith.

> How beautiful upon the mountains
>   are the feet of him who brings good news,

> who publishes peace, who brings good news of happiness,
>> who publishes salvation,
>> who says to Zion, "Your God reigns." (v. 7)

Isaiah is not admiring someone's feet. He is saying, "What a welcome sound is the footfall of a runner bringing good news!" Think of the Greek warrior running from Marathon to Athens in 490 B.C. with the message, "Rejoice! We conquer." He had to get word back to his people, so they wouldn't surrender to the defeated Persians. Or we might think of someone today, pacing back and forth, waiting in suspense for an important phone call. When it finally rings, he jumps in excitement.

What is God's good news to us sinners? Peace, happiness, salvation, "Your God reigns." That's how Isaiah sums it up. The message is not that we can make God victorious, but that his grace has already won the victory over everything that oppresses us. So we must not surrender. The message is not that God loves us, but that he loves us with a love that cannot be defeated, even by our own stupidity. This is the gospel—the finished work of Christ on the cross, his resurrection and ascension and royal authority over everything. There is power within this good news to lift us out of our defeatism (Romans 1:16; 10:14–17). There is no end to the impact of the gospel. It's the only cause in the world that will finally succeed. Isaiah envisions a lone messenger running to the city of God with the good news (Isaiah 52:7), welcomed by the watchmen on the city wall (v. 8), the city bursting into song (v. 9), drawing the nations into the spreading circle of joy, as far as the ends of the earth (v. 10).

Depart, Depart!

> Depart, depart, go out from there;
>> touch no unclean thing;
> go out from the midst of her; purify yourselves,
>> you who bear the vessels of the LORD.
> For you shall not go out in haste,
>> and you shall not go out in flight,
> for the LORD will go before you,
>> and the God of Israel will be your rear guard. (Isaiah 52:11, 12)

Which city will be our home, our identity—Babylon or Zion? The people of God cannot remain as they are. Israel had to leave Egypt. The exiles had to flee Babylon. We too must decide, and get moving. God is telling us to run from every system of false self-salvation, and fast. He expects us to make a clean break, because he has something better for us.

God is not calling for our social withdrawal and isolation but for our spiritual distinction (1 Corinthians 5:9–13). Through Christ, he gives his people the new dignity of priesthood: "you who bear the vessels of the LORD" (cf. Numbers 1:50). To put it in New Testament terms, we have been "approved by God to be entrusted with the gospel" (1 Thessalonians 2:4). So we must be clear in our message and influence. We are bearing a holy thing out to the nations. Anything about us that might make the victory of God ambiguous or unattractive must go. The gospel is so beautiful, we have no right to contaminate it. We must purify ourselves of every "unclean thing."

Isaiah gives us two reasons to remake our lives into a holy pilgrimage, spreading the good news as far as we can (52:12). First, our motivation is not panic but confidence, not loss but gain. Knocked around by life, pitiable in the eyes of the world, still, we are not the Joads. We are priests in procession. God has made us so. Secondly, we have God himself as our strong escort all the way. He is on the move. He goes before his people in victory and follows after to guard the stragglers. His loving presence surrounds us. We have no reason to stay put, and we have two good reasons to press on (cf. Philippians 3:12–14).

While we've been lying asleep in self-absorption and despair, Christ has been busy. He has won the most meaningful victory imaginable on our behalf. He has made us more than conquerors. He is sending us to the nations with a message of pure and endless human happiness, open to all. He is watching over us as we go. He is coming again in final and eternal victory. Let's wake up. Let's be ready. Let's get on with our work, while we still have time. The tone of the gospel is a double-imperative *urgency*.

39

Guilt, Substitution, Grace

ISAIAH 52:13—53:12

God's power is at its greatest not in his destruction of the wicked but in his taking all the wickedness of the earth into himself and giving back love.[1]

THE CHRISTIAN FAITH INCLUDES MIRACLES of divine power. The Red Sea parted for Israel, Jesus was born of a virgin, and so forth. Some people get hung up on miraculous powers. In 1804 Thomas Jefferson took a razor to his New Testament and cut out everything he found incompatible with his rationalism. Only about 10 percent of the text survived the operation.[2] The Christian faith is thoroughly miraculous, and some people choke on that. But they often miss the most outrageous miracle right at the center of the gospel. In Romans 4:5 Paul says that God "justifies the ungodly." That's a real problem. Jesus walked on the water—so what? No one is harmed. But when God justifies the ungodly, he upsets the whole moral order of the universe, doesn't he?

Everybody knows that God punishes bad people and rewards good people. It's his job. But the gospel disagrees. The gospel says that God *justifies* the ungodly. What does that mean? It means that God declares guilty people innocent. It means that God treats bad people as if they were good people. That goes beyond the power of miracle. It's a scandal. Are you open to the mega-miracle and arch-scandal of the gospel? It doesn't matter if you're a conservative person or a progressive person. However you define virtue and vice, you have a sense of right and wrong. You form judgments. You expect God to. But how can he justify the ungodly?

It's a good thing he does. Every one of us is ungodly, and we know it. We've failed to be the people we ought to be. A deep unease about ourselves is why we live in denial. When we discover self-excusing evasion in our politicians, for example, we demand an honest reckoning. But do we require the same unsparing honesty of ourselves? Isn't cover-up the self-righteous strategy of every guilty conscience? Isn't that why we blame others? Finger-pointing is one of our favorite devices for self-justification. And what lies behind that but our own troubled conscience? We may dismiss those feelings as mere social conditioning or our culture's arbitrary invention of right and wrong or our parents' neuroses imposed on us in our youth. But the next time you have a fight with your spouse or roommate or whoever, ask yourself this: Why are you so fiercely passionate to be found *right*? Isn't it because you're not sure you really are? Isn't it because you need to reassure yourself?

There's a reason why we shift the blame. There's a reason why our problems are always someone else's fault. There's a reason why parents blame their children and husbands blame wives and so forth. The reason we continually pass the buck is that we know we can't bear our own guilt. We want so desperately for others to bear it for us. So we dump it on them, without even noticing what's happening in our thoughts. This is a major source of tension in our homes and workplaces and churches.

The Communion service in *The Book of Common Prayer* is insightful when it has believers confessing their sins this way:

> Almighty God, Father of our Lord Jesus Christ, Maker of all things, Judge of all men, we acknowledge and bewail our manifold sins and wickedness, which we from time to time most grievously have committed, by thought, word and deed, against thy Divine Majesty, provoking most justly thy wrath and indignation against us. We do earnestly repent and are heartily sorry for these our misdoings. *The remembrance of them is grievous unto us; the burden of them is intolerable.*

When Thomas Cranmer wrote that centuries ago, he understood that our problem is not just guilty feelings. Our real problem is objective moral guilt before God (Romans 3:19). And our guilt is intolerable, unbearable. If *we* have to answer for what we've done, we'll be crushed.

After years of denial, baseball legend Pete Rose finally admitted to betting on baseball: "People have to understand I wish this would have never happened. But I can't change it, it's happened. And sitting here in my position, you're just looking for a second chance."[3] Every one of us understands that. We're all trapped in consequences we didn't intend but we did set in motion. Every one of us looks at something in the past and agonizes, "If only I could relive that moment! If only I could trade in my record for a better one!" But how can we? It's too late. We're all like Lady Macbeth, washing her hands of her part in murder and moaning, "Out, damned spot! Out, I say! Here's the smell of blood still; all the perfumes of Arabia will not sweeten this little hand."[4] And as Macbeth sees his wife coming unhinged under that distress, he says to a doctor, "Canst thou not minister to a mind diseased, pluck from the memory a rooted sorrow, raze out the written troubles of the brain and with some sweet oblivious antidote cleanse the stuffed bosom of that perilous stuff which weighs upon the heart?" Do you remember how the doctor replies? "Therein the patient must minister to himself."[5] Is *that* our answer—to medicate ourselves with "some sweet oblivious antidote"—entertainment, overwork, romance, achievement? *What makes our unbearable guilt go away? Who can bear it for us?*

Every one of us needs a scapegoat. In the gospel Jesus says to us, "I am the willing scapegoat of the world. At my cross, it's my professional business to be crushed under the unbearable guilt of others. It's my role to bear away other people's guilt. That's what I do, because I love *guilty* people. If you'll trust me, here's the deal. My only guilt will be yours, and your only righteousness will be mine. Is that arrangement acceptable to you? Or will you continue to cope with your guilt by your own devices?"

When we try to shift blame to one another, we create havoc. But there is a redemptive release. It's the miracle and scandal that God justifies ungodly people through the finished work of Christ on the cross. God accepts unacceptable people, God honors shameful people, God treats fools and harlots with royal dignity as Jesus steps into our place at the cross and bears our real moral guilt far away upon himself. That's how God our judge becomes God our justifier. And if *God* forgives you, isn't that enough?

God wants to glorify himself by flooding our lives with sin-bearing mercy in Christ. The only barrier to being awash in freshness and joy and release is when we cling to our guilt by clinging to our own righteousness. All our guilt must go to Christ, and all our righteousness must come from Christ. This is God's way of release for guilty people, and there is no other.

In this famous passage, Isaiah portrays the success, the sufferings, and the significance of the servant of the Lord, with five paragraphs of three verses each:

A¹ The Servant's success: he was repulsive but redemptive (52:13–15)
    B¹ The Servant's suffering: he lived in rejection (53:1–3)
        C The Servant's significance: he was our sin-bearer (53:4–6)
    B² The Servant's suffering: he died in innocence (53:7–9)
A² The Servant's success: he was crushed but victorious (53:10–12)

Isaiah is answering the question, how can the gracious promises of God come true for guilty people? How can the glory of God come down to people who deserve the wrath of God? That question has been lingering in the background. It is *the* question of life. *How can God love us?* Isaiah explains this in his fourth and final Servant Song.

He Was Repulsive but Redemptive

> Behold, my servant shall act wisely;
>> he shall be high and lifted up,
>> and shall be exalted. (Isaiah 52:13)

Isaiah is describing Jesus Christ. His mission into this world succeeded. That's what "act wisely" means. Jesus knew just what to do to achieve his purpose, and it worked. He rose from the dead; he was lifted up to the right hand of the Father and reigns on high with all power and authority.[6] The suffering servant of the Lord is not to be pitied but worshiped. But worship isn't generally people's first reaction. The first thing we notice about a crucified Savior is that he looks, well, crucified.

> As many were astonished at you—
>> his appearance was so marred, beyond human semblance,
>> and his form beyond that of the children of mankind—
> so shall he sprinkle many nations;
>> kings shall shut their mouths because of him;
> for that which has not been told them they see,
>> and that which they have not heard they understand. (Isaiah 52:14, 15)

Isaiah is connecting ("As . . . so . . .") how repulsive Jesus became in suffering for us with how effective he is in purifying us. Jesus was beaten so badly by the Roman soldiers that no one was asking, "Is *he* the servant of the Lord?" The question was, "Is that *human*?" But in a paradox worthy of God, it was his extreme suffering that measures his extreme power to cleanse.

"As many were astonished at you . . . so shall he *sprinkle* many nations." Isaiah is thinking of what Israelite priests used to do. For example, when a leper was cleansed, a priest sprinkled blood on him to show that his disease was washed away and he was healthy now, ready to be accepted back into the community (Leviticus 14:7). That's what Jesus does with moral lepers. And on the Day of Atonement, a priest sprinkled blood on the mercy seat, making Israel fit for the presence of God (Leviticus 16:14). Even the priests themselves had to be sprinkled with "the water of purification" (Numbers 8:7). But Christ is both our priest and our sacrifice, and he doesn't need to be cleansed. In fact, the sprinkling of his blood is pure enough and lavish enough to cleanse "many nations." He touches the unwashed, the unclean, the outsiders, making them fit for God.

This is something new. All the world's top experts never thought of removing our guilt this way. That the servant of the Lord would judge our evil by bearing it himself in his own sufferings—even we who know the gospel struggle to grasp it. But this was the joy set before him—to cleanse the very ones dehumanizing him. One solitary man, abandoned, ground into the dirt under our heel, giving to us in return life-transforming purity—it's the only way lepers like us are healed. Before him we are left in speechless wonder.

Here is the wisdom of God—the undeserved sufferings of Jesus Christ outperforming the best of this world's "sweet oblivious antidotes." And the mission of the church is not to offer the world a Christianized version of their own false salvations but to communicate a good news they've never seen or heard before. If people do not sense that the gospel is saying something unheard of in the usual remedies for human misery, are we speaking clearly?

He Lived in Rejection

> Who has believed what they heard from us?
> And to whom has the arm of the LORD been revealed?
> For he grew up before him like a young plant,
>   and like a root out of dry ground;
> he had no form or majesty that we should look at him,
>   and no beauty that we should desire him.
> He was despised and rejected by men;
>   a man of sorrows, and acquainted with grief;
> and as one from whom men hide their faces
>   he was despised, and we esteemed him not. (Isaiah 53:1–3)

The nations respond to the servant with an awed silence as the gospel reveals his true worth. But in 53:1–3 the believing remnant of Israel laments how few in that nation have believed their witness. The people closest to Christ couldn't understand him. Knowing him personally as a man in the neighborhood—many knew him that way—didn't make unbelief impossible. It took faith to see the glory of God in Jesus of Nazareth. It still does.

How do we break the faith barrier and embrace Jesus Christ crucified as our only Savior? God enables us. His arm of power enters in, flying in low under the defensive radar of our prejudices and awakening in our hearts a new sense of the glory of Jesus. We need God's help to believe, because the truth is, we're more superficial than we realize. We look on the surface of things. We judge by appearances. And Jesus didn't even try to be impressive at that level. He doesn't respect false appearances the way we do. Isaiah says he was "like a root out of dry ground"—an unpromising person appearing in a failed nation. Do not think that if you had been an eyewitness of Jesus, you would have admired him. Not even his miracles made the impact they should have (John 12:37, 38). His own family misjudged him (Mark 3:21; John 7:5). When he traveled with his disciples, it wasn't like the movies. Jesus didn't have a holy glow about him. The woman at the well had no idea whom she was talking to (John 4:25, 26). Even John the Baptist became uncertain about him (Luke 7:18–23; John 1:29–34). Our Lord just wasn't special in ways that count with us. In fact, he became hideous in his sufferings, so that people shunned him: ". . . as one from whom men hide their faces."

Why did the servant of the Lord sink so low? He had to become like us for us to become like him. But if we'd been there, every one of us would have despised and rejected him and turned away to follow after really cool people like Barabbas or Caiaphas or Pilate, depending on our politics or maybe even just our mood at the moment. That's who we are. When the only true remedy for the guilt that tortures us and threatens us with eternal destruction appeared right in front of us, our emotions were dead, our decisions misguided, our minds corrupted. And he accepted it as the price love had to pay to give us our lives back.

He Was Our Sin-Bearer

> Surely he has borne our griefs
>   and carried our sorrows;
> yet we esteemed him stricken,
>   smitten by God, and afflicted.
> But he was pierced for our transgressions;
>   he was crushed for our iniquities;
> upon him was the chastisement that brought us peace,
>   and with his wounds we are healed.
> All we like sheep have gone astray;
>   we have turned every one to his own way;
> and the LORD has laid on him
>   the iniquity of us all. (Isaiah 53:4–6)

Isaiah writes as if we were there at the cross, because we were. If it wasn't our guilt that required the death of Jesus, what did? Remember Rembrandt's painting, "The Raising of the Cross," how he paints himself into the picture as one of the men crucifying the Lord? He not only portrays Jesus; he includes himself in the scene.[7] Isaiah is doing that here, not with a brush on canvas but with a pen on paper. He's not only describing Jesus; he's telling our story too. We cannot say, "If I had been there, *I* wouldn't have shouted 'Crucify him!'"

Isaiah brings us to the heart of his message. Do you see what he's saying? Jesus really was a man of sorrows, but they weren't his own. He didn't deserve them. They were our sorrows. In a way we don't understand, Jesus *substituted* himself for us at the cross. God has done what we'd have no right to do—*God* has shifted the blame to Jesus Christ as he died for guilty people. *God* has pointed the finger. *He* has laid on him the iniquity of us all.

Theologians call this *imputation*, from the Latin verb *imputare*, "to charge (to someone's account)." Guilt must be paid for. It can't be swept under the rug. You know that from your own experience. When you are wronged or injured—even in a fender-bender—someone has to answer for it, either you or the other person. The damage and cost don't just go away. If it's going to be put right, someone has to pay the cost. And so it is with God. There is no way he can turn a blind eye to our evil that is damaging his universe. How did God confront it? How was the damage paid for? Out of love for us, God charged that infinite debt to a substitute. Jesus Christ put himself in the place of sinners, the unbearable weight of their guilt was imputed to him, and he sank under it. "God made him who had no sin to be sin for us, so that in him we might become the righteousness of God" (2 Corinthians 5:21, NIV). This is the love of God.

Substitution is the very meaning of love. In *A Tale of Two Cities*, Sydney Carton takes another man's place at the guillotine and defeats Madame Defarge's lust for revenge. As he's about to die, a young girl also to be executed realizes that Carton has changed places with the condemned man. She tells him, "I think you were sent to me by Heaven."[8] Dying love, real love, comes from God. Our part is to recognize in Jesus the only true love that exists and say to him, "I think you were sent to me by Heaven."

Look at him. By faith look at him hanging there on his cross. What is he saying to you by his sacrifice? "Come to me, all who labor and are heavy laden, and I will give you rest" (Matthew 11:28). "Come, for everything is now ready" (Luke 14:17). "Come to me . . . and I will make with you an everlasting covenant" (Isaiah 55:3). Look at him. By faith, see his dying love for you. What is it worth? His blood is flowing down into pools at the foot of that cross. But it doesn't lie there in waste and loss. It flows out toward us—guilty, sad us. His blood flows out toward a woman who has shamed herself in a desperate craving to be loved. His blood washes her shame clean off her. Then that shame flows back to the cross, where it shames Jesus and is no longer her burden to bear. His blood flows out toward a man held in bondage to lust. He has discovered too late that there is no comfort there, only emptiness and self-hatred. But the blood of Jesus flows out to that man, cleanses him entirely, and takes that painful wrong back to the cross where Jesus suffers for it as his own wrong, freeing that man forever.

The blood of Jesus is flowing out to sinners of all kinds, taking from them their guilt, their shame, their loss, their tears and despair, and giving them a whole new life. Jesus is saying to you right now, "I don't want you to bear your burden one moment longer. Let my chastisement give you peace. Let my stripes heal you." We are all like stupid sheep, wandering off from him through our own futile self-remedies and self-righteous excuses. Who can deny it? But look what God has done. God has laid on Christ the iniquity of us all. Believe it, and entrust your guilt to him. He can't bear it and survive, but he's still willing to bear it.

He Died in Innocence

> He was oppressed, and he was afflicted,
>   yet he opened not his mouth;
> like a lamb that is led to the slaughter,
>   and like a sheep that before its shearers is silent,
>   so he opened not his mouth.
> By oppression and judgment he was taken away;
>   and as for his generation, who considered
> that he was cut off out of the land of the living,
>   stricken for the transgression of my people?
> And they made his grave with the wicked
>   and with a rich man in his death,
> although he had done no violence,
>   and there was no deceit in his mouth. (Isaiah 53:7–9)

The death of Jesus was a miscarriage of human justice, but it was also our Lord's clearheaded choice. He wasn't caught in a web of events beyond his own control. He willingly laid his life down (John 10:17, 18).[9]

Verse 7 compares Jesus to a lamb led to slaughter and a sheep silent before its shearers. What's the point? His death was not a capitulation to weakness but an exercise of deliberate control. He was not overpowered. He *chose* not to fight back. "He stood up in humble service for the sick and wicked, without questions or objections. He received what came, from man or God, without any protest whatsoever."[10]

And there was no way he deserved the abuse he received. Verse 8 laments how thoughtlessly he was gotten rid of. His was just another execution. But verse 9 says that "he had *done* no violence" and "there was no deceit in his *mouth*." In both his actions and his words he died in entire innocence. The final indignity was to be buried not alongside martyrs and saints but with the wicked rich. Who but Jesus has the moral majesty to serve you as your substitute? Only innocent sufferings can atone for guilty sufferings.

If the story of Jesus had ended there in his grave, his heroism would have been admirable but futile. The empty tomb proved that there was more to his death than anyone realized.

He Was Crushed but Victorious

> Yet it was the will of the LORD to crush him;
>   he has put him to grief;
> when his soul makes an offering for sin,
>   he shall see his offspring; he shall prolong his days;
> the will of the LORD shall prosper in his hand.
> Out of the anguish of his soul he shall see and be satisfied;
> by his knowledge shall the righteous one, my servant,
>   make many to be accounted righteous,
>   and he shall bear their iniquities.
> Therefore I will divide him a portion with the many,
>   and he shall divide the spoil with the strong,
> because he poured out his soul to death
>   and was numbered with the transgressors;
> yet he bore the sin of many,
>   and makes intercession for the transgressors. (Isaiah 53:10–12)

The death of Jesus Christ was more than a human plot; it was a divine strategy. At his cross, Jesus was doing "the will of the LORD" (cf. Romans 3:25). And he wasn't embittered by it. He didn't hang from his cross screaming curses at his tormentors, the way other victims did. Nor did he blaspheme God. He perceived in his torments the saving will of the Lord. This is the mystery of the cross. It was on that instrument of human torture that Jesus Christ made his soul an offering to God for other people's sin. The cross, therefore, was no defeat. Isaiah's prophetic eye can see that Jesus was taking the initiative by his death, making the will of God prosper in the most improbable way imaginable. At his cross Jesus achieved the ancient purpose of God with victorious love.

This is why his death produces life in us: "He shall see his offspring." Who are they? All of us who benefit from his death when he justifies us. In verse 12 Isaiah uses a military metaphor to describe this. Jesus divides the spoils of his victory with us as his "strong" partners in God's saving plan (Revelation 2:26, 27). The world perceives his followers as little more than a band of fugitives and losers (Luke 22:35–38). But through Christ's justifying cross-work, we are enriched beyond measure. We possess all things worth possessing (1 Corinthians 3:21–23).

As Jesus stands back and looks at God's saving plan, as he measures the price he had to pay for its success, how does he *feel* about it? "Out of the anguish of his soul he shall see and be satisfied." The Isaiah scroll from Qumran inserts an interpretative word here: "Out of the anguish of his soul he shall see *light*."[11] Anguish was not his final emotional experience. His anguish led to a dawning "light" of victorious joy. Looking on what he accomplished by his passion, Christ is satisfied. Why? Because he's the kind of person who *enjoys* clearing sinners of their guilt and accounting them righteous, though it demands that he bear their iniquities upon himself.

> Here is love, vast as the ocean, lovingkindness as the flood,
> When the Prince of Life, our Ransom, shed for us his precious blood.
> Who his love will not remember? Who can cease to sing his praise?
> He can never be forgotten throughout heaven's eternal days.
>
> On the mount of crucifixion, fountains opened deep and wide;
> Through the floodgates of God's mercy flowed a vast and gracious tide.
> Grace and love, like mighty rivers, poured incessant from above,
> And heaven's peace and perfect justice kissed a guilty world in love.[12]

The Jesus who "suffered under Pontius Pilate, was crucified, died and was buried," to quote the Apostles' Creed, also "rose again from the dead" and now is "seated at the right hand of God the Father Almighty." With supreme power and every moral entitlement, Jesus Christ is acting as the executor of the saving will of God for our guilty human race. He isn't suffering anymore. His offering for sin was complete. And right now, today, all over the world, he's enjoying the satisfaction, the sheer pleasure, of making many ungodly people to be accounted righteous.

The cross isn't a dreamy religious ideal; the cross is a power, it's *working*. The one who descended to unimaginable depths is now enjoying the spoils of complete victory. He's actively saving guilty people today. He treats transgressors as his friends and shares his victory with his former enemies. He stands before the Father, making intercession for the very ones who drove him to death. His cross is a power that evil cannot conquer or even understand, but to God it's everything. Nothing will ever rob Christ of his hard-won right to justify the ungodly.

Who else can love you so miraculously and helpfully? Who else would willingly serve as your scapegoat? *What are you waiting for?*

"The guilt that men are never able to efface, in spite of sacrifices, penance, remorse and vain regrets, God himself wipes away; and men are at once freed from their past and transformed."[13] You can be freed from your past. But Christ is the only way. His sacrifice was good enough for God. Why shouldn't it be good enough for you?

We can respond in either of two ways. One response is to say, "No, that can't be true. It can't be that simple." I remember hearing Joan Baez sing the gospel song, "Oh, Happy Day." Maybe you know the words: "Oh, happy day! Oh, happy day! When Jesus washed my sins away." She sang so beautifully, as she always does. But at the end, with her voice trailing off, she said, "If only it were that easy." Isaiah didn't think it was easy. The suffering servant of the Lord did the most costly thing ever. He suffered the just hell of God's holy wrath against sinners, rather than their bearing it themselves. If there had been an easier way, God would have found it.

Of course, we shouldn't ignore the wrongs we can put right. The gospel doesn't make *that* easy. But the gospel is addressing a deeper question than our injuries to one another. What about our offenses against *God*? How do we make amends at the level of *God's* infinite justice? How can our trinkets of morality down here, conservative or liberal, compensate *God*? The gospel's answer is the perfect Lamb sacrificed for human guilt before God—and God was fully satisfied. All we should do, all we can do, is bow before Christ in our need. The answer *must* be that simple, or we're thrown back on the impossible task of undoing our own guilt. Don't try to be heroic here. This is so much more profound than our moral heroics. Don't trivialize Christ. Revere him.

That's the other response. We believe the gospel. We stop amassing our own imagined righteousness. That pile of dung called our moral superiority over other sinners, which cannot offset our guilt before God but only make things worse—we admit the ugly truth of it all. We revere Jesus Christ crucified for sinners and receive his grace with the empty hands of faith.

If you're an unbeliever, admit that you've gone too far to get yourself out. Let the Scapegoat bear your guilt away, and God will never bring it up again. He promises. Will you receive Christ as your Savior—right now?

If you're a believer, you know the way to refreshment. Take your sins to Christ. Tell him everything. This is his promise: "If we confess our sins, he is faithful and just to forgive us our sins and to cleanse us from all unrighteousness" (1 John 1:9).

Charles Simeon, the Anglican pastor, by his own experience guides us toward the breakthrough we all need:

> In Passion Week, as I was reading Bishop Wilson on the Lord's Supper, I met with an expression to this effect—"That the Jews knew what they did, when they transferred their sin to the head of their offering." The thought came into my mind, What, may I transfer all my guilt to another? Has God provided an Offering for me, that I may lay my sins on His head? Then, God willing, I will not bear them on my own soul one moment longer. Accordingly I sought to lay my sins upon the sacred head of Jesus.[14]

40

When Grace Dances

ISAIAH 54:1—55:13

ISAIAH LOOKS AT THE SIN-BEARING servant of the Lord and has one thing
to say to us: "Break forth into singing and cry aloud" (54:1). In other words,
"Let joyful song *explode* out of you!" We resist that. Isaiah 54:1 may be
one of the most disobeyed commands in the Bible. Our exaggerated sense
of decorum is the last bastion of pride holding out against the gospel. Some
churches make it a virtue. But God doesn't. In his exuberance he's creating
a new world of boisterous happiness through Christ. We must rejoice with
him, or we risk making our hearts impervious to salvation, because that holy
but raucous joy *is* salvation.

When Jesus entered Jerusalem to the loud praises of his followers, the
Pharisees didn't like it one bit. But Jesus said, "If these were silent, the very
stones would cry out" (Luke 19:40). Enthusiasm offends religious people,
because breaking forth into singing and crying aloud entails loss of control.
It brings us down to the level of children, even the vulgar who never learned
their manners. So be it. "If there when Grace dances, I should dance."[1]

As we savor the good news of the sin-bearing servant of the Lord
(52:13—53:12), the mountains of frost and ice within begin to thaw, and
we learn to enthuse. The gospel of a surprising salvation can only make us
laugh, sing, and cheer. John Calvin understood this. His theology teaches us:

> The Church is the place where the Gospel is preached; Gospel is good
> news; good news makes people happy; happy people sing. But then, too,
> unhappy people may sing to cheer themselves up.[2]

Every church should put a notice on its front door: "All face-saving
moralists, take warning! Within these doors your chilly pride is in danger of

melting into exuberant joy. Enter at your own risk. But all sinners depressed with guilt are welcome." Christianity throbs with holy joy for bad people. God made it that way.

The test of a church's faith is not only the wording in its creed but also the gladness in its worship. The gospel demands a carefree spirit. If we aren't going to Hell anymore, if we stand to inherit every blessing Almighty God can think of, if nothing can stand in the way of our restored humanness because it's all ours through the merit of Christ, the friend of sinners—if that can't make us smile, what can?

In Isaiah 54 the prophet uses three images to portray the miracle of God's grace. The servant of the Lord has changed everything by his sufferings, death, and resurrection. Isaiah helps us grasp what the servant's victory is worth to us. Then in chapter 55 the prophet coaches us in how to enjoy this amazing grace.

1. Surprising reversals (54:1–17)
   A A barren woman rejoicing over her growing family (54:1–3)
      B A lonely wife comforted by her loving husband (54:4–10)
         C A poor city beautified with costly jewels (54:11–17)
2. Glad appeals (55:1–13)
   A¹ Come, be satisfied! (55:1–3)
      B¹ The victory of God is certain (55:4, 5)
   A² Return, be changed! (55:6–9)
      B² The word of God is effective (55:10, 11)
         C A renewed world awaits you (55:12, 13)

Isaiah is concluding a major section of his book. In chapters 40—55 he puts front and center God's loving purpose to breathe life back into us. God promises to bring the Jews back from exile in Babylon, which he did. He promises to save us from our deepest captivities within, which he will. And he will not stop until the whole world is renewed. In chapters 54—55 it's time to pause so that the good news can make its full impact.

Surprising Reversals

"Sing, O barren one, who did not bear;
   break forth into singing and cry aloud,
   you who have not been in labor!
For the children of the desolate one will be more
   than the children of her who is married," says the LORD. (Isaiah 54:1)

"Few words could be more important for an understanding of the gospel than surprise."[3] God brings barrenness and joy together—to our surprise. In

Isaiah's culture, infertility marked a woman with shame. He sees the people of God as a barren woman with nothing to be happy about. Did ancient Israel bring God's salvation to the world? No. And it was their own fault. Now to invite this desolate woman to sing for joy seems absurd and cruel. But Isaiah isn't rubbing it in. He's relocating her happiness from herself to the servant of the Lord, the ultimate Patriarch who "shall see his offspring" (Isaiah 53:10). He wants all of us to grasp that our failure is real, but it's not the death of our joy, because Another has succeeded for us, and now we live in him.

The Apostle Paul quotes Isaiah to tease out what this means (Galatians 4:21–31). There are two ways to serve God. One way is to draw on the energy of our own good intentions. The other way is to rely on God's power acting in our weakness. Our virtue can look good, feel good, act good, talk good. But it's sterile. The power of the Holy Spirit may seem impractical, but he makes us fruitful. And the gospel announces that Christ took our failure to his cross, where its shame died, and he has sent us his Spirit, so that we'll thrive forever. Isaiah foresees this grace spreading to the very ends of the earth. He's saying to us, "You *are* barren. But it doesn't matter anymore. You can live in expectancy. God's plan for his people is more and more blessing *by sheer miracle*" (54:2, 3).

Real joy flows from our surprise and relief that Someone Else is what we have failed to be. In ourselves we are this barren woman. We have nothing to be proud of. But we don't have to hang our heads in shame. We should throw our heads back and laugh with delight over our spiritual family multiplying by a power not our own (Colossians 1:3–6). The gospel changes the subject. We look with honesty at our weary ideals that never amount to much, then we look away to God's cheerful power working for his greater glory, our richer joy, and the salvation of the nations, and we *like* it that way. We're a part of something beautifully improbable from beyond ourselves.

My generation longed "to be a cog in something turning."[4] But with our inflated sense of destiny and know-it-all self-righteousness, the movement we created couldn't be the redemption we imagined. Let's hear the gospel again. The human race is dying. We are dying. So we aren't the ones to save the world. God will. The Spirit alone is the Lord and Giver of life, and the church alone is "born according to the Spirit" (Galatians 4:29). That embarrasses our pride. It means we're always dependent. It means we must join *his* movement if we want to be a part of the future. And to be caught up in a miracle we don't deserve makes us happy even now.

"Fear not, for you will not be ashamed;
    be not confounded, for you will not be disgraced;
for you will forget the shame of your youth,

and the reproach of your widowhood you will remember no more.
For your Maker is your husband,
    the LORD of hosts is his name;
and the Holy One of Israel is your Redeemer,
    the God of the whole earth he is called.
For the LORD has called you
    like a wife left[5] and grieved in spirit,
like a wife of youth when she is cast off,
    says your God.
For a brief moment I left you,
    but with great compassion I will gather you.
In overflowing anger for a moment
    I hid my face from you,
but with everlasting love I will have compassion on you,"
    says the LORD, your Redeemer. (Isaiah 54:4–8)

A wife reconciled to her husband is Isaiah's second image of miraculous grace. The striking thing is what the text doesn't say. The faithful city had sunk to the level of a whore (Isaiah 1:21). But now God looks beyond his people's guilt. He doesn't even talk about it. With deep sympathy, he emphasizes not his offended honor but their wounded feelings: ". . . like a wife left and grieved in spirit, like a wife of youth when she is cast off." God is saying, "Yes, I was angry. And I had a right to be. But my servant has taken your guilt away. Believe me that I have cleaned your slate so entirely, you will forget all your heartache under a deluge of my felt love forever."

The gospel is not "He loves me, he loves me not," depending on our own loveliness. The grace of God is a "covenant of peace" (Isaiah 54:10), a permanent arrangement bringing us a wholeness we don't deserve. Therefore, we can enjoy God's grace without fearing that he'll retract it (54:4). We didn't cause his grace to begin with, so we can't reverse it now. God's anger is real, but passing. His love is also real, and lasting—forever. God is the ultimate romantic ("everlasting love"). For all spiritual whores who will receive it, *this is God's word*. Break forth into singing and cry aloud!

"O afflicted one, storm-tossed and not comforted,
    behold, I will set your stones in antimony,
    and lay your foundations with sapphires.
I will make your pinnacles of agate,
    your gates of carbuncles,
    and all your wall of precious stones. . . .
This is the heritage of the servants of the LORD
    and their vindication from me, declares the LORD." (Isaiah 54:11, 12, 17b)

Isaiah's third image of the miracle of grace is a city gleaming with brilliant jewels, a city of such lavish investment as to boggle the mind. Who built this city? Who had the imagination? Who had the wealth? God did. And this city is where his people will live forever (Revelation 21:18–21).

Salvation is a community experience. It took on institutional embodiment in Jerusalem of old, as in the Christian church today. But both the old Jerusalem and the present church cannot be imagined as this dazzling city in Isaiah's vision. He is fully aware of our mediocrity. The hope he offers is not a dreamy denial of reality. It's a promise from God, a promise of costly and lasting renovation. God will replace the church's poverty with wealth, her turbulence with security, and her despair with comfort. It is all his doing (Isaiah 54:16—"Behold, I . . ."), and his resources are endless.

Isaiah explains the literal reality behind his image of the bejeweled city (54:13–17). God's promise to us is not mere survival but his blessing rolling on from generation to generation. Rather than our typical pattern—the death-spiral of privilege leading to complacency leading to judgment—God's people will enjoy endless peace to the full (v. 13). His grace will create a formidably righteous people (v. 14). All who hate them, within or without, will attack to their own destruction (vv. 15–17). The Creator will be our Defender, and who can defeat him? "This is the heritage of the servants of the LORD." And we enjoy it all the more for not deserving it.

Glad Appeals

"Up![6] Everyone who thirsts,
    come to the waters;
and he who has no money,
    come, buy and eat!
Come, buy wine and milk
    without money and without price." (Isaiah 55:1)

The grace won for us by the servant of the Lord is not a theory. It's an experience. And God wants us to enjoy it freely. His invitation is too good to refuse, too urgent even to delay. Isaiah 55:1 lies so close to the heart of God, it reappears at the very end of the Bible as God's final word to us all until Christ returns (Revelation 22:17). *This is the message God wants every member of the human race to hear.* What is he saying? "Don't just sit there thinking about this, theorizing, hesitating, making excuses. Get up. Come over here. I have rich spiritual privilege prepared for you. Buy in—though Someone Else has already paid your bill."

Jesus said, "I am the bread of life; whoever comes to me shall not hunger, and whoever believes in me shall never thirst" (John 6:35). He said, "If anyone thirsts, let him come to me and drink" (John 7:37). Christ overflows with satisfaction. All authentic Christian experience comes from what he provides, not what we provide. But knowing that isn't enough. We must dive into that endless ocean. All that stands between us and God right now is our own sulky unbelief. We don't have to deserve his blessing. We can't earn it. How can we buy what isn't for sale? But God has told us what to do: "Come . . . come . . . come."

> "Why do you spend your money for that which is not bread,
> and your labor for that which does not satisfy?" (Isaiah 55:2a)

Isaiah presses us: "Endless vitality can be yours for nothing. Why don't you run there? *Why?* Where's the payoff you keep sacrificing for here in this worldly system?" We have no reason to refuse God, and we have no reason to cling to our idolatries. That which is not bread *cannot* satisfy, no matter how expensive it is or how hard we try to make it work. Our world is a vast marketplace of unsatisfying but costly remedies for our God-shaped longings. But we're not very smart shoppers.

Calvin and Hobbes discussed this one day in their comic strip. "Getting is better than having. When you *get* something, it's new and exciting. When you *have* something, you take it for granted and it's boring." "But everything you *get* turns into something you *have*."[7]

Our self-chosen disillusionment can even turn against God. We think *he's* against us. In *A Grief Observed*, C. S. Lewis mourned the loss of his wife with these words:

> Her palate for all the joys of sense and intellect and spirit was fresh and unspoiled. Nothing would have been wasted on her. She liked more things and liked them more than anyone I have known. A noble hunger, long unsatisfied, met at last its proper food, and almost instantly the food was snatched away. Fate (or whatever it is) delights to produce a great capacity and then frustrate it. Beethoven went deaf. By our standards a mean joke; the monkey trick of a spiteful imbecile.[8]

When we suffer and our self-pity rages at God and we snuggle up to our most comforting lies, how do we find our way back? Seeing through our lies isn't enough. The only way back is to look again at the servant of the Lord. We despised him and rejected him as he suffered. But he was bearing our griefs and carrying our sorrows. The Lord laid on him the iniquity of us all. But he didn't open his mouth against us or against God. In fact, he makes blasphemers to be accounted righteous. Looking again at him can calm our shrieking hatred and restore us to sanity.

God is calling us back to himself. He explains his metaphor of buying and eating and how much the reality is worth to us.

> "Listen diligently to me, and eat what is good,
>   and delight yourselves in rich food.
> Incline your ear, and come to me;
>   hear, that your soul may live;
> and I will make with you an everlasting covenant,
>   my steadfast, sure love for David." (Isaiah 55:2b, 3)

God's open feast is no soup kitchen. He's serving rich food, the best in the world. How do we taste his delights? By listening diligently to his Word—patient, open-minded, careful poring over his truth in the gospel, thinking it through again and again. That is *the* essential ingredient to the life that is truly life. Jesus said, "The words that I have spoken to you are spirit and life" (John 6:63). Why does the gospel work with life-giving power? Because eager listening to God's Word is the same as coming to *him*: "Incline your ear, and come to *me*."

To all whose hearts leap at the privilege, this is what God gives: ". . . an everlasting covenant, my steadfast, sure love for David." What is he saying? God made a pledge to David (2 Samuel 7). King Saul had failed; so God replaced him with David. But God promised David that his dynasty would rule forever. Human failure couldn't destroy the covenant; it was factored into the covenant. How does this benefit us? Jesus Christ is the heir of the Davidic crown and our true King, if we will have him. And God is committed to the eternal triumph of the throne of Jesus. Not even death could stop him (Acts 13:34). He cannot fail. He covers the failings of his subjects. And God will never back out on this arrangement. He calls it "an eternal covenant, my steadfast, sure love for David."

The voice from Heaven said of Jesus, "This is my beloved Son, with whom I am well pleased" (Matthew 3:17). God's love for us sinners is guaranteed by his love for his Son, who has his full and eternal approval. Why does the Father love the Son so much? John Flavel, the Puritan pastor, with his antiquated English, helps us imagine the conversation between the Father and the Son in eternity past:

> Father: My Son, here is a company of poor miserable souls, that have utterly undone themselves, and now lie open to my justice. Justice demands satisfaction for them or will satisfy itself in the eternal ruin of them. What shall be done for these souls?
>
>   Son: O my Father, such is my love and pity for them that, rather than they shall perish eternally, I will be responsible for them as their Surety.

Bring in all thy bills, that I may see what they owe thee. Lord, bring them all in, that there may be no after-reckonings with them. At my hand shalt thou require it. I will rather choose to suffer thy wrath than they should suffer it. Upon me, my Father, upon me be all their debt.

Father: But my Son, if thou undertake for them, thou must reckon to pay the last cent. Expect no discounts. If I spare them, I will not spare thee.

Son: Content, Father. Let it be so. Charge it all to me. I am able to pay it. And though it prove a kind of undoing to me, though it impoverish all my riches, empty all my treasures, yet I am content to undertake it.[9]

Our salvation is more than a decision we made in time. It flows from a covenant made in eternity. And the Father delights to keep his covenant with his beloved Son by drawing us into the everlasting love of the Triune Godhead (John 17:24–26). He directs our attention away from ourselves to the messianic figure ordained for our salvation:

"Behold, I made him a witness to the peoples,
    a leader and commander for the peoples.
Behold, you shall call a nation that you do not know,
    and a nation that did not know you shall run to you,
because of the LORD your God, and of the Holy One of Israel,
    for he has glorified you." (Isaiah 55:4, 5)

The "him" in the first line refers back to "David" in verse 3, and the "you" in the third line is not the reader but "David" again. The David of ancient history represented the rule of God to the nations from his throne in Israel. They were to rally around him. But only Jesus Christ, the son of David, can play the role of Savior of the world. God has decreed it so (Romans 1:1–5).

The fact of verse 4 has implications in verse 5. Isaiah's second "Behold" shows us the certainty of God's victory through Christ. The prophet sees the nations, even those beyond the known world (as we might say), eagerly running to Christ. What draws them in? The glory of God: ". . . he has glorified you." Ultimate beauty is revealed through the birth, teachings, miracles, humility, authority, sufferings, death, resurrection, and reign of Jesus Christ. The nations are in fact seeing this beauty as the gospel advances today, and Christ's cause will be the only finally successful cause in human history. It's backed up by all the authority of the will of God. That generates urgency.

"Seek the LORD while he may be found;
    call upon him while he is near;
let the wicked forsake his way,

and the unrighteous man his thoughts;
let him return to the LORD, that he may have compassion on him,
   and to our God, for he will abundantly pardon." (Isaiah 55:6, 7)

The banquet of God's grace is free and abundant, but it's also conditional. The reason why we're thirsty (55:1) is that we're wicked (55:7). We have some adjusting to do, and our opportunity is limited. The door is wide-open now, but it will close. What do we need to get busy doing?

To "seek" the Lord is to stop dawdling and to become intentional about him, setting highest value on him, removing everything that keeps us from him, hearing his Word without back-talk, opening up to his will with no preconditions, budgeting our money for his cause first—the ever-widening circle is endless. Seeking the Lord is a whole-life realignment with Christ. We stop treating him as a religious garnish on the side. He becomes our continual feast, our defining center. And the time to move in his direction is *now*.

He is near to us, not far off, not aloof and unavailable. He invites us to call upon him to come still nearer. Our part is to reject ourselves: "Let the wicked forsake his way, and the unrighteous man his thoughts." How could it be otherwise? Our ways and thoughts trivialize God and exalt ourselves, our status quo, our adequacy, our okay-ness (Revelation 3:17). But the truth is, we're wrong. And what's wrong with us is everything we are, right down to our thoughts.[10]

We are so tolerant of our sins, especially if we maintain a superficial, technical righteousness. But we've lost the radical edge of real Christianity in our generation. I hope we're not beyond recovery. We may be. We've forgotten that Christianity is so contrary to our ingrained likes and dislikes, it requires nothing less than a transformation of the magnitude of *a religious conversion*. We American Christians can't just tweak our American ways and American thoughts. We can't just "make a decision for Christ" and leave it at that. We can't join a certain church because it won't challenge our selfish lifestyle and think that's Christianity. Being nice, harmless, churchgoing people, with no repentance, no submission, no forsaking of self, no pursuit of Christ—but all that covered over with a glaze of sentimental religion on Sunday mornings—this is not at all what God has in mind for us. Could the average church today fit into the Book of Acts? The psychology of too many churches, both liberal and conservative, is so filled with certainty about ourselves that there's no room for openness to God. We have drifted from the gospel, and we don't have forever to get back.

If we want to feast at the eternal banquet, God is showing us the way. Could he state it more plainly than in Isaiah 55:6, 7? Our only path forward is as obvious as it is radical. God is calling us to a complete overhaul. God is calling us to place ourselves under his scrutiny, welcoming ways and thoughts completely unfamiliar to us but clearly stated in his Word. God is calling us to reform our lives and our churches with unprecedented newness, because we are not yet living proof of the power of his all-claiming grace. Humbly accepting his call and courageously following through is nothing less than repentance: "Let him return to the LORD." He's worth it. If we submit to the power of repentance, God will not meet our trust with abusive scoldings. He will show us his compassion and generous pardon.

> "For my thoughts are not your thoughts,
>   neither are your ways my ways, declares the LORD.
> For as the heavens are higher than the earth,
>   so are my ways higher than your ways
>   and my thoughts than your thoughts." (vv. 8, 9)

Why do we need repentance so urgently? Because God's thoughts and ways are as high above ours as the heavens are above the earth. The gap is wide. We may not see much wrong in our lives, but what matters is how God sees us. Our intuitive feelings and well-established habits can't be defended; they need to be reexamined. We need to go back to school and enroll in God's course—Human Existence 101. Jesus said, "Unless you turn and become like children, you will never enter the kingdom of heaven" (Matthew 18:3). Our expectations of God are small. The logic of grace doesn't compute with us. We'll never actually get it. But realizing that humbles us, which is the beginning, the middle, and the end of our salvation. If we'll keep listening humbly to his Word, God will surprise us with what he can do.

> "For as the rain and the snow come down from heaven
>   and do not return there but water the earth,
> making it bring forth and sprout,
>   giving seed to the sower and bread to the eater,
> so shall my word be that goes out from my mouth;
>   it shall not return to me empty,
> but it shall accomplish that which I purpose,
>   and shall succeed in the thing for which I sent it." (Isaiah 55:10, 11)

God's people living in the Promised Land were forced to look in faith to a life-source beyond their surroundings. Egypt had the Nile to keep them alive. Mesopotamia had the Tigris and the Euphrates. But Canaan had only the rain—not a constant flow, but a seasonal intervention. If the rains didn't come, people starved. God located his people where they had to live by faith in him not once for all but continually. Even the Jewish exiles in

Babylon carried a memory of this. They understood that rain was the difference between life and death.

God's word is like the rain, Isaiah says. How so? One: true life comes from beyond us. We can't control it; we receive it. Two: true life overcomes death. We can't quench it; it saturates us, and we flourish. Three: true life fulfills the purpose of God. We can't defeat his delight; his delight makes us more than conquerors.

"My word" in verse 11 sums up all of God's gracious promises in the book of Isaiah thus far. The prophet comes full circle from 40:8, where he declared, "The grass withers, the flower fades, but the word of our God will stand forever." Now we know that God's promises not only last, they give us life. We don't keep the hope of the gospel alive; this hope keeps us alive. Like the rain, it may take time for the new life fully to burst forth, but rain never fails. Neither does the promise of God to save sinners. In fact, in the end it will be better than we dreamed.

> "For in joy shall you shall go out
>   and in peace be led forth;[11]
> the mountains and the hills before you
>   shall break forth into singing,
>   and all the trees of the field shall clap their hands.
> Instead of the thorn shall come up the cypress;
>   instead of the brier shall come up the myrtle;
> and it shall make a name for the LORD,
>   an everlasting sign that shall not be cut off." (Isaiah 55:12, 13)

Isaiah concludes chapters 40—55 by lighting this fireworks display of bright hope. Two things stand out. One: the sheer objectivity of the gospel. However you and I may respond to God's promises, the creation will respond. It will explode with joyful freedom when God brings his saving purpose to fulfillment (Romans 8:18–22). This objectivity doesn't mean to shut us out; it means to urge us in. The gospel is not a little psychological uplift; it's tomorrow's world headlines today. Let's believe it.

Two: the magnitude of the gospel. Our salvation includes within its scope the whole created order. That's how big it is. That's what it's worth. Our salvation is not ours alone. God promises to renew everything. Ours is a salvation worthy of no one less than *God*. Let's respect it.

In fact, that magnitude is the point. "It shall make a name for the LORD." The renewed creation, enjoyed by a renewed humanity, ruled by the unchanging Christ—the whole point of this massive salvation is to display forever what kind of person God is. The curse will be reversed. C. S. Lewis's "silent planet" will become Christ's singing planet.[12] And never again will there be another human fall like Adam's. Our salvation will be "an everlasting sign that shall not be cut off," to the eternal glory of God.

Peter Kreeft helps us grasp the practical boldness of this hope for everyone to whom God gives it:

> Now suppose both death and hell were utterly defeated. Suppose the fight was fixed. Suppose God took you on a crystal ball trip into your future and you saw with indubitable certainty that despite everything—your sin, your smallness, your stupidity—you could have free for the asking your whole crazy heart's deepest desire: heaven, eternal joy. Would you not return fearless and singing? What can earth do to you if you are guaranteed heaven? To fear the worst earthly loss would be like a millionaire fearing the loss of a penny—less, a scratch on a penny.[13]

41

Revival and the Heart
of the Contrite

Isaiah 56:1—57:21

WHEN I WAS IN SEMINARY YEARS AGO, J. I. Packer came for a series of special lectures. This one sentence of his I cannot forget: "Do not neglect the revival dimension in your ministry." Thank you, Dr. Packer. I don't intend to.

Revival is often misunderstood. When you drive by a church displaying a sign, "Revival here next week," you can bet there won't be a revival there next week. Revival can't be scheduled. True revival is the wind of the Holy Spirit blowing over a church. The wind blows where it wants to. We hear its sound, but we don't know where it comes from or where it goes (John 3:8). We're just grateful when the Wind blows our way. We pray he will more and more.

What is revival? True revival is God coming down among us, visiting us, dwelling among us in his glory, overflowing into our need (Isaiah 57:15). Revival is the manifest presence of God, the immediacy of God, the kiss of God, the nearness of God in his goodness and power. Revival is a time of refreshing from the presence of the Lord (Acts 3:20). It's a season in the life of the church when God causes the normal ministry of the gospel to surge forward with extraordinary spiritual power.[1] It is not foolish hysterics. It is God becoming overwhelmingly real to us.

Isaiah leads us by the hand toward true revival. His ministry was not intended for people who were spiritually advanced. In chapters 1—39 of his book, Isaiah confronts his own generation with their repeated failure to treat God as if he were really God. They established such a pattern of practical atheism that they disqualified themselves in the sight of God. He had to send them off into exile in Babylon.

In chapters 40—55, the second major section of the book, Isaiah looks beyond his own generation to later times. God promises that, in both the near term and the far term, he will save his sinful people. Near term, the Jews will be released from Babylon to return to the Promised Land. God kept his promise. And why did they have to return to the land? Because that's where Messiah would be born (Micah 5:2). So Isaiah calls a later generation to get ready for the coming glory of the Lord (40:3–5). That's the greater, long-term promise. Isaiah prophesies far in advance the coming of the Messiah as a servant on whom the Lord will lay the iniquity of us all (53:6). All our hopes for ourselves and our world hang on the promised display of God's glory breaking upon us through Christ. God kept his promise. Jesus did come. He *was* the glory of the Lord (John 1:14). He *did* bear our sins (2 Corinthians 5:21). And today we're waiting for, living for, the full and final display of God's glory at the second coming of Christ. Our world is broken. Only Christ can fix it. And he has promised us nothing less than new heavens and a new earth (Isaiah 65:17; 66:22). In revival God gives us a foretaste of that glory right now.

In Isaiah 56—66, the third major section of his book, the prophet shows us the way into ongoing revival as we await the fullness of God's coming kingdom. The structure of his first prophetic sermon looks like this:

A God's people as they should be *and will be* (56:1–8)
   1. Empowered by hope (56:1)
   2. Marked by trust (56:2)
   3. Inclusive of all (56:3–8)
   B God's people as they shouldn't be *but are* (56:9—57:21)
      1. Self-seeking leaders (56:9–12)
      2. A mixed people (57:1–21)
         a¹ Peace for the righteous (57:1, 2)
            b¹ The prostitute and her family (57:3–13a)
               c¹ God our refuge (57:13b)
               c² God our breakthrough (57:14)
            b² The Lord and his friends (57:15–19)
         a² No peace for the wicked (57:20, 21)

Isaiah is showing us that the One who is high and lifted up also dwells with the lowly, and with no one else, in reviving power. The implications are significant.

God's People as They Should Be and Will Be

Thus says the LORD:
   "Keep justice, and do righteousness,

for soon my salvation will come,
    and my righteousness be revealed." (Isaiah 56:1)

The future strengthens us to live well today (1 John 3:3). What do we have going for us? We have the finished work of Christ on the cross more than 2,000 years ago. We have the presence of the Holy Spirit right now. But we also have the future promises of Scripture. God's point here is that his promises for the future are meant to activate us today. Isaiah 56:1 sets the tone for the rest of the book. God is asking, "Have you discovered the power of the future? The fullness of my salvation is on its way to you. Nothing can stop it. I want you to live now on that basis. You are the ones through whom my coming kingdom is to be felt today. You are a living sign of the future. You are a prophetic presence in the world. Live like it."

The justice and righteousness he's talking about—how we actually treat one another—do not not make up a hard, Pharisaical moralism. They're beautiful. They're the outward expression of trust and rest and delight in God:

"Blessed is the man who does this,
    and the son of man who holds it fast,
who keeps the Sabbath, not profaning it,
    and keeps his hand from doing any evil." (Isaiah 56:2)

Look closely. The Sabbath is not keeping our hands from doing any *activity*. The real Sabbath is keeping our hands from doing any *evil*. A true Sabbath rest is busy with justice and righteousness. It's a paradox—busy rest. Can that really work? Sure, because true justice and righteousness aren't driven and perfectionistic but are received by grace. Christ himself is a living Sabbath for people who would be compulsively self-righteous without him. His justice and righteousness are not burdensome but a joyful relief.

What was the Sabbath? It was a weekly celebration of God's perfect creation in the beginning (Genesis 2:1–3). It was a foretaste of God's renewed creation at the end of time (Isaiah 66:22, 23). In other words, the Sabbath was a weekly dress rehearsal for Heaven. The Pharisees never understood that. They couldn't distinguish between the essence of the Sabbath and the form of the Sabbath. The essence is a faith declaring, "My life is no longer business as usual. I've come under God's care, I'm living by his ground rules now, and I'm looking forward to Heaven." In the Old Testament era, that spirit of faith was expressed with certain protocols. For example, you couldn't light a fire on the Sabbath (Exodus 35:3). That outward form of observance was a sign of the Old Covenant (Exodus 31:12–17). But in the flow of the whole Bible, realize that in the transition from the Old Testament to the New, God shifted on a number of fronts from *essence in a Jewish form only* to *essence in many forms.* And the essence of the Sabbath has always been faith enjoying the all-sufficiency of God, faith feeling so loved by God that we rest from our own strategies for self-preservation and live for him. Seeing our lives that way is a real Sabbath rest, and it liberates us to get busy with justice and righteousness.

God's passion for the essence of things more than their forms should encourage everyone who wants to be a child of God:

> Let not the foreigner who has joined himself to the LORD say,
> "The LORD will surely separate me from his people";
> and let not the eunuch say,
> "Behold, I am a dry tree."
> For thus says the LORD:
> "To the eunuchs who keep my Sabbaths,
> who choose the things that please me
> and hold fast my covenant,
> I will give in my house and within my walls
> a monument and a name
> better than sons and daughters;
> I will give them an everlasting name
> that shall not be cut off." (Isaiah 56:3–5)

How could Isaiah say that? Foreigners and emasculated men were, among others, barred from worship (Deuteronomy 23:1–6). After all, foreign cultures were pagan, and emasculation marred God's creation. That point had to be made. But it wasn't God's last word to us. His last word is openness and welcome for anyone whose faith comes to rest in Christ. So don't tell yourself God won't receive you. You might not have a church background. You might feel awkward in church. You might have deeply personal reasons you'd rather not talk about for hesitating. But God wants you to tell yourself this: The one thing that matters to him is that you rest in Christ and choose what pleases him and hold fast to him. If Christ has your heart, God says he'll give you a place in his home *better* than sons and daughters born there who don't treat Christ as their everything. So come on in. To God, insider-ness is no guarantee, and outsider-ness is no obstacle.

When Christ was born, Magi—star-gazers!—came all the way from Persia to worship him, while his own people in Jerusalem wouldn't walk six miles down the road to Bethlehem to check it out (Matthew 2:1–12). When a Roman centurion trusted Jesus implicitly, our Savior said, "Truly, I tell you, with no one in Israel have I found such faith. I tell you, many will come from east and west and recline at table with Abraham, Isaac, and Jacob in the kingdom of heaven, while the sons of the kingdom will be thrown into the outer darkness" (Matthew 8:10–12). The Apostle John wrote, "He came to his own, and his own people did not receive him. But to all who did receive him, he gave the right to become children of God" (John 1:11, 12).

Above all else, God values a heart for Christ. That's how he defines spiritual authenticity. The Jews of old needed to understand that. We need to understand it. We draw lines of exclusion that God wants to erase. He throws the doors wide-open to all alike who will take Christ alone as their legitimacy.

> "My house shall be called a house of prayer
> for all peoples." (Isaiah 56:7b)

God's house of prayer is big and colorful and happily united in Christ, and he wants every one of us to be a part of it. We know from when Jesus kicked the hucksters out of the temple, and quoted this verse, that God is willing to fight for this principle (Mark 11:15–17). What matters in church is what matters to God, especially the gathering in of outsiders (John 10:16), and nothing else matters. When we accept that and implement the implications in our churches, we move toward revival.

Chuck Smith was pastoring a little church in Costa Mesa, California, in the late 1960s, not far from the beach. God began to pour out his Spirit. Teenage kids started getting saved and coming to church. But there was a problem. The oil deposits off the coast of California bubble up little globs of oil that land on the beach now and then, about the size of a quarter. If you step on one, it sticks to the bottom of your foot and you mess up the carpet when you get home. So these young people began coming into church right off the beach. They didn't know they were supposed to wear shoes. All they knew was, Jesus is outta sight and church is cool. God was gathering in outsiders, and it was beautifully authentic. But the new carpets and the new pews at Pastor Smith's church were getting stained. One Sunday morning Chuck arrived at church to find a sign posted outside: "Shirts and shoes please." He took it down. After the service he met with the church officers. They talked it through. They agreed that they would remove the new carpet and pews before they would hinder one kid from coming to Christ.[2] And that wise decision cleared the way for God to visit Calvary Chapel with revival. I was there when they were holding services five nights a week, standing room only. The breakthrough came when they chose to care about what God cares about, and nothing else. That's authenticity—a house of prayer gathering in everyone who will enjoy Christ with us as our Sabbath rest.

God's People as They Shouldn't Be but Are

All you beasts of the field, come to devour—
  all you beasts in the forest.
His watchmen are blind;
  they are all without knowledge;
they are all silent dogs;
  they cannot bark,
dreaming, lying down,
  loving to slumber.
The dogs have a mighty appetite;
  they never have enough.
But they are shepherds who have no understanding;
  they have all turned to their own way;
  each to his own gain, one and all.
"Come," they say, "let me get wine;
  let us fill ourselves with strong drink;
and tomorrow will be like this day,
  great beyond measure." (Isaiah 56:9–12)

Isaiah contrasts the productive Sabbath rest of verses 1–8 with the destructive self-indulgence of verses 9–12. He's asking, "Where are we now, compared to where we should be?" He looks first at the leaders of God's people, and he sees watchmen who are asleep on the job and shepherds who care only for themselves. What he's saying is a warning to everyone in a position of trust.

Peggy Noonan, commenting on a cable news show, described one of our national leaders as "a profoundly unserious person." That's what Isaiah is exposing. He understands that you can't wink at private corruption and maintain public good. He understands that what matters most is not policy but character. Why? Because of God. Even as these leaders in Isaiah's vision are toasting their luck and thinking they've never had it so good, God is calling in their enemies, the "beasts of the field," to "devour" them.

Why is this section here at all? Because justice and righteousness aren't in our DNA. The only power that can create them is faith in Christ. And for that, we need revival—starting with those of us who are leaders. Here's the great thing Isaiah can see. Beyond our own good intentions and smart policies, God is able to stir our hearts to walk in the Spirit rather than the flesh. Isaiah can see that Christ is our real leader. Nations come and go, churches come and go, but Christ will never mislead us. His glory is the one inevitability, and everyone who lives for it now will live in it then.

Where are we as God's people, compared to where we should be? In

57:1–21 Isaiah looks throughout the church generally. He sees mixture there. He sees both authenticity and hypocrisy, both the righteous and the wicked. The darkness is not just "out there"; it's also "in here." Every church is a microcosm of the forces of good and evil. In the church, opposites—not only degrees but opposites—are thrown together. How can you tell who's authentic? The key word here is "peace," especially in verses 2 and 21. The righteous enter into peace, their Sabbath rest, but there's no peace for the wicked. What is Isaiah saying?

His prophetic eye discerns two trends emerging among God's people. One trend is the righteous disappearing.

> The righteous man perishes,
>   and no one lays it to heart;
> devout men are taken away,
>   while no one understands.
> For the righteous man is taken away from calamity;
>   he enters into peace;
> they rest in their beds
>   who walk in their uprightness. (Isaiah 57:1, 2)

Righteous people are perishing, and no one sees the significance of it.[3] In Isaiah's day they may actually have been disappearing for sinister reasons. But even when the righteous aren't valued and recognized and honored, they enter into peace and rest because God takes them away to himself. To be overlooked, even persecuted, but to walk on with God is not a disaster. Not even dying is a disaster. The only real devastation is to lose your integrity before God. It's better to die in obedience than to live in disobedience. In other words, if our living is Christ, then our dying is gain (Philippians 1:21). Death can be a gift, delivering us from evil.

The other trend Isaiah sees among God's people is spiritual adultery (57:3–13a). He senses in the spirit of the times a contempt for God. God's people wanted something new and sexy and exciting. So they were flirting with idols, and the prophetic warnings sounded like mere saber-rattling. God was no longer real to their hearts. What intrigued them was an "anything goes" romp through paganism, however exhausting, however degrading, however stupid. "After all, isn't that how you get by and have some fun along the way?" But to God, it was like getting into bed with a false lover.

> On a high and lofty mountain
>   you have spread your bed,
>   and there you went up to offer sacrifice. (v. 7)

Isaiah understands that God's covenant with us is marital in nature. God loves us with a jealous love, like a man's passion for his wife. Isaiah, Hosea, Jeremiah, and Ezekiel all told us that treating God as if he weren't enough to satisfy us is spiritual whoredom. It's why we must bring our emptiness to Christ and satisfy ourselves again and again. It's why the most important thing about us is our love for Christ, our openness to him alone. It's why our role in the relationship is not control but surrender. It's a constant temptation to spread our love around in sacrifice to other gods, because something in our hearts doesn't believe that he alone is enough to thrill us forever. But we are the ones, even we who treat him so poorly—we are the ones whom he still invites to enter in and find out what his goodness is really worth.

> But he who takes refuge in me shall possess the land
>   and shall inherit my holy mountain. (v. 13b)

That's Old Testament code language to say that in the gospel God is offering us *everything*. If you've been trying to hack out your own existence rather than receiving life as a gift from God, now is the time to start inheriting what you've always really wanted. He is the one—the one we've offended—he is the one who makes it easy for us.

> And it shall be said,
> "Build up, build up, prepare the way,
>   remove every obstruction from my people's way." (v. 14)

God isn't building barriers to keep you away. He's open to you. He even insists that there be no obstacles at all to keep you away. If you can accept Christ, the way to God is open—as far as God is concerned. The hang-up isn't with him. But in our self-pity and unbelief, we treat God as a dead-end rather than our goal. We're the ones slowing down our own progress. What does God do? He keeps the way back to him free of every obstruction, including our own sins.

If you've been wondering how to find God, Isaiah 57:15 is the verse you've been looking for:

> For thus says the One who is high and lifted up,
>   who inhabits eternity, whose name is Holy:
> "I dwell in the high and holy place,
>   and also with him who is of a contrite and lowly spirit,
> to revive the spirit of the lowly,
>   and to revive the heart of the contrite."

Where is God? In two places. He dwells in the high and holy place, where we can't go. And he dwells among the lowly and contrite, where we can go. So the way to find God is obvious. Humble yourself, and he'll find you.

God is not like us. For us, there's no neighborhood too classy for us to move up to, if only we can afford it. But God doesn't value upward mobility. He values downward mobility—not because he feels uncomfortable dwelling in the high and holy place, but because down low is where he finds the people who are open to him.

Would it hurt us to lower ourselves? Not if God is there. Lowliness is the humility that admits, "Where I really belong is at the bottom. What I deserve to be is a nobody." That is so liberating. Life opens up then. Remember Jesus' parable of the wedding feast? Some guests were crowding up to the head table, but the host told them those seats were reserved for others. They were embarrassed. But the people who took the low places were invited to move up to the seats of honor (Luke 14:7–11). Every one of us coming into church should be thinking, *Where is the low place? That's where I belong. I will take the low place. If God wants to honor me further, it's up to him.* The high and holy One does notice, and he visits the lowly with revival. The church I pastor recently received a letter that included these lines:

> I am resolved to humble myself under the mighty hand of God. I strive
> to do all that is within my power to expose, challenge, and change my
> innermost beliefs, values and attitudes. I have committed myself to this.

That is lowliness. That is the authenticity God blesses. I have a History Channel video about the Navy's precision flying team, the Blue Angels. When the team reviews the film of a performance, the leader points out the slight mistakes they made at each point. These are the best pilots in the Navy. But whenever their leader points out a mistake, their standard reply is, "Just glad to be here, sir."[4]

A church filled with that humble openness to Christ is revival-ready. He will dwell among such people. Even if we are involved in spiritual adultery, God will heal us and restore us.

> "I have seen his ways, but I will heal him;
>   I will lead him and restore comfort to him and his mourners,
>   creating the fruit of the lips.
> Peace, peace, to the far and to the near," says the LORD,
>   "and I will heal him." (Isaiah 57:18, 19)

Didn't Jesus say, "Blessed are those who mourn, for they shall be comforted" (Matthew 5:4)? Didn't Paul say, "Christ came and preached peace to you who were far off and peace to those who were near" (Ephesians 2:17)? If we'll stay low before him, he will dwell among us with a peace and a healing and a comfort we can't explain except as a miracle of the Holy Spirit. He offers healing to all, both insiders and outsiders.

> "But the wicked are like the tossing sea;
>> for it cannot be quiet,
>> and its waters toss up mire and dirt.
> There is no peace," says my God, "for the wicked." (Isaiah 57:20, 21)

Peace is not within us. We are by nature restless—never satisfied, never content, never grateful, never relaxed, like the tossing sea. It's because we're wicked. Chuck Colson writes of a despairing young woman, exhausted in an endless round of parties. When a psychologist suggested that she stop, she said, "You mean I don't have to do what I want to do?"[5] Our peace is our drivenness. We need a Savior. And Christ doesn't just confront our wickedness—he *forgives* us. He opens the way to come back. He visits the lowly with reviving life. He says to us all:

> "Come to me, all you labor and are heavy laden, and I will give you rest. Take my yoke upon you, and learn from me, for I am gentle and lowly in heart, and you will find rest for your souls. For my yoke is easy, and my burden is light." (Matthew 11:28–30)

Can anyone else say that to us?

42

Revival and Responsibility

ISAIAH 58:1—59:13

GOD IS MOVING TOWARD the new heavens and the new earth. He has promised the full display of his glory. He has sent Christ his servant to bear human guilt and justify the ungodly, qualifying them for his new world. He pours out his Spirit upon the lowly with reviving tastes of the future glory. "The eyes of the LORD move to and fro throughout the earth that He may strongly support those whose heart is completely His" (2 Chronicles 16:9, NASB).

What he wants now is his church to serve as the model home for the new neighborhood he has promised to build. He wants everyone to be able to look at the church and see the future, so that they can buy in. What kind of church is persuasive in that role? What kind of church is preparing the way of the Lord? What kind of church will God strongly support?

Isaiah tells us. His message is challenging, not because it's all that hard to understand but because it's just plain blunt. Here is the structure:

1. Fasting without a blessing: "Why?" (58:1–5)
    A Tokenism confronted (58:1)
      B Tokenism exposed (58:2–4a)
        C Tokenism rejected (58:4b, 5)
2. Favor for a reason: "If . . . then . . ." (58:6–14)
    A¹ Taking responsibility (58:6, 7)
      B¹ The favor of God (58:8, 9a)
    A² Correcting wrongs (58:9b, 10a)
      B² The favor of God (58:10b–12)
    A³ Choosing delight (58:13)
      B³ The favor of God (58:14)

3. Failure with a remedy: "We know" (59:1–13)
    A Hypocrisy unmasked: "you" (59:1–3)
        B Hypocrisy described: "they" (59:4–8)
            C Hypocrisy confessed: "we" (59:9–13)

Isaiah wants us to take bold new steps for justice and evangelism and renewal in every sense. His wisdom is to take us there not through triumphalistic self-assertion but through the confession of sin.

Fasting without a Blessing

"Cry aloud; do not hold back;
    lift up your voice like a trumpet;
declare to my people their transgression,
    to the house of Jacob their sins." (Isaiah 58:1)

God brings out the big guns of prophetic confrontation. Clearly, he's aiming at the conviction of sin. After verse 1, therefore, what do we expect to read next? What are these sinful people going to be like? Trashing every one of the Ten Commandments?

"Yet they seek me daily
    and delight to know my ways,
as if they were a nation that did righteousness
    and did not forsake the judgment of their God;
they ask of me righteous judgments;
    they delight to draw near to God." (v. 2)

If you moved to a new town and found a church that sought God daily, delighted to know his ways, asked God for righteous judgments, and delighted to draw near to him, you'd join that church. So would I. But Isaiah might not. It's possible for a church to do all these good things with no awareness that, to God, something is deeply wrong. What were these people actually thinking?

"'Why have we fasted, and you see it not?
    Why have we humbled ourselves, and you take no knowledge of it?'" (v. 3a)

The people of God have been fasting. They've even afflicted themselves. (That's the force of "humbled ourselves.") Isn't *that* taking sin seriously? But God is still standing off at a distance, still withholding himself, and they wonder why.

But the question "Why?" is not an openhearted request for instruction.

It's a way of dumping their frustration on God. They thought God was being unfair. They were both pious toward God and angry at God, and it was their very sincerity that explains their anger. They sincerely believed they could obligate God and pressure God. And when their fasting and praying and self-deprivation didn't leverage cooperation out of God, they resented him. What poisoned their souls toward God was not sins like thievery and murder. What poisoned their souls was their religion.

Where did they go wrong? The key is "as if" in verse 2: ". . . *as if* they were a nation that did righteousness." The believers Isaiah is confronting were role-playing righteousness. To be people who seek God, and to be *like* people who seek God—to God, the difference is infinite. Where does he discern their shallowness?

> "Behold, in the day of your fast you seek your own pleasure,
>   and oppress all your workers.
> Behold, you fast only to quarrel and to fight
>   and to hit with a wicked fist.
> Fasting like yours this day
>   will not make your voice to be heard on high.
> Is such the fast that I choose,
>   a day for a person to humble himself?
> Is it to bow down his head like a reed,
>   and to spread sackcloth and ashes under him?
> Will you call this a fast,
>   and a day acceptable to the LORD?" (vv. 3b–5)

We think piecemeal. We don't connect the dots between fasting and seeking God and so forth—good disciplines—and our living Monday through Friday. But God doesn't think piecemeal. He knows we can't compensate for neglect in one area of life by observance in another, especially when fasting is less demanding than labor-intensive involvement with needy people. God doesn't want us to live prayerless lives, running on our own steam. We need to be quiet before him, and fasting is a valid way to do that. But neither does God want us to prove our devotion to him by making ourselves hungry and miserable while disregarding our obligation to make others full and happy. If our Christianity, however sincere, doesn't move us to make our world a better place, it's not only unhelpful to others, it's unacceptable to the Lord. The Bible says, "Religion that is pure and undefiled before God the Father is this: to visit orphans and widows in their affliction, and to keep oneself unstained from the world" (James 1:27).

John Perkins, the heroic African-American Christian leader, writes of "the bigness of the Bible—how it takes in the whole person, both an individual's personal actions *and* social actions."[1] But one of the marks of modern religion is what sociologists call privatization. They mean the tendency for believers to treat their faith as a personal lifestyle option, disconnected from their public responsibilities. Jonathan Edwards knew better.

> Christian love disposes a person to be public-spirited. A man of a right spirit is not a man of narrow and private views but is greatly concerned for the good of the community to which he belongs, and particularly of the city where he resides.[2]

Christianity must be deeply internal and personal. But if it stops there, it's just a spare-time hobby.[3]

The essence of Christianity is love for Christ. That's the power of it, the genius of it. And authentic Christianity expresses that heart for Christ in basically two ways—first, in worship and praise and prayer and lifted hands and open Bibles, all beautiful to God, but, secondly, also in courageous evangelism and defending the weak and feeding the hungry. It's not either/or; it's both/and. But putting ourselves out for others is more contrary to our natural selfishness and therefore more significant to God.[4] To seek him in a way convincing to *him* is what we want, isn't it? What then *does* make our voice be heard on high?

Favor for a Reason

Isaiah now moves back and forth three times between the spirituality God considers authentic and his promises of favor. First, God calls us to take responsibility for our surroundings.

> "Is this not the fast that I choose:
>   to loose the bonds of wickedness,
>   to undo the straps of the yoke,
> to let the oppressed go free,
>   and to break every yoke?
> Is it not to share your bread with the hungry
>   and bring the homeless poor into your house;
> when you see the naked, to cover him,
>   and not to hide yourself from your own flesh?" (Isaiah 58:6, 7)

The NIV translates that last line, "and not to turn away from your own flesh and blood." "Flesh and blood" is family. But Isaiah means more. "Your own flesh"—that's what the Hebrew says—is the human race (cf. Job 34:15). When we feel cold, when we feel hungry, when we feel pain, that misery in our flesh is what all other cold, hungry, suffering people feel too. They are our flesh. We have a responsibility to them, because God cares deeply about all human sufferings, both physical and spiritual. Most of us Americans today are "the haves," both materially and spiritually. All around us are "the have-nots," both rich and poor. Remember the nursery rhyme?

> Hark, hark, the dogs do bark, the beggars are coming to town—
> Some in rags, some in tags, and some in velvet gowns.

That is the world of beggars, rich and poor, that God cares about so deeply. He has blessed us in Christ, to make us a blessing to them (Genesis 12:3).

Are you aware, for example, that 24,000 people die from hunger and hunger-related causes every day, most of them children?[5] And how many are slipping into eternity without Christ? God cares about that. He wants us to do something about it. True revival isn't a private religious joyride. It's the power of a future, better world enabling us to stop saying, "Those people aren't my responsibility." It gets us busy, doing what we can about poverty, illiteracy, slavery, abortion, political manipulation, people being treated like animals, people going to eternal Hell. We don't need three years in seminary to get the motivation to obey God in this way. Three days in Third-World poverty or just three seconds in Hell would motivate us all.

When we suffer, God isn't being cruel to us. He's giving us a gift. He's helping us care more meaningfully for others (2 Corinthians 1:3, 4). But some Christians reverse that. They respond to their pain by turning inward in self-focus. This is not the mind of Christ. Any understanding of Christianity that ends up reinforcing rather than challenging our natural self-absorption—well, God asks, "Is such the fast that I choose?" (Isaiah 58:5).

The symbol of our faith is a cross. Its message is love pouring itself out for others. One time Jesus asked a sick man, "Do you *want* to be healed?" (John 5:6). Why did he ask that? Because misery can be useful. It's a perfect excuse for evading responsibility. But the gospel creates generous, hard-working, available people. The Bible says, "You were called to freedom, brothers. Only do not use your freedom as an opportunity for the flesh, but through love serve one another. For the whole law is fulfilled in one word: 'You shall love your neighbor as yourself'" (Galatians 5:13, 14). God smiles on that kind of Christianity. Here is his promise:

> Then your light shall break forth like the dawn,
>   and your healing shall spring up speedily;
> your righteousness shall go before you;
>   the glory of the LORD shall be your rear guard.
> Then you shall call, and the LORD will answer;
>   you shall cry, and he will say, "Here I am." (Isaiah 58:8, 9a)

Do you want God to answer your prayers? Be his answer to someone else's prayers. Do you want God to come in his immediacy and say to you, "Here I am"? Get close to someone who needs you and say, "Here I am." Here's the paradox at the center of truth: "It is more blessed to give than to receive" (Acts 20:35). Almost nothing in our consumerist American culture encourages us to believe that, but it just happens to be the way life works. Why? Because God is a happy Giver, an intense Lover, a relevant Helper, and he wants us to share in his joy.

Secondly, God calls us to correct the wrongs around us, right down to gossipy finger-pointing.

> "If you take away the yoke from your midst,
>   the pointing of the finger, and speaking wickedness,
> if you pour yourself out for the hungry
>   and satisfy the desire of the afflicted . . ." (Isaiah 58:9b, 10a)

And here is his promise: ". . . then shall your light rise in the darkness and your gloom be as the noonday" (v. 10b). Is your personality gloomy? Is your home a dark place? There may be complex reasons for that. But in it all, don't overlook God's remedy. If you and your family went down to Salama, my church's ministry to downtown Nashville, and you poured yourselves out for the inner city, God says it would cheer you up. And it's not only a remedy for you. God is building the New Jerusalem, where there will be no poverty, no unbelief, no misery. That's where God is taking us. But that eternal city begins in our own cities, as the preaching of the gospel helps every one of us to say, "Maybe I don't need to assemble a perfect little world around me where I get it all my own way. Maybe the passion of my life should be that others may live, both now and forever, to the glory of God." God promises to visit that humility with reviving, noonday light.

Yet another promise, in verse 11, says we'll be "like a watered garden, like a spring of water, whose waters do not fail." This reminds us of the "rivers of living water" Jesus spoke of (John 7:38). How might that actually work? How might those rivers start flowing? James Montgomery Boice proposes one way:

> I would say that one of the best things that could happen to many believers would be for them to be led to give away, all at one time, a substantial part of their savings. That is, they should give a substantial part of their capital. Why? Because there is something about giving away a sizable percentage of one's money—and, of course, the amount would vary entirely from one individual to another—that is spiritually invigorating. And there is seldom a case in which a large gift does not throw the Christian back

on the Lord and increase the feeling that he is all wonderful and that he is more than able to care for the one who trusts him. I have seen this happen in many instances. And I have never known a true Christian to be sorry for even the most sacrificial giving afterward.[6]

If your life is a continual effort to cope with the grim business of survival, just to get by, you don't understand. God has so much more for you than that. He has "a spring of water, whose waters do not fail." Will you trust him enough to follow him into that joy?

Here's another promise, in verse 12: "your ancient ruins shall be rebuilt." John Perkins sees the story of the black race in our country as "two hundred years of slavery, followed by two or three generations of economic exploitation, political oppression, racial discrimination and educational deprivation. . . ."[7] But the damage we inflict, actively and passively, does not defeat God. He is rebuilding the whole world according to the gospel, including human dignity. He intends to do it through us: "You shall raise up the foundations of many generations." God wants to make *you* into a hero in this story of world redemption. The world may never notice you. But God sees.

Thirdly, God calls us to create a culture of God-centered, glad-hearted, regular worship, redefining pleasure itself.

> "If you will turn back your foot from the Sabbath,
>   from doing your pleasure on my holy day,
> and call the Sabbath a delight
>   and the holy day of the LORD honorable;
> if you honor it, not going your own ways,
>   or seeking your own pleasure, or talking idly . . ." (v. 13)

The Sabbath is meant to structure our weekly schedules around glorifying and enjoying God together. The Sabbath is God's appointed release for us from our self-worshiping addiction to work and productivity and efficiency and organization and busyness. The Sabbath is God's way of saying, "No, your highest values will not be professional and commercial. They will only end up destroying you and others through you. Your highest values will be worship and freedom and delight, enriching you and all around you."

For most American Christians today, the Sabbath is the holiday we're least likely to observe. We think we're freeing ourselves from a religious imposition, but in fact we're enslaving ourselves to destructive workaholism, unintentional but real exploitation of our employees, the obliteration of unstructured family intimacy, and, above all, a lost sense of the sacred.[8] If we kept the Sabbath—it's inconvenient, but the important things in life usually are—if we kept the Sabbath, one day in seven, fifty-two weeks a year, we'd automatically add seven and a half weeks of vacation to our year. And not just seven and a half weeks of goofing off. Seven and a half weeks of focusing on God.

God has made a weekly appointment with us. Do we love him enough to keep it? If we do, here's his promise:

". . . then you shall take delight in the LORD,
    and I will make you ride on the heights of the earth;
I will feed you with the heritage of Jacob your father,
    for the mouth of the LORD has spoken." (v. 14)

Delight in God is the most precious treasure in the world. It opens everything else up. It expels sin, it praises Christ, it studies the Bible, it raises kids well, it works hard for the benefit of others, it relieves their sufferings, it builds the church, it goes to Heaven. William Blake understood how important it is not to quench holy delight.

I went to the Garden of Love,
And saw what I never had seen:
A Chapel was built in the midst,
Where I used to play in the green.

And the gates of this Chapel were shut,
And 'Thou shalt not' writ over the door;
So I turn'd to the Garden of Love
That so many sweet flowers bore;

And I saw it was filled with graves,
And tomb-stones where flowers should be;
And Priests in black gowns were walking their rounds,
And binding with briars my joys & desires.[9]

That is *not* authentic Christianity—not to God. He loves delight. And he's calling us to schedule our weekly routines around his great and serious joys, bringing others with us into the atmosphere of holy delight. That means that Sunday is not an extra Saturday. It's not the end of the weekend. It's not the day to get caught up for Monday. It's the Lord's Day, when we set lesser things aside and replenish ourselves and others with all the fullness of God.

That's the kind of church that prepares the way of the Lord—taking responsibility, correcting wrongs, and choosing delight. How do we get there?

Failure with a Remedy

> Behold, the LORD's hand is not shortened, that it cannot save,
>   or his ear dull, that it cannot hear;
> but your iniquities have made a separation
>   between you and your God,
> and your sins have hidden his face from you
>   so that he does not hear. (Isaiah 59:1, 2)

God is powerful. God is listening. He wants to say to every church, "Here I am." But he won't send us his power if we'll only use it to reinforce a kind of Christianity he doesn't identify with. So what *are* these iniquities and sins that turn his face away but that we need urgently to face?

> For your hands are defiled with blood
>   and your fingers with iniquity;
> your lips have spoken lies;
>   your tongue mutters wickedness. (v. 3)

What offends God is the way we hurt one another in what we do and in what we say. Isaiah describes this at length, through verse 8. How we mistreat one another is so significant to God, Paul quotes Isaiah 59:7, 8 in Romans 3:15–17, where he describes how urgently we all need a Savior. Apart from the cross of Christ, verses 3–8 show us what we are—even we, the people of God.

So what's the next step? Is there a way to get traction for forward movement? Yes. Isaiah says in essence, "Confess your sins." In verses 9–13 the pronouns shift from the third person to the first person as we own up to our sins before God.

> Therefore justice is far from us,
>   and righteousness does not overtake us;
> we hope for light, and behold, darkness,
>   and for brightness, but we walk in gloom. (v. 9)

The most important word in that verse is "Therefore." When we melt before God in repentance, we stop asking him "Why?" (58:3) and we accept his assessment of us and its implications: "*Therefore* justice is far from us." We stop pouting, and we start thinking:

> For our transgressions are multiplied before you,
>   and our sins testify against us;
> for our transgressions are with us,

and we know our iniquities:
transgressing, and denying the LORD,
    and turning back from following our God,
speaking oppression and revolt,
    conceiving and uttering from the heart lying words. (Isaiah 59:12, 13)

There is not a hint of self-righteous defensiveness here. Revival always includes confession before God and reconciliation with one another. Revival thrives amid an honest reappraisal of ourselves and our weaknesses. And we *can* risk honesty with him because of the cross of Christ, where his sacrifice absorbs our guilt. God has relocated us in his favor. It's safe now to get real with him. The fastest way into the new heavens and the new earth is the triumph of that grace in the world. And the fastest way to the triumph of grace in the world is the triumph of that grace in the church.

At his cross, Jesus was doing two things at once. He was both bearing our sins far away, and he was teaching us a new way to live. He was saying to guilty sinners, "It's your fault, but it's my problem. I'm taking the responsibility to restore you." Many of us understand the practical implications of that and are giving ourselves away and enjoying the presence of God even in a demanding schedule. If that's you, God is saying to you, "Well done, good and faithful servant. You are the future of the world. Don't stop."

Others of us don't understand. There are two possible explanations for this. One: you're not born-again. You're using Christianity for the glaze of moral legitimacy it seems to spread over a fundamentally selfish lifestyle. God is saying to you, "You need to be rescued from yourself, and only I can do it. Show me you're in earnest, and I will more than meet you halfway." Two: you are born-again, but what you love about your Christian life is not Christ but your Christian life. You don't understand that Christ is not offering you your own perfect little world, but a whole new world where righteousness dwells. But you just don't think beyond yourself. Secretly you're disappointed that God doesn't come through for you with more earthly benefits. God is saying to you, "The sin that makes a separation between us is your irresponsibility. In this real world of urgent need and gospel opportunity, that offends me. But when I can see in you *my* kind of Christianity, your revival will not be far away."

43

Revival and World Renewal

ISAIAH 59:14—60:22

IN C. S. LEWIS'S THE VOYAGE OF THE "DAWN TREADER," the noble mouse Reepicheep is one of the crew sailing eastward as far as they can, all the way to the borders of the kingdom of Aslan, the leonine Christ figure. But when the ship can go no farther, Reepicheep's irrepressible spirit compels him to leave the others behind and sail off still farther east in his little boat, all the way to the very edge of the world and beyond, into Aslan's land.[1] This passage in Isaiah is our little boat in which we sail forward out of the present to the very edge of time and beyond, into Aslan's land. This passage carries us out of today's world of fanatical terrorists and dysfunctional schools and inoperable cancer and broken promises into a future age of worldwide happiness in Christ.

We need Isaiah's prophetic vision. Not long ago I received an e-mail from a member of the church I pastor who said what many of us are thinking these days:

> In the last week or so I have not wanted to turn on the television news or read every article in the paper as I usually do. The world is too ugly and disturbing. Humiliation over the prisoner abuse in Iraq. Fear of the future as we deal with terrorists who openly behead an American for broadcast viewing. Solicitations for pornography constantly in our inboxes. Upside-down morality that elevates tolerance above all else. And then I look in my own heart and see the materialism and criticism and lust. All of this to say—I can't imagine I am the only one who is particularly struck by the darkness and depravity of our world. We can easily feel so hopeless about the world we live in and the future we face.

395

Are you aware that the Bible records many prophecies of a day when the gospel will wash over the whole world under an outpouring of the Holy Spirit?[2] God has committed himself to the future of this world, his grace will triumph permanently and universally, and the races and cultures of this world have a place of honor in God's plan. We have a reason to expect *sweeping spiritual revival* throughout the world, however formidable the opposition. That reason is the Word of God. Remember Genesis 12, where the gospel begins. God promises that in Christ all the nations of the earth will be blessed. How could it be otherwise? The goodness of God is of a spreading nature. Christianity is not a private preference; it's an uncontainable power for world renewal. Jesus said, "I am the light of the world" (John 8:12), and light by its nature illuminates everything around. Even so, the gospel will brighten the world:

All the ends of the earth shall remember
    and turn to the LORD,
and all the families of the nations
    shall worship before you. (Psalm 22:27)

It shall come to pass in the latter days
    that the mountain of the house of the LORD
shall be established as the highest of the mountains,
    and shall be lifted up above the hills;
and all the nations shall flow to it,
    and many peoples shall come, and say:
"Come, let us go up to the mountain of the LORD,
    to the house of the God of Jacob,
that he may teach us his ways,
    and that we may walk in his paths." (Isaiah 2:2, 3a)

I saw in the night visions,
and behold, with the clouds of heaven
    there came one like a son of man,
and he came to the Ancient of Days
    and was presented before him.
And to him was given dominion
    and glory and a kingdom,
that all peoples, nations, and languages
    should serve him;
his dominion is an everlasting dominion,
    which shall not pass away,
and his kingdom one that shall not be destroyed. (Daniel 7:13, 14)

And being found in human form, he humbled himself by becoming obedient to the point of death, even death on a cross. Therefore God has highly exalted him and bestowed on him the name that is above every name, so that at the name of Jesus every knee should bow, in heaven and on earth and under the earth, and every tongue confess that Jesus Christ is Lord, to the glory of God the Father. (Philippians 2:8–11)

After this I looked, and behold, a great multitude that no one could number, from every nation, from all tribes and peoples and languages, standing before the throne and before the Lamb, clothed in white robes, with palm branches in their hands, and crying out with a loud voice, "Salvation belongs to our God who sits on the throne, and to the Lamb!" (Revelation 7:9, 10)

This is not a tangent in the Bible. This is the gospel. If we enjoyed Christ at the present moment, however sincerely, but with a fear that tomorrow he might be forever defeated, would the gospel be good news? The gospel must, and does, announce his final victory. Therefore, you can live now with a sense of personal possession in the future. The Bible says, "All things are yours . . . whether . . . the present or the future" (1 Corinthians 3:21, 22). Whatever your life is now, you are immeasurably rich in what will be. The Bible says, "Neither things present nor things to come . . . will be able to separate us from the love of God in Christ Jesus our Lord" (Romans 8:38, 39). Why do we fear the future? It can only bring us more of the love of God. Step into the boat of the prophetic word and by faith sail away into the age to come, when everyone will be a brother or sister, when crime will be a subject for historical study, when a mighty peace will stand guard over us. If you can see that future, you can face anything in the present.

Revival, then, is more than the awakening of a church. Revival is the future of the world, because God has decreed it. Do you see that in the structure of the passage? It pivots on God's covenant with us.

1. The "Before" Picture (59:14–20)
    A^1 Man in rebellion (59:14, 15a)
        B^1 God in amazement (59:15b, 16)
        B^2 God in action (59:17, 18)
    A^2 Man in retreat (59:19, 20)
2. Pivot: the covenant of Spirit and Word (59:21)
3. The "After" Picture (60:1–22)
    A^1 The Lord our light (60:1–5)
        B^1 The nations accepted (60:6–9)
            C The nations and the church at one (60:10–14)
        B^2 The church transformed (60:15–18)
    A^2 The Lord our light (60:19–22)

Isaiah doesn't tell us when this is going to happen. His intention is simply to strengthen our confidence in the promises of God, because we cannot live without that confidence.

The "Before" Picture

> Justice is turned back,
>   and righteousness stands afar off;
> for truth has stumbled in the public squares,
>   and uprightness cannot enter.
> Truth is lacking,
>   and he who departs from evil makes himself a prey. (Isaiah 59:14, 15a)

Why does the passage begin this way? Because this is how God finds us as he begins his project of world renewal. Interestingly, the four key words in verse 14 all appear at the center of each line in the Hebrew text:

> Turned back is justice, and righteousness stands afar off;
> stumbled in the public squares has truth, and uprightness cannot enter.

The four realities that hold society together are centered in the wording of this verse. But Isaiah is saying that these realities, which should come naturally to us at the core of our beings and at the center of our life together, are in fact outside our experience. To some degree or other, every one of us, every home, every society tells the same story of the human will suppressing the truth (Romans 1:18). Left to ourselves, we are truth-resistant. That's why throughout history every Bedford Falls eventually becomes a Pottersville. Without God's intervention, the center of human social dynamics can be epitomized in Lenin's famous remark summarizing his political modus operandi—"Who, whom?" Who will oppress whom? Knife the other guy before he knifes you, and whoever "departs from evil" ends up the loser! That's the history of the world, because "truth is lacking." And doesn't it often seem that God does nothing about it? But what do Isaiah's prophetic eyes discern?

> The LORD saw it, and it displeased him
>   that there was no justice.
> He saw that there was no man,
>   and wondered that there was no one to intercede;
> then his own arm brought him salvation,
>   and his righteousness upheld him. (Isaiah 59:15b, 16)

Is Isaiah saying that God is taken by surprise? No. His point is twofold.

One: God is not indifferent to wrong. He is incensed. Two: we cannot rescue ourselves. God saw that "there was no man." Only God can save us. How does he do that?

> He put on righteousness as a breastplate,
>   and a helmet of salvation on his head;
> he put on garments of vengeance for clothing,
>   and wrapped himself in zeal as a cloak.
> According to their deeds, so will he repay,
>   wrath to his adversaries, repayment to his enemies;
>   to the coastlands he will render repayment. (vv. 17, 18)

God is a warrior, and he has in himself all the arsenal he needs to win. Clothing is a metaphor for how God displays himself. And a final day is coming when God will appear on the human scene to settle every score with perfect justice, and there will be no hiding place, however remote ("the coastlands"). We should never give up, never give in. The apparent strength of evil is a colossal bluff. This present evil age is weak, it's getting old, it's passing away. Think of the liberation of Paris in 1944, with the Nazis on the run and the people celebrating, and that's a picture, however dim, of the future of the world.

> So they shall fear the name of the LORD from the west,
>   and his glory from the rising of the sun;
> for he will come like a rushing stream,
>   which the wind of the LORD drives.
> "And a Redeemer will come to Zion,
>   to those in Jacob who turn from transgression,"
>   declares the LORD. (vv. 19, 20)

Right now the progress of the gospel can be slow and laborious. But the present is not the measure of the future. The glory of the Lord will rise over the earth like a flash flood, spurred on by the Holy Spirit, sweeping opposition away and dissolving hostility into reverence. That day will bring the final victory of our Redeemer (Romans 11:26, 27).

In ancient Israel, a "redeemer" was a member of the family who shouldered a relative's need as if it were his own. For example, if a person incurred so much debt that he became a slave, a redeemer would buy his freedom back (Leviticus 25:47–49). That's an Old Testament picture of Christ. He is a Redeemer of people who have sinned their way into slavery. And the measure of his commitment to them is the covenant in verse 21.

Pivot: The Covenant of Spirit and Word

> "And as for me, this is my covenant with them," says the LORD: "My Spirit
> that is upon you, and my words that I have put in your mouth, shall not
> depart out of your mouth, or out of the mouth of your offspring, or out of
> the mouth of your children's offspring," says the LORD, "from this time
> forth and forevermore." (Isaiah 59:21)

This is the hinge on which the passage swings from the "before" picture
to the "after" picture. What makes the difference between the world as it is
now and the world of God's promises? God's covenant. Isaiah shifts from
poetry to prose. He puts it in plain language. And twice God declares his
resolve ("says the LORD").

What is a covenant? A Biblical covenant is God pledging himself, binding himself to us so that he becomes our God and we become his people.[3]
We've made the world a mess. But God will not accept defeat, because his
love is not a favorable mood swing. He loves us for reasons deep within his
own being, and he declares his love with a solemn oath (Hebrews 6:13–20).
He guarantees our future, and he explains how he's going to get us there.
He gives us his Spirit and his Word, and he'll never take them away. We
should never separate the Spirit and the Word. God doesn't. And we need
both. Without the Spirit, we get dry. Without the Word, we get weird. But
the Spirit and the Word together are enough to re-create the world. The
Heidelberg Catechism of 1563 teaches us to say:

> I believe that the Son of God, *through his Spirit and Word*, out of the
> entire human race, from the beginning of the world to its end, gathers,
> protects and preserves for himself a community chosen for eternal life
> and united in true faith. And of this community I am and always will be
> a living member.[4]

But there's a problem in this verse. Maybe you've noticed it. Look at
the pronouns. "This is my covenant with *them*." Who are they? "Those in
Jacob who turn from transgression" (v. 20). God's covenant is with repentant
people. No problem there. But then in the next verse he says, "My Spirit that
is upon *you*, and my words that I put in *your* mouth. . . ." Who is that? That's
our problem. It's also the cash value of the verse.

Who does "you" in verse 21 refer to? We might think that the "you"
here is the same as in the next verse: "Arise, shine, for *your* light has come"
(60:1). But that cannot be. Why? Because in Hebrew, unlike English, sec-
ond-person pronouns have gender. And the "you" in 59:21 is masculine,
while the "you" of 60:1 is feminine. Why feminine? Because it's referring to
Zion (cf. 59:20; 60:14). And in Old Testament culture, Zion, the city of God,

is thought of as a feminine entity (Isaiah 37:22). So the masculine "you" of 59:21 isn't Zion, the people of God.

Who is God speaking to? Isaiah doesn't tell us. He is allowing some mystery here. In Isaiah 59:21, out of the blue, we're overhearing a conversation. We're overhearing God promising to give an unidentified someone his Word and his Spirit forever for the benefit of repentant people. Who is that person? The likely answer is the anonymous figure Isaiah has already portrayed to us—the servant of the Lord. In Isaiah 42:6 the servant of the Lord *is* God's covenant with us. In Isaiah 53:10 the servant of the Lord has many spiritual offspring, to whom he gives his own righteousness. Taking into account the categories of the whole Bible, in verse 21 the Father is pledging to the Son how he is going to bless us.

God's promise is not just to us; God has made a promise to his Son. We've been made a part of something vast and ancient and glorious. God has committed himself to renew the world by his Spirit and Word, a commitment based not on what we deserve but on his pledge to his Son. World renewal is as certain as God's faithfulness to himself. So Isaiah urges us, "Brighten up!"

The "After" Picture

Arise, shine, for your light has come,
   and the glory of the LORD Has risen upon you. (Isaiah 60:1)

Think of the sparkling eyes of a child on Christmas morning. Jesus, whose first coming was the dawn of the glory of the Lord, is a sight to cheer us up. God has not abandoned this world. He will never walk away from the place where the blood of his Son was shed. Here is his plan:

For behold, darkness shall cover the earth,
   and thick darkness the peoples;
but upon you the LORD will arise,[5]
   and his glory will be seen upon you.
And nations shall come to your light,
   and kings to the brightness of your rising. (vv. 2, 3)

The key here is that Isaiah is using the metaphor of a city to describe the people of God (cf. 60:14). That explains the political imagery of the chapter. But his message is spiritual. The New Testament tells us that through conversion to Christ we've come "to Mount Zion and to the city of the living God, the heavenly Jerusalem" (Hebrews 12:22). We've joined a spiritual culture that will remake the world. Isaiah 60 has nothing to do with the city of Jerusalem in the modern state of Israel. It has everything to do with the New Jerusalem that the whole world will become (Revelation 21).

Right now our tragic world is suffocating under the thick darkness of evil and unbelief (John 3:16–21). But God will arise, and his glory will be seen. Where? Isaiah says to us, "His glory will be seen *upon you*. And nations shall come to *your light*." The world will be brightened by the glory of God in the church. When God makes his presence manifest among us and we discard all religiosity as so much garbage compared with his surpassing worth, worldly people sense the change and are drawn willingly to God among us. God's glory alone is what makes us compelling.

Isaiah can see masses of people from all over the world migrating into the church, the whole world on pilgrimage to honor the church.

> Lift up your eyes all around, and see;
>   they all gather together, they come to you;
> your sons shall come from afar,
>   and your daughters shall be carried on the hip.
> Then you shall see and be radiant;
>   your heart shall thrill and exult,
> because the abundance of the sea shall be turned to you,
>   the wealth of the nations shall come to you. (Isaiah 60:4, 5)

God has not revealed himself in many religions, but through Christ alone. Isaiah sees the implications of that. It means there is only one culture of salvation in the world, the Christian church. He isn't saying that Christians will be the bosses and everyone else the slaves. That way of thinking belongs to this present evil age. He is saying that the glory of Christ will reunite the human race. The church will no longer be persecuted. The world will no longer be aggressive and hostile. The church will be the lead culture of the world. No more false inferiority or superiority. We'll be at our best in Christ, the world will hurry to be a part of it, and they will not come empty-handed.

> They shall bring gold and frankincense,
>   and shall bring good news, the praises of the LORD.
> All the flocks of Kedar shall be gathered to you;
>   the rams of Nebaioth shall minister to you;
> they shall come up with acceptance on my altar,
>   and I will beautify my beautiful house. (vv. 6b, 7)

The good news of the gospel will go out from the church and will echo back from the nations: "They . . . shall bring good news, the praises of the LORD." And the worship of the nations will be acceptable to God because it will be offered on his altar, the cross. The nations will be true to themselves in all their fascinating human variation, and through the sacrifice of Christ their worship will beautify the house of God.

> Your gates shall be open continually;
>   day and night they shall not be shut,
> that people may bring to you the wealth of the nations,
>   with their kings led in procession.
> For the nation and kingdom
>   that will not serve you will perish;
>   those nations shall be utterly laid waste.
> The glory of Lebanon shall come to you,
>   the cypress, the plane, and the pine,
> to beautify the place of my sanctuary,
>   and I will make the place of my feet glorious. (vv. 11–13)

The best explanation of this is in the New Testament. The Apostle John writes of the New Jerusalem at the end of time, "The kings of the earth will bring their glory into it, and its gates shall never be shut by day—and there will be no night there. They will bring into it the glory and the honor of the nations. But nothing unclean will ever enter it" (Revelation 21:24b–27a). The glory and honor of the nations will be brought into the holy city— human literature and music and dress and all aspects of culture, but purified and consecrated to Christ, flowing into the church, enriching everyone and beautifying the place of God's presence. Can you picture it? Here comes a string quartet from Vienna playing Mozart, here comes a steel drum band from the Caribbean, here comes a pipe band from Scotland in their kilts, here comes a teenage garage band from 1960s California, and all the rest. No one is excluded—except those who are too good for Christ and his church.

God said to Abraham, "I will bless those who bless you, and him who dishonors you I will curse" (Genesis 12:3). How could it be otherwise? The church is the one place of human association where God's mercy is experienced. Because of the cross he says to us, "In my wrath I struck you, but in my favor I have had mercy on you" (Isaiah 60:10). Every faithful church is a gateway into the future of the world. It doesn't seem that way at times. In *The Screwtape Letters*, a senior devil tells a junior devil how to deceive a young Christian.

> One of our great allies at present is the Church itself. Do not misunderstand me. I do not mean the Church as we see her spread out through all time and space and rooted in eternity, terrible as an army with banners. That, I confess, is a spectacle which makes our boldest tempters uneasy. But fortunately it is quite invisible to these humans. All your patient sees

is the half-finished, sham Gothic erection on the new building estate. When he goes inside, he sees the local grocer with rather an oily expression on his face. . . . When he gets to his pew and looks round him he sees just that selection of his neighbors whom he has hitherto avoided. You want to lean pretty heavily on those neighbors. Make his mind flit to and fro between an expression like "the body of Christ" and the actual faces in the next pew. . . . Provided that any of those neighbors sing out of tune or have boots that squeak or double chins or odd clothes, the patient will quite easily believe that their religion must therefore be somehow ridiculous.[6]

Don't be fooled by human ordinariness. God *chose* the most unlikely people for greatness, to magnify his own greatness (1 Corinthians 1:26–29). And he will make all his people great:

> Instead of bronze I will bring gold,
>   and instead of iron I will bring silver;
> instead of wood, bronze;
>   instead of stones, iron. (Isaiah 60:17)

When Christ reigns, everything gets better! He will come to Zion with a plan of urban renewal, as it were, with vast upgrades and state-of-the-art technology and materials, nothing second-rate. Despite every foolish trade we made, squandering what's worth keeping and reaching out for what's cheap, Jesus will give back to us everything that is *best*. Does this mean that we'll live in a city made of metal or, as the last book of the Bible describes it, jewels and pearls and gold (Revelation 21:19–21)? Leave that interpretation to children. Isaiah is inviting us to luxuriate in the wonder that Christ is able to do far more abundantly than all we can ask or think.

The striking thing about verses 15–22 in Isaiah 60 is their finality. Isaiah uses words like "forever" (vv. 15, 21), "from age to age" (v. 15), "no more" (vv. 18, 19, 20), and "everlasting" (vv. 19, 20). Our transformation by God's Word and Spirit will *last*:

> The LORD will be your everlasting light,
>   and your days of mourning shall be ended.
> Your people shall all be righteous;
>   they shall possess the land forever,
> the branch of my planting, the work of my hands,
>   that I might be glorified. . . .
> I am the LORD;
>   in its time I will hasten it. (vv. 20b, 21, 22b)

God stakes his reputation on his promise. He will keep it when the right time comes. He won't need favorable circumstances. He'll come suddenly to change the subject all over the world from our depressing false salvations to Christ as our only Savior, as the final, endless chapter of the human drama.

If this is true, and it is, what are the implications? We've traveled through time. We've seen the future. Now we're back in our world of today. What are the implications of what we've just seen? The Bible says of Abraham that "no unbelief made him waver concerning the promise of God, but he grew strong in his faith as he gave glory to God, fully convinced that God was able to do what he had promised. That is why his faith was 'counted to him as righteousness'" (Romans 4:20–22). The gospel is God drawing back the veil, revealing his strong promises, and saying to us, "Arise, shine, for your light has come." Do not cower in fear, as if the future held nothing for you but death. Believe the gospel. Swallow it whole. You will grow strong as you give glory to God, and your revival will begin even now. "And though this world, with devils filled, should threaten to undo us, we will not fear, for God hath willed his truth to triumph through us. . . . Let goods and kindred go, this mortal life also; the body they may kill; God's truth abideth still; his kingdom is forever."

44

Revival, Preaching, and Prayer

ISAIAH 61:1—62:7

THE FLAVOR OF CHRISTIANITY IS JOY. God's message to the world was distilled into one essential drop by the angel at the birth of Jesus: "I bring you good news of a great joy that will be for all the people" (Luke 2:10).

That's significant, because life stinks. As a teenager, I could pretty much get by on the latest hits from The Beach Boys, Junior Walker and the All-Stars, and The Who. But of course, that just isn't enough happiness to last. Then we face a choice: either go deep into narcotic amusements, or go deep with God. What God offers is "good news of a great joy" for everyone. In this world, that's huge. When real people living real lives in this world demonstrate joy, it's living proof that God saves sinners. Martyn Lloyd-Jones explains the prophetic power of a joyful church:

> As we face the modern world with all its trouble and turmoil and with all its difficulties and sadness, nothing is more important than that we who call ourselves Christian, and who claim the Name of Christ, should be representing our faith in such a way before others as to give them the impression that here is the solution, and here is the answer. In a world where everything has gone so sadly astray, we should be standing out as men and women apart, people characterized by a fundamental joy and certainty in spite of conditions, in spite of adversity.[1]

One of the marks of the early Christians was their joy in God as they lived in a hard world. According to one archaeologist, the apartment buildings of ancient Rome were so shoddily built that "the city was constantly filled with the noise of buildings collapsing or being torn down to prevent it; and the tenants of an [apartment] lived in constant expectation of its coming down on their heads."[2] That was the setting in which the Roman Christians raised their families. The classical world was not all gleaming marble and flowing white togas and sumptuous banquets. It was messy. The streets of Rome were deepest darkness after nightfall. There was no medical care as we know it, no inoculations for children, no retirement benefits, no air-conditioning, no refrigeration. But the early Christians, living in that world, stood out because God gave them a gift from beyond that world. Overflowing acceptance through the cross, God's presence in their hearts, practical wisdom for daily life, and endless enjoyment of him in heaven—isn't that enough to make people happy? They thought so.

Just telling people to be happy won't work. That's annoying. But the gospel doesn't do that. It gives us a hope *beyond* everything that beats us down. The Apostle Peter called it "joy . . . inexpressible and filled with glory" (1 Peter 1:8). That is Christ's gift to the world today. His mission is to bring good news to the poor and to bind up the brokenhearted and to proclaim liberty to the captives and to comfort all who mourn and anoint them with gladness, so that the Lord may be glorified. And he has made us partners with him in that mission.

Isaiah loops two times through the basic understandings that enable us to join the Messiah in his world-renewing mission:

A[1] The Anointed One: his liberating mission (61:1–3)
   B[1] A priestly people: shame replaced with honor (61:4–7)
      C[1] The Lord's commitment: an everlasting covenant (61:8, 9)
A[2] The Anointed One: his saving power (61:10, 11)
   B[2] A prophetic voice: desolation replaced with delight (62:1–5)
      C[2] The Lord's strategy: tireless intercessors (62:6, 7)

Isaiah wants to inspire in us such admiration for our Messiah that we gladly exert ourselves for his cause in our generation.

The Anointed One: His Liberating Mission

The Spirit of the Lord GOD is upon me,
   because the LORD Has anointed me
to bring good news to the poor;
   he has sent me to bind up the brokenhearted,
to proclaim liberty to the captives,
   and the opening of the prison to those who are bound;
to proclaim the year of the LORD's favor,

and the day of vengeance of our God;
  to comfort all who mourn;
to grant to those who mourn in Zion—
  to give them a beautiful headdress instead of ashes,
the oil of gladness instead of mourning,
  the garment of praise instead of a faint spirit;
that they may be called oaks of righteousness,
  the planting of the LORD, that he may be glorified. (Isaiah 61:1–3)

These three verses are all one long sentence, because Jesus was given the greatest anointing of the Spirit in the history of the human race for one reason: to bring good news to the poor. Jesus himself defined his mission this way: "God did not send his Son into the world to condemn the world, but in order that the world might be saved through him" (John 3:17). Here in Isaiah our Messiah announces with seven infinitives all that it means for him to save us.

He defines his ministry as helping people in trouble, people in bondage, people whose hearts are broken. Whose heart hasn't been broken? And is there any devastation like feeling forsaken by God? But Jesus came with a message different from what our emotions tell us. Our emotions tell us that God is against us, we've exhausted our possibilities, life is a waste, so why not just settle into mediocrity and make the best of it? We live in an age of despair. But it's a smiling despair, softened by consumer convenience, driving through for a "happy meal" along the way. Into our age Jesus says, "I came to bear your guilty despair far away, and to replace it with joy inexpressible and filled with glory." He does it single-handedly. He has the Spirit. He has the Word. That's all he needs to remake the whole world, beginning with you and me.

How does he do it? By *preaching*: "The LORD has anointed me *to bring good news* to the poor . . . to *proclaim* liberty to the captives." The NIV translates this, "to *preach* good news." What is the good news? The gospel announces that Christ has won the victory over everything that's against us. If you've committed what you think is the unpardonable sin, if you're broken by your failures, if you fear that your chance at life is over—Jesus announces to you a life so new that, if you understand what he's saying, you'll have difficulty believing it can be yours.

Back in the Old Testament, God was already hinting at this. He established an institution called the Year of Jubilee (Leviticus 25:8–55). Every fiftieth year Israel was to take the whole year off, cancel all debts, return to its original owners all family property that had been sold, and generally be kind and generous to everyone. "Proclaim liberty throughout the land" (Leviticus 25:10)—that was everyone's job for a whole year. It foreshadowed the liberation of Christ (Galatians 5:1). Isaiah is saying that the

Messiah brings that liberation to its fullest realization through the gospel. The cross cancels all our debts. God says we're free to leave the past behind and move on with joyful relief. That is the mission of Jesus into your life. Will you welcome him?

Jesus identified with this passage so closely that he launched his ministry by reading it in a synagogue service in Nazareth (Luke 4:16–21). After he read these verses, he looked around and said, "Today this Scripture has been fulfilled in your hearing." History in the making! All the tangles of sin complicating our lives since the fall of Adam, Jesus at that moment began to loosen. And he continues to free people today through the preaching of the gospel. Every Christian preacher today should be able to say, "The Spirit of the Lord GOD is upon me." And when that is so, then Isaiah 61 is being fulfilled in *your* hearing.

But there's a problem in this passage, or at least a question. Why does Messiah say, "to proclaim the year of the LORD's favor, *and the day of vengeance of our God*"? The year of the Lord's favor is the Jubilee of gospel freedom. We're living in that era now. When I drive north on Franklin Pike and I come over the crest of the hill where suddenly spread before me is the skyline of Nashville, I may by faith see Jesus Christ lovingly spreading his hands out to my city, offering his favor. The Bible says, "Behold, now is the favorable time; behold, now is the day of salvation" (2 Corinthians 6:2b). But what is "the day of vengeance of our God"? When Jesus read this passage at that service in Nazareth, he didn't read these words. He stopped reading at the end of the first line of verse 2. He omitted any reference to the day of the vengeance of our God. Why? Doesn't he fulfill all three verses?

Christ fulfills all the prophecies, but not all at the same time. At his first coming, he inaugurated the year of the Lord's favor. At his second coming, he'll bring in the day of the vengeance of our God, when the door of grace will shut forever. There's a gap in time between the first line of verse 2 and the second line of verse 2, and we're living right now in that interval. It's as if Isaiah looks into the future and sees two mountain peaks far away, one beyond the other. But he can't see how much distance there is between them. So we don't know how long we have. But as long as this season of favor lasts, the Messiah continues to use the preaching of the gospel to take away the ashes of mourning that our dark thoughts heap on our heads and to pour upon us the oil of gladness.

What is the net impact? Does his spreading joy have a morally weakening influence? Verse 3 says, ". . . that they may be called oaks of righteousness." The gospel builds strong Christians—"the planting of the LORD." And his ultimate purpose in it all is "that the Lord may be glorified." This is the mission of Jesus Christ into the world. And he wants us to join him in it.

A Priestly People: Shame Replaced with Honor

They shall build up the ancient ruins;
> they shall raise up the former devastations;
they shall repair the ruined cities,
> the devastations of many generations. (Isaiah 61:4)

Long-standing ruins in our personalities, in our homes, in our world—
God promises to give back everything sin has ruined. And he does it through
us. The mourners of verse 3 become the repair experts of verse 4. Isaiah
uses the language of rebuilding because the Jewish people literally rebuilt
the ruins of Jerusalem after the exile. But that was only a token of a deeper
restoration for us all.

We need this. We have "the devastations of many generations" in
Northern Ireland, in the Middle East, in our homes. That's what sin does.
Sin creates victims, who feel entitled to retaliate, which creates more sin
and more victims who feel entitled to retaliate, which creates more sin and
more victims. . . . Isn't it interesting that in the many wars of history no
one ever stands up and says, "Hey, everybody, I'm firing the first shot. I'm
picking this fight. This war is all my fault"? Every war is a counterstrike;
all shots are return fire, redressing a wrong.[3] Is that convincing? There
are just wars. But where grievances are concerned, every one of us has a
long memory and a short fuse. Every person, every home, every culture
has ancient ruins creating more ruins. And who has ever stopped it? Bob
Dylan sings:

Broken bottles, broken plates, broken switches, broken gates,
Broken dishes, broken parts, streets are filled with broken hearts.
Broken words never meant to be spoken, everything is broken.[4]

Ever since Adam fell, sin has been spreading a culture of death. We'll
never understand ourselves and our surroundings without that background.
This world is not normal. We are not normal. Everything is broken. So
here's a radical proposal: *We need a Savior*. And the only person in the
history of the human race who qualifies is Jesus Christ. He came to re-
create for us a culture of life. And Isaiah's point in verse 4 is that gospel-
liberated people themselves become a creative force for restoration. That's
our mission. God says, in verses 5, 6, that this mission is heroic and will
be perceived as heroic and, in verse 7, that this mission is joyful with a joy
that will last forever. The mission of Jesus and his church will be rebuilding
ruins when every noble human salvation is falling into ruins. Why can we
be confident of that?

The Lord's Commitment: An Everlasting Covenant

> For I the LORD love justice;
>   I hate robbery and wrong;
> I will faithfully give them their recompense,
>   and I will make an everlasting covenant with them.
> Their offspring shall be known among the nations,
>   and their descendants in the midst of the peoples;
> all who see them shall acknowledge them,
>   that they are an offspring the LORD has blessed. (Isaiah 61:8, 9)

God commits himself to us. Remember that the word "justice" means more than legal rectitude; it means the way human life and human society are supposed to be. God *loves* patterns of human wholeness. He loves to see his kingdom coming and his will being done on earth as it is done in Heaven. And he *hates* the "robbery and wrong" of the world as it is today, distorting what he meant us to be. This is who God is: He loves what is right and he hates what is wrong with all the intensity of the divine being. It's unthinkable that God would fail to keep his covenant. Invest yourself in the new world God is building. You can risk it. You can seek first his kingdom and righteousness above your own kingdom, because he isn't just recruiting you; he's promising to bless you.

The Anointed One: His Saving Power

> I will greatly rejoice in the LORD;
>   my soul shall exult in my God,
> for he has clothed me with the garments of salvation;
>   he has covered me with the robe of righteousness,
> as a bridegroom decks himself like a priest with a beautiful headdress,
>   and as a bride adorns herself with her jewels.
> For as the earth brings forth its sprouts,
>   and as a garden causes what is sown in it to sprout up,
> so the Lord GOD will cause righteousness and praise
>   to sprout up before all the nations. (Isaiah 61:10, 11)

Messiah is speaking here. He is delighting in God's strategy for world renewal. It's true that Jesus was "a man of sorrows" (Isaiah 53:3). But not anymore. Now he's greatly rejoicing. God has clothed him with the garments of salvation and covered him with the robe of righteousness. What does that mean? Back in 59:17 God clothed himself with righteousness and salvation. In other words, God asserted himself and displayed himself on behalf of righteousness and salvation in this world. But here we find that he exerts that resolve through the Messiah. In other words, God saves us *through Christ*.

Isaiah sees our Messiah *enjoying* saving us. His influence has all the joy of a wedding celebration, all the fruitfulness of a garden sprouting with new life. He's been doing this for 2,000 years, and he's only begun. Through Jesus Christ, God launched into this sad world an outpouring of joy that will leave the nations in awe. And on this very day in history, at this moment, Jesus is on the move, doing God's saving will all over the world with joyful enthusiasm. Isn't that a cause big enough and bright enough to compel our allegiance?

A Prophetic Voice: Desolation Replaced with Delight

> For Zion's sake I will not keep silent,
>   and for Jerusalem's sake I will not be quiet,
> until her righteousness goes forth as brightness,
>   and her salvation as a burning torch.
> The nations shall see your righteousness,
>   and all the kings your glory,
> and you shall be called by a new name
>   that the mouth of the LORD will give.
> You shall be a crown of beauty in the hand of the LORD,
>   and a royal diadem in the hand of your God.
> You shall no more be termed Forsaken,
>   and your land shall no more be termed Desolate,
> but you shall be called My Delight Is In Her,
>   and your land Married;
> for the LORD delights in you,
>   and your land shall be married. (Isaiah 62:1–4)

Here is the meaning of human history. God intends to prove, through Christ, how much he can love and bless ruined human beings. And his love is of the nature of delight. The Jewish people long ago thought they were forsaken. Sometimes we do too. But God comes and changes the subject. The gospel announces that, if you are in Christ, God *delights* in you. His love must be described with that kind of emotional language. God says, "I even have a pet name for you now—Hephzibah ('My delight is in her'). You're no longer defined by your past. I redefine you with a new name of my own choosing. I am rewriting your future, and nothing can change it."

In the gospel God looks us right in the eye and levels with us. This is what he says: "I will never leave you nor forsake you" (Hebrews 13:5). A New Testament scholar unpacks the unusual force of that statement: "Never,

never, never, in any circumstance whatsoever, God will not fail."[5] And the love of God that will never fail is a passionate gladness. It becomes our high-octane joy in revival, and Isaiah devotes his life to promoting it. "For Zion's sake I will not keep silent."

Isaiah 62:1 is a neglected Biblical emphasis today. The prophet is deeply moved. Something grips him. What is it? Zion, the city of God, the church, is reduced to contempt. Salvation is not going forth from her like a burning torch. The nations see nothing of God in the human landscape. Isaiah's heart is broken for God's people in his generation. When salvation is not going forth as a burning torch, God is saying, "Your life passion should be defined with these three words: *for Zion's sake*. When they lay you in your grave, this should be the epitaph on your gravestone: 'For Zion's sake.' That should be the statement your life makes, because I have appointed my church as the human delivery system for joy inexpressible overflowing onto a dying world. That's my plan, *and there is no Plan B*."

Over the last thirty years or so we American Christians have diminished our very capacity for revival, and we're laying a foundation of sand for the future. We've jury-rigged our own hybrid version of Christianity that doesn't even think in terms of the loyalty inherent in the words "for Zion's sake." So many Christians today are living a conveniently free-floating way of life, it doesn't *feel* misaligned. It feels normal, and costly involvement feels like a super-spiritual option. But to God, church-hopping, self-protecting, me-first-Christianity isn't even recognizable. "For Zion's sake" defines a way of life that works and prays and tithes and gets involved. Church membership vows could be summarized with these three words: "for Zion's sake." But our generation is disinclined to that kind of gutsy intentionality.

What's happening to us? We're being changed not by the gospel but by a hyper-individualistic ethos of devotion to self. Complicating that is the fact that many people have been wounded by the church. Personally, the worst experiences of my life have been within the church. Why go back in? Because of God. God has made an everlasting covenant with his church, and her salvation *will* go forth like a burning torch. That's the future of the world.

Isaiah has been showing us in his prophetic crystal ball a future day when the nations will run toward Christ through his church. Maybe you need to embrace Christ by re-embracing his church. If your relationship with your church is ambiguous and sporadic and subject to convenience, the problem is not your relationship with your church. The problem is your relationship with Christ. He has made his loyalty clear. He even delights in his church. He is committed to the revival of the world through the revival of the church. To God, the most important thing in all of created reality is his church, a crown of beauty in his hand. Your own greatest happiness is the revival of your church. Are you praying for your church? Are you praying for the outpouring of the Holy Spirit? Or will God have to wait to find people who will share the burden of his heart? About 200 years ago Timothy Dwight, president of Yale and a leader in the Second Great Awakening, wrote these words:

> I love thy church, O God; her walls before thee stand
> Dear as the apple of thine eye and graven on thy hand.
> For her my tears shall fall, for her my prayers ascend,
> To her my cares and toils be given, till toils and cares shall end.[6]

He wasn't saying, "I'll spend all my time in committee meetings down at church." He wasn't saying, "I'll isolate myself socially within my church subculture." He was saying, "I will partner with my church for the renewal of the world, to the glory of God." Paul wrote, "We are workers with you for your joy" (2 Corinthians 1:24, NASB). Real joy takes *work*. In the nineteenth century Charlotte Elliott wrote these lyrics:

> Christian, seek not yet repose,
> Cast your dreams of ease away;
> You are in the midst of foes—
> Watch and pray.[7]

Why don't we write lyrics like that today? Do we understand something they didn't back then? Or is it we who have forgotten something? Maybe this is how our generation would rewrite those lines:

> Christian, seek an early retirement,
> Cast your burdens far away;
> You are on the eighteenth green—
> Putt and pray.

Why do we laugh? Why don't we weep? If God were to pour out his power upon us, would we use it for Zion's sake? Or would we use it to reinforce patterns of religious selfishness that know nothing of his cross? Maybe our first step toward revival is recommitment to our own membership vows. God has made a vow, and he's calling us to join him in his resolve.

The Lord's Strategy: Tireless Intercessors

> On your walls, O Jerusalem,
>   I have set watchmen;

> all the day and all the night
>   they shall never be silent.
> You who put the LORD in remembrance,
>   take no rest,
> and give him no rest
>   until he establishes Jerusalem
>   and makes it a praise in the earth. (Isaiah 62:6, 7)

We are the "watchmen," like sentries on the city wall, keeping our eyes peeled for what God is doing in the world today. We encourage one another about these momentous events. We also speak to God. In fact, with language I wouldn't have dared to use, our prayers are to *give God no rest* until a revived church astonishes the world.

Jonathan Edwards wrote a famous appeal to the Christians of his day to unite in prayer for revival. At the end of his appeal he wrote this:

> It is very apparent from the Word of God that he often tries the faith and patience of his people, when they are crying to him for some great and important mercy, by withholding the mercy sought for a season; and not only so, but at first he may cause an increase of dark appearances. And yet he, without fail, at last prospers those who continue urgently in prayer with all perseverance and "will not let him go except he blesses."[8]

Otto Kristian Hallesby was a Norwegian theologian who resisted the Nazis during World War II and suffered for it in a concentration camp. He understood what it means to pray all the way through until God answers. He said that prayer is like mining. Prayer is like boring holes deep into the rock of human hearts. It's work. It tries our patience. We can't see results. But in God's time, he places the dynamite and lights the fuse, and the rocks crumble. God has called us to give him no rest until he makes a revived church the praise of the earth.[9]

God is, as it were, overcome by prayer. Jacob wrestled with God, and God said to him, "You have striven with God and men, and have prevailed" (Genesis 32:28). Jesus compared prayer to a man pounding on his neighbor's door late at night until, "because of his impudence," the neighbor gets up and helps him (Luke 11:8). The Apostle James says that the prayer of a righteous person "has great power as it is working" (James 5:16). And God has positioned you and me in this generation to pray down his power upon the ministry of the gospel and not quit until the whole world is praising God.

Bill Bright, founder of Campus Crusade for Christ, recently died. Here are excerpts from a *Christianity Today* interview with him several years before his death:

CT: What is your condition?

Bright: I've lost 60 percent of my lung capacity and it keeps going down. One day I'll breathe my last, which is fine. I can say I've lived a pretty exciting life. But since it was announced to me that there is no cure for the disease, I've entered into a different relationship and a more wonderful intimacy with the Lord. James says to rejoice when you're having difficulties. Paul speaks of rejoicing when you suffer. I know the reality of what they were saying. . . .

CT: Your health is declining.

Bright: But my spirit is soaring.

CT: Do you feel you have completed the mission for which you were put on earth?

Bright: [God] doesn't need Bill Bright any more than he needs a twig on a tree. He created us in his image, and he loves us . . . but he can raise up sticks and stones to worship him. So, it's not as though my departure is going to leave a big hole. . . .

CT: What would be your parting words to believers?

Bright: . . . Jesus said, "Come unto me, all you who are weary, and I will give you rest. Peace I leave with you." So my word to believers would be: Let us awaken out of our Laodicean spirit and return to our first love, as the church at Ephesus was admonished to do. And let us share this most joyful news with everybody on the planet.[10]

45

Revival and the Wrath
of the Lamb

ISAIAH 62:8—63:14

ISAIAH STARTLES US WITH THE COMPLEXITY OF GOD. He structures this passage around three main points. First, God assures us that he's preparing a place for us so great we'll never want to leave (62:8–12). Thirdly, God reminds us of his steadfast love throughout our history—and in spite of us too (63:7–14). But between those two statements God reveals the triumphant anger of Christ, the bloodied victor in a war of vengeance against human evil (63:1–6). Future promise, past faithfulness, bloody vengeance, all in one passage. Why? Because God is not a simplistic person. He is complex. And his complexity is the hope of the world.

Isaiah invites us to look at the grandeur of God. His text is a Biblical Grand Canyon. We step up to the edge, we take a long, thoughtful look, and we see more of God than we've ever seen before. That's helpful. How so? We look at the world today, we see the brutality, the sufferings, the insecurity of our own lives, and we wonder, "God, are you asleep? Why don't you do something about all this? You have the power. Why don't you *act*?" That's the way we think, looking at our surroundings. But when we look beyond this world and enlarge our vision of God and accept him for all that he is, our frustrations melt, and we are strengthened to face anything. We need the perspective of Mr. and Mrs. Beaver. Remember them, in *The Lion, The Witch and the Wardrobe* by C. S. Lewis?

> "Is—is he a man?" asked Lucy.
> "Aslan a man!" said Mr. Beaver sternly. . . . "Aslan is a lion—*the* Lion, the great Lion."

"Is he—quite safe? I shall feel rather nervous about meeting a lion."

"That you will, dearie, and no mistake," said Mrs. Beaver, "if there's any who can appear before Aslan without their knees knocking, they're either braver than most or else just silly."

"Then he isn't safe?" said Lucy.

"Safe?" said Mr. Beaver. "Don't you hear what Mrs. Beaver tells you? Who said anything about safe? 'Course he isn't safe. But he's good. He's the King, I tell you."[1]

Christ is not safe, but he's good. If we'll trust him enough to accept him rather than squeeze him into the mold of our own demanding preconceptions—when we open up with that kind of trust, we've prepared the way of the Lord (Isaiah 40:3). We are revival-ready.

In this passage Isaiah oscillates—he doesn't vacillate, he oscillates—between the kindness and the severity of God.

A¹ The Lord's future promise: securing a holy city (62:8–12)
    1. His word reassuring us (62:8, 9)
    2. His openness welcoming us (62:10–12)
  B The disturbing vision: a victorious warrior (63:1–6)
    1. Who is this? (63:1)
    2. Why is his apparel red? (63:2–6)
A² The Lord's past record: loving a backward people (63:7–14)
    1. His goodness carrying us (63:7–9)
    2. His Spirit leading us (63:10–14)

This passage answers the prayer of our hearts when we sing "Be Thou My Vision." Without a vision of Christ before us, we're overwhelmed. Without a clear view of Christ in his glory, all we can see is the world around us, and we're thrown back on the defensive. We feel threatened. We then become aggressive and complicate our problems still further. But with Christ himself clearly before us, when his glory weighs upon us as it should, we know what to fear and what not to fear.

The Lord's Future Promise

The LORD has sworn by his right hand
    and by his mighty arm:
"I will not again give your grain
    to be food for your enemies,
and foreigners shall not drink your wine
    for which you have labored;
but those who garner it shall eat it

and praise the LorD,
and those who gather it shall drink it
   in the courts of my sanctuary." (Isaiah 62:8, 9)

God has two ways to relate to people, with two different sets of ground rules—the Old Covenant and the New Covenant. The Old Covenant says, "Do the right thing, and I will bless you. You will live. Fail to do the right thing, and I will curse you" (Deuteronomy 27—28). The New Covenant says, "You have failed. You've broken my law, and by now you're way beyond your capacity for self-correction. But I save sinners. I've done everything for you through my grace in Christ. Enter into him by the merest faith, and you will live."

The subtlety is that the Old Covenant/New Covenant distinction is both historical and existential. In other words, God established an Old Covenant relationship with Israel in Biblical times. But even back then God led believers into personal New Covenant freedom. And each of us today struggles through Old Covenant frustration into New Covenant rest as we come to the end of ourselves and trust in Christ to do for us what we can't do for ourselves. Each of us re-lives the ancient story, personally and spiritually.[2]

If you're angry with God because he seems so far away, understand why. You're in Old Covenant thinking. Our natural moral calculations always overestimate what we've done and what we deserve and underrate what God has done. This is why the Old Covenant is an unworkable arrangement. Our deepest beings are too infested with hostility toward God for merit-based pay to work. We fail God more than we know. Then we blame him and get bitter and small and hateful. If that's where you are with God right now, hang on. Trust him as much as you can, and let him lead you forward. He has something better for you. According to his New Covenant arrangements, everything he demands he also provides, freely and forever, through the finished work of Christ on the cross. You need to believe that.

In this passage God promises that Old Covenant defeat is not his last word to his people. When his New Covenant purposes are fulfilled, they will eat and drink and do everything for the glory of God (1 Corinthians 10:31). "Foreigners shall not drink your wine . . . those who gather it shall drink it in the courts of my sanctuary." That's Biblical code language for life in its fullness, never again to be disturbed, in the presence of God. That's where he's taking his people. In fact, it's what he's offering the nations:

Go through, go through the gates;
   prepare the way for the people;
build up, build up the highway;
   clear it of stones;

lift up a signal over the peoples.
Behold, the LORD has proclaimed
    to the end of the earth:
Say to the daughter of Zion,
    "Behold, your salvation comes;
behold, his reward is with him,
    and his recompense before him."
And they shall be called The Holy People,
    The Redeemed of the LORD;
and you shall be called Sought Out,
    A City Not Forsaken. (Isaiah 62:10–12)

What does Isaiah see in his mind's eye? A walled city, formerly desolate and forsaken but now repopulated with redeemed people, the gates of the city open, a newly resurfaced highway leading from the ends of the earth into this city, and the nations invited to come enjoy the victory of God with his people. It's a picture of the future, when the church and the world will become one. God proclaims to the end of the earth a coming salvation. All who welcome the call are made "The Holy People" by the grace of Christ. They will enter the New Jerusalem, redeemed out of the wreckage of every failed human culture, to the eternal glory of God.

The final victory of grace isn't Isaiah's wishful thinking. These imperative verbs and these future tense promises are a prophetic way of saying, "This is *God's* will. Christ is preparing a place for us. And the way in has been made easy, like a built-up highway, so that anyone who desires Christ may enter in." Every living church today is an entry-point into the eternal city. And we don't want to complicate God's will. Our gates, as it were, are wide-open. The only obstacle to living in the fullness of Christ forever is Christ. How could it be otherwise? If he isn't what you want, then Heaven isn't what you want, because Heaven is Christ. But the way in is open. Not even our sins can keep us out. Christ is the way, Christ is the reward, and Christ is the barrier. If you can accept him, you're in. And across your life, along with all others in the New Covenant community, the hand of God will write these words: "Holy," "Redeemed," "Sought Out," "Not Forsaken."

The Disturbing Vision

Who is this that comes from Edom,
    in crimsoned garments from Bozrah,
he who is splendid in his apparel,
    marching in the greatness of his strength?
"It is I, speaking in righteousness,
    mighty to save."

Why is your apparel red,
    and your garments like his who treads in the winepress?
"I have trodden the winepress alone,
    and from the peoples no one was with me;
I trod them in my anger
    and trampled them in my wrath;
their lifeblood spattered on my garments,
    and stained all my apparel.
For the day of vengeance was in my heart,
    and my year of redemption had come.
I looked, but there was no one to help;
    I was appalled, but there was no one to uphold;
so my own arm brought me salvation,
    and my wrath upheld me.
I trampled down the peoples in my anger;
    I made them drunk in my wrath,
    and I poured out their lifeblood on the earth." (Isaiah 63:1–6)

This is a solemn passage. Let's think it through with two questions. First, what are Edom and Bozrah? Edom was a nation south of Israel, and Bozrah was their capital city. Edom was a long-standing enemy of God's people, going all the way back to the personal rivalry between Jacob and Esau, the founder of Edom (Genesis 25:30; 27:41). Edom hated Israel so bitterly that, in the prophetic worldview, that nation became more than a nation. It became the epitome of malice toward God and his people. In other words, "Edom" represents the human being at its worst—despising God, finding itself in earthly joys, and persecuting God's people because of their loyalty to a higher world.

Augustine saw the human race divided into the city of God and the city of man. The city of God is everyone who loves God, even to the extent of contempt toward self. The city of man is everyone who loves self, even to the extent of contempt toward God.[3] Each one of us lives in one city or the other. And our true loyalty stands out in the way we treat God's people. Bob Dylan sang about this:

Go ahead and talk about him because he makes you doubt,
Because he has denied himself the things you can't live without.
Laugh at him behind his back just like the others do,
Remind him of what he used to be, when he comes walkin' through.

Stop your conversation when he passes on the street,
Hope he falls upon himself, oh, won't that be sweet
Because he can't be exploited by superstition anymore
Because he can't be bribed or bought by the things that you adore.

When the whip that's keeping you in line doesn't make him jump,
Say he's hard-of-hearin', say that he's a chump,
Say he's out of step with reality as you try to test his nerve
Because he doesn't pay tribute to the king that you serve.

He's the property of Jesus
Resent him to the bone
You got something better,
You've got a heart of stone[4]

That's Edom against the people of God. Which side are you on?

Secondly, and this is Isaiah's own question, *who is this* coming from Edom, blood-spattered with the gore of the enemies he has slaughtered? The prophet is speaking as one of those watchmen on the wall (Isaiah 62:6). He's looking and longing for God to come and rescue us from the madness of this world, from the madness in our own hearts. Suddenly, out in the distance, from Edom, he sees someone coming. Who is this—friend or foe? Why is his clothing spattered red? Has he been treading grapes in a winepress? Has he been making wine? Could the explanation be that simple and reassuring? No. He's been taking vengeance on his enemies. He's been fighting for redemption. And he's done it alone—not with a great army, but all by himself. We didn't help him. We don't even see him until his victory is already complete. Look at him out there, the way he's approaching us, marching in the greatness of his strength. He's not even tired. He's energized, he's awesome, he is terrible in his wrath. *Who is this?*

This is a vision of Jesus Christ, the Savior. The Apostle John was given a similar vision:

> Then I saw heaven opened, and behold, a white horse! The one sitting on it is called Faithful and True, and in righteousness he judges and makes war. His eyes are like a flame of fire. . . . He is clothed in a robe dipped in blood. . . . From his mouth comes a sharp sword with which to strike down the nations, and he will rule them with a rod of iron. He will tread the winepress of the fury of the wrath of God the Almighty. On his robe and on his thigh he has a name written, King of kings and Lord of lords. (Revelation 19:11–16)

And elsewhere in the Revelation John watches this present age in its death throes: "Then the kings of the earth and the great ones and the generals and the rich and the powerful, and everyone, slave and free, hid themselves in the caves and among the rocks of the mountains, calling to the mountains and rocks, 'Fall on us and hide us from . . . the wrath of the Lamb'" (Revelation 6:15, 16).

Let's not fear the wrong things. God said to Isaiah, "Do not call conspiracy all that this people calls conspiracy, and do not fear what they fear, nor be in dread. But the LORD of hosts, him you shall regard as holy. Let him be your fear, and let him be your dread" (Isaiah 8:12, 13). God wants us to fear wisely. He wants to redirect our fears from passing human crises to the final divine crisis. He wants us to concern ourselves most urgently with this question: *Who is this?*

The answer is not simplistic. He is the Lamb. But he is also the Lion. Do you see the repeated anger-words in verses 3–6? Isaiah rolls out the vocabulary of "anger" and "wrath." Do you see the word "vengeance" in verse 4? Jesus Christ is not safe. But he is good. Don't try to get him to fight for your side, whatever it may be. He has his own cause to fight for. His "year of redemption" has come. He's out to rid the whole world of every last particle of human evil. You and I had better be on his side. And we can be. He wants us to be. He is "mighty to save" (v. 1), and he wants to be mighty for you and me. But we must seek first his kingdom and righteousness.

There are two things everyone must understand about the wrath of the Lamb. One: if *the Lamb* is angry with you, there can be only one reason. You deserve it. The Lamb of God is "gentle and lowly in heart" (Matthew 11:29). So if the Lamb is angry with you, it's only because you've rejected love and tenderness and redemption. A review of Tony Hendra's book, *Father Joe: The Man Who Saved My Soul*, starts out like this:

> Saints are perhaps always best evoked by sinners. And it would be hard to think of someone more at ease in the world of modern sin than Tony Hendra. He is and has been a brilliant satirist, an alum of National Lampoon in its glory days, an architect of the peerless parody rock documentary, "This is Spinal Tap," a man who has known (and tells us of) serial sex and drugs and rock and irony. But this extraordinary, luminescent, profound book shows us something wonderfully unexpected and deeply true. These ideas of sin that we have are not really sin. Or rather: they are the symptoms of sin, not its essence. And its essence is our withdrawal—our willful withdrawal—from God's love.[5]

The reason for the wrath of the Lamb, the essential sin that will spatter your blood on his robe at his second coming, is your rejection of his love. Let the Lamb love you.

Two: if you've suffered injustice from others and you're angry, let the Lamb fight for you. You can either churn inside and dream of sweet payback and plot your revenge and turn your soul into acid, or you can let the Lamb defend you—to the degree that you deserve defense. The gospel says, "Beloved, never avenge yourselves, but leave it to the wrath of God, for it is written, 'Vengeance is mine, I will repay, says the Lord.' To the contrary, 'if your enemy is hungry, feed him; if he is thirsty, give him something to drink.' . . . Do not be overcome by evil, but overcome evil with good" (Romans 12:19–21). Let the Lamb defend you.

To stabilize us as we wait for Christ to come with his final intervention, Isaiah invites us to look back at the faithful love of God thus far.

The Lord's Past Record

> I will recount the steadfast love of the LORD,
>   the praises of the LORD,
> according to all that the LORD has granted us,
>   and the great goodness to the house of Israel
> that he has granted them according to his compassion,
>   according to the abundance of his steadfast love. (Isaiah 63:7)

Isaiah heaps words upon words in an attempt to describe the love of God. He begins and ends this summary verse with God's "steadfast love." Why? Because the steadfast love of God surrounds us. And felt assurance in his love is the oxygen of our souls, keeping us alive, stabilizing us again and again, all the way.

The Bible says, "Keep yourselves in the love of God" (Jude 21). How? By going back and rethinking what he has done for us, as Isaiah does in verses 8, 9. God chose us. He became our Savior. He has shared in our afflictions. He has given us his presence. He has redeemed us and carried us every step of the way. The highest love is steadfast love for people who don't deserve it. That is God's love for his people. It's the meaning of our lives. It's the story of salvation coming down into our world.

Think of how the Christian church began, a little band of frightened people in an outpost of the Roman Empire, with all the powers of society against them. But God loved them. This is how one scholar helps us to see it:

> Within the space of *thirty years* after the death of Christ the gospel had been carried to all parts of the civilized and to no small portion of the uncivilized world. Its progress and its triumphs were not concealed. Its great transactions were not "done in a corner." It had been preached in the most splendid, powerful and enlightened cities; churches were already founded in Jerusalem, Antioch, Corinth, Ephesus, Philippi and at Rome. The gospel had spread in Arabia, Asia Minor, Greece, Macedon, Italy and Africa. It had assailed the most mighty existing institutions; it had made its way over the most formidable barriers; it had encountered the most deadly and malignant opposition; it had traveled to the capital and had secured such a hold even in the imperial city as to make it certain

that it would finally overturn the established religion and seat itself on the ruins of paganism. Within thirty years it had settled the point that it would overturn every bloody altar, close every pagan temple, bring under its influence everywhere the men of office, rank and power, and that "the banners of the faith would soon stream from the palaces of the Caesars." All this would be accomplished by the instrumentality of Jews—of fishermen—of Nazarenes. They had neither wealth, armies nor allies. With the exception of Paul, they were men without learning. They were taught only by the Holy Ghost, armed only with the power of God, victorious only because Christ was their captain, and the world acknowledged the presence of the messengers of the Highest and the power of the Christian religion. Its success never has been and never can be accounted for by any other supposition than that God attended it.[6]

It doesn't matter what forces and trends are against Christ today. Until he returns, he'll always have enemies. Count on it. Don't worry about it. What does change along the way is our responsiveness to his steadfast love. It isn't his enemies that disempower us. We do it to ourselves:

> But they rebelled
>   and grieved his Holy Spirit;
> therefore he turned to be their enemy,
>   and himself fought against them. (Isaiah 63:10)

It wasn't the Assyrians or Babylonians who defeated Israel long ago. They defeated themselves by saying no to God. They were thinking, *We're okay. We can handle this ourselves. We don't want* that much *of God. You know how he complicates things.* When they rebelled against God, things couldn't just go on as before. God is not mocked. When a child runs into the street right in front of a car, the dad pulls his child to safety angrily. If a neighbor rescues the child, he doesn't get angry. Only love cares enough to get angry and rebuke and discipline. So it is with God. If our lives grieve his Holy Spirit, he won't support our stupidity. The Bible says, "God *opposes* the proud" (James 4:6). When the church is knocked back on the defensive by surrounding social forces, the problem is not the church's relationship with those surrounding forces. The problem is the church's relationship with God. We need to be saved from ourselves, first and foremost. If we will embrace his steadfast love, he will show us what it means that our God is a Mighty Fortress.

Therefore, the question Isaiah asks twice in verse 11 is *the* question of every generation: "Where is he?" The important questions of life are always God questions. If you see yourself as you are—helpless, guilty, needing a great Ally—this becomes *the* question of your life. Where is he? Stop everything else until you find the answer to that question. Nothing else matters. Look beyond yourself. Look beyond your sins. Look beyond your fears. Where is *he*?

Where is he who led his people in order to make a glorious name for himself (Isaiah 63:14)? Other generations experienced him. Now it's our moment. Where is he in our experience? Like the prodigal son coming to his senses, when we go to our Father in honesty, admitting everything, right down to the details—and there is no true repentance in generalities but only in specifics—when we go to our Father with that kind of trust, while we're still a long way off—and every one of us is a long way off—while we're still a long way off, he sees us and runs to us and embraces us and kisses us. This is God. When we go into repentance, our experience of our complex God becomes simple—steadfast love through the blood of the Lamb.

46

Revival and the
Descent of God

ISAIAH 63:15—64:12

ISAIAH 64:1 IS AS GOOD A DESCRIPTION OF REVIVAL as we'll find: God comes down to us. That language is figurative. With God, there is no up or down. But figures of speech in the Bible always point to a literal reality. What is the reality behind Isaiah 64:1? The felt presence of God. Isaiah says "at your presence" three times in verses 1–3. And why God's *felt* presence? Because when God comes down, "the mountains . . . quake." God's presence is like a fire burning brushwood or causing water to boil, Isaiah says. Then he says, in effect, "What I'm talking about is God making his name known to his adversaries, so that the nations tremble before him" (v. 2b). He's talking about God intervening. He's talking about God shaking up this world and changing his enemies into his worshipers.

But Isaiah isn't just talking about this. He's *longing* for it. The most important word in the whole passage is the first word in 64:1: "Oh." The most important punctuation mark in the passage is the exclamation point at the end of that sentence (v. 2). Isaiah isn't theorizing. He's praying, and with passion. For Zion's sake he is not keeping silent, until her salvation goes forth as a burning torch. He is taking no rest and is giving God no rest until God's people are a "praise in the earth" (Isaiah 62:1, 7). He is gripped by a cause greater than himself. There is no greater joy for him than the descent of God to earth.

Isaiah is teaching us how to pray. We don't learn to pray by listening to one another. We learn to pray by reading the Bible. God wants us to pray with boldness and passion for the growth of his kingdom. Isn't that what the Lord's

Prayer emphasizes? Before we pray for our daily bread, we're taught to pray that God's kingdom will come (Matthew 6:9–13). God also invites us to make our requests about everything known to him (Philippians 4:6). If it matters to us, it matters to him (1 Peter 5:7). God invites us to tell him everything. He's listening. But how can we overlook the main thing God tells us to pray for— the power of his kingdom today? When we're passing around prayer requests in our small groups, is his cause the first thing we mention? Are we praying with God's priorities? Do we understand that all our own happiness is in the victory of God? Are we longing for the descent of God upon us at our church? What could be greater for you, for your family, for your city?

The structure of the text shows that Isaiah is not arguing a case in logical sequence. He's too deeply moved for that. His thoughts are a freely interwoven mixture of highs and lows.[1]

> A[1] Longing: the love of God (63:15, 16)
>   B[1] Lamentation: our hardened hearts (63:17–19)
> A[2] Longing: the presence of God (64:1–5a)
>   B[2] Lamentation: our long-standing sins (64:5b–7)
> A[3] Longing: the touch of God (64:8, 9)
>   C Appeal: the unrestrained God (64:10–12)

What God wants for us is a passion for his glory to be unrestrained, coming down into our experience in new ways. This matters. Typical American Christianity today just isn't enough to meet the challenge of our times. We need God to come down.

Longing: The Love of God[2]

> Look down from heaven and see,
>> from your holy and beautiful habitation.
> Where are your zeal and your might?
>> The stirring of your inner parts and your compassion
>> are held back from me. (Isaiah 63:15)

There is a clue here to Isaiah's message. The Hebrew words translated "are held back" reappear in 64:12, the last verse in the passage, as "restrain yourself." The same Hebrew word lies behind the two English translations. This prayer begins with Isaiah agonizing over the way God is withholding his compassion from his people, and it ends with Isaiah asking God to stop restraining his love and power. *The whole prayer is for God to visit us without holding himself back at all.* There he is in his holy and beautiful heavenly palace, as it were. We're down here in our mediocrity. What's the answer? Not more of us. The only answer is more of God.

Look how Isaiah describes God: ". . . the stirring of your inner parts." Does God have inner parts? Not literally. But God does have deep feelings for us. The Jerusalem Bible translates this, "the yearning of your inmost heart." Or it could be translated, "the turmoil of your inner being." What God feels for us he feels deeply, not superficially or sporadically. But sometimes he withholds from us the experience of his love, and at other times he pours out an experience of his love. God is committed to us. The work of Christ on the cross is finished. The Holy Spirit has come. The Triune God never changes. But our experience of him does change, and he is the one who changes it. That's why we should pray.

There is a difference between doing church in our own power and entering into the presence of God. You can pray about that. God wants you to. He's teaching you to. This is a good prayer. God himself gave it to us. Isaiah isn't attacking God by his questioning here. He isn't doubting God. He's asking God, "*Where* are your passion and your power in our experience down here? Where are your zeal and your might being demonstrated here in our generation? The love you do feel so deeply within yourself you're withholding from us. Come down!"

> For you are our Father,
>   though Abraham does not know us,
>   and Israel does not acknowledge us;
> you, O LORD, are our Father,
>   our Redeemer from of old is your name. (Isaiah 63:16)

If the ancient patriarchs could get into a time machine, hit the fast-forward button, and reappear among the people of God at Isaiah's time, Abraham and Israel would look at them and say, "Who are you?" The people of God have drifted. They've become less than they used to be. They need renewal. Every generation does. Every generation needs to rediscover afresh in its own experience what Christ is worth and what it means to live flat-out for him. If the Reformers appeared today and toured the Protestant churches of our nation, would they identify with us? Or would they turn away in bewilderment? What then do we need? Not the patriarchs. Not the Reformers. They're all dead. But God is our Father and our Redeemer. However far we've drifted, and we have, he still identifies with us and loves us more than the patriarchs or Reformers ever could, by an infinite degree.

Lamentation: Our Hardened Hearts

> O LORD, why do you make us wander from your ways
>   and harden our heart, so that we fear you not?
> Return for the sake of your servants,
>   the tribes of your heritage. (Isaiah 63:17)

This is disturbing. But let's not misunderstand. Isaiah is not blaming God for the failure of this generation. He isn't saying that God forced them to sin. *They* have wandered from God's ways. *They* do not fear God. And they're responsible for that. But the prophet looks more deeply, and he sees the discipline of God at work. When we wander from God, that doesn't put him in a helpless position of hand-wringing and wondering what to do next. If we wander from his ways, God may teach us a lesson by handing us over to the power of our sins and hardening us, so that we *can't* come back.

We tell ourselves we can fool around with some darling sin and then, when we feel like it, just drop it and come back to God, no big deal. Where did we learn to think that way? Does the Bible teach us to trivialize God? Sin is a power beyond our control (John 8:34). When we find our hearts hardened with lethargy and self-pity and even blaming God himself, so that we don't even want to return to him, what then? We pray that *God* will return to *us*. Do you see it here? "Return for the sake of your servants." We are utterly dependent on God. When we have wandered from his ways and no longer fear him, our hope is not in ourselves at all. Our hope is that in his mercy God will return to us.

Longing: The Presence of God

Oh that you would rend the heavens and come down,
    that the mountains might quake at your presence—
as when fire kindles brushwood
    and fire causes water to boil—
to make your name known to your adversaries,
    and that the nations might tremble at your presence! (Isaiah 64:1, 2)

In other words, "O Lord, we need an unusual divine event. We're thankful for your steady blessings day by day. But these are desperate times. We're in a pathetic condition. We need more blessing than we've ever seen before. We need the unmistakable intervention of *God*!" Have you ever been in a worship service when you became aware that Someone had entered the room and you were in the presence of God and you had to do business with him? God is able to come down and visit us in unusual power. We know this from Isaiah 64:1.

The history of God's people illustrates how God can do this. In 1735 God visited New England. Jonathan Edwards recorded what he saw in his own town:

> The town seemed to be full of the presence of God. It never was so full of love, nor of joy, and yet so full of distress, as it was then. There were remarkable tokens of God's presence in almost every house. It was a

time of joy in families on account of salvation being brought unto them; parents rejoicing over their children as new born, and husbands over their wives, and wives over their husbands. . . . Our public assemblies were then beautiful. . . . The assembly in general was, from time to time, in tears while the Word was preached, some weeping with sorrow and distress, others with joy and love, others with pity and concern for the souls of their neighbors.[3]

And God is coming down into our world today. Take China. Chinese Christianity has grown from around one million believers in 1950 to somewhere between 80 to 100 million today—and in the face of persecution. But God is coming down, and there's nothing any human government can do to stop him. He's making the mountains of human opposition quake at his presence, and through the gospel he's turning enemies into worshipers.

It's important for us know that much of the American Christianity we take for granted today is subnormal. Churches here and there are growing with the power of God upon them. But as a whole, American Christianity is drifting into historic inconsequentiality. And yet we seem to be satisfied with our condition. We feel little urgency and longing. We're hardly aware of our mediocrity. We've lost the vision of the prophets and apostles. We've forgotten that to whom much is given, much is required (Luke 12:48). What should we do? We must choose to accept the inconvenient, disturbing, question-provoking, ego-humbling, prayer-stimulating, church-changing, prophetic burden that the glory of God would come down upon us today. Let's embrace the longing. Let's live with it. Let's pray with it. Let's die with it on our hearts. And as we pray, let's stay open to God.

When you did awesome things that we did not look for,
    you came down, the mountains quaked at your presence. (Isaiah 64:3)

What does God's work in the past teach us? Not how predictable he is, but how surprising he is. He never acts out of character. He never contradicts his own Word. But he is never at a loss for new ways to break through. Israel was cornered at the Red Sea. The Egyptian army was bearing down on them. What happened? The sea opened up. Nobody was expecting that. The whole world was stumbling in darkness, with no way forward. What happened? The Savior of the world was born in a barn. Nobody was expecting that. We were condemned in our inexcusable guilt, without a defense. What happened? Our Judge endured our penalty at the cross. Nobody was expecting that. He was dead and buried. All the hopeful expectations he had created were exploded. What happened? He rose from the grave, ascended to the Father, and began pouring out his Spirit to make his murderers into his friends. Nobody was expecting that.

He is still full of surprises. Within my memory, the American church of the 1950s and 60s was stuck in a rut, getting stale, lacking a prophetic voice, and as the 60s progressed, our nation started tearing itself apart. What happened? God came down. He changed the subject, and crazy, longhaired young people all across the country started running toward Christ in many thousands of improbable conversions. Nobody was expecting that. And it's time for us to pray again, "Oh, that you would rend the heavens and come down and do awesome things we're not looking for! Surprise us again!"

> From of old no one has heard
>   or perceived by the ear,
> no eye has seen a God besides you,
>   who acts for those who wait for him. (Isaiah 64:4)

Unlike our idols, God *acts*. No one has ever trusted God in vain. We may ask for the wrong things, but we can never get ahead of God with true thoughts of his greatness and true longings for his power. We'll never enlarge our vision of him too greatly. We'll never ask him to do his revealed will and hear him reply, "Well, I'll try." He is able to do immeasurably more than all we ask or think (Ephesians 3:20, 21). Stretch your vision of God, all the way out to the full extent of the Bible, and then *expect* God to be true to himself. Jesus said, "According to your faith be it done to you" (Matthew 9:29).[4]

> You meet him who joyfully works righteousness,
>   those who remember you in your ways. (Isaiah 64:5a)

God meets not the brilliant one, not the lucky one, but the one who is joyfully, humbly going along in the simple, ordinary path of obedience. That's where God can be found—not with a guru on a mountaintop, but right where you are, if you're willing. You don't need to run from your life; it's where God wants to meet you. You don't need to wait for ideal conditions. You just need to use the life you do have to remember God and his ways. Are God's ways your ways? Is he the center of your lifestyle? For all of us, that's an adjustment worth making.

Lamentation: Our Long-Standing Sins

> Behold, you were angry, and we sinned;
>   in our sins we have been a long time, and shall we be saved?
> We have all become like one who is unclean,
>   and all our righteous deeds are like a polluted garment.
> We all fade like a leaf,

and our iniquities, like the wind, take us away.
There is no one who calls upon your name,
 who rouses himself to take hold of you;
for you have hidden your face from us,
 and have made us melt in the hand of our iniquities. (Isaiah 64:5b–7)

Day by day, as you and I move into the future, we are not writing our lives on a blank page. The page of our heart is already crowded with stains and things crossed out and misspellings and incomplete erasures. We're complicated. Isaiah uses four similes—you see the word "like" four times—to help us recover a more realistic self-awareness.

First, we're like an unclean leper. I could warn everyone I meet, "Hi, I'm Ray Ortlund, and I'm contagious with the leprosy of sin. You'd better keep your distance. I might mess up your life." Secondly, even at our best moments, when we do what's right, we're not as good as we look. All our righteous deeds are like a polluted garment. It's not just our sins that stink; our righteousness stinks. Thirdly, our vitality fades away like a brittle, autumn leaf. We're easily depleted. We just don't last. Fourthly, our iniquities, like the wind, take control of us and move us in directions we never meant to go. And we're not very good at taking hold of the only One who can save us. You and I do not need to be delivered from our enemies; primarily, we need to be delivered from ourselves. So we look to the very One we have offended as all our hope.

Longing: The Touch of God

But now, O Lord, you are our Father;
 we are the clay, and you are our potter;
 we are all the work of your hand.
Be not so terribly angry, O Lord,
 and remember not iniquity forever.
 Behold, please look, we are all your people. (Isaiah 64:8, 9)

This way of praying glorifies God because it expresses our radical need for him. We're the clay, he's the potter, and we need his touch to redesign us and reshape us to be more the way he wants us to be. God holds all power over us, like a potter over clay. Does that discourage prayer? Is his sovereignty, the potter-clay relationship—is that a disincentive to prayer? We can pray with confidence for this very reason: *We are the clay; he is the potter.* He is able to touch us again. We need it, again and again. And God has many methods of touch. Isaiah is not asking that God wouldn't discipline us but that God wouldn't discipline us to the extent we deserve, because by God's own choice we are his people and under his hand.

Appeal: The Unrestrained God

> Your holy cities have become a wilderness;
> > Zion has become a wilderness,
> > Jerusalem a desolation.
> Our holy and beautiful house,
> > where our fathers praised you,
> has been burned by fire,
> > and all our pleasant places have become ruins.
> Will you restrain yourself at these things, O LORD?
> > Will you keep silent, and afflict us so terribly? (Isaiah 64:10–12)

The Jews returned from Babylon to the literal ruins of Jerusalem. The temple had been burned down. Everything was a wreck. And that mattered, because Jerusalem at that time represented the government of God on earth. But the Jews came back to a depressing scene with memories of how great it had once been. So they appealed to God: "Look at this mess, Lord. Look what we've been reduced to. Look at how your cause has suffered. And it's our fault. We deserve nothing. But your name is upon us. So we turn to you. Can you ignore us? You've put so much of yourself into us. Will you restrain yourself at the sight of your cause here in the ruins of weakness?"

The greatest prayer we can pray is for God to do his will, for his glory, in his way, by his gospel, in our generation, *without restraint*. That's a prayer God loves to hear and is ready to answer. He's the one who gave us this prayer in the first place. He creates newness out of ruins when we bow low before him and say, "Lord, as far as I'm concerned, don't restrain yourself at all. Have your way with me and with us all, freely and entirely. Just let us be a part of your movement today."

47

Revival and the
Eagerness of God

ISAIAH 65:1–25

I NOTICED AN AD IN AN AIRLINE MAGAZINE offering a dating service. Here's the line that caught my eye: "See if you're a victim of bad luck or a soul in need of a massive intervention." Interesting question. Am I a victim of bad luck, or am I a soul in need of a massive intervention? A preacher couldn't put it better than that.

The gospel is for souls in need of a massive intervention. The church is a free dating service, matching you with the perfect Lover of your soul. He wants to change your story from victimhood to an intervention. Even if you're not interested in him, he is still eager to get to know you and to develop a fulfilling relationship with you. And with God, you don't have to be an attractive, successful, thin, young, intelligent professional to find love. You can be ugly. You can be a failure. If you think you have something to offer God, the date's off. But if you see yourself as a soul in need of a massive intervention, God is ready right now.

Isaiah has taught us to put an "Oh!" in our prayers. He has taught us to long for God to come down and make his presence felt in our generation. "Look down from heaven and see, from your holy and beautiful habitation. Where are your zeal and your might?" (63:15). That's how we should pray. Isaiah 65—66 is God's answer to that prayer. He promises an intervention of the magnitude of new heavens and a new earth. Rather than God restraining himself, what does Isaiah show us as chapter 65 begins? God is so eager, he's being found by people who aren't even longing for him.

The structure of the text begins and ends with a vision of the eager God, the findable God, the God who says to us, "Here I am!"

A¹ The eagerness of God now (65:1)
  B¹ The pleading God offended (65:2–7)
    C Our authenticity with God (65:8–16)
  B² The creating God rejoicing (65:17–23)
A² The eagerness of God forever (65:24, 25)

Isaiah wants to change our despairing thoughts of a remote, uninvolved God to confidence in an eager God of massive intervention in the lives of people who are so clueless that God himself comes down to find them.

The Eagerness of God Now

> I was ready to be sought by those who did not ask for me;
>   I was ready to be found by those who did not seek me.
> I said, "Here I am, here I am,"
>   to a nation that was not called by my name. (Isaiah 65:1)

This is hardly a dignified picture of God. "Here I am, here I am"—he's trying to get the attention of self-important little people who order their lives as one massive snub of him. But God wants to be noticed. He almost humiliates himself to get on our radar screens. In fact, he did humiliate himself. He came down in Jesus, taking the form of a servant (Philippians 2:3–8). God is so persistent in his overtures that many of the people who find him weren't even looking for him ("a nation that was not called by my name"). God does not wait for us to show an interest in him. He makes the first move. An old hymn marvels at this:

> I sought the Lord, and afterward I knew
> He moved my soul to seek him, seeking me;
> It was not I that found, O Savior true; no, I was found of thee.

> Thou didst reach forth thy hand and mine enfold;
> I walked and sank not on the storm-vexed sea;
> 'Twas not so much that I on thee took hold as thou, dear Lord, on me.

> I find, I walk, I love, but oh the whole
> Of love is but my answer, Lord, to thee;
> For thou wert long beforehand with my soul; always thou lovedst me.[1]

This is the way of God. He requires of us no spiritual pedigree or talent. He just says, "Here I am!" with heart-awakening power. And *anyone* may welcome him.

The New Testament says that when the gospel is being preached, the voice of Christ himself comes through (Romans 10:14, NASB). Paul said, "We are ambassadors for Christ, God making his appeal through us" (2 Corinthians 5:20). Through us, even us, God is saying to our city, "Here I am! And I am so ready to meet you, you don't even need to be seeking me to find me." The church is where people who wouldn't be caught dead in church can find God. You don't need to be religious. In fact, religion can be a problem.

The Pleading God Offended

> I spread out my hands all the day
>   to a rebellious people,
> who walk in a way that is not good,
>   following their own devices. (Isaiah 65:2)

God "spread[ing] out his hands" is God pleading, even begging. He's patient. He gives ample opportunity. But with some people it's a wasted effort. Why? The problem is the human mind. The ESV translates this, "following their own *devices*." The NASB translates it, "following their own *thoughts*." That's what Isaiah means by "devices"—the structures we assemble in our thoughts to manage God and keep him at a distance, because seeing him clearly, in his grace and humility, is counterintuitive and threatening. But there's an irony here we shouldn't miss.

In the first century the Apostle Paul noticed something that bothered him. He saw that comparatively few Jewish people accepted Jesus as their Messiah. But Gentiles were running to Christ in droves. Why wasn't the opposite happening? Israel had a rich background with God. They had been schooled in the messianic prophecies for centuries. Accepting Jesus should have been easy. But too many turned away. At the same time, Gentiles, who had never been covenanted with God and had no training in the Bible, got it. Why? Paul wanted an answer. He found it right here in Isaiah 65:1, 2, which he quotes in Romans 10:20, 21. What he found here in Isaiah is that Israel's problem was not a lack of information or preparation. Their problem was summed up in the word "rebellious" in verse 2: "I spread out my hands all the day to a *rebellious* people."

What does that word mean? It means stubborn, rigid, never satisfied. It's the opposite of the "contrite and lowly spirit" of 57:15. Isaiah's prophetic eyes see God explaining himself, being reasonable, opening his arms, patiently pleading, but for some people even that isn't enough. It's what Paul saw in his day—God reaching out to his covenanted people again and again, through the prophets, for example, but supremely through Christ. But he couldn't get through to them. Why? The people he had loved so much just wouldn't listen. So here's the irony: The people with the most exposure and the best opportunity rejected Christ, while the people on the outside, with all the disadvantages, loved him. "He came to his own, and his own people did not receive him" (John 1:11; cf. Isaiah 53:3).

Spirituality does not run along bloodlines. Our children need more than exposure to the gospel; they need the Holy Spirit-given miracle of responsiveness to the gospel. And by nature they are disinclined to it, as we all are. Do you realize that every generation of the church is about twenty years away from apostasy, apart from the reviving mercies of God? We need him that much, again and again, with wave after wave of grace restoring us, every generation afresh. "If the LORD of hosts had not left us a few survivors, we should have been like Sodom, and become like Gomorrah" (Isaiah 1:9).

The irony goes deeper. When Isaiah's people rejected God, they didn't become nonreligious. They were very religious. But they were following their own thoughts, their own ideas and intuitions, which were pagan:

> . . . a people who provoke me
>   to my face continually,
> sacrificing in gardens
>   and making offerings on bricks;
> who sit in tombs,
>   and spend the night in secret places;
> who eat pig's flesh,
>   and broth of tainted meat is in their vessels. (Isaiah 65:3, 4)

This is not the worship God had authorized through Moses. The people couldn't find God this way. But they didn't want to find God. They were intrigued by the mysterious rites of the surrounding pagan cultures.

The human mind is deeply pagan. Our natural thoughts do not submit gladly to God but look for ways to manipulate his power for our own ends. When the Israel of Paul's day rejected God's grace in Christ, they remained thoroughly religious. But they were following their own thoughts—in essence no different from any other attempt to harness the divine. Connecting Romans 10:1–3 with 11:1–6, we can see that zeal for legalistic self-righteousness is comparable to Baal-worship.

Every man-made religion, whether pagan or puritanical, ends up not only dishonoring God but also mistreating people. Its message to people is, "Keep to yourself, do not come near me, for I am too holy for you" (Isaiah 65:5). Human religion, whatever form it takes, is a mechanism for self-righteous exclusion and sanctimonious comparing and elitism and self-exaltation. It feels holy, it feels pious, but God says it provokes him to his face continually. *One of the most important discoveries we must make in all of life is the difference between true holiness and false holiness.* We don't always know evil when we get involved in it, especially when it presents itself in a religious form. We must know that God is offended ("These are a smoke in my nostrils," v. 5) by any religion, however much it may even quote the Bible, that rebels against the authority of his grace and sets its own self-serving preconditions.

But the God we have offended—this same God is eager to help us. He welcomes any sinner who will reach out and grasp his hand extended in Christ. He's still saying today, "Here I am." It's what he's saying to you right now.

Authenticity with God

> Thus says the LORD:
> "As the new wine is found in the cluster,
>   and they say, 'Do not destroy it,
>   for there is a blessing in it,'
> so I will do for my servants' sake,
> and not destroy them all." (v. 8)

In this metaphor, someone is harvesting grapes to make wine. He cuts a cluster down from the vine. Some of the grapes are good, others bad. But you don't throw the whole bunch away just because some of the grapes have gone sour. If some taste good, you keep the whole bunch and then separate the good from the bad. This is a picture of what God does among all who claim to be his people. He discriminates carefully; he looks beneath the surface of things before he decides to gather in or throw away.

Isaiah wants to correct one of our hidden assumptions, common even today. Many people assume that outward identification with the church is enough to get by. God seems to accept it. "Why shouldn't he? We don't mind God-talk. We can even handle Jesus-talk." Isaiah confronts that misunderstanding with his doctrine of the remnant. He is saying, "The truth is, God is patiently putting up with spiritually artificial people who are mixed in among his responsive people. But a harvest is coming when the true and the false will be forever separated."

> "I will bring forth offspring from Jacob,
>   and from Judah possessors of my mountains;
> my chosen shall possess it,
>   and my servants shall dwell there.
> Sharon shall become a pasture for flocks,
>   and the Valley of Achor a place for herds to lie down,
>   for my people who have sought me.
> But you who forsake the LORD,

> who forget my holy mountain,
> who set a table for Fortune
>   and fill cups of mixed wine for Destiny,
> I will destine you to the sword,
>   and all of you shall bow down to the slaughter,
> because, when I called, you did not answer;
>   when I spoke, you did not listen,
> but you did what was evil in my eyes
>   and chose what I did not delight in." (vv. 9–12)

What is the difference between the people God will accept and the people God will reject? It's the difference between having Christ and not having Christ. God saves sinners *through Christ*. That's the gospel. But how do you know if you have Christ? That's what Isaiah is explaining here. His answer is that authentic faith in Christ proves itself with openness to his Word and delight in his pleasures. But not listening when God speaks and not choosing what God likes is how we ruin ourselves. Being deaf to his Word and dull to his delights, while still attending church, is hypocrisy.

Why is that a deal-breaker in the sight of God? Here's one reason: "You . . . who set a table for Fortune and fill cups of mixed wine for Destiny, I will destine you to the sword" (vv. 11, 12a). That's odd, but insightful. Back in Isaiah's day people contrived idolatrous rituals to bend Fate and Luck their way. But down inside us all is a fear of the future, a deep insecurity, a passion for control, an unbendable will that looks for any way but God's way. It's the spirit of the poem *Invictus* by William Ernest Henley:

> It matters not how strait the gate,
> How charged with punishments the scroll,
> I am the master of my fate;
> I am the captain of my soul.[2]

Not many people say it that bluntly, but to be the master of one's fate and the captain of one's soul can feel so reassuring. It's why idols attract. What we choose and what we make, we can control. We'll climb any mountain except God's holy mountain, because it's hard for us to trust him and surrender to his will. We fear that if we yield to God, he'll ruin everything. But our mechanisms for control are disasters. Our holy mountains are hellish. We should know that by now.

How do we get out of our folly? Look again at the mercies of God in Christ, and ask him to make you a living sacrifice to his good will (Romans 12:1, 2). A spirit of openness to God's Word and delight in his pleasures comes from his triumphant grace. Being a servant of God is more than making sure you don't do any really big, bad sins. It isn't just rejecting what offends God. It's embracing what delights God. It's trusting that what pleases him will please you too. Yield to his love, his ways, his future for you. Everything hinges on that, now and forever.

Now Isaiah looks far into the future. He's directing our thoughts all the way forward to ultimacy, to finality, to Heaven and to Hell. Verse 12 looks into our lives now; verse 13 connects our present with our eternal future with the word "Therefore":

> Therefore thus says the Lord GOD:
> "Behold, my servants shall eat,
>   but you shall be hungry;
> behold, my servants shall drink,
>   but you shall be thirsty;
> behold, my servants shall rejoice,
>   but you shall be put to shame;
> behold, my servants shall sing for gladness of heart,
>   but you shall cry out for pain of heart
>   and shall wail for breaking of spirit." (vv. 13, 14)

God is holding his hands out to us, but they aren't weak and helpless hands. God loves authenticity, wherever he finds it; he hates hypocrisy, wherever he finds it. However mixed his people are now, God will make his own judgments unmistakably clear and final and powerful. And Isaiah's argument ("Therefore") is that who we are now will count forever.

Each one of us is standing at a fork in the road with only two eternities possible, either Heaven or Hell, and there will be no self-deception in either place. What is Heaven like? It's like eating, drinking, rejoicing, and singing for gladness of heart forever. What is Hell like? It's like hunger, thirst, shame, crying out in pain, and wailing in brokenness of spirit in despair forever.

To many people today, the very idea of Hell is offensive. Will God send nice people to Hell just because they don't believe in Jesus? Isn't sincerity what God wants, no matter what brand name your religion happens to have? This objection seems unanswerable. But it is answerable.

The problem with this objection is that it doesn't understand the gospel at all. It's the Biblical gospel that raises the subject of Hell, right? So Hell is a gospel problem. But what does the gospel say? It says that God saves bad people, not nice, sincere people. To claim that there can't be a Hell because God accepts anyone who is nice and kind and tolerant is to claim that we're saved by our own moral attainments. That might sound sweet. But where does it leave all the not-nice, unkind, intolerant people in the world? Is there any hope for all the *bad* people? The gospel says there is. The gospel says that bad people can be saved, because Jesus Christ obeyed God *for* bad people. But the popular ethic of self-salvation, however benign and reasonable it seems, is in fact cruel and exclusionary and snobbish. And God says that cruelty, exclusionism, and snobbishness belong in Hell.

For another thing, the gospel says that Christ himself went to Hell for us. That's what happened at the cross. Don't you realize that *every* sinner goes to Hell? All sin is punished in God's moral universe, every single sin without exception. No one gets away with anything. But sinners go to Hell in one of two ways—either personally or substitutionally, either in themselves and in their own experience throughout eternity or in Christ and in his infinite sufferings on the cross. And the love of God for us is not that he decided not to punish the guilt of our sins, but that Christ gave himself as our substitute in his passion and death. He endured our Hell on the cross. If you want to believe in a loving God, is there any greater love than the dying love of the cross?[3]

Do not be offended by the strong doctrine of Hell. Do not be fooled by plastic counterfeits. Only the gospel of Christ crucified offers bad people hope and displays the costly love of God. If you come to God as "the God of truth" (Isaiah 65:16)—not the God of nice people but the God of truth—then God wants to encourage you. He is preparing a place for you. Look where he's taking his servants.

The Creating God Rejoicing

> "For behold, I create new heavens
>   and a new earth,
> and the former things shall not be remembered
>   or come into mind.
> But be glad and rejoice forever
>   in that which I create;
> for behold, I create Jerusalem to be a joy,
>   and her people to be a gladness." (vv. 17, 18)

About five seconds into this new world, you and I will turn to one another and say, "Cancer, terrorism—what were they? Hmmm. Can't seem to remember. No matter. Here we go!" As Isaiah paints a picture of the new heavens and the new earth, to which God has been leading his people for so long, the prophet uses images from life as we know it now to communicate life as we'll know it then (vv. 19–25). For example, "The young man shall die a hundred years old" (v. 20). But Isaiah doesn't mean that people will live a very long time before they die. There will be no death (Revelation 21:1–4). Isaiah is saying to us, "The life you've always longed for but has always eluded you, always kept just out of reach—that life is what God is preparing for his servants." The place to which is God taking us is *the* human experience that defines the very meaning of joy. C. S. Lewis came to this conclusion:

> If I find in myself a desire which no experience in this world can satisfy, the most probable explanation is that I was made for another world. If none of my earthly pleasures satisfy it, that does not prove that the universe is a fraud. Probably earthly pleasures were never meant to satisfy it, but only to arouse it, to suggest the real thing. . . . I must make it the main object of life to press on to that other country and to help others do the same.[4]

In the end, there will be only one commandment for God's servants to obey forever and ever: "Be glad and rejoice forever in that which I create" (Isaiah 65:18). For those who refuse to rejoice in what God creates, Jeremy Taylor, the seventeenth-century Anglican bishop, summed it up: "God threatens terrible things, if we will not be happy."[5] How could it be otherwise? Hell is simply eternal souls, who don't want God, getting their way. And Heaven is eternal souls, who long for God, getting all they want—God himself in infinite, joyful measure. And new as it will be, the setting for our lasting joy will be new heavens and a new earth, analogous to where we live now. It will not be alien but recognizable. We will finally be home—with God.

The Eagerness of God Forever

"Before they call I will answer;
    while they are yet speaking I will hear.
The wolf and the lamb shall graze together;
    the lion shall eat straw like the ox,
    and dust shall be the serpent's food.
They shall not hurt or destroy
    in all my holy mountain,"
    says the LORD. (vv. 24, 25)

How big is your hope? Is the wingspan of your hope big enough to get you soaring? Is your hope big enough, imaginative enough, human enough to include whole nations and the entire created order, with wolves and lambs and lions thrown in for good measure? Hope on this grand scale—this is the gospel.[6] It's big. It offers both the prospect of personal intimacy with God forever and a renewed world of peace and righteousness. It isn't just one or the other. God has a plan for you and for this whole world. The Lord Jesus Christ died for this, and he will not be denied.

Your enjoyment of God can begin now. It *must* begin now. Enter into Christ with nothing but need. He will re-create you. The gospel says, "If anyone is in Christ, he is a new creation. The old has passed away; behold, the new has come" (2 Corinthians 5:17). If you are in Christ, God has not just patched up your old you. He has made you *new*. And you will enjoy God forever in endless newness.

Every day you and I are tempted to throw this hope away. But what for? This broken-down, fifth-rate world? It isn't worth it. "What no eye has seen, nor ear heard, nor the heart of man imagined, what God has prepared for those who love him . . ." (1 Corinthians 2:9)—*that's* what we're living for. Not the weekend, but The End.

If you are not a Christian believer, or if you are a believer, God is saying this to every one of us: "Here I am! Interested? Even if you're a bad person, I'm still here. In fact, I will save you. Look to Christ. If you'll look honestly, you will conclude that I can be trusted. You will yield control. You will choose what I delight in. And I will prepare a place for you in the new heavens and the new earth. I will do it *eagerly*."

48

Revival and Worship

ISAIAH 66:1–24

AT 9:40 ON THE MORNING of November 1, 1755, Lisbon was struck by an earthquake. It was All Saints' Day, and the churches of Lisbon were filled with worshipers. Thirty churches were destroyed. Within six minutes 15,000 people died. Survivors ran down to the waterfront and got on ships in the harbor to escape the aftershocks, only to be hit by three tsunami waves that then swept over the city. Thousands more died. Lamps, candles, and cooking fires were upset in homes all over the city and started uncontrollable fires that burned for days. More people died. Within a week 30,000 people were dead, and one of Europe's great cities lay in ruins.

The philosopher Voltaire in France saw this tragedy as proof positive that no reasonable person can believe in God. How can a good and all-powerful God create a world like this? Voltaire mocked the facile optimism of Alexander Pope in England who had affirmed, "Whatever is, is right." Gottfried Wilhelm Leibniz, the German scholar, had proposed that we live in "the best of all possible worlds." Voltaire despised that way of thinking. Isn't it painfully obvious that this world is *not* right and *not* the best of all possible worlds? Voltaire reasoned, "If this is the best of all possible worlds, what can the rest be?"[1]

God agrees with Voltaire. This world is not what he had in mind at the creation. But he's doing something about it. And he's not just patching up this broken world; he is out to renew it wonderfully. Isaiah 65—66 is God's ultimate answer to our longings for his intervention. His answer is nothing less than "new heavens and a new earth" (Isaiah 65:17; 66:22).

In the beginning God created the heavens and the earth. It was perfect. Then we ruined it. We were deceived into thinking that we'd be better off defining for ourselves what our existence should be. We didn't realize we were pulling a lever to make God's perfect creation into our perfect hell. What did God do at that point? Two things at once. On the one hand, he sealed off our evil so that it couldn't have its fully devastating impact. He judged us—but in mercy. On the other hand, he gave us a promise that, through Christ, he would reverse all the damage we've done (Genesis 3:15). In effect he said, "It's your fault, but it's my responsibility. I'm taking you on as my personal project. You need a Savior, and I'm providing him. In Christ the world has hope." Isaiah is unpacking how big this promise is and how you and I can be a part of it.

Isaiah's final chapter is primarily about worship. The problem with the whole world is false worship, and we enter into God's promised future through true worship.

A¹ True worship: trembling at God's word (66:1, 2)
  B¹ False worship: offering pig's blood (66:3, 4)
    C¹ Persecution for God's people (66:5, 6)
    C² Prosperity for God's people (66:7–14)
  B² False worship: eating pig's flesh (66:15–17)
A² True worship: declaring God's glory (66:18–21)
    D Conclusion: eternal life or eternal death? (66:22–24)

As God revives his people in true worship, we become a prophetic presence in a dying world, a living invitation to all to join us in the delights of God that will last forever.

True Worship: Trembling at God's Word

Thus says the LORD:
"Heaven is my throne,
  and the earth is my footstool;
what is the house that you would build for me,
  and what is the place of my rest?
All these things my hand has made,
  and so all these things came to be,
    declares the LORD.
But this is the one to whom I will look:
  he who is humble and contrite in spirit
  and trembles at my word." (Isaiah 66:1, 2)

Isaiah isn't saying it was wrong for Solomon to build a temple. He isn't saying it was wrong for the returning Jewish exiles to rebuild the temple. But there is a temptation inherent in every outward form of worship. The temptation is to think we can wall God in, control God, extract from God his blessing by honoring him in a certain way. But there is not one verse in all the New Testament telling us that God cares about our church buildings, for example. Even here in the Old Testament, when he did authorize a temple, he warned his people of the potential misunderstanding built into every created tool for worship. What God blesses is not buildings and liturgies and styles; what God blesses is a trembling heart. We can make even the Biblically authorized worship of the one true God into false worship in his sight. How? By doing all the "right" things, but not listening to his Word. What God blesses—and when this understanding enters our hears, the blessings flow out upon us as we never dreamed possible—what God looks upon with favor is simple: a humble trembling at his Word, setting no preconditions (Acts 7:44–53).[2]

We shouldn't think of our singing only as our worship, but the sermon is something else—a large-group Bible study. True worship is also listening to God's Word with a longing to hear, a desire to believe, an intention to obey. Preaching a sermon is worship. Hearing a sermon is worship. The one to whom God looks with favor is not the one with the fanciest liturgy—or the plainest—but the one who is humble and contrite in spirit and trembles at his Word.

What complicates this is that God uses preachers to communicate his Word. And every preacher is imperfect. Every preacher gives the listener some reason not to listen. We preachers don't mean to, but we do. Our responsibility is to minimize the complications. Your responsibility is to overlook the complications and listen to God. Paul commended the new believers in Thessalonica: "When you received the word of God, which you heard from us, you accepted it not as the word of men but as what it really is, the word of God" (1 Thessalonians 2:13). When you can see in your Bible that the minister's message is coming from that Bible, it changes everything. What you are hearing is not his brainstorm; you are hearing the Word of God.[3] And receiving it not as the word of a man but as the Word of God is the true worship of deeply reverent listening.

Beware of sitting back in church and rating the service, evaluating how it suits you. What's happening is more significant than that. We are all before Christ, and he is evaluating us (Revelation 2—3). Don't be a sermon connoisseur, taking a taste here, a sip there, according to your likes and dislikes. If you worship *as God defines worship*, you will receive his Word with a trembling eagerness, whatever he says (James 1:21). And he will give you more than you could ask or imagine.

One mark of revival is a ravenous hunger for the truth of the gospel. A minister in the Church of Scotland saw unmistakable evidences of God's touch upon his people during the revivals of his time:

"It was a common thing, as soon as the Bible was opened, after the pre-liminary services, and just as the reader began"—here, you will observe, it was the simple reading of the Word without preaching; yet such was the power upon the minds of the people, that "it was a common thing, as soon as the Bible was opened, after the preliminary services, and just as the reader began, for *great meltings* to come upon the hearers. The deep-est attention was paid to every word as the sacred verses were slowly and solemnly enunciated. Then the silent tear might be seen stealing down the rugged but expressive faces turned upon the reader. . . . It was often a stirring sight to witness the multitudes assembling during the dark winter evenings—to trace their progress as they came in all directions across moors and mountains by the blazing torches which they carried to light their way to the places of meeting. The Word of the Lord was precious in those days; and personal inconvenience was little thought of when the hungering soul sought to be satisfied."[4]

The hungering soul seeking to be satisfied with a word from God—that's what it means to be humble and contrite. That's the worship God blesses. That will be the culture of the new heavens and the new earth. If you want to be a part of it then, you've got to become a part of it now.

False Worship: Offering Pig's Blood

"He who slaughters an ox is like one who kills a man;
　　he who sacrifices a lamb, like one who breaks a dog's neck;
he who presents a grain offering, like one who offers pig's blood;
　　he who makes a memorial offering of frankincense,
　　　　like one who blesses an idol.
These have chosen their own ways,
　　and their soul delights in their abominations;
I also will choose harsh treatment for them
　　and bring their fears upon them,
because when I called, no one answered,
　　when I spoke, they did not listen;
but they did what was evil in my eyes
　　and chose that in which I did not delight." (Isaiah 66:3, 4)

Slaughtering an ox and sacrificing a lamb and so forth—these were all legitimate acts of worship. The Levites presided over this worship. But God is saying, "This Biblically authorized worship is, to me, pagan. It's disgust-ing. Away with it!" Why? "Because when I called, no one answered, when I spoke, they did not listen."

Jesus said that the upright Pharisees were like whitewashed tombs, outwardly beautiful but full of death and filth (Matthew 23:27). They were offering God unclean worship, no matter how Biblical it may have seemed, because they were willful, misguided, and unteachable. Even today church becomes, to God, pagan ritual if we are not listening to his Word. He can see the manipulative motivation behind it. To "do church" in the finest style, but with a closed heart, is evil in God's eyes. It is choosing what he does not delight in, and he will destroy it.

Why does God care so passionately about the authenticity of our worship? Because every church service is where the new creation is struggling to break in, where human hearts are deciding whether their Christianity will *resist* the future God has promised or whether their Christianity will *become* the future God has promised. And true worship is so counterintuitive that, as it rises and sweeps through a church, inevitably it will be criticized.

Persecution for God's People

> Hear the word of the LORD,
>   you who tremble at his word:
> "Your brothers who hate you
>   and cast you out for my name's sake
> have said, 'Let the LORD be glorified,
>   that we may see your joy';
> but it is they who shall be put to shame.
> The sound of an uproar from the city!
>   A sound from the temple!
> The sound of the LORD,
>   rendering recompense to his enemies!" (Isaiah 66:5, 6)

Isaiah is looking at God's people in this present age of mixture and conflict. What does he see? Two groups of people—true worshipers, and their "brothers" rejecting them. It happens in liberal churches. It happens in conservative churches. Religious people who settle for a form of godliness but are threatened by its power always resist God. They may build beautiful temples, but the humble and contrite are not welcome, because longing for God to come down and change everything isn't what religious people want. So again and again in churches something like this can be heard: "You're always saying you want to glorify and enjoy God. Let us help you. Let's see how joyful you are as we show you to the door."

Why doesn't everyone welcome joy? Because religion is a mechanism for reinforcing the status quo, while joy is the power of the future, claiming and transforming all that we are. And for some church people—well, they just never figured on getting *that* much of God (see John 9:1–41). He and all who love him embarrass them.

If you long for revival, if you're willing to sacrifice your religious culture for the sake of the new creation, you will be persecuted. Count on it. There is no easy way for God's kingdom to come into this world, including the religious world. So ask yourself, "Is my precious hide so important that I can't suffer for the in-breaking kingdom of God?" Personally, at times I've felt, "Well, yes, my precious hide *is* that important!" That's when I've been the most miserable. Jesus said, "Blessed are you when others revile you and persecute you and utter all kinds of evil against you falsely on my account. Rejoice and be glad, for your reward is great in heaven, for so they persecuted the prophets who were before you" (Matthew 5:11, 12). He doesn't apologize for the cost of serving him. He looks us right in the eye and says, "You're getting beaten up for me? Feeling sorry for yourself? Get over it. Your reward is great. What if prophet-assassinating people *liked* you?" God will punish all persecutors with startling effect. Our privilege is so to prize his smile that we happily bear witness to his worth, come what may. The future is ours.

Prosperity for God's People

"Before she was in labor
she gave birth;
before her pain came upon her
she delivered a son.
Who has ever heard such a thing?
Who has seen such things?
Shall a land be born in one day?
Shall a nation be brought forth in one moment?
For as soon as Zion was in labor
she brought forth her children.
Shall I bring to the point of birth and not cause to bring forth?"
says the LORD;
"Shall I, who cause to bring forth, shut the womb?"
says your God. (Isaiah 66:7–9)

Isaiah turns his eyes far into the future, looking all the way through the troubles of the present to the end of the age. Delightfully, the church appears as a mother. And a miraculous thing is happening. This mother is giving birth without labor pains. In fact, she's bearing not just one child but a whole nation of children. Isaiah foresees the gospel advancing effortlessly in the conversion of multitudes of people with unheard-of rapidity. Imagine waking up tomorrow morning to find that everyone in your city has converted to Christ. Miracles on that grand scale are the promise of God. He commits himself to it. We saw a precursor to this miracle of new life on the great

Day of Pentecost, when 3,000 people were born again all at once (Acts 2:41). We see this power in every true revival along the way. But we haven't seen anything yet. The story of the church will be *the* final chapter of human history, with unprecedented human joy.

> "Rejoice with Jerusalem, and be glad for her,
>   all you who love her;
> rejoice with her in joy,
>   all you who mourn over her;
> that you may nurse and be satisfied
>   from her consoling breast;
> that you may drink deeply with delight
>   from her glorious abundance." (Isaiah 66:10, 11)

God sends his blessing out upon the nations through his church. Isaiah makes that obvious: "So *I* will comfort you; you shall be comforted *in Jerusalem*" (v. 13). The comfort God gives he gives through the ministry of his church. And he is promising an end to our mourning over the barrenness and inadequacy of the church, the church with nothing to offer. Isaiah sees a mother with more than enough milk, suckling her contented child. In the ways of God, his church provides the whole world with the only true comfort that exists, and it is the very comfort of God himself. That's why, in verse 10, Isaiah calls us to stand up and cheer for the church. He's saying, "Identify with your church. Let your loyalty be obvious through thick and thin. Why? *Your life depends upon it.* It is Zion's children who will drink deeply with delight from her glorious abundance forever."

What we must see in Isaiah's prophecy is this: Right now we all tend to be muddled and mixed and unclear about where we stand. But in fact we are shaping our eternal destinies. We are either entering into true worship or settling for false worship disguised as true worship. Our lives have one meaning or the other. And it doesn't matter what we intend; what finally matters is what we *are*—in the sight of God. Who we really are will become clear, the truth about us will last forever, and there are only two possible outcomes. God is offering us new life (vv. 7–9), delightful comforts (vv. 10, 11), "peace . . . like a river" (v. 12), his own presence and power (v. 14). But if we draw back now, for whatever reason, there is only one alternative—the fiery rebuke of God. That too will last forever.

False Worship: Eating Pig's Flesh

> "For behold, the Lord will come in fire,
>   and his chariots like the whirlwind,
> to render his anger in fury,

and his rebuke with flames of fire.
For by fire will the LORD enter into judgment,
and by his sword, with all flesh;
and those slain by the LORD shall be many.

Those who sanctify and purify themselves to go into the gardens, following one in the midst, eating pig's flesh and the abomination and mice, shall come to an end together, declares the LORD." (vv. 15–17)

Isaiah sees God angrily destroying all false worship, whether primitive or modern, liberal or conservative, forever. God will ride down in his war chariot, as it were, to complete his mission of ridding his world of our filthy idols and false salvations. Isaiah is talking about Jesus: ". . . when the Lord Jesus is revealed from heaven with his mighty angels in flaming fire, inflicting vengeance on those who do not know God and on those who do not obey the gospel of our Lord Jesus. They will suffer the punishment of eternal destruction, away from the presence of the Lord and from the glory of his might, when he comes on that day" (2 Thessalonians 1:7–9).

It's tempting for religious people to think of God's final judgment with a certain satisfaction: "Finally the 'bad' people will get what's coming to them!" But God wants everyone to think again. Look at Isaiah 66:17. All self-sanctification and self-purification are, to God, pagan and nauseating. He will put an end to it all through Christ. Do we realize that when we pray for God's kingdom to come and his will to be done on earth, we're praying for the end of religion, the end of the world? We're praying for the fiery holiness of God to burn away all our idolatries. No more pig's flesh offered as worship! Only a trembling sincerity to hear God's Word. That is the future of the world. And God uses his true people to bring in that future.

True Worship: Declaring God's Glory

"For I know their works and their thoughts, and the time is coming to gather all nations and tongues. And they shall come and shall see my glory. . . . And some of them also I will take for priests and for Levites, says the LORD." (Isaiah 66:18, 21)

If we were to flip on our TVs right now, we would see the most sophisticated communications technology in the history of man declaring the glory of diet plans and new improved bathroom cleansers and low-rate credit cards. These are the self-trivializing works and thoughts of man, our stupid self-salvations. Thank God, the time is coming when all nations and tongues will see his glory! And right now he is sending missionaries and preachers and laypeople to the ends of the earth to spread the good news about true and worthwhile salvation in Christ. "They shall declare my glory among the nations" (v. 19).

Paul taught us to see gospel ministry with Isaianic vision when he explained that winning the nations for Christ is a priestly service. Evangelism too is worship. Our worship at our church is to offer our city and the nations to God, acceptable to him through Christ, sanctified by the Holy Spirit (Romans 15:16, 17). He receives all kinds of people, including unlikely people, as his "priests and . . . Levites," for his glory. Isaiah foresaw it. Paul launched it. We participate in it. It's how God remakes the world.

Conclusion: Eternal Life or Eternal Death?

"For as the new heavens and the new earth
   that I make
shall remain before me, says the LORD,
   so shall your offspring and your name remain.
From new moon to new moon,
   and from Sabbath to Sabbath,
all flesh shall come to worship before me,
   declares the LORD.

And they shall go out and look on the dead bodies of the men who have rebelled against me. For their worm shall not die, their fire shall not be quenched, and they shall be an abhorrence to all flesh." (Isaiah 66:22–24)

This seems a chilling way for a great book to conclude. At least the music ends with a minor chord. Isaiah began by confronting false worship (1:10–15); he concludes by celebrating true and endless worship (66:22, 23). He began by invoking the heavens and the earth as witnesses to the magnitude of the evil that God's people had committed (1:2); he concludes by envisioning new heavens and a new earth as the only adequate venue for the endless dignity of God's people (66:22). But his vision also closes with the final destiny of all who rebel against God's purpose of grace. Their destiny is Hell.

What is Hell? It is hearing the voice of Jesus say, "Depart from me, you cursed, into the eternal fire prepared for the devil and his angels" (Matthew 25:41). Hell was not prepared for you but for the devil. Heaven was prepared for you (John 14:2, 3). All you have to do to go to Hell forever is stay on your present course of self-salvation. The outcome of your rejection of God will be God's eternal rejection of you, because rejecting his free salvation is the sin of all sins. It is rejecting Heaven. And how can people who reject Heaven end up there? God knows when he's not welcome, and he knows what to do about it. "Hell says not merely a temporary no but an eternal no to sin. . . . Hell is especially for those who think they are too good to be helped by God. . . . Hell receives those who imagine themselves good; Jesus receives those who know themselves sinners."[5]

Does Isaiah's final warning about Hell embarrass you? It didn't embarrass Jesus. In Mark 9:48 he quotes Isaiah 66:24 to describe Hell. Not only is he frank about human suffering in this world, he's frank about human suffering in the next world. The way Isaiah describes Hell, it's as if the New Jerusalem will have a cemetery beside it. I don't think he means that literally. But he is saying that side by side there are only two final destinies for each one of us—eternal life or eternal death—and we must choose now.

In fact, we are choosing. Every one of us is constantly reaching out for one or the other—for our own self-salvation for our glory or for God's salvation for his glory. Every one of us is living a life that reveals the true tilt of our souls, one way or the other. And Isaiah 66:24 seems to be saying that Hell will have no power at all to torment those beyond its reach. Hell will not cancel or even diminish the joy of Heaven. Hell will not blackmail the universe until the redeemed consent to suffer its miseries too, at least a little. Hell will have no veto power over Heaven. Holy delight will triumph forever.[6]

Before we get defensive about Isaiah's uncensored display of eternal worship versus eternal dying, there are two things to think about.

One: as awful as Hell is, we deserve it. If you've never come to realize that you deserve Hell, if you're still angry at God and offended that he allows a fallen world, you don't understand yourself. There is a reason why this world is one massive tragedy. The reason is, we've made it this way—you and I. And Hell is just the eternal extension of the spiritual conditions we're creating right now. When Lord Byron, the exciting bad boy everyone envied at the time, found himself on his thirty-sixth birthday alone, his vitality already spent, he sat down and wrote these lines:

> My days are in the yellow leaf;
> The flowers and fruits of love are gone;
> The worm, the canker, and the grief
> Are mine alone![7]

What is Hell but that—extended into eternity? It's what we deserve, because it's what we have chosen and made. We *deserve* the bitter outcomes of the folly we have embraced again and again.

Two: God himself came down into this world and suffered Hell out of love for us, to save us from our folly. It's time for us to humble ourselves. It's time to change the subject in our minds from blaming God for ruining the world to owning our real moral guilt before him, so that we can receive his saving love in Christ.

It was on a Friday morning when they took me from the cell
and I saw they had a carpenter to crucify as well.
You can blame it on Pilate, you can blame it on the Jews,
you can blame it on the devil. It is God that I accuse.
It's God they ought to crucify instead of you and me,
I said to the carpenter hanging on the tree.

Now Barabbas was a killer, and they let Barabbas go.
But you are being crucified for nothing here below,
and God is up in heaven and he doesn't do a thing
with a million angels watching and they never move a wing.
It's God they ought to crucify instead of you and me,
I said to the carpenter hanging on the tree.[8]

Don't you see by now? The crucified God saves sinners. Don't you see in his sufferings the measure of how much he loves God-haters like us? Don't you see that it's time to stop raging at him and to start worshiping him? It's time. And for every one of us, time is rapidly coming to an end.

Notes

Preface

1. John D. Woodbridge, ed., *More Than Conquerors* (Chicago: Moody Press, 1992), p. 209.
2. J. I. Packer, in Clyde E. Fant, Jr. and William M. Pinson, Jr., eds., *20 Centuries of Great Preaching, Volume 11: Maier to Sangster* (Waco, TX: Word Books, 1971), p. 270.

Chapter One: Introduction to Isaiah

1. William Henry Green, *The Pentateuch* (New York: John Wiley, 1863), pp. 194, 195.
2. Arturo G. Azurdia, III, *Spirit Empowered Preaching* (Fearn, UK: Christian Focus, 1998), p. 16.
3. D. F. Pears and B. F. McGuinness, trans., *Tractatus Logico-Philosophicus: The German Text of Ludwig Wittgenstein's Logisch-philosophische Abhandlung* (London: Routledge & Kegan Paul, 1961), p. 149.
4. Barry G. Webb, *The Message of Isaiah: On Eagles' Wings* (Downers Grove, IL: InterVarsity Press, 1996), p. 13.
5. Oswalt, I:3. On p. 175 of his second volume, Oswalt identifies Isaiah as "everywhere agreed to be the finest theological mind in Israel."
6. N. H. Ridderbos, in J. D. Douglas, et al., eds., *The New Bible Dictionary* (Grand Rapids, MI: Eerdmans, 1973 reprint), p. 574.
7. Quoted in John Eliot Gardiner, liner notes to *Bach: Cantatas—Christmas*, Archiv Produktion 463 589-2, p. 1.
8. *Institutes*, 3.7.2. Cf. Timothy George, *Theology of the Reformers* (Nashville: Broadman, 1988), p. 59.
9. Rashi, Ibn Ezra, Radak; Babylonian Talmud, Megilla 10b, Sota 10b.
10. Cf. Gregory Zilboorg, "Fear of Death," *Psychoanalytic Quarterly* 12 (1943): 465–475.
11. Ernest Becker, *The Denial of Death* (New York: The Free Press, 1973), p. 4. I thank Dr. Tim Keller for drawing my attention to Becker.
12. *Ibid.*, p. 6.
13. William James, *The Varieties of Religious Experience: A Study in Human Nature* (New York: Collier Books, 1961 reprint), p. 124.
14. J. I. Packer, "Saved by His Precious Blood: An Introduction to John Owen's *The Death of Death in the Death of Christ*," in *A Quest for Godliness: The Puritan Vision of the Christian Life* (Wheaton, IL: Crossway Books, 1990), p. 130.
15. *Lutheran Book of Worship* (Minneapolis: Augsburg, 1978), p. 199.
16. James H. Charlesworth, ed., *Old Testament Pseudepigrapha* (New York: Doubleday, 1985), II:163, 164.

Chapter Two: Our Urgent Need: A New Self-Awareness I

1. Paul Tournier, *Escape From Loneliness* (Philadelphia: Westminster Press, 1962), p. 163.
2. William Kilpatrick, "Faith & Therapy," *First Things*, February 1999, p. 23.
3. Quoted in Gerhard von Rad, *Old Testament Theology*, trans. D. M. G. Stalker (New York: Harper & Row, 1965), II:33, footnote 1.

4. Motyer, p. 116: "Those who fail to delight in a piece of literature such as this are indeed hard to please."

5. "To a Louse, on Seeing One on a Lady's Bonnet, at Church," in Alexander Smith, ed., *The Complete Works of Robert Burns* (London: Macmillan, 1921), p. 74.

6. *Institutes*, 1.1.1.

7. One thinks of the pathetic ghost of Jacob Marley in Charles Dickens's *A Christmas Carol*.

8. Jonathan Edwards, *Works* (Edinburgh: Banner of Truth Trust, 1979 reprint), I:669.

9. John Piper, *Desiring God: Meditations of a Christian Hedonist* (Sisters, OR: Multnomah, 1996), p. 89.

Chapter Three: Our Urgent Need: A New Self-Awareness II

1. The Westminster Larger Catechism of 1648 asks, "What is repentance unto life?" The wise answer is, "Repentance unto life is a saving grace, wrought in the heart of a sinner by the Spirit and word of God, whereby, out of the sight and sense not only of the danger but also of the filthiness and odiousness of his sins, and upon the apprehension of God's mercy in Christ to such as are penitent, he so grieves for and hates his sins as that he turns from them all to God, purposing and endeavouring constantly to walk with him in all the ways of new obedience." Thomas Watson, in *The Doctrine of Repentance* (Edinburgh: Banner of Truth Trust, 1994 reprint), p. 22, articulates the spirit of true repentance:

"My sin is ever before me" (Psalm 51:3). David does not say, "The sword threatened is ever before me," but "my sin." O that I should offend so good a God, that I should grieve my Comforter! This breaks my heart!

2. Cf. Philip Schaff, *History of the Christian Church* (Grand Rapids, MI: Eerdmans, 1970 reprint), VII:160.

3. Derek Kidner, in *The New Bible Commentary*, 4th edition (Downers Grove, IL: InterVarsity Press, 1994), p. 634.

4. Brief but profound exposition of the sixth commandment, "You shall not murder" (Exodus 20:13), can be found in the Westminster Larger Catechism, Questions 134–137, and the Heidelberg Catechism, Questions 105–107.

5. Martin Luther, quoted in Dietrich Bonhoeffer, *Life Together*, trans. John W. Doberstein (New York: HarperCollins, 1954), p. 9.

6. Richard F. Lovelace, *Dynamics of Spiritual Life: An Evangelical Theology of Renewal* (Downers Grove, IL: InterVarsity, 1979), pp. 113, 114.

7. Watson, *Repentance*, pp. 97, 98.

Chapter Four: Our Urgent Need: A New Self-Awareness III

1. Cf. Raymond C. Ortlund, Jr., *God's Unfaithful Wife: A Biblical Theology of Spiritual Adultery* (Downers Grove, IL: InterVarsity, 2003).

2. D. Martyn Lloyd-Jones, *What Is an Evangelical?* (Edinburgh: Banner of Truth Trust, 1992), pp. 9, 10.

3. Whittaker Chambers, *Witness* (New York: Random House, 1952), pp. 13, 14.

4. Geoffrey Barlow, ed., *Vintage Muggeridge: Religion and Society* (Grand Rapids, MI: Eerdmans, 1985), pp. 91, 92.

5. Bruce D. Chilton, *The Isaiah Targum*, The Aramaic Bible, Volume 11 (Collegeville, MN: The Liturgical Press, 1987), p. 4.

6. This is contrary to the ESV, which has "they," but in line with the RSV, NASB, NIV, and NRSV, I emend the third-person verb of the Hebrew text to the second person, as appears in a few Hebrew manuscripts and Targum.

7. Cf. Walter A. Elwell, ed., *Evangelical Dictionary of Theology* (Grand Rapids, MI: Baker, 1984), p. 919.

Chapter Five: The Transforming Power of Hope and Humility

1. C. S. Lewis, *Mere Christianity* (New York: Macmillan, 1958), p. 104.

2. Cf. Peter D. Miscall, *Isaiah* (Sheffield, UK: JSOT Press, 1993), p. 25.

3. According to United States government figures (www.whitehouse.gov/omb/budget/fy2003), the cost of military spending in 2003 was 368 billion dollars. From 1998 to 2003, the defense budget grew at the average rate of 7 percent per year, while the budget for the Corps of Engineers shrank at the average rate of 1 percent per year.

4. Richard Lovelace, *Dynamics of Spiritual Life: An Evangelical Theology of Renewal* (Downers Grove, IL: InterVarsity Press, 1979), p. 184: "When men's hearts are not full of God, they become full of the world around like a sponge full of clear water that has been squeezed empty and thrown into a mud puddle."

5. In saying "Do not forgive them," Isaiah is not forbidding divine forgiveness. He is expressing his Spirit-given sense of the outcome appropriate to his generation. The negative imperative can be used "to express the conviction that something cannot or should not happen," according to GKC 109e, which paraphrases our text with, "and thou canst not possibly forgive them."

6. Oswalt, I:113.

7. John Piper, *God's Passion for His Glory* (Wheaton, IL: Crossway Books, 1998), p. 76.

8. Glenn Leggett, ed., *12 Poets* (New York: Holt, Rinehart and Winston, 1958), p. 43.

9. Edward J. Young, *The Book of Isaiah* (Grand Rapids, MI: Eerdmans, 1965), I:134.

Chapter Six: The Enriching Power of Loss and Gain

1. Horst Meller and Rudolf Sühnel, eds., *British and American Classical Poems* (Braunschweig, Germany: Georg Westermann Verlag, 1966), p. 238.

2. See in this context Isaiah 2:2, 11, 12, 17, 20; 3:7, 18; 4:1, 2.

3. Elisabeth Elliot, *Shadow of the Almighty: The Life & Testament of Jim Elliot* (New York: Harper & Brothers, 1958), p. 19.

4. C. S. Lewis, *Mere Christianity* (New York: Macmillan, 1958), p. 160.

5. If the emendation proposed by BHS is valid, as it may be, verse 13 also reads, "he stands to judge *his people.*" Cf. RSV, NEB, REB.

6. Cf. Jonathan Edwards, *Works* (Edinburgh: Banner of Truth Trust, 1979 reprint), I:428, 429.

7. Lewis, *Mere Christianity*, p. 94.

8. Oswalt, I:140.

9. Isaiah's imagery appears on some of the Judaea Capta coins from the Roman conquests of the first century A.D., picturing a Jewish woman seated dejectedly on the ground, her hands tied behind her back. Cf. David Hendin, *Guide to Biblical Coins*, 3rd edition (New York: Amphora, 1996), pp. 206, 217.

10. Cf. Isaiah 11:1; Jeremiah 23:5; 33:15; Zechariah 3:8; 6:12. "The fruit of the land" may emphasize the humility of his human roots in the line of Abraham. The words "branch" and "fruit" should be capitalized, to make the messianic metaphor clear.

11. Jonathan Edwards, *Charity and Its Fruits* (Edinburgh: Banner of Truth Trust, 2000 reprint), pp. 327, 328.

Chapter Seven: Receiving the Grace of God in Vain

1. Peter D. Miscall, *Isaiah* (Sheffield, UK: JSOT Press, 1993), p. 31, notes the sevenfold repetition of the verb √*aśâh* in verses 2–5. God's generous "doing" is juxtaposed with the vineyard's disappointing "doing".

2. Derek Kidner, in *The New Bible Commentary*, 4th edition (Downers Grove, IL: InterVarsity Press, 1994), p. 637.

3. Oswalt, I:159.

4. C. S. Lewis, *The Great Divorce* (New York: Simon & Schuster, 1996), pp. 20–22.

5. Cf. Raymond C. Ortlund, Jr., *Supernatural Living for Natural People: Studies in Romans Eight* (Fearn, UK: Christian Focus, 2001), pp. 43–53.

6. D. Martyn Lloyd-Jones, *A Nation Under Wrath: Studies in Isaiah 5* (Grand Rapids, MI: Baker, 1998), p. 75.

Chapter Eight: The Triumph of Grace over Our Failure: Isaiah

1. Peter Brown, *Augustine of Hippo: A Biography* (Berkeley, CA: University of California Press, 1967), p. 375.

2. A. W. Tozer, *The Knowledge of the Holy* (New York: Harper & Row, 1961), p. 76.

3. Cf. *IBHS*, 12.5.

4. Elizabeth Barrett Browning, "Aurora Leigh," quoted in James Dalton Morrison, ed., *Masterpieces of Religious Verse* (New York: Harper & Brothers, 1948), p. 16.

5. Cf. George M. Marsden, *Jonathan Edwards: A Life* (New Haven, CT: Yale University Press, 2003), pp. 460–463.

6. H. C. G. Moule, *Charles Simeon* (London: Inter-Varsity, 1956 reprint), p. 28.

7. Matthew 13:14, 15; Mark 4:12; Luke 8:10; John 12:39–41; Acts 28:25–27.

8. Quoted in T. H. L. Parker, *John Calvin: A Biography* (London: J. M. Dent & Sons, 1975), p. 90.

9. See Richard Baxter, "Directions Against Hardness of Heart," in *A Christian Directory* (Ligonier, PA: Soli Deo Gloria, 1990 reprint), pp. 171–176.

Chapter Nine: The Triumph of Grace over Our Failure: Judah I

1. Cf. Peter Brown, *Augustine of Hippo: A Biography* (Berkeley, CA: University of California Press, 1967), pp. 365–375.

2. C. S. Lewis, *Reflections on the Psalms* (New York: Harcourt, Brace & World, 1958), p. 62.

3. The ESV reads in 7:1 that the northern alliance "could not yet mount an attack against it." But the word "yet" is not in the Hebrew text and obscures the force of the verse in Isaiah's authorial strategy. He is not saying that they had not succeeded *yet*; he is saying that they would not succeed *at all*.

4. Cf. Walter C. Kaiser, Jr., *A History of Israel* (Nashville: Broadman & Holman, 1998), p. 365.

5. Derek Kidner, in *The New Bible Commentary*, 4th edition (Downers Grove, IL: InterVarsity, 1994), p. 639.

6. John D. W. Watts, *Isaiah 1—33* (Waco: Word Books, 1985), p. 93.

7. John Murray, "Faith," in *Collected Writings* (Edinburgh: Banner of Truth, 1977), II:260.

8. The correct translation of Isaiah 7:14 should probably be "Behold, the *young woman* shall conceive and bear a son . . ." rather than "Behold, the *virgin* shall conceive and bear a son. . . ." Cf. RSV, NRSV, NEB, REB, NJPS; NASB margin: "maiden." The virgin conception of Jesus is not established by the Hebrew word *calmâh* in this verse; it is established by the narratives of Matthew 1:18–25 and Luke 1:26–38. It is unnecessary, and a misplaced effort, to insist upon the meaning "virgin" for the Hebrew word in Isaiah 7:14 in order to validate the doctrine of our Lord's virgin birth. Isaiah's word simply means "young woman," even as the masculine equivalent *'elem* means "young man." Virginity or non-virginity is not the point of the word. The message of Isaiah 7:14 is not the virginity of the mother but the God-with-us significance of the child. Matthew makes his emphasis explicit at the end of his verse 23: ". . . which means, God with us." He clearly records the virginity of Mary, to be sure; but the God-with-us-ness of Jesus is the point of his quotation of Isaiah 7:14, consistent with Isaiah's message.

9. W. H. Griffith Thomas, *The Principles of Theology: An Introduction to the Thirty-Nine Articles* (London: Church Book Room Press, 1963 reprint), p. 136, summarizes the Old Testament with apostolic wisdom. He sees it as a book of unfulfilled prophecies, unexplained ceremonies, and unsatisfied longings, all of which are resolved in the New Testament's focus on Jesus Christ, who fulfills in his life the prophecies, explains in his death the ceremonies, and satisfies in his resurrection our longings. Matthew and the other writers of the New Testament read every page of their Old Testaments this way.

10. D. A. Carson, "Matthew," in *The Expositor's Bible Commentary*, ed. Frank E. Gaebelein (Grand Rapids, MI: Zondervan, 1984), VIII:76.

Chapter Ten: The Triumph of Grace over Our Failure: Judah II

1. BDB, s.v. *qin'âh*; cf. J. G. Hava, *Al-Faraid: Arabic-English Dictionary*, 5th edition (Beirut: Dar el-Mashreq, 1982 reprint), s.v. *qana'a*.

2. Cf. M. W. Elliott, "Remnant," in T. Desmond Alexander and Brian S. Rosner, eds., *New Dictionary of Biblical Theology* (Leicester, UK: Inter-Varsity Press, 2000), pp. 723–726.

3. Jonathan Edwards, *Works* (Edinburgh: Banner of Truth Trust, 1979 reprint), I:309.

4. I thank Pattie Dixie of the South American Mission Society in Britain for providing a record of these events and journal entries.

5. Cf. Stephen Charnock, *Discourses Upon the Existence and Attributes of God* (Grand Rapids, MI: Baker, 1979 reprint), II:89-175.

6. Quoted in W. A. Criswell, "What Happens When I Preach the Bible as Literally True," in Earl D. Radmacher, ed., *Can We Trust the Bible?* (Wheaton, IL: Tyndale House, 1979), p. 92.

7. Kenneth P. Minkema, ed., *Jonathan Edwards: Sermons and Discourses, 1723–1729* (New Haven, CT: Yale University Press, 1997), pp. 465, 466.

Chapter Eleven: The Triumph of Grace over Our Failure: Israel I

1. Cf. H. D. Lewis, "Philosophy of Religion, History of," in *The Encyclopedia of Philosophy*, ed. Paul Edwards (New York: Macmillan, 1967), VI:279.

2. Cf. J. I. Packer, *Knowing God* (Downers Grove, IL: InterVarsity Press, 1973), pp. 134–142; "Anger," in T. Desmond Alexander and Brian S. Rosner, eds., *New Dictionary of Biblical Theology* (Leicester, UK: Inter-Varsity Press, 2000), pp. 381–383.

3. Cf. David Powlison, "Anger Part 1: Understanding Anger," *The Journal of Biblical Counseling* 14 (1995): 42, footnote 13.

4. "Quake's Power = Million Atomic Bombs?", CNN.com, December 29, 2004.

5. C. S. Lewis, "The Trouble with 'X'. . .," in *God in the Dock: Essays on Theology and Ethics*, ed. Walter Hooper (Grand Rapids, MI: Eerdmans, 1973 reprint), p. 155.

6. Winston S. Churchill, *The Second World War: Triumph and Tragedy* (Boston: Houghton Mifflin Company, 1953), p. ix.

7. Quoted in Iain H. Murray, *Jonathan Edwards: A New Biography* (Edinburgh: Banner of Truth Trust, 1987), p. 442.

8. Cf. Motyer, p. 110.

9. Cf. John D. W. Watts, *Isaiah 1—33* (Nashville: Word, 1985), p. lv: "The core of the Vision's theological message, however, is that Yahweh is the Lord of History. He calls and dismisses nations. He determines their destinies. He divides the ages and determines the eventual courses of mankind."

10. *ARAB*, I:110.

11. Paul Tournier, *Guilt and Grace* (New York: Harper and Row, 1962), p. 145.

12. *The Works of John Newton* (Edinburgh: Banner of Truth Trust, 1988 reprint), III:607, 608.

Chapter Twelve: The Triumph of Grace over Our Failure: Israel II

1. A. W. Tozer, *The Knowledge of the Holy* (New York: Harper & Row, 1961), p. 9.

2. C. S. Lewis, *The Weight of Glory and Other Addresses* (Grand Rapids, MI: Eerdmans, 1974 reprint), pp. 1, 2.

3. The route of the invading army can be traced with Yohanan Aharoni and Michael Avi-Yonah, *The Macmillan Bible Atlas* (London: Macmillan, 1968), map #154.

4. Richard F. Lovelace, *Dynamics of Spiritual Life: An Evangelical Theology of Renewal* (Downers Grove, IL: InterVarsity Press, 1979), p. 183.

5. Christopher Hitchens, "Where Aquarius Went," *The New York Times Book Review*, December 19, 2004, p. 10.

Chapter Thirteen: Our Response to the Triumph of Grace

1. By repeating the literary marker "in that day," Isaiah is dovetailing chapter 12 with 10:20, 27; 11:10, 11 as the immediate context.
2. Verse 6 shifts to feminine singular forms, but only because Isaiah is referring to the people of God corporately as the "inhabitant of Zion." The grammatical form must change, but the logic of corporate address remains.
3. See Will Metzger, *Tell the Truth: The Whole Gospel to the Whole Person by Whole People*, 2nd edition (Downers Grove, IL: InterVarsity Press, 1984), pp. 21–27, regarding the difference between testimony and witness.
4. Leon Morris, *The Gospel According to John* (Grand Rapids, MI: Eerdmans, 1973 reprint), pp. 425, 426.
5. *World Pulse*, November 12, 2001, p. 5.
6. Quoted in Derek Thomas, *God Delivers: Isaiah Simply Explained* (Durham, UK: Evangelical Press, 1991), p. 119.
7. Oswalt, I:295.

Chapter Fourteen: The Supremacy of God over the Nations I

1. Miroslav Volf, *Exclusion and Embrace: A Theological Exploration of Identity, Otherness and Reconciliation* (Nashville: Abingdon Press, 1996), p. 304. I thank Dr. Tim Keller for drawing my attention to Volf.
2. *Ibid.*, p. 302.
3. Cf. Luke 17:26–30; Acts 17:31; 2 Corinthians 1:14; Philippians 1:10; 2:16; 2 Thessalonians 2:1, 2.
4. Seth Erlandsson, *The Burden of Babylon: A Study of Isaiah 13:2—14:23* (Lund, Sweden: C. W. K. Gleerup, 1970), argues that the Babylon in view here is not the Babylon of the Neo-Babylonian Empire but the Babylon of the Assyrian Empire in Isaiah's own time.
5. I would translate verse 5 ". . . to destroy the whole earth," as in the ESV margin, because the parallel line refers to "the heavens." Again, in verse 9, I would prefer ". . . to make the earth a desolation," because verse 10 locates this within a cosmic setting.
6. Cf. Daniel I. Block, *The Gods of the Nations: Studies in Ancient Near Eastern National Theology*, 2nd edition (Grand Rapids, MI: Baker, 2000), p. 150.
7. Paul Johnson, *Intellectuals* (New York: Harper & Row, 1988), p. 10.
8. Cf. Paul C. Vitz, *Psychology as Religion: The Cult of Self-Worship* (Grand Rapids, MI: Eerdmans, 1977), pp. 28–36, 57–65.
9. Arnold J. Toynbee, *A Study of History: Volume XII, Reconsiderations* (London: Oxford University Press, 1961), p. 488.
10. "Is the Shorter Catechism Worthwhile?" in John E. Meeter, ed., *The Selected Shorter Writings of B. B. Warfield* (Phillipsburg, NJ: Presbyterian and Reformed, 1970), I:383, 384.
11. Dr. Ray Ortlund, Sr., *Light from the Cradle* (Hollywood: Haven of Rest Ministries, 1987), p. 5.

Chapter Fifteen: The Supremacy of God over the Nations II

1. Nathaniel Hawthorne, *The Scarlet Letter: A Romance* (Edinburgh: William Paterson, 1850), p. 303.
2. The Septuagint omits the heading to the oracle but interprets the second *ba'rab* in verse 13 as "in the evening," as do Targum, the Vulgate, and the Syriac. Cf. F. Delitzsch, *Biblical Commentary on the Prophecies of Isaiah* (Grand Rapids, MI: Eerdmans, 1969 reprint), I:386.
3. Oswalt, I:435, proposes that "these verses [15–18] make a fitting summation to the message of chapters 13–23."
4. J. Gresham Machen, "Christianity and Culture," in *Education, Christianity and the State* (Jefferson, MD: The Trinity Foundation, 1987), pp. 45–59.

Chapter Sixteen: The Supremacy of God over the Nations III

1. Peter Brown, *Augustine of Hippo: A Biography* (Berkeley, CA: University of California Press, 1967), pp. 297, 298.

2. Cf. 2 Corinthians 4:18; Hebrews 11:1–16; 12:22–29.

3. Marcus Dods, ed., *The Works of Aurelius Augustine, Bishop of Hippo: The City of God* (Edinburgh: T. & T. Clark, 1872), II:47.

4. Jacques Ellul, *The Meaning of the City* (Grand Rapids, MI: Eerdmans, 1970), pp. 1–23.

5. Isaiah 24:21; 25:9; 26:1; 27:1, 2, 12, 13.

6. John W. Whitehead, *Grasping for the Wind: The Search for Meaning in the 20th Century* (Grand Rapids, MI: Zondervan, 2001), tells the story, on a grand scale, of how Western society experimented with new constructions of human meaning in the chaotic, tragic twentieth century.

7. Isaac Watts, "Come, We That Love the Lord," verse 4.

8. Cf. Cyrus H. Gordon, "Leviathan: Symbol of Evil," in *Biblical Motifs: Origins and Transformations*, ed. Alexander Altmann (Cambridge, MA: Harvard University Press, 1966), pp. 1–9.

9. Alexander Pope, "Essay on Man," in *12 Poets*, ed. Glenn Leggett (New York: Holt, Rinehart and Winston, 1958), p. 78.

10. Flannery O'Connor, "Novelist and Believer," in *Mystery and Manners* (New York: Farrar, Straus & Giroux, 1969), p. 159.

11. See 1 Corinthians 15:24, 25; Revelation 12:3, 9; 13:1; 20:1–3, 7–10.

12. Jeremiah Burroughs, *A Treatise of Earthly-Mindedness* (Orlando, FL: Soli Deo Gloria, 1991), pp. 1–76.

Chapter Seventeen: Our One Security: God's Sure Foundation

1. Alexander Solzhenitsyn, *'One Word of Truth . . .': The Nobel Speech on Literature, 1970* (London: The Bodley Head, 1972), p. 27.

2. Malcolm Muggeridge, *The End of Christendom* (Grand Rapids, MI: Eerdmans, 1980), pp. 50–52.

3. Cf. Richard Owen Roberts, *Spiritual Drunkenness* (Wheaton, IL: International Awakening Press, 1993).

4. Cf. Isaiah 7:9; 12:2; 26:3, 4; 28:16; 30:15; 31:1; 32:17; 43:10; 50:10.

5. "Colorful Sayings of Martin Luther," *Christian History*, Issue 34, p. 27.

6. Cf. Elizabeth Achtemeier, "Isaiah of Jerusalem: Themes and Preaching Possibilities," in Christopher R. Seitz, ed., *Reading and Preaching the Book of Isaiah* (Philadelphia: Fortress, 1988), p. 32.

7. C. S. Lewis, *The Last Battle* (New York: Scholastic, 1995 reprint), pp. 168, 169.

8. Friedrich Nietzsche, *Beyond Good and Evil*, trans. Marianne Cowan (Chicago: Henry Regnery, 1969 reprint), pp. 73, 74.

9. Cf. A. W. Tozer, "Miracles Follow the Plow," in Warren W. Wiersbe, comp., *The Best of A. W. Tozer* (Camp Hill, PA: Christian Publications, 1997 reprint), pp. 239–243.

Chapter Eighteen: God's Power on God's Terms

1. C. S. Lewis, *The Abolition of Man* (New York: Macmillan, 1965 reprint), p. 91.

2. Cf. Raymond C. Ortlund, Jr., *Supernatural Living for Natural People: Studies in Romans Eight* (Fearn, UK: Christian Focus, 2001), pp. 123–133.

3. Cf. Paul Johnson, *A History of the Modern World from 1917 to the 1980's* (London: Weidenfeld and Nicolson, 1983), p. 698: "What is important in history is not only the events that occur but the events that obstinately do not occur. The outstanding non-event of modern times was the failure of religious belief to disappear. . . . What looked antiquated, even risible, in the 1980's was not religious belief but the confident predictions of its demise once

provided by Feuerbach, Marx and Comte, Durkheim and Frazer, Wells, Shaw, Gide and Sartre and countless others."

4. Cf. Iain H. Murray, *Revival and Revivalism: The Making and Marring of American Evangelicalism, 1750–1858* (Edinburgh: Banner of Truth Trust, 1994), p. 116.

5. *The Evening Standard*, London, March 4, 1966.

6. Cf. Bob Dylan, "When He Returns," *Slow Train Coming* (1979), verse 3:

Surrender your crown on this blood-soaked ground, take off your mask,
He sees your deeds, he knows your needs even before you ask.
How long can you falsify and deny what is real?
How long can you hate yourself for the weakness you conceal?
Of every earthly plan that be known to man, he is unconcerned.
He's got plans of his own to set up his throne when he returns.

7. Flannery O'Connor, *Wise Blood* (New York: Farrar, Straus and Giroux, 1967 reprint), p. 22.

8. *Institutes*, 3.3.16.

9. Jonathan Edwards, *Charity and Its Fruits* (Edinburgh: Banner of Truth Trust, 2000 reprint), p. 58.

10. Jonathan Edwards, *The Religious Affections* (Edinburgh: Banner of Truth Trust, 1997 reprint), p. 28.

11. Roger Rosenblatt, "What Really Mattered?" *Time*, October 5, 1983, p. 25.

Chapter Nineteen: The Counterintuitive Ways of God

1. Cf. D. A. Carson, "When Is Spirituality Spiritual?" in *The Gagging of God: Christianity Confronts Pluralism* (Grand Rapids, MI: Zondervan, 1996), pp. 555–569.

2. J. R. R. Tolkien, *The Return of the King, Being the Third Part of The Lord of the Rings* (Boston: Houghton Mifflin, 1994), p. 820.

3. Cf. Kenneth P. Minkema, ed., *Jonathan Edwards: Sermons and Discourses, 1723–1729* (New Haven, CT: Yale University Press, 1997), pp. 91–96.

Chapter Twenty: Our Only True Hope

1. "Let's Roll," *World*, August 17, 2002, p. 26.

2. Cf. Jonathan Edwards, *Works* (Edinburgh: Banner of Truth Trust, 1979 reprint), II:158.

3. Cf. Malcolm Muggeridge, "The Great Liberal Death Wish," *Imprimis*, May 1979, p. 5.

4. C. S. Lewis, *The Lion, the Witch and the Wardrobe* (New York: Scholastic, 1995 reprint), p. 80.

5. The ESV reads, "Each will be like a hiding place. . . ." This is a valid translation. But the distributive use of the Hebrew noun, while possible here, seems less apt than an indeterminate use of the noun to attract attention to the messianic figure. Cf. Motyer, ad loc.

6. Cf. William J. Dumbrell, "The Purpose of the Book of Isaiah," *Tyndale Bulletin* 36 (1985): 111–128.

Chapter Twenty-one: Finding God in Failure

1. C. S. Lewis, *Surprised by Joy: The Shape of My Early Life* (New York: Harcourt, Brace & World, 1955), pp. 228, 229.

2. The English translation differs here, but the underlying Hebrew word is the same.

3. The ESV reads, "We wait for you." But the word order of the Hebrew lays the emphasis on "for you."

4. Oswalt, I:597, writes with spiritual wisdom: "If the believer is called to abandon his or her own haste in patient waiting on the Lord, it is with certainty that there always comes a divine 'Now!' . . . Those who are consumed by their own plans are always taken unaware by God's work."

5. According to the rabbinic notation in the Masoretic text, verse 20 marks the exact midpoint in the book of Isaiah.

6. Cf. Barry G. Webb, "Zion in Transformation: A Literary Approach to Isaiah," in David J. A. Clines, Stephen E. Fowl, and Stanley E. Porter, eds., *The Bible in Three Dimensions* (Sheffield, UK: Sheffield Academic Press, 1990), pp. 65–84.

Chapter Twenty-two: The Two Final Outcomes

1. Martin Luther, *A Commentary on St. Paul's Epistle to the Galatians* (London: James Clarke & Company, 1953), p. 40.

2. I acknowledge my debt to C. S. Lewis here. Cf. Wayne Martindale and Jerry Root, eds., *The Quotable Lewis* (Wheaton, IL: Tyndale House, 1989), #666-706.

3. The ESV translates this, "For the LORD is enraged against all the nations." That is a valid rendering. But Isaiah is using a syntactical device suggesting possession, as in verses 6 and 8. His rhetorical strategy should not be obscured in our translation.

4. Lance Armstrong, with Sally Jenkins, *It's Not About the Bike: My Journey Back to Life* (New York: Berkley Books, 2001), p. 113.

5. Oswalt, I:624, 625.

6. Curiously, the NIV of Deuteronomy 28:2 weakens the sense with "All these blessings will come upon you and *accompany* you."

Chapter Twenty-three: In Whom Do You Now Trust?

1. Mihajlo Mihajlov, *Underground Notes* (London: Routledge & Kegan Paul, 1977), p. 174.

2. "The Rabshakeh" is an Assyrian title of uncertain meaning. But clearly the function of this person was that of chief spokesman for the king. Cf. KB3, s.v.

3. The ESV reads in verse 4, "On what do you rest this trust of yours?" A more literal rendering would be, "What is this trust that you trust?" Taking this into account, one can locate the seven uses of "trust" in this paragraph.

4. BDB, ad loc., p. 105. Cf. Wehr, s.v. *baṭaḥa*, p. 77.

5. P. G. Wodehouse, *The Code of the Woosters* (Woodstock and New York: The Overlook Press, 2000), p. 20.

6. Cf. John White, *The Fight: The Christian Struggle* (Downers Grove, IL: InterVarsity, 1977), p. 98.

7. Edith Schaeffer, *The Tapestry* (Waco, TX: Word Books, 1981), p. 356.

8. Edith Schaeffer, *L'Abri* (Wheaton, IL: Tyndale House, 1969), pp. 124, 125.

Chapter Twenty-four: That All the Kingdoms of the Earth May Know

1. J. R. R. Tolkien, *The Two Towers, Being the Second Part of The Lord of the Rings* (Boston: Houghton Mifflin, 1994 reprint), p. 696.

2. Tony Carnes, "Manhattan Ministry a Year Later," *Christianity Today*, November 18, 2002, p. 28.

3. For example, this is the premise of John F. Kennedy, *Profiles in Courage* (New York: Harper & Brothers, 1956).

4. An Assyrian palace relief depicts their assault on an ancient city, possibly Gezer in Israel, with scenes of outrageous cruelty. Cf. Carel J. Du Ry, *Art of the Ancient Near and Middle East* (New York: Harry N. Abrams, 1969), p. 104. According to R. D. Barnett, *Assyrian Palace Reliefs in the British Museum* (London: The Trustees of the British Museum, 1970), p. 19, "War, in fact, was the principal activity of the Assyrians."

5. *ANET*, p. 288.

6. "Oh, What a Beautiful Mornin'," from Rodgers and Hammerstein's *Oklahoma!*

Chapter Twenty-five: Peace and Security in Our Days?

1. James I. Packer, *The Collected Shorter Writings of J. I. Packer, Volume 4: Honouring the People of God* (Carlisle, UK: Paternoster Press, 1999), pp. 235, 236.

2. Hans J. Hillerbrand, ed., *The Reformation: A Narrative History Related by Contemporary Observers and Participants* (Grand Rapids, MI: Baker, 1981 reprint), p. 354.

3. Isaiah uses the ambiguous "in those days" to show that the national crisis of chapters 36—37 and the personal affliction of chapter 38 and its aftermath in chapter 39 are connected, but also to allow that these events are not necessarily sequential, which, in fact, they are not. Cf. Motyer, pp. 285, 286, 290, 291.

4. Comparing Isaiah's text with the simpler account in 2 Kings 20:1–11, we see that Isaiah has arranged his text to highlight 38:21, 22. He juxtaposes the full extent of God's grace (verse 21) with Hezekiah's ungenerous slowness to believe (verse 22). The Chronicler refers explicitly to the pride that went before Hezekiah's fall (2 Chronicles 32:24–31).

5. W. S. Plumer, *Earnest Hours* (Richmond: Presbyterian Committee of Publication, 1869), p. 290. I thank Rev. Iain Murray for sending me this quote via e-mail.

6. Malcolm Muggeridge, *Chronicles of Wasted Time, Chronicle I: The Green Stick* (New York: Quill, 1982 reprint), pp. 258, 259.

7. Octavius Winslow, *Personal Declension and Revival of Religion in the Soul* (London: Banner of Truth Trust, 1962 reprint), pp. 169–186.

Chapter Twenty-six: God's Glory, Our Comfort

1. C. L. Sulzberger, *The American Heritage Picture History of World War II* (New York: Crown Publishers, 1966), pp. 298, 299.

2. David Remnick, "Seasons in Hell," *The New Yorker*, April 14, 2003, p. 77.

3. Christopher R. Seitz, in *The Anchor Bible Dictionary* (New York: Doubleday, 1992), III:472, 473, reviewing the recent history of Isaiah studies, writes:

> To applaud prophetic genius in respect of ethical insight was one thing; but to claim for this same genius the ability to foresee events centuries in advance went beyond enlightened logic.
>
> But the startling impressiveness of Isaiah's message outperforming "enlightened logic" is the point. God wanted his people to be certain that he governs history according to his own preordained and, to the unprophetic eye, unforeseeable plan. Without that scandal, the message to the exiles would have carried no force.

4. Cf. Matthew 3:3; 4:14–16; 8:17; 12:17–21; 13:14, 15; 15:7–9; Mark 7:6, 7; Luke 3:4–6; 4:17–19; John 1:23; 12:37–41; Acts 8:27–35; 28:25–27; Romans 9:27–29; 10:16; 10:20, 21; 15:12.

5. The ESV reads, ". . . that her warfare is ended, that her iniquity is pardoned, that she has received . . ." This is a valid translation of the Hebrew conjunction. It interprets verse 2 as the content of the comforting message. But the conjunction can also be causal, in which case verse 2 explains the occasion of the message. This interpretation is to be preferred, because verses 3–5, 6–8, and 9–11 provide the content of the message. "Cry to her" in verse 2 is matched by "A voice cries" in verse 3, "A voice says, 'Cry'" in verse 6, and the heralds of verse 9.

6. The ESV reads "her warfare." But an interpretation more relevant to the exiles' actual situation is "servitude." Cf. BDB, s.v. *ṣābā(')*, sub 3, b.

7. *Institutes*, 3.3.2.

8. Cf. Raymond C. Ortlund, Jr., "Revival: Blessing or Problem?" *Reformation & Revival Journal* 11 (Summer 2002): 10–17.

9. John Piper, "A Passion for the Supremacy of God," *Spirit of Revival*, March 2002, p. 5.

10. Cf. Gerhard von Rad, *Old Testament Theology* (New York: Harper & Row, 1962), I:146; Walther Eichrodt, *Theology of the Old Testament* (Philadelphia: Westminster Press, 1967), II:29–35.

11. The ESV text reads "all its beauty," while the alternative in the margin is "all its constancy." The marginal reading is to be preferred, since this Hebrew word is used frequently in the Old Testament for God's steadfast love. Cf. Francis I. Andersen, "Yahweh, the Kind and Sensitive God," in Peter T. O'Brien and David G. Peterson, eds., *God Who Is Rich in Mercy* (Grand Rapids, MI: Baker, 1986), pp. 41–88. Presumably, the ESV text evi-

dences the interpretative logic lying behind the Septuagint's "glory," also evident in BDB, s.v. *ḥesed*, sub I, 4. But the Greek interpretation is a clumsy stab at the sense, in connection with Isaiah's botanical figures of speech in the context. "Glory"/"beauty" is an unexampled sense of *ḥesed*. The fact that 1 Peter 1:24, 25 quotes the Greek tradition does not validate that interpretation of this one word. Peter's argument depends on the net force of the whole statement in Isaiah's text, which affirms that God's word *abides*. "The living and *abiding* word of God" in 1 Peter 1:23 is confirmed by the Isaianic "but the word of the Lord *remains* forever" in 1 Peter 1:25, which both the Hebrew and Greek traditions share in common. The Septuagint's mistranslation of *ḥesed* is immaterial to the point Peter is making, and the meaning of *ḥesed* in Isaiah 40:6 must be established by its usage throughout the Hebrew Bible.

12. C. S. Lewis, *Reflections on the Psalms* (New York: Harcourt, Brace & World, 1958), pp. 94, 95.

Chapter Twenty-seven: God's Uniqueness, Our Assurance

1. Cf. Os Guinness, *The Gravedigger File: Papers on the Subversion of the Modern Church* (Downers Grove, IL: InterVarsity, 1983), pp. 49–70.

2. David F. Wells, *God in the Wasteland: The Reality of Truth in a World of Fading Dreams* (Grand Rapids, MI: Eerdmans, 1994), pp. 88–17.

3. Quoted in Daniel J. Kevles, "The Final Secret of the Universe?" *The New York Review of Books*, May 16, 1991. I thank Dr. John Piper for drawing my attention to Misner's comment.

4. J. I. Packer, *Knowing God* (Downers Grove, IL: InterVarsity, 1973), p. 5.

5. *Confessions*, I.iv.

6. The ESV translates, ". . . the path of justice," an arguable rendering. But Isaiah is not thinking of the social order. He is thinking of the natural order. God is before him as the Creator, not the Judge. Cf. R. N. Whybray, *The Heavenly Counsellor in Isaiah xl 13–14* (Cambridge, UK: The University Press, 1971), pp. 17–18. Oswalt, II:56, paraphrases, ". . . the right way to do things."

7. Whybray, *Heavenly Counsellor*, pp. 71–75; *ANET*, pp. 64, 68.

8. See Wayne Grudem, *Systematic Theology: An Introduction to Biblical Doctrine* (Grand Rapids, MI: Zondervan, 1994), p. 158.

9. A. W. Tozer, *The Knowledge of the Holy* (New York: Harper & Row, 1961), p. 11.

Chapter Twenty-eight: God's Greatness, Our Renewal

1. Viktor E. Frankl, *Man's Search for Meaning: An Introduction to Logotherapy* (New York: Washington Square Press, 1969 reprint), pp. 117, 118.

2. Cf. Basil Jackson, "Psychology, Psychiatry and the Pastor," *Bibliotheca Sacra* 132 (1975): 3–15.

3. David Laing, ed., *The Works of John Knox* (New York: AMS Press, 1966 reprint), V:24. I thank Rev. Iain Murray for drawing my attention to Knox here.

4. Theodore G. Tappert, ed., *Luther: Letters of Spiritual Counsel* (Philadelphia: Westminster Press, 1955), p. 145.

5. Cf. Radak, as cited in Solomon Mandelkern, *Veteris Testamenti Concordantiae Hebraicae atque Chaldaicae* (Tel Aviv: Schocken, 1967 reprint), p. 1017: "In Arabic the meaning of the verb is 'to be tense (impatient), firm and strong.' And this is the sense of 'Wait for the Lord; be strong and let your heart take courage' (Psalm 27:14)." BDB, s.v., proposes the seminal meaning of the root as "twist, stretch," the tension of enduring, waiting. KB3, s.v., comments, "perhaps denominative from I קָו, קַו with the basic meaning to be taut." But, of course, with "the LORD" as the object of this waiting, this agony will also be joyful.

6. *The Works of Jonathan Edwards* (Edinburgh: Banner of Truth Trust, 1979 reprint), I:xxv.

Chapter Twenty-nine: The Reality of God in an Unreal World

1. Cf. Phillip E. Johnson, *Darwin on Trial* (Downers Grove, IL: InterVarsity Press, 1993).

2. Quoted in D. A. Carson, *The Gagging of God: Christianity Confronts Pluralism* (Grand Rapids, MI: Zondervan, 1996), p. 53.

3. Fyodor Dostoevsky, *The Brothers Karamazov*, trans. Ignat Avsey (Oxford, UK: The University Press, 1994), p. 103.

4. Cf. Eugene H. Merrill, *Kingdom of Priests: A History of Old Testament Israel* (Grand Rapids, MI: Baker, 1987), pp. 474, 475. Cyrus's statement of policy on repatriation can be read in Mordechai Cogan, "Cyrus Cylinder," in *The Context of Scripture, Volume II: Monumental Inscriptions from the Biblical World*, ed. William W. Hallo (Leiden: E. J. Brill, 2000), pp. 314–316.

5. Cf. Genesis 1:4, 10, 12, 18, 21, 25, 31.

6. Calvin comments, "God has no need of outward and natural means for aiding his church, but has at his command secret and wonderful methods, by which he can relieve their necessities, contrary to all hope and outward appearance." John Calvin, *Commentary on the Book of the Prophet Isaiah*, trans. William Pringle (Grand Rapids, MI: Eerdmans, 1948), III:267.

Chapter Thirty: A Delusion, a Servant, a New Song

1. *Institutes*, 1.11.8.

2. Henry Chadwick, trans., *Augustine's Confessions* (New York: Oxford University Press, 1992), p. 201.

3. Robert H. Fischer, trans., *The Large Catechism of Martin Luther* (Philadelphia: Fortress Press, 1959), p. 9.

4. A. Leo Oppenheim, *Ancient Mesopotamia: Portrait of a Dead Civilization* (Chicago: The University of Chicago Press, 1964), pp. 183–227.

5. Clark Pinnock, et al., *The Openness of God: A Biblical Challenge to the Traditional Understanding of God* (Downers Grove, IL: InterVarsity Press, 1994), p. 7. For an admirable response, see Bruce A. Ware, *God's Lesser Glory: The Diminished God of Open Theism* (Wheaton, IL: Crossway Books, 2000), pp. 102–121.

6. Piotr Bienkowski and Alan Millard, eds., *British Museum Dictionary of the Ancient Near East* (London: British Museum Press, 2000), p. 131.

7. Does this Biblical language warrant a female view of God? Cf. Roland Mushat Frye, "Language for God and Feminist Language: A Literary and Rhetorical Analysis," *Interpretation* 43 (1989): 45–57.

8. Jonathan Edwards, *Works* (Edinburgh: Banner of Truth Trust, 1979 reprint), II:244.

Chapter Thirty-one: God's Way to Reformation

1. Elisabeth Elliot, *Shadow of the Almighty: The Life & Testament of Jim Elliot* (San Francisco: HarperCollins, 1989 reprint), p. 13.

2. Marilynne Robinson, *The Death of Adam: Essays on Modern Thought* (Boston: Houghton Mifflin, 1998), p. 78.

3. Quoted in Jim Elliff, "Reformation or Revival?" *Heartcry! A Journal on Revival and Spiritual Awakening*, Fall 1997, p. 21.

4. Jesus said, "I am the good shepherd" (John 10:11). Cf. Leon Morris, *The Gospel According to John* (Grand Rapids, MI: Eerdmans, 1971), p. 509, footnote 34: "It is important that the word 'good' here is one that represents, not the moral rectitude of goodness, nor its austerity, but its attractiveness. We must not forget that our vocation is so to practice virtue that men are won to it; it is possible to be morally upright repulsively."

5. Francis A. Schaeffer, *Speaking the Historic Christian Position into the 20th Century* (privately published, Wheaton College, 1965), pp. 125, 126.

6. C. S. Lewis, *Miracles: A Preliminary Study* (New York: Macmillan, 1967), pp. 96, 97.

7. Cf. R. E. Watts, "Exodus," in *New Dictionary of Biblical Theology*, ed. T. Desmond Alexander and Brian Rosner (Downers Grove, IL: InterVarsity Press, 2000), pp. 478–487.

8. "Excerpts from Jim Elliot's Diary," *His*, April 1956, p. 9.

Chapter Thirty-two: God's Way to Revival

1. The ESV reads, "Yet you did not call upon me, O Jacob." That translation is not wrong. But the emphasis of the Hebrew falls on "me." This should be visible in our English rendering, because the personal emphasis informs all the other statements in the paragraph.

2. Robert B. Cialdini, "The Science of Persuasion," *Scientific American*, February 2001, p. 76.

3. Brian H. Edwards, *Revival! A People Saturated with God* (Darlington, UK: Evangelical Press, 1990).

4. *Sermons of Robert Murray M'Cheyne* (London: Banner of Truth Trust, 1972 reprint), p. 16.

5. Cf. Jonathan Edwards, *Works* (Edinburgh: Banner of Truth Trust, 1979 reprint), I:539: "It may here be observed that from the fall of man to our day the work of redemption in its effect has mainly been carried on by remarkable communications of the Spirit of God. Though there be a more constant influence of God's Spirit always in some degree attending his ordinances, yet the way in which the greatest things have been done towards carrying on this work always have been by remarkable effusions at special seasons of mercy."

6. Gerhard von Rad, *Old Testament Theology*, trans. D. M. G. Stalker (New York: Harper & Row, 1962), I:208.

7. According to *Current Thoughts and Trends*, June 2001, p. 4. The pious negativism that discredits our witness is visible in the wording of the metric Psalm 100 in some modern hymnals. Its original in the Genevan Psalter of 1551 says, "Sing to the Lord with cheerful voice, him serve with *mirth*." That wording is Biblically accurate. But it was corrupted by later editors to "Sing to the Lord with cheerful voice, him serve with *fear*." There is no depth of perdition low enough for such editors.

8. Moshe Halbertal and Avishai Margalit, *Idolatry*, trans. Naomi Goldblum (Cambridge, MA: Harvard University Press, 1992), p. 10.

9. Gerald A. Larue, *Babylon and the Bible*, Baker Studies in Biblical Archaeology (Grand Rapids, MI: Baker, 1969), pp. 51–54, 69.

10. Christopher R. North, "The Essence of Idolatry," *Beihefte zur Zeitschrift für die alttestamentliche Wissenschaft* 77 (1958): 159, writes, "The conflict in Israel down to the Exile was the conflict between Yahweh and Baal. The Baals and Astartes were fertility gods and the type of religion they represent is 'sexy.' Not that there are not creator-gods in fertility religions. But the gods and goddesses with their marriages and illicit loves are so many parts of the stream of life and are borne along on its current. They are personifications of natural process. To make, and worship, iconic representations of them is the most natural thing in the world."

11. A. W. Tozer, *The Pursuit of God* (London: Marshall, Morgan & Scott, 1961), p. 20.

Chapter Thirty-three: God's Surprising Strategies

1. J. B. Phillips, *Your God Is Too Small* (New York: Macmillan, 1955), p. vi.

2. See chapter 29, footnote 4 in this book.

3. Cf. C. S. Lewis, *God in the Dock* (Grand Rapids, MI: Eerdmans, 1970), pp. 243, 244.

4. The ESV reads, "yourself," but the literal rending is "himself."

5. *The Church Hymnary: Revised Edition* (London: Oxford University Press, 1927), #520.

6. Theodore G. Tappert, ed., *Luther: Letters of Spiritual Counsel* (Philadelphia: Westminster, 1955), p. 133; cf. Blaise Pascal, *Pensées* (Franklin Center, WI: The Franklin Library, 1979), #194; J. I. Packer, "Mystery," in *Concise Theology* (Wheaton, IL: Tyndale House, 1993), pp. 51–53.

7. C. S. Lewis, *The Silver Chair* (New York: Collier Books, 1970 reprint), pp. 16, 17. Italics his.

Chapter Thirty-four: Gods That Fail and the Collapse of Their Cultures

1. Henrik Ibsen, *Four Major Plays*, trans. James McFarlane and Jens Arup (Oxford, UK: Oxford University Press, 1998), p. 126. Italics his.

2. Cf. Tim Keller, "Post-everything," *by Faith*, June-July 2003, pp. 29, 30.

3. Herbert Schlossberg, *Idols for Destruction: Christian Faith and Its Confrontation with American Society* (Nashville: Thomas Nelson, 1983), p. 7.

4. The ESV reads, "Recall it to mind, you *transgressors*." This is valid. But the idea of rebellion, also inherent in the Hebrew, is more to the point. Cf. Isaiah 1:2; 66:24.

5. *Hymns for the Living Church* (Carol Stream, IL: Hope Publishing Company, 1974), #47.

6. John Newton, *Works* (Edinburgh: Banner of Truth Trust, 1988 reprint), III:608, 609.

7. The ESV reads, "I will take vengeance," which is not wrong. But the syntax of the Hebrew front-loads the word "vengeance" for emphasis.

8. *Humanist Manifestos I & II*, American Humanist Association, 1973. Italics theirs. For an explanation of how we arrived at our modern hubris, see Francis A. Schaeffer, *How Should We Then Live?* (Old Tappan, NJ: Fleming H. Revell, 1976), especially pp. 57–78.

9. T. S. Eliot, "The Hollow Men," in Glenn Leggett, ed., *12 Poets* (New York: Holt, Rinehart and Winston, 1958), p. 287.

10. Walter Hooper, ed., *They Stand Together: The Letters of C. S. Lewis to Arthur Greeves (1914–1963)* (New York: Macmillan, 1979), p. 465. Italics his.

Chapter Thirty-five: God's Commitment to God Is His Assurance to Us

1. Cf. 48:1, 5, 6 (twice), 7, 8, 12, 14, 16, 20. Besides being translated as "hear," this verb is variously rendered "announce," "listen," and "proclaim."

2. C. S. Lewis, *The Four Loves* (New York: Harcourt, Brace, Jovanovich, 1960), p. 175. On pp. 175, 176, Lewis writes:

> We must always keep before our eyes that vision of Lady Julian's in which God carried in his hand a little object like a nut, and that nut was "all that is made." God, who needs nothing, loves into existence wholly superfluous creatures in order that he may love and perfect them.

Chapter Thirty-six: Not with Swords' Loud Clashing

1. The ESV reads, "that my salvation may reach to the end of the earth." It is more likely, however, that the sense of the Hebrew should be construed as translated above, making the servant himself the salvation of the world.

2. Richard F. Lovelace, *Dynamics of Spiritual Life: An Evangelical Theology of Renewal* (Downers Grove, IL: InterVarsity, 1979), p. 90.

3. Jonathan Edwards, *Works* (Edinburgh: Banner of Truth Trust, 1979 reprint), I:xlvii.

Chapter Thirty-seven: Why Do We Have Ears on the *Outside* of Our Heads?

1. Matthew 11:15; 13:9, 43; Luke 8:8; 14:35; etc.

2. Cf. BDB, p. 182, sub I, 2.

3. Malcolm Muggeridge, *Christ and the Media* (Grand Rapids, MI: Eerdmans, 1977), p. 92.

4. The ESV correctly translates 50:10, ". . . and *obeys* the voice of his servant." But the Hebrew idiom uses the verb translated "listen" in 51:1, 7.

5. Quoted in John Piper, *The Legacy of Sovereign Joy* (Wheaton, IL: Crossway Books, 2000), 104.

6. Oswalt, II:337.

7. Cf. John Stott, quoted in Muggeridge, *Christ and the Media*, p. 123.

Chapter Thirty-eight: *Wachet Auf*

1. Cf. Michael David Coogan, ed. and trans., *Stories from Ancient Canaan* (Philadelphia: Westminster, 1978), pp. 75–115.

2. C. S. Lewis, *The Screwtape Letters* (New York: Simon & Schuster, 1996 reprint), p. 15:

> There are two equal and opposite errors into which our race can fall about the devils. One is to disbelieve in their existence. The other is to believe, and to feel an excessive and unhealthy interest in them. They themselves are equally pleased by both errors, and hail a materialist or a magician with the same delight.

3. Andrew Hurley, trans., *Against All Hope: The Prison Memoirs of Armando Valladares* (New York: Alfred A. Knopf, 1986), pp. 16, 17.

4. Bruce D. Chilton, *The Isaiah Targum*, The Aramaic Bible, Vol. 11 (Collegeville, MN: The Liturgical Press, 1987), p. 102.

5. Martin Luther, *A Commentary on St. Paul's Epistle to the Galatians* (London: James Clarke & Company, 1953), p. 40.

6. See C. S. Lewis, "The Inner Ring," in *The Weight of Glory and Other Addresses* (Grand Rapids, MI: Eerdmans, 1974 reprint), pp. 55–66.

Chapter Thirty-nine: Guilt, Substitution, Grace

1. J. N. Oswalt, "Isaiah," in *New Dictionary of Biblical Theology* (Downers Grove, IL: InterVarsity Press, 2000), eds. T. Desmond Alexander and Brian S. Rosner, p. 222.

2. Michael Massing, "America's Favorite Philosopher," *The New York Times Book Review*, December 28, 2003, p. 7.

3. According to abcnews.go.com, January 7, 2004.

4. Shakespeare, *Macbeth*, Act 5, Scene 1.

5. *Ibid.*, Act 5, Scene 3.

6. Cf. Acts 2:33; Ephesians 1:20–23; Philippians 2:9–11.

7. Francis A. Schaeffer, *How Should We Then Live?* (Old Tappan, NJ: Fleming H. Revell Company, 1976), pp. 98, 101.

8. Charles Dickens, *A Tale of Two Cities* (London: P. R. Gawthorn, Ltd., 1946), p. 312.

9. The willing intentionality behind Christ's sufferings is implicit in the reasoning of Peter, who calls Christians to *choose* to follow the example of Jesus (1 Peter 2:18–25).

10. Hallvard Hagelia, *Coram Deo: Spirituality in the Book of Isaiah, with Particular Attention to Faith in Yahweh* (Stockholm: Almquist & Wiksell, 2001), p. 475.

11. E. Y. Kutscher, *The Language and Linguistic Background of the Isaiah Scroll (I Q Isaa)* (Leiden: E. J. Brill, 1974), p. 543.

12. "Here is Love," William Reese (1802–1883).

13. Paul Tournier, *Guilt & Grace: A Psychological Study* (New York: Harper & Row, 1962), p. 184.

14. Quoted in H. C. G. Moule, *Charles Simeon* (London: Inter-Varsity, 1956 reprint), pp. 25, 26.

Chapter Forty: When Grace Dances

1. Edward Mendelson, ed., *W. H. Auden: Collected Poems* (New York: Vintage International, 1991), p. 745.

2. T. H. L. Parker, *John Calvin: A Biography* (London: J. M. Dent & Sons, 1975), p. 87.

3. Dan B. Allender and Tremper Longman, III, *Bold Love* (Colorado Springs: NavPress, 1992), p. 71.

4. Joni Mitchell, "Woodstock" (1970).

5. The ESV reads, ". . . like a wife deserted . . . ." That is a possible translation; but it may create a presumption of guilt on the husband's part, which cannot be Isaiah's intention. He is not interested in how the marriage fell apart but in how it's being restored, because this Husband is *not* a deserter. Here and in verse 7 the Hebrew can also be translated with

the less loaded verb "leave," the reality of which is clarified in verse 8: "I hid my face from you."

6. The ESV reads, "Come, everyone who thirsts, come to the waters. . . ." The Hebrew text, however, calls for an initial word different from the imperative "Come." The Hebrew interjection incites interest and urges on. Cf. ESV Zechariah 2:6, 7.

7. Quoted in Richard Winter, "Still Bored in a Culture of Entertainment," *Perspectives*, The Francis A. Schaeffer Institute, Spring 2002, p. 4.

8. C. S. Lewis, *A Grief Observed* (New York: Seabury Press, 1973), p. 17.

9. John Flavel, "The Redemption Betwixt the Father and the Redeemer," in *The Works of John Flavel* (Edinburgh: Banner of Truth Trust, 1968), I:61.

10. Oswalt, II:443, writes, "We humans want God's gifts, but we are always fearful of letting the Giver into our lives, lest we should lose our illusory feeling of control."

11. The ESV reads, "For you shall go out in joy and be led forth in peace." This is a valid translation. But I wish to make visible the emphatic word order in the Hebrew text.

12. C. S. Lewis, *Out of the Silent Planet* (New York: Macmillan, 1965).

13. Peter Kreeft, *Heaven: The Heart's Deepest Longing* (San Francisco: Ignatius Press, 1989), p. 183.

Chapter Forty-one: Revival and the Heart of the Contrite

1. Raymond C. Ortlund, Jr., *When God Comes to Church: A Biblical Model for Revival Today* (Grand Rapids, MI: Baker, 2000), p. 9.

2. I have verified this story in a phone conversation with Pastor Smith, for which I thank him. He has my deep respect for daring to obey the implications of the gospel at that defining moment.

3. The epidemic of forced resignations by faithful pastors in the modern church would be analogous to what Isaiah saw back then.

4. "Blue Angels: Around the World at the Speed of Sound," AAE-10037 (1994).

5. Charles W. Colson, "The Enduring Revolution: 1993 Templeton Address," *Sources*, No. 4, 1993, p. 7.

Chapter Forty-two: Revival and Responsibility

1. John Perkins, *Let Justice Roll Down* (Glendale, CA: Regal Books, 1976), p. 108. Italics his.

2. Jonathan Edwards, *Charity and Its Fruits* (Edinburgh: Banner of Truth Trust, 2000 reprint), p. 169.

3. Cf. Os Guinness, *The Gravedigger File: Papers on the Subversion of the Modern Church* (Downers Grove, IL: InterVarsity Press, 1983), pp. 71–89.

4. Cf. Jonathan Edwards, *Works* (Edinburgh: Banner of Truth Trust, 1979 reprint), I:428.

5. According to www.thehungersite.com, May 5, 2004.

6. James Montgomery Boice, *Philippians: An Expositional Commentary* (Grand Rapids, MI: Zondervan, 1971), p. 290.

7. Perkins, *Let Justice Roll Down*, p. 105.

8. Cf. Judith Shulevitz, "Bring Back the Sabbath," *The New York Times*, March 2, 2003; Nan Chase, "Ancient Wisdom," *Hemispheres*, July 1997, pp. 118, 119.

9. "The Garden of Love," in *Blake: Poems* (New York: Alfred A. Knopf, 1994), p. 61.

Chapter Forty-three: Revival and World Renewal

1. C. S. Lewis, *The Voyage of the "Dawn Treader"* (New York: Macmillan, 1972 reprint), pp. 212, 213.

2. Cf. John G. Lorimer, "Encouragements from the Promises and Prophecies of Scripture," in *The Revival of Religion: Addresses by Scottish Evangelical Leaders Delivered in Glasgow in 1840* (Edinburgh: Banner of Truth Trust, 1984), pp. 185–233.

3. Cf. Walther Eichrodt, *Theology of the Old Testament* (Philadelphia: Westminster Press, 1961), I:36ff.; *Westminster Confession of Faith*, chapter 7.

4. *Ecumenical Creeds and Reformed Confessions* (Grand Rapids, MI: The Christian Reformed Church, 1984), p. 26.

5. The ESV translates this, "but the LORD will arise upon you," which is not wrong. But the emphasis of the Hebrew word order favors "but upon you the LORD will arise."

6. C. S. Lewis, *The Screwtape Letters & Screwtape Proposes a Toast* (New York: Macmillan, 1962), p. 12.

Chapter Forty-four: Revival, Preaching, and Prayer

1. D. Martyn Lloyd-Jones, *Spiritual Depression: Its Causes and Cure* (Grand Rapids, MI: Eerdmans, 1965), p. 23.

2. Jerome Carcopino, *Daily Life in Ancient Rome* (New Haven, CT: Yale University Press, 1940), pp. 31, 32.

3. Cf. Cornelius Plantinga, Jr., *Not the Way It's Supposed to Be: A Breviary of Sin* (Grand Rapids, MI: Eerdmans, 1995), pp. 57–60.

4. Bob Dylan, "Everything is Broken" (1989).

5. Ceslas Spicq, *Theological Lexicon of the New Testament*, trans. James D. Ernest (Peabody, MA: Hendrickson Publishers, 1994), I:400.

6. *The Church Hymnary: Revised Edition* (London: Oxford University Press, 1927), #210.

7. *Hymns for Today's Church* (London: Hodder & Stoughton, 1982), #355.

8. Jonathan Edwards, *Works* (Edinburgh: Banner of Truth, 1979 reprint), II:312.

9. O. Hallesby, *Prayer* (Minneapolis: Augsburg, 1944 reprint), pp. 75–77.

10. "Bright unto the End," *Christianity Today*, October 1, 2001, pp. 56–59.

Chapter Forty-five: Revival and the Wrath of the Lamb

1. C. S. Lewis, *The Lion, the Witch and the Wardrobe* (New York: Collier Books, 1972 reprint), pp. 75, 76. Italics his.

2. Cf. Douglas J. Moo, *The Epistle to the Romans* (Grand Rapids, MI: Eerdmans, 1996), pp. 25–27.

3. Marcus Dods, ed., *The Works of Aurelius Augustine, Bishop of Hippo: The City of God* (Edinburgh: T. & T. Clark, 1872), II:47. See Chapter Sixteen above.

4. Bob Dylan, "Property of Jesus" (1981).

5. Andrew Sullivan, "The Saint and the Satirist," *The New York Times Book Review*, May 30, 2004, p. 1.

6. Albert Barnes, *Notes on the New Testament: Acts* (Grand Rapids, MI: Baker Book House, reprint of the 1884–85 edition), p. vii. Italics his.

Chapter Forty-six: Revival and the Descent of God

1. Claus Westermann, *Isaiah 40—66: A Commentary* (Philadelphia: Westminster Press, 1969), p. 392: "This psalm is probably the most powerful psalm of communal lamentation in the Bible."

2. I gratefully acknowledge my debt to Martyn Lloyd-Jones, *Revival* (Wheaton, IL: Crossway Books, 1987), pp. 291–316.

3. *Jonathan Edwards on Revival* (Edinburgh: Banner of Truth Trust, 1995 reprint), p. 14.

4. Cf. *The Church Hymnary: Revised Edition* (London: Oxford University Press, 1927), #450: "Thou art coming to a King; large petitions with thee bring, for his grace and power are such none can ever ask too much."

Chapter Forty-seven: Revival and the Eagerness of God

1. *The Hymnal of the Protestant Episcopal Church in the United States of America* (New York: The Church Hymnal Corporation, 1940), #405.

2. Roy J. Cook, comp., *One Hundred and One Famous Poems* (Chicago: The Reilly & Lee Co., 1958), p. 95.

3. Cf. Tim Keller, "Preaching Hell in a Tolerant Age: Brimstone for the Broad-minded," *Leadership Journal*, Fall 1997, www.christianitytoday.com.

4. C. S. Lewis, *Mere Christianity* (New York: Macmillan, 1958), p. 106.

5. C. S. Lewis, *George MacDonald: Anthology* (London: Geoffrey Bles, 1970 reprint), p. 19.

6. Cf. Cornelius Plantinga Jr., *Engaging God's World: A Reformed Vision of Faith, Learning and Living* (Grand Rapids, MI: Eerdmans, 2002), pp. 12–14.

Chapter Forty-eight: Revival and Worship

1. Cf. John R. W. Stott, *The Cross of Christ* (Downers Grove, IL: InterVarsity Press, 1986), pp. 311, 312, quoting Voltaire's *Candide*.

2. Cf. David Peterson, *Engaging with God: A Biblical Theology of Worship* (Grand Rapids, MI: Eerdmans, 1992), p. 141.

3. The Second Helvetic Confession of 1566, in Philip Schaff, ed., *The Creeds of Christendom* (Grand Rapids, MI: Baker Book House, 1990 reprint), III:237, affirms: "*Proinde cum hodie hoc Dei verbum per praedicatores legitime vocatos annunciatur in Ecclesia, credimus ipsum Dei verbum annunciari et a fidelibus recipi. . . .*" ("So then, when today this Word of God is proclaimed in church through lawfully called preachers, we believe that the very Word of God is being proclaimed and received by believers.")

4. Charles J. Brown, in *The Revival of Religion: Addresses by Scottish Evangelical Leaders Delivered in Glasgow in 1840* (Edinburgh: Banner of Truth Trust, 1984 reprint), pp. 316, 317. Italics added.

5. Thomas C. Oden, *Life in the Spirit: Systematic Theology, Volume Three* (New York: HarperCollins, 1992), p. 450.

6. Cf. C. S. Lewis, *The Great Divorce* (New York: Macmillan, 1973 reprint), p. 120.

7. Tom Peete Cross and Clement Tyson Goode, eds., *Heath Readings in the Literature of England* (Boston: D. C. Heath and Company, 1927), p. 764.

8. I gratefully acknowledge Dr. Roy Clements for this poem.

Scripture Index

General Index

Ibsen, Henrik, 306
Idolatry, 20, 50, 52, 54, 55, 171, 175, 183,
    184, 241, 245, 248, 262, 263, 267, 268,
    269, 270, 271, 273, 274, 275, 276, 283,
    293, 301, 303, 305, 308, 309, 313, 317,
    319, 368, 381, 442,454
"Imagine" (song), 306
Invictus (Henley), 442
Isaac, 378

Jacob (Israel), 196, 252, 281, 379, 416, 423
James, William, 20
Jefferson, Thomas, 351
Jesus Christ,
    birth of, 90, 113, 300, 351, 407, 433
    death of, 31, 41, 46, 60, 80, 99, 121, 145,
        148, 149, 161, 176, 198, 229, 235,
        252, 258, 282, 284, 289, 299, 311,
        316, 335, 343, 348, 354, 355, 356,
        357, 358, 359, 360, 377, 393, 394,
        403, 408, 421, 428, 431, 433, 444,
        457
    Everlasting Father, 99
    Immanuel, 91, 92
    Judge, 126, 433
    King, 99, 100, 116, 124, 184, 236, 239,
        369, 420
    Lord, 100, 184, 186
    Messiah, 62, 114, 117, 124, 128, 184,
        185, 297, 320, 325, 335, 376, 409,
        410, 412, 413, 439
    Mighty God, 99, 111
    our substitute, 31, 121, 161, 194, 219,
        260, 274, 324, 357, 358, 359, 360,
        368, 376, 385, 394, 433, 444
    Prince of Peace, 99
    Redeemer, 47, 133, 137, 212, 259, 311,
        399
    resurrection of, 302, 348, 354, 358, 360,
        433
    Savior, 92, 97, 99, 100, 114, 265, 285,
        325, 326, 370, 384, 393, 405, 411,
        424, 433, 442
    Second Coming of, 113, 116, 148, 176,
        237, 367, 410
    servant of the Lord, 272, 273, 274, 324,
        325, 326, 327, 334, 335, 336, 337,
        338, 339, 355, 356, 363, 365, 368,
        401
    true Vine, 72–73
    Wonderful Counselor, 99
John the Baptist, 60, 72
Judgment of God, 62, 81, 83, 92, 125, 126,

130, 143, 156, 198, 199, 200, 311, 312,
    443, 454
Justice, 44, 46, 52, 72, 132, 146, 175, 198,
    272, 273, 361, 377, 380, 412

Keller, Tim, 214
Kelly, Gene, 121
Key, Francis Scott, 116
Kilpatrick, William, 25
Knowing God (Packer), 242
Knox, John, 251, 278
Kreeft, Peter, 374

L'Abri, 211, 280
Last Battle, The (Lewis), 156
Latimer, Hugh, 221
Law of God, of Moses, 67, 137
Leadership, 44, 59, 60
    false leaders, 60
Lebanon, 166, 244, 403
Legalism, 269
Leibniz, Gottfried Wilhelm, 447
Lenin, Vladimir, 398
Lennon, John, 162, 306
Les Miserables, 139
Leviathan, 148
Lewis, C. S., 58, 103, 110, 156, 159, 187,
    239, 283, 304, 313, 368, 373, 395, 419,
    445
Liddell, Eric, 174
Lion, the Witch and the Wardrobe, The
    (Lewis), 419
Lloyd-Jones, Martyn, 15, 42, 71, 407
Lord of the Rings trilogy (Tolkien), 54, 176
Lovelace, Richard, 38, 114
Luther, Martin, 26, 33, 148, 155, 195, 251,
    268, 302, 331, 336, 347
Lutheran Church, Affirmation of Baptism,
    21

Macbeth, 353
    Lady Macbeth, 352
Machen, J. Gresham, 137
Magi, the, 301, 378
Magnificat, Maryís, 129
Maher-shalal-hashbaz, 90, 91
Manís Search for Meaning (Frankl), 249
Mao Tse-tung, 183
Mary, mother of Jesus, 82, 129
Mary, Queen, 221
M'Cheyne, Robert Murray, 291
Melanchthon, Philipp, 251

Index of
Sermon Illustrations

We have become the "plastic culture" we protested in the sixties, 145

Francis Schaeffer tells his wife that if the Holy Spirit were taken out of the Bible, sadly, most churches wouldn't change much, 211

John Piper: our view of God, and our understanding of the glory of God, is small and uninformed, 236

C. S. Lewis: the world is full of praise for poetry, wine, actors, mountains, etc., but we are called to something higher—praising God, 239

Supremacy of God
A. W. Tozer: God is as high above an archangel as an archangel is above a caterpillar, 77

Tolerance
Dorothy Sayers: what the world calls tolerance is actually the despair that comes from not taking a stand on anything, 257

Trust in God
Sarah Edwards, on her husband Jonathan's death: "The Lord . . . has made me adore his goodness, that we had my husband so long," 105

After three missionaries are kidnapped, mission director learns to pray, "God, even if we never know what has become of them, you will still be God," 124

Martin Luther: faith in God or faith in idols?, 268–269

Truth
Flannery O'Connor: "the truth does not change according to our ability to stomach it," 173

Two Worlds
In Lewis's *The Last Battle*, Peter and friends saw blue sky and sunshine, while the Dwarfs only saw a stable, 156

Eric Liddell runs for the glory of God, while Harold Abrahams has a point to prove, 174

Comfort at Todd Beamer's funeral, but hopelessness at memorial service for all who died on United airliner, 179

Augustine: two cities—the city of man (love of self) and the city of God (love for God), 423

Bob Dylan song: some are "the property of Jesus," some have "a heart of stone," 423–424

Unbelief
Luther: the root of sin is unbelief and voluntary darkness, 331

Watchfulness
W. S. Plumer on the necessity of being watchful against carelessness and compromise, 227

Bach's cantata *Wachet auf* ("Sleepers, Awake!") enjoins us to watch for Christ's return, 341

Wrath of God
Jonathan Edwards sermon "Sinners in the Hands of an Angry God," 101

Witness
Francis Schaeffer: if he had only one hour to present the gospel to someone, he would spend the first fifty minutes on divine judgment, 198

Edith Schaeffer on God's calling her and her husband to begin a new way of ministering to the lost, 211–212

Thomas Cranmer recants his faith but later stands firm, to death, 221–222

Young man tells Francis Schaeffer that every time he comes to L'Abri, he feels like a human being, 280

Chuck Smith and fellow pastors take out the church's carpet rather than turn away teens who have oil on their feet, 379

Jonathan Edwards: Christian love reaches out to the whole community, 388

Martyn Lloyd-Jones: "In a world where everything has gone so sadly astray . . . here is the solution, here is the answer," 407

Bill Bright, toward the end of his life: "Let us share this most joyful news with everybody on the planet," 417

C. S. Lewis: the fact that this world can't satisfy our desires shows that we were made for to press to another one, "and to help others do the same," 445

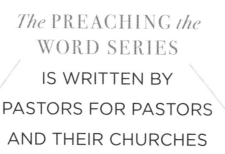

The PREACHING the
WORD SERIES
IS WRITTEN BY
PASTORS FOR PASTORS
AND THEIR CHURCHES

crossway.org/preachingtheword